THE Murder of SHEREE

WAYNE MILLER

Published by
Wilkinson Books
an imprint of

Information Australia
A.C.N. 006 042 173
75-77 Flinders Lane
Melbourne VIC 3000
Telephone: (03) 9654 2800
Fax: (03) 9650 5261

ISBN 1 86350 219 X

Copyright © 1996 Wayne Miller

Cover Design and Page Layout:
Paul Martinsen

Printed and bound in Australia by
McPherson's Printing Group,
Maryborough, Victoria.

All rights reserved. This publication is copyright and may not be resold or reproduced in any manner (except excerpts thereof for bona fide study purposes in accordance with the Copyright Act) without the prior consent of the Publisher.

Every effort has been made to ensure that this book is free from error or omissions. However, the Publisher, the Editor, or their respective employees or agents, shall not accept responsibility for injury, loss or damage occasioned to any person acting or refraining from action as a result of material in this book whether or not such injury, loss or damage is in any way due to any negligent act or omission, breach of duty or default on the part of the Publisher, the Editor, or their respective employees or agents.

Miller, Wayne, 1957 - .
The murder of Sheree.

ISBN 1 86350 219 X

1. Beasley, Sheree. 2. Lowe, Robert. 3. Murder - Victoria - Rosebud. I. Title

364.1523099452

Dedicated to Sheree Joy Mandile (Beasley)
Born February 25, 1985 - Murdered June 29, 1991, aged six years.
And the men and women of the Victoria Police Force.

ABOUT THE AUTHOR

IN HIS 13 years in the Victoria Police, Wayne Miller won awards ranging from Recruit of the Year in 1975 to several commendations for investigative ability. In 1983 he was dux of Detective Training School; the following year he went undercover buying drugs in the drug squad. When he resigned in 1988, he was an instructor at the Sergeants' Course.

He started his journalistic career at The West Australian newspaper and was appointed chief police reporter after just 12 months. After two years at Sydney's Daily Telegraph Mirror, Miller transferred to the Herald Sun as chief police reporter.

In 1995, he won a Walkley Award for his 28-page special report on the Sheree Beasley case. He lives in Melbourne with his wife and family.

ACKNOWLEDGEMENTS

◆

THANKS MUST go to the following people.

Lorraine Lowe, Benjamin Lowe, Jonathan Lowe, Anthony Mandile jnr, Jill and Anthony Mandile snr, Kerri and Steve Ludlow, Neil and Denise Greenhill and their daughters Adele and Harmony, Joy and Leslie Greenhill, Margaret and John Hobbs, for sharing their grief, heartache and inner secrets with me.

Victoria Police Chief Commissioner Neil Comrie, his Media Director John Allin, Superintendent Peter Halloran, Det Chief Insp Laurie Ratz, Det Insp Paul Hollowood, Det Insp Dannye Moloney, Det Sen Sgt Dale Johnson, Det Sen Sgt Geoff Alway, Det Sen Sgt Jeff Calderbank, Det Sgt Alex Bartsch, Sgt Matthew Wood, Donna Wood, Sgt Keith Joyce, Det S/C Andrew Gustke, Det S/C Paul O'Halloran, Det S/C Murray Gregor, Sen Const Steve Batten.

Herald Sun Editor-in-Chief Steve Harris, photographer Heath Missen, artist Lisa Nolan, reporters Fay Burstin, Allison Harding, Anita Quigley, Kristin Owen, Brad Newsome, Carolyn Webb, Greg Thom, Paul Anderson, Leanne Hall, Jane Willson, all from the *Herald Sun*, Lesley Jackson, Sue Motherwell from the *Herald Sun* Library, reporter Tim Pegler from *The Age*, Professor Stephen Cordner, Melissa and Pauline Montalto, Peter Reid, Barry Dickins, Karen Joseph, Rev Dr Gordon Powell and his wife Gwen, Dr Brian Dunn, Richard Lowe in New Zealand, Alistair Leithead from the *Evening Chronicle* in Newcastle-Upon-Tyne, England, proof readers Sandra Dexter and Inspector Bruce McKenzie, publisher Michael Wilkinson, production manager Berith Ostrom, designer Paul Martinsen and my wife Janice and our darling children whom I hardly saw for 18 months.

Special thanks to Hoggy.

Some proceeds from the sale of this book are being donated to Sheree's four sisters Crystal, Jacinta, Rhianhon and Stevi.

FOREWORD

THIS EXCEPTIONAL book had its genesis when I asked Wayne Miller to place a murder case under a microscope...to tell it how it really is; for the victim's family, the murderer, the police and the local community. I wanted him to go behind the headlines of daily news.

Wayne was then chief police reporter for the *Herald Sun*, Australia's largest selling daily newspaper, and had reported crime for several years with the *Daily Telegraph Mirror* in Sydney and the *West Australian* in Perth. He is a crime reporter with a difference - he had been a policeman in Victoria for 13 years prior to becoming a journalist. He has seen crime from all sides - as an investigator, and now as an observer.

Wayne nominated the Sheree Beasley case because he could not understand how a married man in his 50s, with children, could have such a generous and loving facade yet abduct, sexually molest and then brutally murder a six-year-old girl who was unknown to him.

As editor in chief I'd seen the effect of this crime on our community. Wayne spent four months, working long hours, examining and exploring the issues of the case.

I knew Wayne could write but what he delivered was compelling. The day his groundbreaking 28-page special report appeared in the *Herald Sun*, it was clear by the phone calls and correspondence to our office that it had touched a nerve.

It was no surprise to me when Wayne won a Walkley Award - the highest award for journalistic excellence - for this report.

Knowing there was much more to tell, I encourged Wayne to start writing this book.

He continued with many interviews over countless hours, mountains of research, sometimes at personal cost, both financially and emotionally.

Foreword

When I read the first draft of the book, it was in one all night sitting. The horror of Robert Lowe, his life and his crime, is all here. But it is much more than a crime book. Wayne takes us inside the minds of the police, Sheree's family, and the most disturbing journey of all, inside Robert Lowe's evil mind.

The most experienced homicide officer on the case said he never understood evil until he encountered Robert Lowe.

Very few books have the ability to change our perceptions. This book does that.

Steve Harris
Editor-in-Chief
The Herald and Weekly Times Ltd

PREFACE

◆

IN JUNE 1994, my editor-in-chief, Steve Harris, asked me to dissect a murder investigation for the *Herald Sun*. I chose the 'Sheree Beasley investigation'.

All I knew of the case then was Robert Arthur Selby Lowe had been charged with kidnapping and murdering Sheree. I soon learned, though, that it was an extraordinary case, so extraordinary that much of it sounded like fiction. Sadly, it was not.

After the feature article appeared in the *Herald Sun* in December 1994, Steve suggested I write a book. There were many powerful motivators.

Lowe's greatest fear is being exposed to the public. I know, from conversations with many people, and from reading some of his letters from prison, that he does not want anybody to know about his sordid life. That thought alone helped me finish this work.

Sheree's mum, Kerri Ludlow, told me many times she wanted the public to know all about the murder and more importantly, about Lowe. She saw his public exposure as her only real means of revenge.

It was very fortunate for me that everybody I approached - police, Sheree's family, the Lowe family and Lowe's psychotherapist Margaret Hobbs - spoke of their involvement, and how they had been affected. I spent countless hours with these people before, during and after the trial, piecing together the nightmare that had dominated so many lives for so long. Along the way I realised I had come to know some very special people.

I marvelled at their ability to not only maintain their sanity but make brave, sound decisions and, when it was required, take firm action in the face of incredible pressure and strain.

Preface

Hundreds of police and civilians were involved in this investigation. I must firstly thank all Sheree's relatives, particularly Kerri Ludlow and her father Neil Greenhill, for their time, and for allowing me into their inner sanctum when their grief was at its worst.

A very special thank you also to Lorraine Lowe and her sons Jonathan and Benjamin, for speaking to me many times over many hours. Margaret Hobbs graciously gave me many, many hours of her time also, enabling me to gain some sort of insight into Robert Lowe's dark mind. (Robert Lowe declined to talk to me. He said an interview could serve "no useful purpose".)

It was impossible, and unrealistic, to talk to everyone involved in this investigation for the purpose of this book. While I have shown the types of enquiries undertaken by the police by highlighting the actions of a handful of detectives, it would be a mistake to believe those men and women were the only ones carrying out those duties. Scores of detectives did door knocks, and chased countless fruitless leads, working in the cold and at night, while their families waited for them to come home.

CHAPTER ONE

◆

SHE WALKED the streets of Melbourne in a daze. She knew the city so well, yet she was lost. It had slowly dawned on Lorraine Sangster that the road she was following was not leading to her intended destination. Her life, and the way to lead it, had been mapped out for her by the Exclusive Brethren, a fundamentalist Christian group she had been born into. But Lorraine had grown increasingly dissatisfied with the church. The rules she had lived by were not for her. What had seemed normal and logical for decades now seemed ridiculous and meaningless. She thought it stupid, for example, that God would spurn her if she had her hair cut short, or kissed a boy or man. She had come to realise that what she had thought was normal was very unconventional indeed.

Her childhood had been sheltered and restricted. At school she had shown promise at hockey but church rules forbade playing competitive games. On Sundays, children were not allowed to bounce a ball. Girls were not even permitted to knit. In accordance with church laws, the Sangsters had no radio, no pre-recorded music, and no television. It was strict and there was a sense of belonging but now she was a woman, nothing the church preached seemed to work for Lorraine. She felt she didn't belong. She knew the Exclusive Brethren were good at heart and well-motivated but she felt she was living a lie. She had never felt so lonely in her 28 years - she just knew she was missing out on something. But what was the alternative? After all, the brethren taught that the world outside was full of bad people.

Wearing a simple blue cotton dress, Lorraine ambled in the sunshine along Flinders Street to Brunton Avenue, and found herself approaching the Melbourne Cricket Ground. She walked through the cool, dappled shadows of the trees in the cricket-ground's car park. It was March 1969.

Dreamily she plodded on. From inside the stadium she heard voices pouring from a public address system. She was overwhelmed by an urge to see the crowd, or even just be close to the arena, just to get the feeling of the event. Perhaps something would happen which would help her decide what to do with her life. She was curious about the Billy Graham crusade but hadn't planned to go inside, for while tens of thousands revered Billy Graham as a man of God, Lorraine's church saw him as an instrument of Satan.

Ten years earlier Lorraine had broken the brethren's rules when she slipped into the MCG with two teenage girls from the church. The trio watched Billy Graham in awe. Lorraine was consumed by guilt - she knew she shouldn't be there - but she found it very stirring. The huge, happy crowd, the glorious music, the singing, the joy. She had never heard a big choir before and she was captivated by the music. She wondered why God would be upset if the brethren had an organ or piano in church. It didn't make sense. Lorraine went home wide-eyed but dared not tell a soul. Then two church elders came to her home and spoke to her in front of her parents. Someone from the church had also been to the crusade and had seen the girls there. Hit by pangs of conscience, he had confessed - and reported the girls for good measure. The elders wanted to know if it was true.

Lorraine confessed but she couldn't help noticing her father's face. He was smirking. Lorraine remembered how on school holidays years before, he had taken the family to a rented house in Sorrento on the Mornington Peninsula. The house had a radio and the kids would listen to *Kindergarten of the Air*. Lorraine always remembered its signature tune - "Boys and girls come out to play ...". Her dad listened to the radio too. He argued that it wasn't their radio - it just happened to be there.

Charles and Greta Sangster had also been in church-trouble. Charles had broken a new rule that members could not be connected in any way with a non-member, in particular with shares in business. Charles was the director of a laundry firm and had shares in it, so he had to sell them.

The elders continued their cross-examination.

"How do you think the Lord would feel about your sin, in going into the enemy's camp?" Lorraine felt awful. She apologised and said she would ask their forgiveness. Secretly though she still remembered the thrill of the crusade.

To atone, the elders said, she must attend a special meeting - her own trial - while the congregation would 'take up matters of care and concern' following the usual Wednesday night meeting. It was Lorraine's only chance to express her regret at her sin. The brethren would judge whether she was repentant, and whether they could forgive her.

The Exclusive Brethren's main meeting place was in Prospect Hill Road, Camberwell. From the outside, the building looked a little like a flying saucer. It was a circular building, shaped so everyone could see and be seen. It was surrounded by a high cyclone-wire fence to keep non-members out. Guards kept watch at the gates. Inside the building, the elders sat in a ring in the centre, and the congregation looked on from the surrounding seats. High above there was a gallery behind a balcony.

Lorraine and one of the other girls who had offended sat in the second row of the church through the first bible study class so they wouldn't have to stand up and walk too far to speak into the microphone. Lorraine was petrified. She was thankful the other girl had to speak first. The girl stood and an elder questioned her while about two thousand brethren looked on.

"Is it true you attended the Billy Graham crusade?" he said into the mike.

"Yes, with sorrow," lied the 15-year-old.

Then it was Lorraine's turn. With her head bowed, she sobbed as she admitted her guilt, mortified at the sound of her voice echoing round the hall.

"Yes, I went to the crusade. I knew I should not have done this thing. I will never do it again."

A deep discussion followed as to whether there was evidence of repentance and whether the brethren, and therefore God, could forgive the girls. The alternatives were to be 'shut up' for a time, where Lorraine would not be allowed to circulate and would be virtually in 'house prison' until she reached repentance; to be considered repentant and then forgiven; or to be judged wicked and be excommunicated forthwith. The elders took her tears to be those of repentance.

The Murder of Sheree

AS LORRAINE continued walking towards the stadium, she searched through other memories, questioning her relationship with the church. She had been confused and unhappy for years.

She had lived with her two sisters and parents in Payne Street, Surrey Hills, until she was about eleven, when, in 1951, the family moved to Finch Street, East Malvern. Lorraine went to Tooronga Road State School then Malvern Girls' High for a few years before she went to MacRobertson Girls' High on a scholarship.

All brethren women wore a narrow velvet band around their heads to show the angels they were subject to God-ordained authority. At Malvern Girls' High School one morning the headmistress called Lorraine to the platform at assembly. In front of the school she told Lorraine to take the black belt off her head because it wasn't part of the school uniform. The schoolgirl felt humiliated when she had to tell the headmistress she wasn't allowed to.

Lorraine was lost in the bush when she was twelve. She and two younger girls had gone on an adventure while on a family picnic. Lorraine spent the night leading her two little friends to safety. She was terrified, and prayed desperately through the night that if God rescued her, she would commit her life to Him. The decision excited her. The girls were found shortly after first light and the following Sunday night Lorraine told her parents she wanted to be a Christian.

She felt she had to tell someone outside the family. She racked her brain before she thought of the elderly school caretaker. His house was on the schoolgrounds and he was always leaning on the schoolgate as the kids arrived. Lorraine looked for him but for the first time he wasn't there. She walked up to his front door and rang the bell. When he answered, Lorraine told him solemnly, "I have decided to commit my life to Jesus and be a Christian." The caretaker looked at her for a minute. A faint smile crossed his face.

"Just a minute," he said, and disappeared inside. Lorraine could hear him talking with his wife but she could only make out a few sharp words. Eventually the smiling caretaker returned with a bunch of flowers, dripping with water, which he pushed into her hands.

At 17, Lorraine took up nursing at Bethesda Hospital. She adored nursing; it was all she had ever wanted to do but she hated living away from home and was often homesick. Still, she enjoyed the freedom. She got away with doing lots of things, like eating a steak at a restaurant; and listening to her room-mate's radio on her days off. She taught herself how to type and she learnt shorthand.

The brethren did not like Lorraine living under the same roof as unbelievers. Somehow Lorraine fobbed them off but she left nursing at the end of 1958 anyway, due to ill health. Then she landed a secretarial job in an insurance company in Collins Street.

The church rules were getting stricter. Now Christmas and birthdays could not be celebrated. Lorraine lived back at home for the next two years until her parents fell foul of the church and were excommunicated. At a church meeting one evening, somebody stood up and announced that the congregation no longer 'had fellowship' with Charles and Greta Sangster. Lorraine's parents told the girls they had decided to leave the church because of 'false teaching'. The brethren said it was for challenging the truth.

The family went home straight after the meeting so the girls could pack and leave. Greta gave each of her three daughters some sweets and kissed them goodbye. Lorraine, younger sister Margaret and elder sister Elwyn boarded temporarily with an elderly woman before moving to a flat in Riversdale Road, Camberwell.

When it became illegal for members to live under the same roof as non-members, the young women moved from the flat into a house in Barkers Road, Hawthorn.

Charles and Greta were trying to persuade their daughters to leave the brethren. The girls felt the pull but they had been brought up to believe in the church, and none of them were ready to throw it all away and incur God's wrath. Leaving also meant having no contact with their friends or relatives and Lorraine knew nobody outside the brethren. She missed her parents terribly and she often cried herself to sleep. It was 1961 and Lorraine was just shy of her twenty-first birthday.

Another busy day at the Collins Street office was over. On her way to the tramstop, Lorraine looked up and saw her father, standing still and alone, watching her. Lorraine wanted to speak to him but she was too frightened. Members were not allowed to acknowledge ex-members, who were considered unclean. She walked quickly past her dad without speaking to him but not before she saw the look on his face. He was heartbroken. Lorraine walked on with tears streaming down her face. She didn't see her father for another eight years.

Margaret surprised Lorraine when she moved back home with her parents. Lorraine didn't feel she could break the rules but she couldn't afford the rent, so she moved in with a young couple and their three children for several months. She was happy there but the brethren told her she had to move on. She had to live with 'family'. Lorraine moved in with an uncle and aunt and their family in Prospect Hill Road, Camberwell.

Lorraine applied for a secretarial job with Professor Richard Bennett at St Vincent's Hospital. To her surprise, she got the job. She was terrified when she first started. The job was really beyond her; she was terribly naive and didn't think she would last the three months probation. Professor Bennett was the chairman of various boards and held meetings, attended by numerous surgeons, in the library adjacent to Lorraine's office. Many times Lorraine would get calls from the operating theatres, asking her to pass on urgent messages to the surgeons. She would open the library door and just stand in the doorway, not knowing who she was supposed to speak to. Usually no-one took any notice of her.

She went to evening classes at Suzan Johnston's School of Deportment where she learned how to run an office and, best of all, how to interrupt meetings. The first time she did it the 'SJ' way, she was bursting with pride.

The professor became the first person Lorraine could relate to outside the church. She saw him as a kind, fatherly man, similar to her dad. Lorraine gradually came to realise that not all people outside the brethren were bad.

But she felt inadequate and disorientated and it was a constant worry. In conversation, for example, she dreaded people asking for her opinion of a well-known actor or sportsman. Every time it happened she would explain apologetically that she didn't know who they were.

One lunchtime, Lorraine offered to do some shopping for a young doctor who worked in her department. He asked if she would call into a bookshop in Elizabeth Street and buy *Portnoy's Complaint* for him. Pleased to be of assistance, Lorraine strolled in with a smile and asked the salesgirl for the book. There had been a furore since its release and it was banned in parts of Australia. The salesgirl called the manager, who strode from his office and told Lorraine he was surprised she wanted the book. Lorraine wondered what he was talking about. He said he would never stock such filth. When Lorraine went back to work and reported what had happened, the whole department laughed at her. She realised it was a good-hearted jest.

It was against church rules to talk about the brethren to outsiders but Lorraine didn't mind that. She was frightened people would laugh at her and not understand. The more she learnt about the outside world, the more uncomfortable she became with the teachings and the ways of the church.

Lorraine had only been to a couple of parties but they had been so long ago she couldn't remember them. She had never been to a public sports match of any kind. She had never been to a picture theatre. She had never worn make-up or jewellery. She had never worn trousers or jeans.

In the 1960s the brethren were not allowed to go to the beach. They couldn't go on a holiday. They couldn't eat anything made with 'unclean hands' (ie. take-away food). They couldn't become members of anything other than the brethren (ie. a club or a union). As the rules got tighter things became tougher for Lorraine at work. Brethren weren't allowed to eat or drink with non-members, so she couldn't eat in the lunchroom. Instead, she went out and sat on a seat somewhere. Or she just ate while walking. Lorraine kept her background a dark secret from everyone at work, particularly the professor. She often wondered what they thought of her.

Lorraine tried to ring her father, who was the chief electrical engineer at the State Electricity Commission office in St Kilda Road. It was a risk for if the brethren found out she could have been excommunicated. The man in Charles Sangster's office told Lorraine her father was overseas for a few months. She missed him terribly.

AS LORRAINE approached the arena she heard a choir in full song. It sounded so rich and joyful and uplifting. Lorraine hadn't gone to the city for any particular reason but now she was sure she had been subconsciously drawn by the crusade. She was hoping to hear and *feel* something like she had in 1959. Just what, she wasn't sure. Was it a sense of belonging she was after? She hadn't felt anything but sorrow and bewilderment for such a long time. She concentrated on the singing.

"...And now I am on my way home,
Surely goodness and mercy shall follow me,
All the days, all the days of my life...
And I shall dwell in the house of the Lord forever,
And I shall feast at the table set for me..."

Lorraine leant against the wall of the sports ground and began to cry. As her hands felt the cold bricks in the wall behind her, her heart brimmed with joy. She felt a tremendous rush of release. She knew instinctively she could leave the brethren without leaving the Lord, and without losing her faith. She was on her way home.

A church counsellor inside the stadium was listening to the same singing. He walked to the centre of the ground and stood next to his friend and minister, the Reverend Gordon Powell. Like many before him that day, and like many more to come, the man was deeply moved by the Reverend Billy Graham's words. Robert Lowe, a 32-year-old Englishman declared to the crowd of 85,000 that he had committed his life and his soul to the Lord.

Her joy intermingled with trepidation, Lorraine walked along the banks of the Yarra River to the city centre and caught a tram home. She had to leave the church immediately. Once she had made up her mind, she knew she could not live a double life. Yet she felt totally uninformed and unprepared for a life in the 'real' world without the fellowship of the brethren. She knew the brethren would never speak to her; never even acknowledge her if they saw her, just as she had ignored her dad, and others who had left. But already committed to leaving, Lorraine felt a sense of pride.

It is easy to live within a system where all the decisions and rules of life are made for you and all you have to do is comply, she told herself.

It takes much more courage to leave than to stay.

She felt also a sense of loss and futility. She felt suddenly devastated that she had wasted almost thirty years in a system she now thought was false. She had never doubted her faith or love for the Lord - she knew that was real and personal - but she had lived a deprived and sheltered life, believing that was what God wanted. She was shattered now to realise she was following the false teaching of men. She hoped God would realise the life she had led was not her choice but what she had been born into. She had carried it out in the sincere belief it was what God required of her. And she hoped, no matter what happened or what had gone before, that nothing the brethren had done to her would ever separate her from her own faith.

As the tram rumbled along St Kilda Road, Lorraine looked out at the trees lining the boulevard. The first rusty brown and red leaves had begun to fall. As she contemplated the change of season, Lorraine took stock of her life. It hadn't been all bad. She realised she knew many lovely and sincere people. She had a large extended family. Yet she still needed her mum and dad.

She ran home from the tram stop, dashed inside her aunt and uncle's home, and picked up the heavy black telephone handle. Wondering if her parents had returned from their overseas trip, she frantically dialled their number.

"Dad, I want to come home," Lorraine said. She was crying with joy and relief.

Charles could hardly believe his ears. They spent the next evening together for the first time in too many years.

WHEN SHE got home from work the following Monday, Lorraine waited until after dinner to tell her uncle and aunt of her decision. They were very upset but more because they would miss her. Just by telling them she wanted to leave the brethren, Lorraine had placed a terrible burden on them. If they supported her, they would be considered part of the 'plot' and could be barred from the fellowship. They could lose all contact with their own family.

To protect themselves, the aunt and uncle rang an elder and told him what was happening. Lorraine went to her room and began packing her meagre belongings into two cases.

A few minutes later she heard the door bell chime. The elders had arrived. There were about twelve of them, dressed in business suits. Some wore hats. They were very serious; they were witnessing a very solemn event. Everybody who spoke did so in a hushed tone.

The elders walked along the hallway. Two of them spoke to Lorraine from her bedroom doorway. These men were determined she was not going to leave. Lorraine was petrified, yet she was equally determined to carry out her plan. One of the elders asked her to meet with them in the loungeroom.

Lorraine left her scattered clothes and half-full cases and walked to the doorway of the loungeroom. The elders gathered round like a murder of crows. Lorraine trembled as the elders spoke of her folly and explained again the crime she was committing. Lorraine thought of her father waiting for her.

An elder said they would pray Lorraine would be hindered from leaving as they began quoting the Bible. Lorraine fled back to her room. She was too frightened to shut the door but she continued packing.

One elder had brought his wife with him. The woman walked softly into Lorraine's room and embraced her. She kissed Lorraine on the cheek and then knelt down. She neatly folded Lorraine's clothes and placed them gently in the cases. Lorraine couldn't believe she would take such a risk.

The elders had moved back towards Lorraine's bedroom. A couple of them stood in the doorway while the rest gathered in the hallway. They continually asked Lorraine why she was leaving. They couldn't understand.

Lorraine felt sick. As she packed she told them they were not the only Christians. They denied that and told her she was turning her back on the Lord. She was about to enter the world of the Devil. The woman helping Lorraine became very upset.

Lorraine pushed the cases shut and looked up. She couldn't see the elders now. She thought she might sneak out without them seeing her. But when she emerged from her bedroom, she found them in the hallway, kneeling. Six of them faced one wall, six faced the other. Lorraine's last obstacle was a twenty-four legged barrier. When the elders saw her, they began to mournfully pray aloud. With leaden dread, Lorraine slowly picked her way between the black legs. Occasionally she accidentally bumped a leg or back with her cases. As she moved through the men, holding her breath, the praying grew louder. Different sections of the Bible were being recited, some with venom, some with mercy, some with genuine love. They prayed she would turn back from the path of destruction.

"Lord, prevent. Intervene in this action."

"Lord, have mercy on her soul."

Lorraine quickly stepped over the last pair of calf muscles. As the praying reached a crescendo, above the chanting, Lorraine heard one clear voice.

"Lord, we commit her to Satan for destruction of the flesh".

Lorraine flinched. She opened the front door, took a breath and stepped out without looking back. Her aunt and uncle were in the kitchen and her aunt was crying. Lorraine hadn't had time to say goodbye properly but she wasn't about to go back now. She knew they understood.

She struggled out the front door and clambered into the taxi she had ordered. Lorraine cried all the way to her parents' home yet she felt invigorated. She had no doubt she was doing the right thing but she was afraid. The taxi driver occasionally glanced in his mirror but he said nothing.

Mr Sangster met his daughter at the door and gave her a long hug. Lorraine went straight to the kitchen and sat in her old seat at the table. Her mother had a hot cup of chocolate ready. Margaret was there too. Everything was just as Lorraine remembered it. The same clock on the wall, the same furniture, the same stove, the same well-stocked pantry, the handsome but worn carpet in the hall.

When Margaret and her parents went to their rooms to retire, Lorraine sat on the edge of her bed in the very formal visitor's room. Where did she belong? She tried to envisage what was to come, but she couldn't see anything. The world outside the brethren seemed huge and wild and frightening. But it was exciting too, and she knew she had to follow her heart.

After midnight she crept into the kitchen and put the kettle on to make herself a hot drink. While she was sitting there her father came in and sat beside her. Lorraine wept when he put his arms around her. She went to bed filled with joy.

THE NEXT day Lorraine had her waist length hair cut to her shoulders. Then she told Professor Bennett the story of her background and what had just happened. He was very understanding. He told his staff and they united in helping Lorraine cope with her new life.

One weekend the professor asked Lorraine to stay and babysit. At the time the British serial *"Coronation Street"* was popular on television. The professor asked Lorraine to watch it while he and his wife were out and tell them later what had happened. Lorraine panicked. She had never touched a television, or watched one for that matter. One of the professor's sons showed her how to turn the set on and off. But not having seen a film at all before, and not knowing the plot or the characters, she became confused. To her shame she found she could not tell the professor or his wife anything about the story the next morning.

Her workfriends opened up new doors for her. A pathologist, Dr Thelma Baxter, took Lorraine to her first concert - *"Fiddler on the Roof"* - and to a restaurant - The Society - in Bourke Street. Lorraine practised winding up spaghetti for several weeks before she would go. Dr Baxter also gave Lorraine a ticket to see the Melbourne Symphony Orchestra. She had the best seat in the house, right in the front row. The live music thrilled her. She got the fright of her life when the man next to her nudged her and said, "You are allowed to breathe, you know!"

LORRAINE DECIDED not to mix with ex-brethren. Many who had left had given up their faith but that was not an option for Lorraine. She made up her mind to seek out what was real and true, and not throw everything overboard just because a system had failed her. She decided she would try to establish herself in a church of long-standing reputation.

She settled on Scots Church in Collins Street, Melbourne, mainly because it was big and she could lose herself in it while she found her feet. The minister was Reverend Gordon Powell, who had officiated at

The Murder of Sheree

the Billy Graham Crusade. Church was difficult at first - it was so different to what she was used to - but she persevered and with time became more relaxed.

One Sunday Mr Powell announced the Presbyterian Church was arranging a six week world tour. Lorraine and her sister Margaret decided they would go. They flew to the United States, Europe and the Holy Land. They saw the Passion Play at Oberammergau. When she returned, Lorraine knew her experiences had re-built her faith. She allowed herself a little self-satisfied smile.

Her greatest dream now was to live a 'normal' life. She wanted dearly to be a housewife in a nice home. But she had never kissed a man other than her father. She wondered what it would be like to be kissed. She wondered if she would ever find a man who might want to care for her, love her, or even marry her. She couldn't imagine who might take an interest in her.

CHAPTER TWO

IT WAS Christmas 1970 and Lorraine wanted to relive the excitement and anticipation of the Christmases she had experienced as a child. She arrived at Scots Church very early, about an hour before the service, and sat in the second front row, staring at the beautiful stained-glass windows. She was alone in the church, apart from the organist, who was practising quietly. Lorraine thought it was a bit like being at her own personal service. Then an uneasy feeling crept over her and suddenly she felt very lonely. She prayed to God for a friend for Christmas. That was all she needed, she thought, and pictured a girlfriend, a soul mate - someone she could trust. She prayed like that for about half an hour. The euphoria of being in control of her own life had vanished. She felt poorly equipped for her new life ahead.

Lorraine enjoyed the service so much she couldn't believe it when the hour ended and the congregation began filing out. The worshippers slowly shuffled toward Reverend Gordon Powell at the doorway, who was waiting to shake the hands of his flock as they left. In front of her, just two metres away, Lorraine could see the back of a tall, slim, dark-haired man who was wearing a modern blue shirt with very narrow red stripes. She didn't really notice him - it was more the shirt he was wearing.

Outside it was warming up. It was a bright day with a light, gusty wind and the promise of a hot afternoon. On the steps of the church, the man with the nice shirt walked up to Lorraine and started talking to her.

"I'm supposed to be going to Mr Powell's for lunch," he said. Then he turned and pointed to his white Holden Kingswood parked near the intersection of Russell and Collins Streets. He grinned widely. "Maybe I'll have to catch a tram."

Lorraine could see he had left the car's headlights on. She felt a little awkward but she was pleased he was talking to her. He introduced himself as Robert Lowe. She thought that was a nice name. Robert said his church was Brighton Baptist Church. He never did explain why he was at Scots Church that day.

The pair chatted pleasantly for a few more minutes about the service. Lorraine felt at ease. Robert was easy to talk to and he made her feel as if she was the only woman in the world. He was well-mannered, and his deep, rich voice was as smooth as honey. And he spoke so clearly. Lorraine thought his voice would sound wonderful on radio. She cast a quick eye over him when she felt he wasn't watching her. He stood about six feet tall, and had a slim but athletic build. He was nice.

Robert said he would ring her and suggested that they might be able to go out together. Then they went their separate ways. That night Lorraine lay in bed wondering if Robert Lowe was the answer to her prayers.

FOR THE next two months Lorraine didn't see him at church. It was early March before he rang her at work and asked if she would like to go for a drive. Lorraine recognised his voice immediately but she wasn't wildly excited. After all, he had taken his time getting back to her. In fact, she felt rather anxious about going out with him, as she had never been out with a man before. But Robert seemed very kind and considerate so she had no real worries about going out with him when the day came.

LORRAINE WORE her best dress - a pale blue, sleeveless number. Robert picked her up after lunch on the Saturday in his Kingswood, his company car, and they drove to the Dandenong Ranges, in outer-eastern Melbourne. They drove along the fern-lined black ribbons that wend their way through Olinda, Sassafras and Sherbrooke Forest. They had a delightful afternoon tea in a tea house. Lorraine loved every minute of it. Robert was kind, and easy to talk to. His manners were perfect and he was great fun. He didn't talk about himself much but he asked Lorraine a great deal about herself. She told him almost everything. Everything except the brethren.

Robert did talk a little about himself. His family lived in New Zealand, where they had moved after migrating from England. He laughed as he described himself as the 'black sheep' of the family. Lorraine laughed a little too, but she had no idea what he was talking about. She didn't dare quiz him. After all, she thought her own history was pretty weird. She felt she had enough to be ashamed of.

Robert said he had considered going to a bible college and maybe doing full-time missionary work. Lorraine wondered if that would be a good idea for her too, to help unlearn some of the brethren's teachings. Then Robert took Lorraine into his confidence. He had decided, he said, to follow Christ after the Billy Graham crusade the year before. He wanted to commit his whole life to Christian work. As he explained to her how he had walked up to the stage to be received, she realised where she was at the same time. But she didn't tell him.

As Robert drove Lorraine home in the late afternoon, he talked of how he had come to Melbourne to attend the Melbourne School of Textiles. He was a salesman for Dupont, a division of Dunlop, selling dacron fibrefill to the furniture industry. His prospects looked good.

Lorraine felt a little dreamy. It had been such a wonderful day. Robert dropped her at home just before dinner and gave her his important-looking business card with his home phone number written on the back. Lorraine had been charmed off her feet.

IT TOOK a while for the relationship to blossom. Initially Robert rang Lorraine only once a fortnight. Occasionally they went out for dinner after work. Sometimes they went to a church function together. And they became involved in a missionary organisation and went to a couple of youth camps at Creswick and Warburton.

Lorraine was impressed by Robert's sporting abilities. He played a bit of squash and he coached and played rugby at Power House, in South Melbourne. Lorraine watched him play a couple of times and decided he was very good. He had his own cricket gear and had played for years but he had retired by the time Lorraine came to know him. But he coached a junior team and went to the Test matches at the MCG. His other hobby was listening to short wave radio. Lorraine noticed he didn't have many friends, but then neither did she. He was new in Melbourne and had a busy work and sport schedule, so it was not unusual that he didn't have a lot of mates. Lorraine had been in her new world for only a short time, too. Robert was probably the best friend she had. People liked talking to him. Women liked him but he wasn't a flirt. He brought out the best in people. He made a gathering come alive. Lorraine was proud to be seen with him.

The couple spent their courting hours chatting about their pasts and their families. As their relationship grew, Robert revealed a little more about himself. Lorraine loved listening to him talk.

Robert's dad Eric was a well-to-do accountant and part-owner of a drapery business called Lowe and Moorhouse, in Newcastle-Upon-Tyne, England. Lorraine learnt Robert had been born there with the proverbial silver spoon, in 1937. He had the best possible upbringing and had gone to one of the finest boarding schools in the land. And the family was well connected. Robert's godfather, Uncle Ronnie - Ronald Selby Wright - was the minister of Edinburgh's Presbyterian Church and later became chaplain to Queen Elizabeth II. Eric Lowe joined the RAF and, due to the war, was separated from his wife, while Robert and older brother Graeme boarded at St. Mary's Primary School in the Scottish Border Country. But tragedy struck when Eric died in 1945, at the age of 33. He had returned home from his tour of duty but soon after was found dead in bed from a brain haemorrhage. Robert, then eight, was called into the headmaster's office.

"Are you Robert Lowe?" the headmaster asked.

"Yes sir," the little boy said.

"Your father's dead. Now go back to class."

Young Robert was a sensitive, artistic boy with a passion for painting, especially watercolours. He was a budding sportsman as well, excelling at high-jump and winning several school tennis championships. Then he went to the exclusive Sedbergh School in Cumbria, from 1951 until 1955. He holidayed with other lads on fishing expeditions in Scotland.

As a teenager, Robert liked school. He was smart and did well academically. He continued to shine at sport, particularly rugby and cricket. He wanted to join the RAF like his dad but he was rejected. He didn't tell Lorraine why. Mrs Lowe remarried, to Dr Peter MacKinlay, and in November 1956 travelled with her husband and sons Robert and Richard back to her native New Zealand. (Graeme came later).

They settled in Levin, about 95km north-east of Wellington, where Dr MacKinlay started up a general practice. Shortly after, Robert moved to Auckland, boarding there while he worked for a local accounting firm.

"That was probably the loneliest period of my life," Robert told Lorraine. "The loneliness used to eat into me."

Shortly after arriving in Melbourne in 1968, Robert trained at the Melbourne School of Textiles, secured his job with Dunlop Dupont, and moved into a boarding house in Hudson Street, Caulfield. He told Lorraine how he came to be at the MCG in March '69. Reverend Gordon Powell, as chairman of the 1969 Billy Graham Evangelistic Association Crusade, had asked his congregation at Scots Church for volunteers to act as ushers, counsellors, and general helpers for the upcoming crusade. Robert had volunteered.

"With the realisation of the seriousness of the matter, I responded, offering my services as an usher and counsellor - thinking I knew a little!" Robert said. "How wrong I was in thinking that. But at least I did the right thing because by so doing I had to attend the Christian Life and Witness courses. And it was at those in the Independent Church opposite that I committed myself to the Lord and became a Christian."

LATER THAT year Graeme Smith, the Victorian Director of Campaigners for Christ, met Robert at the Brighton Baptist Church. Robert had gone there with a couple of other men. Graeme liked Robert, who was always very polite, well-mannered and immaculately dressed. Graeme was delighted when he later saw Lorraine and Robert together. It was obvious they were very much in love. From then on he always saw them together, hand-in-hand.

Not long after, Robert stopped going to Brighton Baptist Church, and started worshipping at the Chelsea Baptist Church with Lorraine. Robert soon became the Sunday School teacher and with Lorraine eventually looked after the youth work too, which entailed monthly outings, calling on families during the week, and organising functions. Robert threw himself into the church with a great deal of gusto.

Lorraine had scores of picture slides from her recent overseas trip, especially of the Holy Land. Robert arranged a night at a fellow worshipper's home so Lorraine could show her slides of Israel. On the night, Lorraine ate her dinner, readied herself and waited for Robert to pick her up.

She greeted him with a smile but she saw something was wrong. He was acting strangely - he was distant and uptight. She asked him what was wrong but he didn't answer. They got in his car and much to Lorraine's surprise he took off like a maniac. He drove round and round the block, not heading anywhere, at great speed. The tyres were squealing as he drifted round corners and the car was fishtailing. Lorraine sat mortified, rocking from side to side. Then Robert stopped the car for a few seconds. He sat looking straight ahead. Lorraine was about to ask why he was behaving so strangely when he took off again, spinning the wheels. Lorraine was imploring, "What's the matter?" But Robert didn't hear her. His eyes were fixed on the road. Without turning his head he finally said angrily: "I don't want you to go tonight."

Lorraine reminded him it was he who had organised the night and that people were expecting them. After about half an hour of more maniacal driving, Robert calmed down and drove to Chelsea. Everybody could see something was wrong when the couple walked in because Lorraine was still trembling. Robert recovered from whatever it was that was troubling him and everybody had an enjoyable night. Lorraine thought he must have had a really bad day at work.

BY OCTOBER 1971, the relationship was blossoming. Which was why Lorraine was so puzzled when she found a letter from Robert, hand-delivered in the letterbox, telling her he would not see her again. The note told Lorraine she should not fret but console herself by concentrating on the positive things in their relationship. Not only did Lorraine have no idea what Robert was on about, she had not seen it coming. She thought Robert was as much in love with her as she was with him. She was devastated, and she turned to Mr Powell.

The minister had taken Robert under his wing at Robert's stepfather's request. Dr MacKinlay had written to Reverend Powell from New Zealand, asking him to look after Robert's interests. Apparently Robert had been in some kind of trouble - it was never specified - and the family hoped Robert could have a fresh start. But the churchman didn't tell Lorraine that. Although he had never heard of Robert or Peter MacKinlay he resolved to help where he could. Like everybody else he thought highly of Robert.

Mr Powell told Lorraine it was not the first time that Robert had broken somebody's heart. He had ditched another girlfriend who, broken-hearted, had moved to Ballarat.

After a few weeks Lorraine told a friend what had happened. The women hatched a plan to confront Robert at his home. As Lorraine and her friend arrived in Hudson Street, they saw Robert pull up in his car. Lorraine ran from her car and jumped in beside him and asked him, breathlessly, what was wrong. He said he was concerned they were getting too close. Lorraine felt he was scared of commitment, and told him so. They talked for about half an hour. Then Robert said he would see her again.

It was October 25 and Lorraine was crocheting a cotton top for Robert's birthday. It was mainly white with a blue band around it and a collar. She sat up half the night getting it finished for her man's birthday the next day. At 2am Lorraine's dad came out to see what she was doing. With a chuckle he said she was just like her mother. Greta had done the same thing before they were married. Charles made his daughter a hot drink while he laughed about 'silly women'.

Robert was thrilled the next day when Lorraine handed him the top. That night they went out for dinner to celebrate.

One Saturday evening in June 1972, Robert and Lorraine went for a drive to Queenscliff, at the south-west entrance to Port Phillip Bay. It was a lovely day out - driving, chatting, listening. On the way home, as they approached Geelong, Robert remembered it was time to listen to one of his favourite programs, a Christian radio show. He parked near a tin shed and attached an antenna wire to it to improve the reception. The program, from Radio HCJB in Quito, Ecuador, came in loud and

The Murder of Sheree

clear on Robert's little short wave set. The couple sat cuddling, listening to the program. Lorraine wasn't affected by the program much - it was about commitment - but she was surprised at Robert's reaction to it. He asked her to marry him. Lorraine was surprised but she was also very, very happy.

When they got home, Robert - just having a bit of fun - knelt down in front of Mr Sangster and asked for permission to marry Lorraine. Lorraine's parents were delighted. Robert was a steady young man, an obvious achiever, who was a true Christian to boot. The following Monday, Lorraine walked to work in the rain. She thought about her past, and considered her future. She certainly felt blessed. She had made the right decision in 1969. She would have a wonderful life, with a caring, kind man. She felt ready to burst. Everything seemed to be shining in colours Lorraine had never seen before. She never forgot that feeling of completeness, of being loved.

THE HAPPY couple had their engagement party at the Sangster home, which was now a unit in Beaconsfield Parade, Albert Park. It was a quiet but joyous affair, attended by members of Lorraine's family and a few friends from church. Lorraine had never had a party for herself before.

Robert and Lorraine became inseparable. One night while they were driving in the city, they stopped to post some letters at the Melbourne GPO. Robert parked the car next to the public toilets in Elizabeth Street and Lorraine jumped out of the car to post the mail. Dashing back to the car, she slipped down the steps and fell, breaking a bone in her foot. She cried out in pain. She couldn't move and lay there for a few minutes before a passerby saw her. Robert was so sorry he hadn't seen what had happened, otherwise he would have jumped to Lorraine's aid. The public toilets had blocked his view.

A FEW weeks before the wedding, Lorraine and Robert bought a house in Albert Street, East Malvern. Robert shifted in alone to save paying rent in Hudson Street. The following Saturday, Lorraine helped her fiance pack and shift his things. Lorraine looked around the boarding house as she moved towards Robert's room. The house was quite presentable and very tidy. She was completely taken aback when she stepped into Robert's room. It wasn't just untidy, it was dirty. Under the mat beside his bed were papers and old food wrappings. There was dirty clothing everywhere and dirty underwear was scattered across the floor. Lorraine took the mess home and put it through the wash, but her mum told her to throw most of it away. The women bought new underpants for Robert as most had gone to holes. Lorraine was amazed but then she hadn't lived with brothers. Maybe that was what happened when men lived alone.

Robert's family were delighted with the news of the wedding but Graeme couldn't spend time away from work. Richard couldn't make it to his brother's wedding either. Robert was terribly disappointed. He asked Noel Sampson, a medical student the couple knew from St Vincent's, to be a groomsman, and Graeme Smith to be best man. Graeme was a little bewildered but nonetheless pleased to officiate. He knew Robert but he wasn't that close to him.

They were married at Camberwell Baptist Church at 5pm on October 10, 1972. Lorraine was 32. Her new husband was 35. Professor Bennett topped the day off when he flew back from London two days early to propose a toast.

Lorraine shifted into their comfortable new home, which they had bought for $24,000. Robert had borrowed $12,000, and when the couple scratched up everything they had, it came to exactly $12,000. Lorraine was so happy, she thought it was all meant to be. She was starry-eyed for months. There was a little hiccup when Robert was retrenched as soon as they came back from their honeymoon but he soon got another job. He was doing nicely as a travelling salesman and bringing in a good income. Lorraine revelled in preparing hot dinners for her new husband and loved watching him eat her food. She would wait to hear if he liked his meals and he never let her down. It was a wonderful home, with a pretty front garden and a neat, spic-and-span interior. Life was as good as it gets.

Richard Lowe came to visit his older brother and new sister-in-law while he was in Australia on business. Over dinner, the discussion turned to Christianity, Billy Graham and heaven and hell. Rick asked his brother, "If you died now, would you go to heaven?"

"Oh, yes," Robert said. "I'm now a Christian, I've changed."

"If you'd died before Billy Graham, for crimes you have committed?"

Lorraine knew what he meant. Innocent, unknowing crimes against God's laws.

"I'd have gone to hell," Robert said.

Lorraine thought that was a bit harsh but she knew how seriously Robert took God's laws. She thought he was being unnecessarily hard on himself.

LORRAINE and Robert were lying in bed. Robert was looking at the ceiling. He turned his head on the pillow so his wife couldn't see his face.

"You may not always have me around," he said.

"What do you mean?" Deep lines furrowed her brow. She thought he might be going to die. Robert didn't answer. Then Lorraine thought perhaps he was just joking. He was a bit of a jokester. He was probably playing devil's advocate.

IN JUNE 1974, their first son was born. Robert was thrilled. He just burst into tears when he first saw the baby. Robert was with Lorraine at the birth until the last hour or so when things went wrong. Lorraine's specialist had to call in two other experts and they sent Robert out of the theatre. The baby was born in shock. Lorraine briefly nursed her son before he was placed in a special cot and not moved for forty-eight hours. Robert raced to Lorraine's parents' home to break the news and then rang his parents in New Zealand. He decided Lorraine could name the boy but because of a family tradition, Robert insisted on having the name Selby - his mother's maiden name - inserted somewhere. When they were first married, Robert's mother had tried to get them to take on the surname of Selby-Lowe, but Lorraine didn't like it. The baby was christened Benjamin Selby Lowe.

ROBERT WAS a couple of hours late for dinner when her neighbour came in saying Robert was on the phone. (Robert wouldn't allow Lorraine to have the phone connected for some years because there was a public phone box just down the street.)

Lorraine was relieved he had rung but she was confused when Robert asked her to grab some identification and catch a taxi to the Prahran police station. He said the police didn't believe he had a wife and young son. Lorraine arrived at the station with Benjamin who was not quite 18 months old. The policeman behind the counter asked Lorraine her name and checked her address. One policeman smiled as he watched Benji sitting on the counter, playing with a rubber stamp. Then Robert came out of an interview room, grinning and full of confidence. He strode across the pale green linoleum, thanked the police, shook hands with some unenthusiastic officers, and then left with his wife and son. Robert took Lorraine and Benji out for dinner on the way home. Robert told his wife the police must have taken down a wrong car registration number. They were obviously looking for somebody else. He told Lorraine this often happened with company cars, and the police did their best to be awkward. Despite his ordeal, Robert seemed relaxed and they had a fun night out. Robert made a big joke about it.

"That's one way to get you out for dinner without a babysitter," he chimed.

Over dinner he explained he had been talking to a woman that afternoon. Maybe the woman had had second thoughts after talking to a stranger, he said, and handed in his car number, but there was nothing to it. Lorraine wasn't all that worried. She knew Robert was an extrovert and, being a salesman, took the opportunity of speaking to everyone he met. He had previously told Lorraine he liked to 'chat up' men and women, which he said meant just talking to strangers. Unfortunately some people misinterpreted his friendliness and sometimes became alarmed at a stranger speaking with them. Lorraine had seen this happen herself. Once Robert had approached an elderly lady who was walking past their church one night and asked if she would like to join them in church. The woman simply glared at him and said: "Do I know you, young man?" But usually he got a good reaction when Lorraine was with him. Once Robert caught the train to work with Lorraine, who always travelled in the same compartment each day. When Robert sat down he said brightly, "Good morning, everyone!" with a cheeky look on his face. Everybody laughed and conversations actually took place on a commuter train.

ROBERT BECAME youth director of the Worldwide Evangelistic Crusade and ran youth meetings and youth camps. He belonged to the Baptist Lay Preachers and preached in churches all over Victoria. When Lorraine and Robert joined the Camberwell Baptist Church, Robert met Bill Naylor, a representative of Radio HCJB. When Bill heard that Robert was also interested in the radio station, he encouraged him to become involved. Robert became a representative. He threw himself into it and eventually became Australian chairman of the World Radio Missionary Fellowship. It was all voluntary, but it involved a lot of work and a lot of time. There were monthly and weekly meetings to arrange and attend, as well as national conferences. Robert helped arrange for missionaries to go out to their work, organised visas and sent them to language school. Overseas folk involved with the World Radio Missionary Fellowship often stayed with the Lowe's. Life was busy.

SECOND SON Jonathan MacKinlay Lowe was born in 1976. The couple tried for more children but Lorraine suffered four miscarriages, including one when she and Robert were camping in Bairnsdale. There was a tremendous storm and lightning hit the tree next to their tent. The next day Lorraine miscarried. Robert desperately wanted to have a little girl but finally they gave up trying.

IN 1979 the family moved to Mannering Drive, Glen Waverley, almost in the shadow of the spire of the Police Academy. The home had four bedrooms and was brand new. It was a pseudo-Spanish style home, popular in the early and mid 70s, painted white and mission brown. The brick front fence blocked out the street and completed a garden courtyard between the front door and gate. The front garden was not spectacular but it was pleasant and well-manicured, with a little birdbath placed in the centre of the lawn. It looked still and peaceful.

The Lowe's were initially $2000 short for the deposit on their new home but Robert imported a new line of Korean wall clocks and sold them at an exhibition in one week, making up the shortfall. As a salesman he almost always exceeded expectations. He spoke well and was always meticulously dressed. He dabbed black hair dye on his grey hairs to make himself look younger. He relied heavily on motivational tapes and attended motivational and mind power conferences where he bought books and tapes. He seemed to need the stimulation constantly to keep himself psyched up at work. Occasionally he turned his hand to other sales ventures for some quick cash. In the early 1980s he spent a week flying around Tasmania hawking 'Ma Evan's Hair Tonic'. Robert told Lorraine he went with Alex Jesaulenko, the Australian Rules football legend.

In addition to the monthly radio church meetings at home and countless voluntary hours spent on the organisation, Robert still found time to continue with his junior cricket coaching at the Waverley Junior League at Larpent Reserve. He spent any spare time lavishing attention on Lorraine. Not only did he regularly bring home gifts but he would ring her three or four times every day from work just to say "Hello, I love you."

Whenever anybody was ill, Robert was so reassuring and comforting. He often hugged his wife and sons. The four of them loved to spend a Friday night around the open fire in winter. They did everything together.

Sometimes some very funny things happened. Lorraine blushed but she couldn't help but laugh when Robert drove home almost naked one hot afternoon from the swimming pool. He was cross as he explained how some mischievous kids had stolen his clothes while he was doing laps. Then he saw the funny side too. Lorraine and Robert often fell about laughing when they mentioned it.

Occasionally Robert would lose his temper over little things. One weekend the family was staying at the Sangster's holiday unit in Florence Avenue, Rosebud. It was early morning, and the boys - Benjamin was about seven and Jonathan about four - were jumping about on their bunks. Lorraine and Robert were trying to have a bit of a lie-in but the little guys were up to high jinks.

Lorraine was worried they would fall off the bunks and she asked Robert to check on them. He found them jumping on the bed. The elastic on their pyjama pants had given way and their pants had fallen down. The little boys were laughing and jumping around naked from the waist down. Robert thought they were being dirty. He grabbed both of them and belted them on their bottoms and legs with his rubber thong. Jonathan ran into his mum and dived into her bed sobbing.

Benji was a hyperactive child and was on Phenobarb for several years. Robert showed his temper another time when the family and Mrs Sangster drove to Rosebud for the weekend. Lorraine was sitting next to Robert, and Mrs Sangster was sitting in the back between the two boys in their safety seats. The boys were shrieking and laughing. Lorraine could tune out but Robert could not and he asked Benji to be quiet.

As Benji rocked back in his seat laughing, Robert decided he had had enough. He swung the car into the emergency lane, got out and stomped around to the back seat where Benji was sitting. The father abruptly pulled his son from the car, pulled his pants down and smacked his bottom hard. When he finished, Robert pulled Benji's pants up, jumped back in the car and drove off.

Benjamin stood on the side of the road, watching the car's back wheels spin as it took off at high speed. The traffic was heavy and Lorraine was frightened for Benji, but Robert wouldn't stop. Through the rear window she saw Benji running after the car with his hands out, crying. Lorraine tried to get Robert to turn across the median strip, but he wouldn't. He wouldn't even speak. He didn't say anything.

Finally he relented and swung around but to Lorraine it seemed like an eternity before they drew up beside Benji, still running and crying, but it may have been only five minutes. Robert didn't say anything to his son. He just put him in the car and drove on. Mrs Sangster comforted her grandson and Lorraine turned around and held his hand all the way to Rosebud. Lorraine thought Robert over-reacted with the boys at times but as a man and head of the household, he was in charge of discipline.

IN THE early 1980s, Richard Lowe, by now a successful businessman in Wellington, flew to Melbourne and went to church with his brother's family. He was amazed when he saw his older brother preaching from the pulpit. Rick couldn't believe how good Robert was. He read a passage from the Bible and then talked, without notes, about the virtues of what he had read. He was sensational. It seemed to Rick that Robert's transformation was complete. This was a different man to the one he had visited on a prison farm in New Zealand.

AS THE boys grew older, Robert bought a small yacht and occasionally went sailing with them at McCrae, a popular summer holiday spot about 60km south of Melbourne, on the Mornington Peninsula. The nearest boat ramp to their unit was at McCrae. If the truth be known Robert was a pretty crummy sailor but the boys went with their dad to keep him happy. The family would spend the weekend at the unit and go sailing when the weather permitted. If it was too windy, or too calm, Robert would take the boys to the Rosebud mini-golf down the road. Afterwards, he might buy them an ice-cream or sweets at the Lighthouse Milkbar on Nepean Highway.

It was on the weekends that Lorraine would stop occasionally and reflect on how her life had changed since she had left the brethren. Life was good. Husband, two sons, nice home, holiday unit, a reasonable income. She couldn't imagine life being any better. She was so caught up in being the model mum and wife that when the dark clouds started looming, she didn't see them.

In 1984, Robert asked Lorraine to come to the Springvale Magistrates' Court. He told her he had been wrongly accused of something and the court needed to see they were a respectable family. He needed to show everybody they were wrong in accusing him.

Puzzled, Lorraine met Robert and his lawyer Peter Ward outside the court. Lorraine was pleased when Mr Ward said the whole thing would be 'vigorously denied'. He told her not to worry. Robert said he was completely innocent and was very angry that accusations had been made against him. Two girls, both about twelve years old, testified against Robert but they could not identify him in court. They were not even sure what he had done. They admitted they did not see him do anything. Then they cried and said they could not give any details of any offence.

Mr Ward said it was disgraceful that Robert had been put through such an ordeal. Especially when he was so worried about his wife who had had a fourth miscarriage and was just out of hospital. Everybody turned and looked at Lorraine. She didn't really understand what was going on, she was ill and on medication, yet she was furious at being used publicly in such a way. She stormed off home before the case ended. Robert came home later and said the whole thing was a lie and it was over. He said it was not his idea that she come to court and he would never use her in that way.

She was angry with him though and warned him to modify his behaviour. He told her he wasn't doing anything wrong. Lorraine didn't want to talk about it because it made her feel dirty. She did start to wonder, though, about Robert's behaviour, mainly thinking he may flirt when she was not with him. She never believed he did anything like expose himself - which was what he had been charged with - for he strongly denied that.

Instead, she worried and wondered what he had done. After all, something must be getting him into trouble. Gingerly she asked for details. Robert told her that when somebody became 'known to police' and the police lost a court case, they were determined to prove themselves right, even if they had to tell lies.

He told her the police had been harassing him. He said they kept records and would get him for 'loitering', when he had done nothing wrong. They would ask for proof of identification just to annoy him. Robert said the police were liars who were very clever at seeming friendly, but were ready to ambush unsuspecting people, especially Christians.

He told her never to trust the police. In fact, it was just as dangerous to allow them into the house as any stranger, probably more so. Robert admitted he had 'a bit of a problem' in that he needed to talk to people, especially women, which had sometimes drawn police attention, but he denied absolutely ever being unfaithful, or committing any crimes.

Lorraine started to wonder if Robert had some sort of a 'kink' but she deliberately put those thoughts out of her mind. She was determined to make her marriage work and didn't want to *know* about any threat to her new life. She was also acutely aware that she had led a very sheltered life. Robert told her most people had brushes with the law. Lorraine would have known this if she had regularly mixed with the general run of people, he said. He promised Lorraine there was nothing to worry about. He would never, ever hurt her. Lorraine was all he ever wanted and he had no need for anyone else.

From that point on, Lorraine harboured a dislike for the police that bordered on hate. She hadn't realised how manipulative and petty they could be.

The Murder of Sheree

GRETA SANGSTER was in St Georges Hospital. She had had her first heart attack in the late 1970s and Lorraine had nursed her mum at home for some time, gradually getting her back on her feet. Greta had a heart condition and the family knew she could die at any time. Lorraine loved having her mother living with her, even though she had to bed-nurse her and care for two pre-schoolers as well. Just before Charles died he asked his daughter to look after her mother. Lorraine knew her father would have been pleased. And Robert was very good with Greta too. But she took a turn and was admitted to hospital. After a little while she seemed to pick up but suddenly she had a major heart attack, and died.

Robert delivered the eulogy and he performed admirably. It was a graveside funeral and he spoke well. Everybody was impressed. He spoke of Mrs Sangster's kindness, her generosity, her love, her acceptance of him into the family and her love for the things of God. Afterwards, Lorraine went to pieces. A crowd came in for afternoon tea at her home and she was glad Robert was there to help. It was at times like this Robert was at his best.

The next day, as he was leaving home, Robert mentioned, almost in passing, that he had to go to court. He said he had been charged with a crime but the whole thing was a set up by the cops.

That night Robert came home upset and wouldn't tell Lorraine what had happened, other than to speak ill of the police. He told her she had to believe he was innocent because there might be bad publicity. When his case came up in court, he said, the policeman giving evidence nodded to the press, who immediately started taking notes. Such a small incident would not normally get into the papers but the police had deliberately made the whole thing public. Robert had only been playing with a banana at the beach one day when he was charged with wilful and obscene exposure.

The next morning he was out of bed very early. He headed off to the local store and bought the morning newspapers. He found a small article in *The Sun* headed 'Banana Strut Man', which detailed what had really happened. Robert had been caught walking around in a pair of brief swimming trunks, with a banana stuffed down the front. Then he had approached several young girls and made lewd suggestions to them. Robert bought all *The Sun* newspapers from the stores around the area so people from the church or the boys' school would not find out.

Lorraine didn't see the article but some parents at the school did. The school received a few anonymous threatening phone calls, making vile comments about Benjamin and Jonathan. Lorraine was angry. She told the boys their father had been accused of some stupid behaviour, which he denied was true, but it had been mentioned in the paper and some people were causing trouble. But things soon settled down again and life went on as usual. The school staff were very kind to Lorraine and the boys, and the headmaster refused to have the boys removed from the school as was requested by some parents. However the staff did suggest to Robert that he not come onto the school grounds for a short time. Just to keep people happy.

WHEN THE family wasn't staying in Rosebud on a weekend, Robert might take the boys to a football match at VFL Park in nearby Mulgrave to watch Hawthorn play. Or he might go and watch Jonathan playing cricket or footy. Robert was bitterly disappointed when Benjamin didn't take up cricket and football. He did his best to get him interested in cricket, but Benji preferred basketball. Robert was thrilled when Jonathan excelled in cricket.

Sundays, of course, were reserved for church. The family now worshipped at Syndal Baptist Church. Robert occasionally saw his best man, and Graeme was always impressed when he saw Robert with his family. When he looked at Robert, Graeme saw a devoted and proud father. A good man who gave every indication of being committed to Christian work.

Shortly after the newspaper story appeared, the Lowes left Syndal Baptist Church. Robert said he simply wanted to belong to a smaller church. He said there was nothing for him to do at a big church. He wanted to be used and feel useful, and get the boys more involved. So the family started attending Knox City Presbyterian Church. Lorraine liked it and her whole family became very involved. Lorraine played the piano during the services. She was asked to teach the Sunday School, which she did, and she loved it. Robert helped her as she was a bit shy doing it on her own.

At times Lorraine worried about her husband's brushes with the police but not sufficiently to do anything about it. And anyway, what could she do? If Robert said there was nothing happening, why should she doubt him? She wished the cops would leave him alone. When Pastor Ross Brightwell asked if anybody could think why Robert should not be sworn in as a church elder, Lorraine didn't feel she had anything to say. Robert may have had a 'kink' or been a flirt but that was all.

As an elder, Robert had families consigned to him to care for and visit. He did it well, and people, especially older women who lived alone, loved him calling. Lorraine and Robert spent their Saturday nights at home preparing the next day's lessons for Sunday School or for a sermon Robert would deliver. The Sunday School kids adored him.

BY 1990, Robert was working for Maria George Pty Ltd, a small rag trade firm in Flinders Lane, Melbourne. His job was to sell beads, pearls, and other items to Myer and other retailers who carried fabrics and haberdashery. He was great at his job. Occasionally he went interstate, usually to NSW and Tasmania. The boys were in Caulfield Grammar and doing very well. And Robert had paid off the house. He depended on Lorraine to run the house and care for his needs and those of the boys. He depended on her in his missionary work and Lorraine was always there to support him. If Robert arranged a meeting at home, he expected her to handle the supper, or entertain overseas visitors. Lorraine depended on Robert for financial and emotional support. After her parents died, she had no-one else who really cared for her. She looked to him for leadership and advice. Socially she depended on him, too. She never liked going out without him and preferred to stand beside him or even in his shadow. Lorraine wouldn't entertain at home without him. Most weekends they had somebody around for a meal, usually from the church or the mission. Lorraine encouraged Robert to take one of the boys camping for a night to enable them to spend more time together. Lorraine would have spent special time with a daughter.

The family never wanted for anything. Lorraine worked as a medical typist to supplement the family income, using any extra money for special holidays away. She and Robert had been planning Robert's retirement for years. They planned a tour of England and New Zealand, visiting all the places Robert had once called home. Robert had had some scrapes with the law that Lorraine didn't understand but apart from that things were nigh on perfect. She was living out her dream - a normal wife in a normal home. Many times she thanked the Lord for her good fortune.

CHAPTER THREE

◆

BUT ROBERT could be exasperating. He was very strong-willed and he despised being told what to do. And not just with Lorraine. In the late 1980s the police pulled him over for a random breath test on Burwood Highway in the eastern suburb of Burwood. Neither he nor Lorraine had been drinking but Robert refused to co-operate.

"Won't she do?" he asked, jerking a finger towards his wife. He spoke to the officers as if they were his minions.

"No sir, it has to be the driver," said one of the constables.

"Well, we'll swap seats and then you can test her," Robert said. He went to get out of the car but the officer intervened.

"No sir, it doesn't work like that."

Lorraine was embarrassed. Robert was being a real pill. As the conversation continued, it occurred to her that he was going out of his way to upset the police. It crossed her mind that the police might dislike Robert as much as he hated them. She admired the police for the way they handled Robert. They kept their cool, and eventually Robert took the test. He blew what he knew he would. Zero.

ROBERT OFTEN talked about Lindy and Michael Chamberlain. He was outraged that the police had charged the Seventh Day Adventist pastor and his wife over the disappearance of their daughter Azaria from Ayers Rock in 1980. To Robert, it was further evidence of police harassing Christians. He was cock-a-hoop when the couple were pardoned. And it reinforced to Lorraine what Robert had been telling her about the police for years.

When Caulfield Grammar's physical education teacher Mark Bensen left the boys' school for being 'irregular', it was no surprise to Lorraine that Robert brought him home and made a fuss over him.

"This is how people are unfairly treated, Lorri," Robert told his wife, pointing to the man sitting next to him. There had always been constant visitors to the Lowe household for church matters but the most frequent visitor now was Mark Bensen. Robert and Mark spoke nearly every night in the loungeroom, sometimes for hours on end. Lorraine walked past the loungeroom one night and overheard the word 'valium' several times. Maybe Mark, his career in tatters, was on medication, Lorraine mused. She felt sorry for him losing his job. She would have been disgusted and shocked if she knew Mark Bensen couldn't help himself when it came to molesting children, particularly boys. She would have been even more shocked had she known her husband had a history of criminal behaviour himself.

Robert was 19 when he stole a car in England and tried to run down a policeman, earning himself a hefty fine of 21 pounds (this was 1956) and bringing shame on himself and his family. He had been arrested and charged several times in New Zealand between 1959 and 1965. Charges of indecent assault on a male and theft brought only fines. But two other charges of wilful and obscene exposure - three and a half years apart - brought six months imprisonment each.

In 1964, the court branded Robert Arthur Selby Lowe a "rogue and a vagabond". Certainly Lorraine knew Robert had been troubled by police for offences he had not committed. But she would not have believed he had been interviewed more than a dozen times and had appeared in court on charges of indecent behaviour, loitering for homosexual purposes, wilful and obscene exposure and theft. She would have been devastated to know some had been committed since they were married.

The Springvale court charges were laid after Robert was caught at Waverley Gardens Shopping Centre fondling his erect penis in front of a number of girls. The following year he was arrested after he had been caught near Batesford Reserve, Chadstone, sitting on the ground outside the public toilets with his pants pulled down, masturbating. Just a few minutes earlier he had been following two young girls and making obscene suggestions before they ran away. The Chadstone area was a favourite 'beat'.

Robert kept his criminal life a dark secret. The thoughtful phone calls Robert made to his wife each day were to prevent her trying to call him at work. If she had, she wouldn't have been able to find him, for he had had nine different employers over the years. She still thought he worked for the company he had started with, but he had left there years ago. He was a good salesman - great, in fact. But when his behaviour in company cars was attracting police attention, his employers had to 'let him go'.

ON MELBOURNE Cup Day - November 6, 1984 - six-year-old Kylie Maybury set off for the local Food Plus store. It was only a 150 metre walk from her home in Gregory Grove, Preston, to the shop in Plenty Road. Her last known movement was to buy a bag of sugar in the shop at 5pm and walk outside. There was one other sighting, not confirmed, in a fast food store in Preston East. A little girl matching Kylie's description bought a big serve of chips from the Kentucky Fried Chicken store. Police said later that if it was Kylie, she would have been driven there by her abductor.

She had been snatched from under her mother's nose. Julie Maybury was waiting at home for the sugar to make a cup of tea. Within fifteen minutes the alarm was raised. At 12.45am Kylie's body was found face down in a gutter in Donald Street, less than a kilometre away from where she went missing. She had been raped, held for several hours, and then murdered. Police believe she was enticed into a car and driven away. An autopsy found traces of valium in Kylie's body, but nobody in her family, or anybody she knew, had access to the drug. Police later recovered a pink Strawberry Shortcake purse in Tyner Shreet, Wantirna South, near the Knox City Shopping Centre, in Melbourne's outer eastern suburbs. Kylie had such a purse with her when she was abducted. The located purse still had money in it.

Despite an intense investigation, and the offer of a $50,000 reward, Kylie's murder still remains unsolved. Her death and the circumstances surrounding it has destroyed those close to her. Her father and grandfather both committed suicide. Neither were suspects, although they were interviewed by the police as a matter of course.

In a plea for public assistance, Julie Maybury came forward and wept at a press conference. "Kylie was very beautiful," she said. "I just want to tell other mothers who have got daughters to be careful because I don't want it to happen to them."

MARGARET HOBBS had a reputation for being a lay-expert on people suffering from compulsive disorders, especially men who were repeat sex offenders. After she arrived in Australia from the United Kingdom in 1968 with her husband John, some belongings and a Diploma of Mental Welfare, she got a job as a probation and parole officer with the Victorian Mental Health Authority.

After dealing with exhibitionists and other compulsive disorder sufferers, she gradually 'gravitated' to exploring the more serious offences of incest, paedophilia, and rape. None of this evolution was planned, it just happened. When one day Margaret realised she had been in the public service for ten years treating these men, she took her expertise into the private world of outpatient psychotherapy. She rapidly built a reputation as *the* woman to seek out for treatment for wilful and obscene exposure and other compulsive behavioural disorders.

In Melbourne's Pentridge Prison, Margaret had treated some of the worst (captured) sex offenders in Victoria such as the 'Silver Gun Rapist' Peter Vaitos, 'Mr Stinky' Raymond Edmunds and Brendon Megson, known as 'Mr Baldy'. She drew up a loose profile of the background of exhibitionists/serial rapists. She found they were men who were never sure of their own sexuality. They usually didn't get along with women or they had a history of bad relationships with women. Typically they had fathers who seemed to be dominant but really it was their mothers who were in charge.

Often these men had been either physically or emotionally without a father. More than likely they had been abused or 'fixated' at some sexual level, beyond which they hadn't matured. They were usually non-assertive but often very aggressive and lacking in a sense of responsibility. Usually they felt they hadn't reached their potential and were always looking for pastures new. And many of them had a very religious background.

Margaret had learnt long ago that these men were very ignorant about sexuality. Some could have sex with their wives and ten minutes later be down the local shops exposing themselves. If, as youngsters, they had flashed at some girl or woman and got a thrill, it became a conditioned response, an answer to stress or depression. Most of the men Margaret saw professionally told her when they behaved that way, they were looking for some sort of response, some reassurance they were men. Of course, they wouldn't get it. Even if they did, they would run a mile. The men weren't looking for fear, they were looking for attention. It was all very narcissistic. Margaret saw their behaviour as misdirected, projected anger. It was all to do with the final act of social revenge. All the men Margaret saw loosely fitted the same profile.

Margaret could be an imposing figure. She was always very sympathetic but if someone started playing games - as sometimes happens in therapy - she would rule with an iron fist. Mucking about was counterproductive and a waste of time. Margaret would let any errant patient know that quick-smart. She enjoyed her work, helping these men overcome their problems.

In the week following Kylie Maybury's murder, Margaret was reading of the latest developments in the investigation in the newspaper. She took an interest in the story because she knew most of her patients would be troubled by it. Some would be angry it was motivating them to offend again. Others would be titillated. These sorts of things sometimes hampered her patients' recovery process. *Poor little girl,* Margaret thought. Just then, Robert Lowe walked into her clinic. Margaret put down the newspaper and greeted him. After shaking hands, they sat down - Margaret on her favourite loungechair, Robert on a leather armchair opposite. Margaret thought he was well-motivated to change his ways but smiled wryly to herself. *They all only come after they've been caught,* she thought. Robert had a court case pending at Springvale Magistrates' Court. He told Margaret he was married with two children and that he wanted to change. Margaret saw Robert a number of times and then wrote a report for his court appearance.

She wrote:

```
His behavioural problem is a chronic one having
been established over some 15 years and has been
strengthened and conditioned by non-detection. He
```

```
has not been afforded the opportunity of treatment
due to this non-detection and continuing mistaken
beliefs. He expresses great relief that he has
finally been caught......
```

AT COURT the offensive behaviour charge was marked "withdrawn". Robert was placed on a $500 twelve month good behaviour bond for wilful and obscene exposure, on the condition that he continue seeing Mrs Hobbs.

Robert told his wife that although the court had found him guilty, he had done nothing wrong. He was angry he had been convicted for something he hadn't done and on top of that he had to see Mrs Hobbs to satisfy the court. Lorraine was mad about it too, and not just because of the conviction. She didn't like her husband off visiting another woman one or two nights a week. Every time Robert came home from seeing Margaret, he would be chirpy and happy. She hated that. Lorraine came to dislike Margaret because of the intimacy the psychotherapist enjoyed with her husband.

When Robert asked his wife to visit Margaret with him, Lorraine was unsure whether to go. Robert explained that Margaret liked to talk to the spouses of her patients, to help them understand what was happening in therapy.

Lorraine went, and she hated it. Robert was calling Margaret 'Marg' and was so familiar with her. Then the horror began. Margaret explained that Robert was an exhibitionist. She explained what that meant for a man like Robert. He liked to expose himself. But the signs were good and he showed that he wanted to change. It shouldn't take long with a little application. Margaret went on to explain why it happened and how she planned to treat him but Lorraine had switched off. She was frightened by what she was hearing and her brain, almost involuntarily, was shutting out what she didn't want to hear. By the time she left the building, she had put the matter to rest, although she did think about it for a day or two. Then she went back to concentrating on her domestic duties.

Robert told Lorraine he had only visited Margaret a few times and had no need to see her any more. In fact, Margaret saw him frequently.

He presented as a very suave, sophisticated, well-dressed man with impeccable manners. He stood when Margaret entered the room, he always rang when he was late and hardly ever missed a session. He was very well-educated and motivated to change. And it was flattering for Margaret to talk to a man who hung on her every word. A man who took written notes of her pearls of wisdom. He was a promising patient.

Robert had a tremendous acquittal rate for exposure and offensive behaviour charges. Wilful and obscene exposure is a relatively minor crime in the world of criminal investigations. As such, it is usually handled by junior, inexperienced uniformed police officers, often many years younger than Robert Lowe. As an articulate, well-respected family man and devoted churchman, he could - and always did - perform a treat when any police officer *dared* to suggest he might have done something improper. And as a career deviant, Lowe had studied and looked for ways around the law. A text book pedant, he would fondle himself flamboyantly inside his trousers in front of young girls, knowing he could not be charged with the offence of 'exposure'. And he learnt that young victims often could not give evidence on oath because they were too young to understand what an oath was in a court of law. A youngster's uncorroborated evidence against a model citizen would often result in an acquittal. Self-satisfied, Robert Lowe would walk from court with a smug look, sometimes stopping to smile at the police who had arrested him.

IT WAS a hot December afternoon in 1984 - so hot you could smell the bitumen on the road, as if it had just been poured. Pauline Montalto, 6, and her 11-year-old sister Melissa were in Tyler Street, Preston. It was literally just around the corner from Donald Street, where Kylie Maybury's body had been found seven weeks earlier. The sisters both noticed the strange man dressed in slacks, brown shoes and a 'daggy' jumper. Melissa watched as the man, with a funny look on his face - a look she had never seen before - pulled plums and apples from his pants and threw them over the back fence of a foster home. There were kids everywhere in the backyard. Most of them were jumping in and out of the pool, trying to cool off. Some of them got out of the water and went to the fence to see

The Murder of Sheree

who was throwing the fruit. Melissa and Pauline rode their bikes closer to get a better look at the man. As they approached him, he moved to the other side of Tyler Street and ran into the front yard of a house. He crouched down behind a low brick fence. Then he called out, "Come here".

The girls crossed the road and stood in the gutter with their bikes, talking with the man across the naturestrip and footpath.

"What's your name?" he asked Melissa as he looked around.

The girl gave the man a false name. She couldn't look him in the face. She didn't know why that was. She stared at his brown shoes.

"Where do you live?" he asked.

Melissa gave a false address. She noticed the man had his hands in his pockets. He looked like he was rubbing himself.

"Do you go to school?"

"Yes." Melissa tightly held onto the handlebars of her bike. She looked at her little sister, then back at the man.

"What do you do at school?"

"School work. Sport. I play volleyball and basketball."

A strange grin came over the man's face. "What did you say? You play with boys' balls?"

Melissa's upper lip curled with disgust.

"No, I never said that." She knew instantly what he was all about.

"Have you got brothers?"

Melissa noticed that the man was slowly curling his body as he spoke, kneeling and bending. He was breathing quicker.

"Yeah, I've got two." She said. She had a quick look around to see if there were any other adults around. Nobody.

"Have you ever seen their dicks?"

Melissa blushed and said she hadn't. The man was now in a funny sort of a squatting position and still trying to get lower to the ground.

"You must have seen them. Do you want to see one?' He smiled and Melissa noticed it was a crooked smile. Nasty. His teeth looked a bit black in some places.

"No," she said quickly.

The man was now lying on the ground. He could not be seen from across the road because of the small front yard fence. He was speaking in a half-whispered, urgent voice.

"Do you want to go with me?"

Melissa shook her head and felt a funny feeling in her stomach. She shook her head vigorously but her eyes never left his face. The man's eyes darted around wildly. He was talking to Melissa but he wasn't looking at her much. Melissa thought he looked nervous or worried.

He kept saying it over and over. "Do you want to go with me?"

The little girl shook her head.

"Do you want to go with me?"

"Nooooo," she said. "I told you. No way."

"Do you want to go with me? Come on."

Melissa and Pauline's uncle drove up and parked his car with a screech. The man ran to his car, parked about 30 metres away, and sped off. Melissa's uncle wrote down the registration number.

In January, 1985, Robert Lowe was interviewed by Preston CIB after receiving complaints that a strange man had tried to get some girls into his car. The detectives checked the details of the suspect's car. It was registered to Lorraine Lowe from Glen Waverley. The driver, her husband Robert, had been charged before with sex offences. Lowe denied all knowledge of what had gone on. He denied even being in the area at the time Pauline and Melissa were accosted. But he matched the description. The car was the same model and colour that the girls had reported. There was even a pair of brown shoes in the boot. And Lowe's employer was based in Preston. But the girls couldn't say exactly what the man had done that had frightened them. And Lowe would admit nothing, even when confronted with the facts. He resorted to a 'no comment' record of interview and despite his prior convictions, refused to acknowledge he had any sort of problem.

The detectives had no doubt he would offend again. They had already checked with other police who had charged Lowe and found he was prone to stonewalling, lying, refusing to admit anything. But it was the married man's word against the allegations of two young girls. The detectives knew they had the right man, despite Lowe's protestations. They submitted a brief of evidence for offensive behaviour but knew it wouldn't get past first base. They were right. The inspector would not recommend prosecution. It made them angry. But what else could they do? The law is the law.

THE MORE Margaret saw Robert, the more she realised he differed from her other patients. In private practice she found every man with a pending court case would curb his illegal activities; he would be remorseful, especially towards his own family and his victims; and would suffer anxiety or depression in varying degrees. Robert Lowe cared not one iota. In fact, he clearly enjoyed behaving the way he did. And while most offenders might offend once or twice a month, Lowe admitted he was offending sometimes five times a week. Margaret learnt years later he was offending three or four times that much.

Margaret had developed a two-year program for patients which showed them how to alter their 'conditioned responses' to women. Gently, gradually, Margaret would train the men how to stop themselves from attacking or approaching women. She attained a remarkable success rate. In the early stages of the program she asked the men to write down what they did each day, what they thought about and how they behaved towards potential or actual targets. She decided it would be just the thing for Robert but as soon as she saw the results of his writings, she was very, very concerned. He had regular 'beats' - schools, beaches, swimming pools and public toilets in Black Rock, Beaumaris and St Kilda - he 'worked' as he cruised in his company car. Anywhere there were little girls, and occasionally boys, Robert would be on the prowl. He did not see children, only 'targets'. Margaret was surprised at the lack of sympathy Robert had for his victims, particularly given he was a dad too. There was never any remorse. She talked to him about his victims, and about how they must have felt.

"You've got two boys yourself, Robert. How would you feel if it happened to them?"

Robert just shrugged his shoulders and looked at the floor. It was of no concern.

"What about the people paying you good money to work for them? You're spending hours a week doing this Robert."

No response.

Robert differed from other exhibitionists in more sinister ways. Most 'flashers' keep a distance from their victims. Robert Lowe liked to get close, to try to touch them, to try to get them into cars, to make filthy suggestions to them. Margaret saw that as very dangerous territory. He was certainly a serial offender, whose behaviour was becoming more brazen and whose targets were getting younger. His fantasies were terribly powerful. But as time went on, she realised he was not trying to reform. He was only playing at being a patient. Psychotherapy was just another way of exposing himself, only verbally. By 1985, Margaret was annoyed and distressed that, if anything, his behaviour was getting worse. She had never had a failure before. For her case notes, she wrote a report outlining his behaviour:

```
He would use pornography, invariably stolen, he
was a compulsive shoplifter, leaving pornography
and retrieving it when picked up by targets. Their
actions legitimised his belief that he could talk
to them. In this way he deviated from the more
often encountered offender. Regressive, immature
behaviour and difficulties relating to mature women.
He was also approaching both sexes, and appeared
to be arbitrary and inconsequential.

The fateful provision of many victims for him
serves as permission-giving for compulsive offenders
and allows them to justify their behaviour in
terms of victim's presence and culpability. The
victim of a sexual attack is sheer bad luck. The
victim's fate is sealed as soon as they wander
into the sight of the hunter. This aspect was most
ingrained in Mr Lowe. He rationalised that they
shouldn't be there, they wouldn't look if they
weren't interested, if they did that signalled
that they were willing participants, etc.

These attitudes are deployed in the behaviour termed
cruising and grooming. It means preparing the target
and finding vulnerable children. Where there is a
cruising for victims and an active manipulation of
circumstances and relationships to ensure contact
with potential targets, the behaviours occur with
cognitive distortions to justify, and with the
```

offender, develop an increasing ability to select vulnerable and isolated targets. A source of concern for Mr Lowe was the age of his targets and his close interaction with them. It seemed to convey a sense of daring and bravado but such was the strength of his drive that he appeared to give insufficient consideration to the outweighing probability of apprehension. All discussions on these aspects showed a lack of commitment to stop. He failed to modify them to any significant degree.

His failures to respond to therapy I considered to be due to features not typically present in exhibitionists and which I thought suggested the existence of a sociopathic disorder. An absence of guilt or remorse was consistently present and (he) could not be swayed on any grounds including morality and spirituality. There were no signs of anxiety or depression and indeed he appeared to derive great satisfaction from outwitting the police.

He is an inveterate liar but responded to absolutely specific questions. He believed he could truthfully deny allegations if they deviated slightly from the facts. His lack of responsibility, his refusal to see the wrongness of his behaviour and his inability to learn from his past experiences were a further indication of more serious indications of more serious pathology. I terminated Mr Lowe's sessions.

Margaret did not see Robert from 1985 until March 1987 when he came in for one session. Then he stayed away again, reappearing on August 4. He told Margaret he was more in control of his behaviour and wanted to make a fresh start in therapy. He saw Margaret sporadically throughout 1988 and 1989 but he did not appear to have changed. In late 1988, he was arrested in the Latrobe Valley in eastern Victoria and questioned over a series of exposures and offensive behaviour offences. He denied the crimes, which took place near schools and swimming pools, and asked Margaret how he could complain about the treatment he had received from the police. For some reason which Margaret never learned, Robert escaped prosecution.

From what he was saying, it seemed to Margaret that his criminal behaviour was escalating. He complained to Margaret that there had been unpleasant threats to his family after the Banana Strut Man story appeared in *The Sun*. But he seemed quite oblivious to the effects on his wife and children. He complained bitterly about his perceived unjust treatment by the elders of the Syndal Baptist Church after the newspaper article appeared. Robert mentioned to Margaret that his relationship with Lorraine was deteriorating and that he was very unhappy with his life. Margaret felt he was now making little investment in family life and he was alienating himself as a father. He showed little interest in his sons' schoolwork, hobbies or sport. He did try some of what Margaret suggested, by moving away from children as victims and approached prostitutes in the St Kilda area. But none of them would have a bar of him and he found it totally unsatisfying. He was on unfamiliar turf with consenting adults. And as he told Margaret, 'lying' with a prostitute was against his moral code.

Margaret was sure his failure to respond to therapy was due to features not typically present in exhibitionists. When he failed to try to reform, Margaret again terminated the counselling sessions.

She had learnt a great deal about the charming man who first came to see her in 1984. She knew him far, far better, yet she realised he was so heavily defended that she didn't really know what made Robert Lowe tick. He deflected any attempts to make contact with the 'inner man'. She saw a man who lied at almost every opportunity, even about things he didn't need to lie about. Margaret often wondered what type of fear it was that made him do that. She felt certain he had never exposed himself to any woman or girl older than 14. His 'targets' always indicated the flavour of paedophilia.

By April 1990, Robert was back. He told Margaret that the police had been to his employer in relation to an alleged attempted child abduction. He was adamant that nothing had happened but a child he had judged to be about five had been with two other girls he had followed. He'd spoken to her in the garden of a home. Robert could not give a clear and concise account of what had happened - he was always vague whenever he was detailing offences he was alleged to have committed. Margaret was worried that he had done something but she'd never learn what it was from him. Several weeks later Robert lost his job again.

He later told Margaret that a few weeks after that session, while he claimed he was looking for work, he was involved in an incident with two young girls in Flinders Street. He said they were primary school girls and thought they were both about 10-years-old. Margaret was very concerned.

She compiled another report:

```
In 1990, he was a rep with Invicta which gave him
a lot of time on the road. He spent a large
proportion of his working life patrolling "beats",
in this respect he became a predatory opportunist.

He had a regular patrol of beach suburbs and would
be around when school was finishing or at lunchtime,
carried his bathers with him, spent time at swimming
pools where he would initiate conversation.

Extended his behaviour throughout his many trips
interstate and within Victoria and perhaps indulged
even more because he was off his home ground.
Carried disguises in hats and glasses to confuse
identification.
```

Despite all the counselling, Robert simply refused to change his behaviour, even though he was paying lip service to Margaret's concerns. She could see he was refining his prowlings. He studied it like a professional. As far as Margaret was concerned, the danger bells were ringing loud and clear. Robert had been to court enough times for the same types of offences to warrant imprisonment. She felt he needed to be punished so he could see his behaviour was unacceptable. But she never even thought of reporting him to the police. She had always represented the defendant in court, proffering reports and giving evidence on their behalf from the witness box. And there was the issue of confidentiality. She would never entertain the idea of breaching a confidence. She had to play by the rules within the judicial system and hope they would get tough with him.

IT WAS October 1990. Lorraine walked to the wooden letter box and grabbed the mail. *Typical,* she thought, *they've all got windows on the front. More bills.* She opened the rates bill, the gas bill and another one she couldn't make out initially. Then she saw it was an account from a lawyer for services rendered.

Lorraine paced the house all day. She tried to busy herself but couldn't concentrate on anything. From 4.30pm onwards she kept walking into the loungeroom, watching for the company car to pull into the driveway. Then, at 5.10pm, Robert walked in and cheerily kissed his wife on the cheek. He saw immediately that he was in trouble.

"What's this?" she demanded, throwing the paperwork into his hand.

Robert was stunned for a moment. As he read the document, his mind went into overdrive. He said he knew Tony Nicholson through Margaret Hobbs and it was probably just some silly administrative error. He would take care of it tomorrow.

Robert spent the rest of the night behaving as if nothing had happened. Lorraine wanted to believe him but she watched him constantly for any signs of guilt. There were none. Maybe he was telling the truth.

The next night Robert came home and triumphantly told Lorraine he was right. It was something to do with a court case but it had nothing to do with him. Tony Nicholson had pulled the wrong file out of his ledger and sent it to the wrong place.

But Lorraine still felt uneasy. She wondered if Margaret Hobbs knew anything about it. When Robert was at work, she rang Margaret and asked angrily, "Who is this Tony Nicholson?" Margaret told her he was her son-in-law and he had done some legal work for Robert but she wouldn't elaborate. Lorraine said that, despite herself, she wanted to come into a session with Robert to find out what was going on.

LORRAINE WAS sitting in Margaret's clinic, nervously taking in her surroundings, when Robert breezed in a few minutes later from work. Languidly he sat in the leather chair, looking right at home. He wasn't at all nervous or concerned at confronting his wife. Rather he seemed to be looking forward to it. Lorraine sat on the two seater couch to Robert's left. Margaret sat in front of him. She found it hard to contain her excitement. Lorraine's presence could be just the thing to force Robert to modify his behaviour. Margaret had already decided she would play only a minor role. She would start off the proceedings and then sit back, watch and wait. She might steer the conversation but what she really wanted was Robert and Lorraine to thrash out the whole issue.

She looked at Lorraine and saw she was sitting on the edge of the couch, trembling. Lorraine looked nervously at Robert, then at Margaret, then her brown, flat shoes. She knew it was time to pull her head up for air, to find out what was going on. She realised that she had been ignoring some things but this sort of stuff - therapists, lawyers letters and visits from the police - seemed to be getting out of hand. Suddenly she felt a hot surge of anger build up from somewhere deep down inside her and erupt into words.

"What's going on Robert?" she said forcefully. It was the first time she had ever really confronted him. She had learnt from childhood that it was not a woman's role to question her man. Her brow was furrowed; her eyes fixed on his face. Margaret noticed that despite the anger, there was fear too.

Robert gazed back calmly. Then he looked at Margaret with a hint of a questioning look. Lorraine got the impression he wanted her to start quizzing Margaret. But Lorraine wanted him to talk.

"This disgusting behaviour; why don't you stop?" She was pleading. Margaret noticed Lorraine's dress was quivering. Both women looked expectantly at the patient. Robert sat back in his chair. As he reclined, he tilted his head back and looked down his nose at his wife. After a few seconds pause to add to the tension, he said, with an air of superiority, "Because I choose not to."

Then he smiled, his upper lip turning down a little at the sides, revealing the dark teeth. Margaret was absolutely stunned. *God, that was cruel,* she thought. She knew Lorraine was aware Robert had a problem but there was no doubt she was unaware of the scope and range of his behaviour.

Lorraine's mouth dropped open and she jumped a little. For a few seconds she just stared at him and then Margaret saw the colour rush from her face. The therapist had never seen that vicious side of Robert before. It was as if he had slapped Lorraine across the face. Margaret felt he was allying himself with her against his wife. She realised he was saying to Lorraine, "This is the other woman in my life".

Margaret looked back at Robert. His lips were stuck in a broad smug smile. He was having the time of his life. She looked back at Lorraine. Her eyelids were fluttering as if the cogs in her brain had jammed. She was gasping for air and looked as if she might faint. Instead, she stood up and ran from the room. Margaret gave chase and tried to speak to her but Lorraine ran and ran and ran. She was gripped with a terror she could not understand. She didn't really understand what she was running from. The loving husband, the church elder - her lover and the father of her two boys - the man she adored, had just told her that he wasn't going to stop running all around Melbourne exposing his penis to little girls and boys. And he didn't care! Why? What was wrong? Was it her? Had she done something wrong? Was it her fault? *"Because I choose not to!"* What sort of therapy was that? What had Margaret been telling him? That it was all right to do that sort of thing? Maybe she had been teaching him these things. Maybe they were having an affair. *Maybe I'm going mad.* When Lorraine ran out of breath, she suddenly realised the bind she was in. The only place she had was her home. But what did that mean now? She panicked and broke into a run again. She was running away from him but she didn't know where she was running to.

Margaret was quite taken aback. It was the revelation of Robert's bad side he had never shown before. She had never seen this snide behaviour in him.

Later that afternoon, as Lorraine walked from room to room in a muddle, the phone rang. It was Margaret. At first Lorraine didn't want to talk but eventually they had a conversation. Margaret had spoken to Robert for a full hour after Lorraine had left but he showed no remorse at what he had done. Margaret realised what that meant.

"Why don't you divorce him Lorraine?" Margaret said. "He'll never change."

"No, no, I couldn't possibly divorce him," Lorraine said. "Who would look after us?"

Lorraine had invested nearly 20 years of what already had been a wasted life in Robert, her sons and her home. She couldn't see how she could start life again.

"Well, he'll never change Lorraine. If you don't divorce him, you'll be sorry," Margaret said.

After she hung up, Lorraine walked into the dining room and looked at the family photos on the wall. Her husband smiled back at her, his arms draped round his young sons. Then she sat at the dining room table, with her hands folded lightly in her lap. She remembered all the happy family dinners they had had at that very table. She could see Robert just over there, laughing and eating, the life of the party. In a flash she recalled something she had never thought about before. It was something she hadn't even realised she had noticed. In her mind's eye she could see Robert eating while someone else at the table was talking. He had a funny smirk on his face and his eyes were a little glazed. Lorraine struggled to identify the look. It occurred to her that he was remembering something, something that was his little secret. She realised she had seen that look many times but had never wondered about it before. Now she was curious as to what it was about but she knew she couldn't ask him. He would never discuss it. She bowed her head and sat perfectly still. She became acutely aware of the bible in the book shelf next to her although she didn't look at it. Robert had often talked about how God did not want any married couple to divorce. Lorraine believed that too. Now she felt she was bound in invisible chains and wrapped in a straitjacket. She didn't move for an hour.

Two weeks later Margaret threw Robert out of therapy again when he told her that he was going to plead not guilty to the Flinders Street offences. Margaret felt the colour come to her face. He was treating it all as a bit of a joke.

"I cannot support this irresponsible attitude you have towards your victims, Robert. I don't want to see you any more," she said.

Robert began to argue but Margaret stood up and walked to the door. She opened it and said firmly, "Leave Robert, I don't want anything to do with you at all".

There was a nasty argument. Then he began gently pleading with her.

"You can't do this to me," he said. He enjoyed making people feel guilty.

"I'll do what I like," Margaret said and put him out.

A few weeks later Robert rang and asked Margaret for a court report.

"Don't be ridiculous Robert. I don't have one good thing to say about you." Margaret chuckled a little.

"Well, I want you to write a report anyway," he said.

Margaret did write a report. It described Robert's past criminal behaviour and his attitude to reforming. In closing, Margaret wrote:

```
I am of the opinion that he truly believes that he
is indulging in harmless behaviour. It does need
the intervention of the courts to instil in him
the illegality of his actions. The censure of the
court at this time will assist with any on-going
therapy once it  has been clearly demonstrated to
Mr Lowe that his behaviour is unacceptable to the
community.
```

Margaret could have said it simpler - send him to jail. She sent the report to his lawyers and presented herself at the Melbourne Magistrates' Court on November 9, 1990. But Robert's lawyers decided not to tender the report. Robert was fined $750.

Robert stayed away from therapy for a while, although he did ring Margaret sporadically.

"I still need you Marg," he would say, but he never turned up.

He felt pretty good about himself. After the court case he behaved like a man who had removed a minor irritation. He had outwitted the police and could now get back to what he did best - frightening children and trying to abduct them - with the latest impediment out of the way. He was getting better in the execution of his crimes and he was growing bolder. He was refining his craft. He felt invincible.

CHAPTER FOUR

◆

IN 1990, at age 24, Kerri Greenhill was reeling. She'd had precious little contact with her parents since she was two, had had a string of broken, tumultuous relationships, dabbled in drugs, been chronically unemployed - and seemingly permanently pregnant - her only son had died of cot death and she was living in virtual poverty with three kids to care for. And a month after baby Shane died in May 1990, his father, Shane senior, died of a drug overdose. He couldn't face life without his son. Two funerals in a month. Kerri was like the punchdrunk boxer who is always in there fighting, but invariably ends up on the canvas. In his head he hopes he will fight on and win - in his heart he knows he's going down again. She was learning how to roll with the punches.

Kerri's teenage parents Neil and Marie Greenhill found it very difficult bringing up a baby girl. Kerri was adopted by her paternal grandparents Leslie and Joy Greenhill when she was about two and a half years old. Kerri lived with them in Preston but moved out on her own when they shifted to Rosebud in the early 1980s.

At age 17, Kerri met and fell in love with Anthony Mandile, a tall, strong, handsome young man just a few months her senior. Within months she was pregnant and in late 1984, the couple married in the backyard of Kerri's uncle's home in Highett. The Mandiles set up home in half a house in Mulgrave.

Their first child was due on St Valentines Day but Sheree Joy Mandile, was born eleven days late on February 25, 1985, at Dandenong and District Hospital, weighing 3189 grams. Kerri couldn't believe how beautiful she was. She was perfect.

The new baby behaved herself when she went home. She never suffered from colic and slept right through from 11pm to 6am. She was a bundle of joy. Kerri was so proud, she entered Sheree in every baby contest she could find. By the time Sheree was 4 weeks old, she had won three trophies and several ribbons in beautiful baby competitions in shopping centres all around Melbourne's south-eastern suburbs.

When Sheree was 6-months-old Kerri took her to see her great-grandmother Joy at Rosebud. Kerri and Joy took Sheree to the beach and plonked her in the shallows. She loved it. Whenever it was hot, Kerri would put Sheree in a big plastic tub. She was like a frog in a pond.

When Sheree was just over a year old, Kerri was working as a receptionist in an electrical store. Anthony worked at his father's tool-making firm in Braeside, in Melbourne's outer southern suburbs, while his mother Jill looked after baby Sheree.

But Kerri missed her daughter and it wasn't long before she left work to stay with her baby. She took Sheree to a playgroup when she was two but they asked Kerri not to bring her back. Sheree was a fidget and she disrupted the other kids too much. Sheree was Action-Girl. She rode her three-wheeled bike round and round. She rushed into everything full tilt. Everybody who saw her said she had 'been here before'.

On May 30, 1987, the couple's second daughter, Crystal, was born but the marriage was in trouble. Not long after, Anthony and Kerri split. Kerri moved to Waterloo Place, Mornington and Sheree went to three-year-old kindergarten. She adored it. Already she was a shining extrovert. She was always the star of the show, centre stage. At home, she loved dancing in the loungeroom for her mum or dad or grandparents. She often sang Carly Simon's *You're So Vain* (she called it *Clouds in My Coffee*) and knew all the words to Don McLean's *American Pie*. When she sang along with the radio or cassettes, she mimicked the actions she had seen the singers perform on the television. Sheree thought she was it and a bit when Kerri bought her a plastic microphone. She took it everywhere and sang and sang and sang. And she loved dancing too, anywhere, anytime. By the time she was 4 she was riding a two-wheeler bike with no training wheels.

Kerri was now seeing Shane Beasley, a troubled young man from Frankston, the gateway to the Mornington Peninsula in Melbourne's outer south-east. Kerri and her daughters took his name. Shane was a regular on the Frankston drug scene, popping sedatives such as Rohypnol and using heroin regularly. It was inevitable that the drugs would cause problems.

Sheree was home when her mum's new de-facto was brought home comatose by friends after overdosing on different types of drugs. Kerri called ambulances to their home in Elm Court, Frankston, where the paramedics used Narcan, a synthetic drug, to instantly jolt him back. Not long after, Shane was admitted to Frankston hospital after overdosing on Rohypnol. Kerri had medical problems of her own and was hospitalised, too. The Department of Health and Community Services stepped in. Sheree went to live with Granddad Neil, and Crystal went to her Grandma Marie.

Neil cherished the eight months Sheree spent with him and his wife Denise, and two daughters Adele and Harmony at their Epping home. He had always felt guilty about not being more involved in Kerri's upbringing. Only 18 when she was born, and battling to keep his marriage together, he could not cope with a baby. Now he was able to care for his daughter's own child - a child who was the spitting image of her mother. It was like making up for lost time, lost memories, a lost daughter. It was a wonderful time.

Eight months later Kerri was well enough for the girls to return home. Soon Kerri was pregnant again and in 1989 she bore another daughter, Jacinta. Sheree carried on as if she was Jacinta's mother. She fussed over her as if it was the most natural thing in the world. Kerri sometimes looked at her oldest daughter and thought: *She's only five. More like five going on forty-five.*

Sheree started school in prep at Frankston's Monterey Primary School in 1990 but she was not alone on her first day. Chloe, Kerri's German Shepherd that Sheree had ridden around the backyard when she was a toddler, followed her to school and waited for her outside. A grown up now, Sheree insisted on making herself seven lunches for school. Kerri smiled when she saw them three days later, stale and hard.

School was okay but having fun was more interesting. Every day was just a build up to the weekend.

"How many more days do I have to go to school?" Sheree would ask her mum.

The Murder of Sheree

Kerri would tell her.

"Why do I have to go to school? I know how to spell my name, I know how to write my name." She had an answer for everything.

Anthony and his parents saw the girls almost every weekend. Jill and her husband Anthony senior would pick up their granddaughters from Kerri on the Friday afternoon and drop them back on Sundays. Jill and Anthony liked to take the girls to the big slides at Jells Park reserve, and for drives through the Dandenongs. Sometimes they watched videos, went to the movies, or visited relatives. Sheree loved to dance around the house. Kylie Minogue songs were favourites, as was the tune *Wild Wild West* by The Escape Club. Occasionally on her way home from the Mandiles, after a hectic weekend, Sheree would stop to pick some azaleas from the front garden to give to her mum.

Not a day went past when people wouldn't stop and laugh at Sheree's happiness. Her zest for life rubbed off on everybody. She loved the movie *ET* and believed it was all true. She loved all the Disney classics too. Sheree was a happy little girl but things weren't so rosy for the adults in her life. Kerri, pregnant again, split with Shane. There were arguments about the drugs. Kerri was trying to get them out of her life, for herself and for her girls. Shane was trying but he was unable to escape. He left their home in Elm Court in Frankston, but occasionally returned to see his Jacinta. Terrible fights would erupt. Kerri took out a restraining order to keep him away.

In early February 1990, Kerri gave birth to Shane junior. Kerri was over the moon.

Sheree was in her element with a little brother to look after. She was always the first out of bed in the morning and she would check on him to see if he was still asleep. Ten weeks after Shane was born, Sheree bounded into her mum's room to check on her baby brother in the bassinette. While Kerri slumbered peacefully, Sheree looked in the bassinette.

"Mum," she said quietly, "Baby Shane's still asleep."

As Kerri roused, she eyed the digital clock next to the bed. It was 8.03am. Shane was usually awake at 6am, crying for a bottle.

The mother felt a sharp pang in her stomach as she turned her head and looked at the bassinette. Sheree was looking on, puzzled.

"Pull the baby's doona off," Kerri yelled. Sheree did, then turned to her mum. Wide-eyed, she said, "He's not moving".

Kerri felt sick and jumped out of bed. She peered at the baby but without even touching him, she knew. He was dead. Sheree didn't know what was wrong, but she knew it was something terrible. Crying uncontrollably, she dashed outside and ran up and down the court, screaming hysterically.

Sheree went to her brother's funeral. Kerri felt it was right she should know what death was.

A short time after Shane's death, Sheree spent the weekend with her grandmother Jill Mandile. The rain had stopped and a brilliant burst of sunlight drenched the back of Jill's home. Sheree ran out to the balcony and saw a rainbow. She pointed at it and said to her grandma, "My baby brother's up there". Jill blinked back the tears and gave her a hug. She could see that Sheree was growing up quickly.

Four weeks after Shane died, his father was dead too. Drugs had claimed another victim.

BY MID 1990, Steve Ludlow had moved into Elm Court with Kerri. They met at a local hotel. Steve was four years Kerri's junior. She wondered if things would work out this time.

Sheree, meanwhile, was blossoming. A born organiser, she had her own gang at school. She rode her bike everywhere. She would rush home from school, and often without even saying hello, she'd drop her bag, get on her bike and hit the road. She showered and dressed herself. Kerri enjoyed watching her grow up.

Sheree bossed her shy little sister Crystal. Crystal idolised her. Sheree was always showing Crystal the way. Whenever photos were being taken, Sheree posed with a broad grin. Crystal would sit next to her with a frown. Sheree would elbow her and say, "Come on, smile". But sometimes she would accidentally hit her too hard and Crystal would cry.

There was mischief in Sheree too. One day Kerri bought $200 in groceries and stocked the fridge and cupboards. The next morning, Kerri found the shopping in Jacinta's cot. Eggs, flour, sugar, cold meat, tubs of

The Murder of Sheree

margarine, peanut butter. Everything was opened and smeared all over the place. Crystal and Jacinta had raw egg sandwiches with egg shells, and the cheese was squeezed and squished through their fingers. The fridge was empty. Kerri looked around but she couldn't find Sheree. Then she saw her in the loungeroom watching television. She said she didn't know what her mum was talking about.

IN JANUARY 1991, Lorraine and Robert Lowe spent a weekend at the family unit in Rosebud. It was a quiet weekend and the weather had been dirty. Leaving Benjamin and Jonathan at the unit, the couple went for a drive around the back roads of Red Hill. Just for fun, Robert and Lorraine decided to collect pinecones.

Out on the Mornington-Flinders Road, they stopped their car and raced around trying to outdo each other. They both searched the south side of the road; Lorraine near a clump of pine trees, Robert near a small drain running under a driveway. The pickings were slim and just who collected the most - well, who could remember? That wasn't the point. At times like this Robert was such fun to be with.

KERRI, STEVE, the girls and faithful Chloe moved from Frankston to South Road, Rosebud, a small coastal holiday resort town, later the same month. South Road cuts across Parkmore Road, a 400 m long dirt track that leads to Nepean Highway. The highway is the town's lifeline, linking it to affluent Portsea at the end of the Peninsula and busy Melbourne to the north. Ever since it was founded, Rosebud has been a popular holiday spot, particularly for young families because of its safe, shallow beaches. High tide in Rosebud is the summer, when the waves of tourists and daytrippers wash through the town, swelling its numbers to overflowing. On hot days, particularly weekends, it is nigh on impossible to secure a parking spot in the town. Low tide is April through to November, when the visitors have ebbed back to their homes, away from the cold winds and deserted beaches. To Kerri and Steve, this was ideal for the family. A new life, a quiet life - a good life for the girls. No drugs, no memories of a dead baby boy in a new bassinette. Kerri's de facto parents lived just down the road. Steve's parents lived in Rosebud too.

Sheree loved it. She went to Rosebud Primary School, with good old Chloe still following her there every day. More than once the school rang Steve, asking him to come and get the dog, which was sitting outside the classroom door.

Sheree had a new bike, a pink Roadmaster she got from Santa. She rode like the wind everywhere and people noticed her all over town. Her schoolteacher, Jill Young, had seen her a couple of times when it was nearly dark. About 5pm one day, she approached the little girl and asked her why she was hanging around near the school.

"I'm riding my bike and I'm having fun and Mum knows I'm here, so it's okay," she said.

"Well, it's not okay. So go home and be careful," the teacher said.

Fairies and 'flying' in costume around the house or the back yard with magic wand in hand became the latest fancy. In late April 1991, the fairy also went to dancing lessons at the Stage Door Dance Academy in Rosebud. She was sure she would be a world famous dancer one day. She promised her mum that when she was famous, she would buy her a Honda Accord motor car. In late June, a man was spotted near the dance school, asking children to get into his car. The dance school proprietors Sheron and Steve Brown told all their charges to be careful. One woman was concerned for Sheree. She had noticed Sheree got herself ready for dancing and always came to classes on her bike. Sheree was always very attentive in class and tried hard all the time.

Sheree and Crystal often went roller skating when they stayed with the Mandiles. Sheree adored it. She rolled up to Jill once when she was at the Caribbean Rollerama in Scoresby and said, "Look, Nan, look how good I am and how fast I am," before heading off to the speed skating area. She thought she was an accomplished skater. She couldn't speed skate at all, but she thought she could.

Luckily for Kerri, it was never hard to get Sheree to go to bed. The reason she went so readily was because she wanted the next day to happen, and it wouldn't unless she went to sleep. After the noisy baths, the messy teeth-cleaning and toilet stops, the girls would toddle off to bed. Sheree would kneel by her bed and say her prayers.

"Now I lay me down to sleep,

The Murder of Sheree

I pray the Lord my soul to keep
If I should die before I wake,
I pray the Lord my soul to take
God Bless Mummy and Daddy, Crystal and Jacinta."
Then she'd jump into bed and fall asleep, exhausted. Tomorrow's fun was just one sleep away.

CHAPTER FIVE

◆

ON MARCH 1, 1991, scores of students from Heathmont Secondary College were at the Croydon Swimming Pool for the annual swimming carnival. Around 9.30am three boys were sitting on the grass near the cyclone wire fence that surrounds the pool grounds when they noticed the funny old codger just outside the fence. He was wearing a green baseball hat and although he had his hands in his trouser pockets, it was obvious he was fondling himself. The boys could see he had an erection. They guessed he was about forty years older than them. What they didn't know was that in sexual maturity, he was a few years their junior.

The old guy walked over to the fence and with a strange, glazed look on his face, started talking to the boys.

"I'm waiting to meet some girls, about sixteen or seventeen. They're coming on the bus," he told them. "I'm going to have sex with them, I'm going to lick them," he sneered.

The boys snickered as teenage boys do and looked at each other, trying not to laugh out loud. What a weirdo! They had the sense to tell one of the teachers, Fiona Henshaw, about him. Fiona and another teacher, Phillip Reynolds, ran into the street, just in time to see Robert Lowe run to his little blue Toyota Corolla. He sprinted to the back of the car and raised the hatchback, obscuring the rear number plate before jumping in and revving the engine like mad. His car was jammed between two other parked cars and he was having trouble getting out. After some quick toing and froing and much gear crunching, he fled with tyres squealing but not before Mr Reynolds yelled, "You're gone pal, we've got your number." Lowe sped around the corner, his work cases lurching in the back seat.

The teachers called the police who didn't take long to determine the car belonged to a rag trade company. The owner wasn't keen on giving the particulars of the driver but the Croydon police finally learned who it was. When Lowe was interviewed he admitted he was 'in the vicinity' but was merely 'resting' in his car. He was warned to stay away from areas where schoolchildren congregate. No charges were laid. For Lowe it was another sweet victory. He adored this game. He knew he wasn't 'exposing' himself - his penis was in his trousers. In his mind he was walking a thin line, staying within the legal boundaries and deriving immense sexual satisfaction. And just to add to the titillation, he was frustrating the police.

ROSEBUD PRIMARY School put on a special 'Stranger Danger' training program for the youngsters in April 1991. The children were taught not to get into cars with strangers or even to talk to them. It was better to run away to the houses with the yellow badges on the letterboxes. Sheree, too, learnt about the bad men; the strangers who try to take little girls and boys away from their mums and dads. A young man in his 20s followed her home from school. He did not run after her - he just walked - but he repeatedly called out, "Come here!" Sheree walked quickly, panicking, then she ran as fast as she could. She burst in the door, flustered and crying, and spat out breathlessly that a man had followed her home. Kerri checked outside but there was nobody there. She soothed her daughter and cuddled her.

That night, when the meals were finished and the dishes were done, Kerri sat at the kitchen table with Sheree on her lap.

"I would never, ever let anything happen to you," Kerri said. "I would die before that would happen." And she meant it. After what happened to baby Shane, Kerri knew she couldn't stand the pain if anything happened to any of her girls.

"And I promise I'll never go with a strange man, mummy," Sheree said. Then she bounced off to bed.

But something was happening to other girls in Melbourne. An abductor/rapist dubbed 'Mr Cruel' by the media, was breaking into homes at night, tying up families and escaping with young girls, holding them captive for a day or two, and then releasing them. But his latest victim,

Karmein Chan, was not released. She had vanished completely. Eventually she would be found dead, shot in the head by a small calibre firearm. But she was missing for almost 12 months.

Robert had talked often to his family about the fate of several girls who had been abducted and never found, like Eloise Worledge, who went missing in 1968 from her Beaumaris home. Sometimes he asked Lorraine if she had any theories about how Eloise had been taken from her room. He had talked about other girls who had been abducted. Now he talked incessantly to Lorraine about Karmein. He was fascinated. He talked about her over breakfast, while they were driving in their car, as they lay in bed at night. Lorraine felt very sorry for the Chan family but Robert was driving her to distraction. Sometimes she told him to stop talking about Karmein but he persisted. He mentioned Karmein almost every day.

Another man was fascinated by Karmein's disappearance. A prisoner in Pentridge prison, serving a life sentence, had tried to extort $15,000 from Karmein's parents. He had telephoned them and threatened to kill their daughter unless they came up with the money. The Spectrum task force, which was investigating Mr Cruel's crimes, tracked down the prisoner and interviewed him. He admitted the offence and said he needed the money to have somebody outside prison killed. The police knew then they had reached the bottom of the barrel. The would-be extortionist received a further five years on top of his life sentence.

There was a remote link between Robert Lowe's Knox City Presbyterian Church and the Karmein Chan mystery. Pastor Ross Brightwell's daughter was in the same year as Karmein at the same school, the Presbyterian Ladies College in Hawthorn. Robert sometimes prayed for Karmein with his family around the kitchen table. Once, as a church elder he led a prayer in church for her to be returned safe and well. People could see he really did feel for that little girl. He even kept newspaper clippings of the case but they were hidden among his work papers in his car. Nobody, not even Lorraine, knew he had them. Nor did she know a magazine article on the parents of missing children was concealed in religious books in Robert's study.

The Murder of Sheree

EVEN THOUGH Rosebud was a great place to live, each week was still a struggle with no regular income, and no car to get around in. Still, it was pretty, quiet and away from the troubles of the big smoke.

Kerri and Sheree were coming home after a fun day shopping in May, 1991, but they missed the bus. They hitch-hiked instead with their full bags and were given a lift by a kind passerby. He seemed a reasonable bloke, chatting pleasantly as he drove. He dropped them home and went on his way. The people in Rosebud were nice. In some parts of Melbourne you wouldn't get a lift at all.

An hour's drive away in Glen Waverley, the Lowe's were putting the finishing touches to their plans for a trip to Mildura, in Victoria's far north-west. Robert's work would take him there for a week at the start of the June school holidays and Lorraine and the boys could join him. They were all looking forward to it.

The pilot announced he intended putting the plane down for an engine check. There was no need to worry, it was just routine. The passengers would be on the ground for about half an hour and were free to get out and stretch their legs. The plane landed softly on the thick snow which stretched as far as one could see. The passengers scrambled out, happy for a break in the journey. It was night, and what struck Lorraine first was how bright the stars were. They seemed like great flickering lights hanging in the sky, closer than she had ever seen them before. She walked away from the other passengers and stood alone, staring up at the sky. Despite the cold she somehow felt a soothing warmth.

One particular star attracted her attention, for it seemed to be made up of many moving colours. As she fixed her eyes on the star, she seemed drawn nearer and nearer to it, as though subjected to a magnet pull. Suddenly she was off the ground and floating towards it. Everything was happening slowly but in a flash Lorraine was quite close to the bright star. As she approached she could see that the moving colours were really people. Busy, happy women, dressed in shiny green, blue, red and yellow robes, were buzzing about with laden trays, setting food down and generally all talking at once. There was an air of great expectancy and excitement.

Lorraine's attention was drawn to a man sitting at the centre of the table. His clothes were purple, clear and shining, as though they were made of stained glass. She crept up closer, longing to join in the fun and celebrations, to hear what everybody was saying. The man in purple noticed her and stared straight into her eyes. It was the Lord.

He spoke softly to her. "You are very welcome at my table, but we are not quite ready yet." Then he smiled. Lorraine felt accepted and wanted and loved. She knew she would never forget that smile.

Lorraine woke with a start and looked around. She was at the holiday unit in Rosebud with her family. She was so elated she knew she wouldn't get back to sleep. She shook Robert to tell him what had happened but he just grunted and reminded her it was 3am. She dressed and went outside. It was cold and dark but her heart seemed on fire. She went for a long walk along the beach, trying to fathom whether the dream was a message of some kind. She thought of it often during the next four years. That warm sense of welcome and acceptance was often the only thing that kept her going.

ON SATURDAY June 22, 1991, Robert and his son Benjamin borrowed Pastor Ross Brightwell's car - it had a tow bar - and put a refrigerator in the trailer. Robert often advertised the unit for rent in the church magazine for fellow Christians, usually during the school holidays. But the old refrigerator was really too small for a family on holidays. Robert and Benjamin drove down the Frankston freeway, through Frankston, and then up and over Olivers Hill along the Nepean Highway. They drove along the Peninsula Freeway, then on to the bayside suburb of McCrae, passing the Lighthouse Milk Bar, the mini-golf, the lighthouse and the boat ramp before arriving at the holiday unit. Father and son installed the fridge. The unit had that still, empty smell from being shut

The Murder of Sheree

up too long. As they inspected the place they noticed some wall tiles in the shower had come loose. They needed regluing and grouting. Robert told Benji he would come back one day and fix them. Then they headed back home, taking the same route.

Maybe the thought of the upcoming trip to Mildura, with no chance of exposing himself with his wife and boys around, triggered the evil spark. For even though he had his son sitting beside him, Robert's mind - and eyes - started to wander. He spied a vivacious little girl on a pink bike riding along the Nepean Highway. She was riding unsteadily, lurching a little from side to side and she struggled to push the big pedals down. Left, right, left, right. But she was smiling and laughing. Happy and carefree. Robert didn't say anything and Benjamin didn't notice Sheree at all. As they headed home along the freeway, Robert was strangely silent. Already he was planning.

Two days later, instead of hawking Maria George's wares, Benjamin's dad drove to the Mornington Peninsula again. Robert Lowe sat waiting in his blue Corolla, like some predatory animal that stalks the sick or very young. He parked near the McCrae boat ramp where he'd gone sailing with his boys. Just over the road was the mini-golf course. Next door was the milkbar he'd been to many times before. Eventually his patience was rewarded. There was the little girl again. The pink helmet enveloped her head and rested low on her ears. A few passing motorists saw her and smiled. Others were worried about her unsteadiness, fearing she might stray onto the road into the path of a car. But those onlookers only saw her for a few seconds as they went on about their business. Only Robert Lowe was concentrating on her.

Sheree rode along the Nepean Highway from the milkbar, slowly making her way back home to her sisters and her mum, and Steve. It was a long ride for a little girl - just over a kilometre - but she loved the freedom she felt on that bike.

Robert Lowe started his car, his eyes and mind totally focussed on the target. He followed at a distance that would not alarm Sheree nor draw the attention of adult passersby, his body as tense as a cat ready to pounce on a small bird. Sheree made her way past the freeway turn off and turned into the dirt track known as Parkmore Road. She lumbered on, past the two telephone booths, the giant pine tree and the wooden fence that strained to contain the Parkmore Caravan Park. Sheree often popped in there to look at the birds in the big aviary but now she didn't have time. Singing and talking to herself, she rode on, past the thick, weatherbeaten and straggly bushes that lined the road, past the holiday houses and neat brick homes. The gravel crunched and spat under the Corolla's wheels as it followed the same route.

Four hundred metres from the Nepean Highway, Parkmore Road forms a T-intersection with South Road, just across from number 43. Lowe watched through the windscreen as Sheree rode across the intersection to her home. She rolled around the back and ran inside the white fibro house. Lowe sat in Parkmore Road for a minute or two. He examined the house and its surrounds. In his rear vision mirror he saw there was a kink in Parkmore Road. The bushes at the side obscured the view to the highway and beach just beyond it. Now he was bristling with excitement. He smiled and turned into South Road. Next Saturday would be ideal.

CHAPTER SIX

◆

ROBERT ROSE at 7am on Saturday, June 29, 1991. The day was as dark and cold as his intent. He told his wife he would drive to Rosebud and fix the loose bathroom tiles after going to his regular prayer meeting, which were held in various homes on the first, third and fifth Saturdays of each month. Robert checked the garage but he couldn't find the grout gun. A few minutes later he came back inside mumbling to himself. Lorraine usually bought him muffins or crumpets to take to the morning prayers, as they always ended with a big breakfast, but she had been so busy she had forgotten to buy them. Robert stomped and snarled about having to do everything himself but Lorraine couldn't see what all the fuss was about.

"Why don't you just buy them when you stop to buy the grout?" she asked.

In a huff he grumbled something and then drove off. As he drove, he smiled. He had a wonderful day planned. Today he could set the trap after days of planning. He just needed the little girl to step into the frame.

At 7.45am, while Robert was praying at the home of Pamela and Willem Vandenberg in Brae Court, Nunawading, with several other worshippers, Sheree Beasley was bounding out of bed, ready for another day. At eight o'clock she asked her mum if she could go to the Lighthouse Milk Bar but was told she couldn't. Kerri made breakfast for Crystal and Jacinta while Sheree insisted on making her own. When Kerri went back to bed for a while, Sheree took her mum brekkie in bed. Cordial and toast.

Sheree finally had her own way at 10 o'clock. She was at the milkbar buying bread for her mum - and a small bag of sweets for herself. Robert had just begun eating breakfast with his friends. He casually told them he would be wearing his handyman hat in Rosebud that afternoon, fixing tiles. At 11 o'clock, with a cheerful wave, Lowe set off in his blue Toyota Corolla, south down Springvale Road towards Rosebud. He was now consumed by sinister intent. As he drove through the congested Springvale shopping centre, Kerri rose again to see her girls playing in the backyard.

Half an hour later, Sheree asked Kerri if she could take Crystal to the mini-golf near the Lighthouse Milk Bar. Kerri said maybe but not until after lunch. So, just after midday, bored with sitting still, Sheree went for a ride down Parkmore Road towards Nepean Highway.

Lowe was now in the area he had reconnoitred twice in a week. Just before 1pm, Sheree was at home again, asking if she could buy some more sweets. Again Kerri gave in and asked her daughter to run an errand to the 'Silver Heirlooms' clothes shop on the highway. Kerri handed over a note and an envelope. The note was for Sandra Gaisford, the proprietor of the clothes shop. The other was an envelope with $20 inside. On the front Kerri wrote a the list of things she wanted bought.

"There'll be one dollar left and you can buy lollies with that. All right, Sheree?"

"Yes, mum. Yes, yes, yes." Sheree was laughing and jumping up and down.

While Kerri was talking to her daughter, local handyman Todd De Young was driving along the Nepean Highway. As he drove past Parkmore Road, in his peripheral vision he spied a blue car parked next to the two phone boxes in Parkmore Road, about twenty metres from the highway. He didn't see the driver. He didn't see Sheree either, who was happily pedalling down Parkmore Road.

She popped into Silver Heirlooms and handed Sandra Gaisford the note, before riding home. She forgot to go to the milkbar.

"You'd forget your head if it wasn't screwed on," Kerri laughed. Sheree laughed too. Oh, well. She could go for another ride on her bike. It was now past lunchtime and the girls' tummies were grumbling. Kerri wrote out a list for Sheree on the same envelope she had forgotten to take to the milk bar. Kerri wrote 'cigarettes, a pastie, a sausage roll, some corn chips and a bottle of Coke'. The envelope still had $20 in it. At 1.50pm, Sheree set off for the milkbar again.

Just after 2pm, Sheree left the Lighthouse Milkbar with all the goodies she'd been sent for. A chill wind blew off the bay, driving inside those who had tried to make the most of a gloomy day. Gai and James Henley and their three children left the Rye Pier and walked back to their car. It was no longer the sort of day to spend outside.

The Henleys drove along the Nepean Highway back towards McCrae. They moved into the right hand lane as they drove past the Rye Safeway store. Gai noticed a car driving towards her on the other side of the road. She saw a little girl wearing a bicycle helmet, sitting on the front seat, visibly upset. Gai then turned her gaze to the driver. At that moment, he stared back and their eyes locked. The man was angry, with a sour look on his face, so sour it made her look away. Gai didn't think he looked like an exasperated parent. It made her feel uncomfortable.

Janine Kent drove into Parkmore Road and saw a pink child's bike lying on the road. The front wheel was still spinning. Janine thought a child might have run off to play. She tutted and picked up the bike and wheeled it to the side of the road, where she placed it up against a huge pine tree. At least that way it wouldn't get run over.

KERRI HAD set the kitchen table and was telling Jacinta to stop whinging for lunch when Steve walked into the room.

"Sheree should be back now," Kerri said flatly. It was just a comment.

"I'll go and look for ya," Steve volunteered. He turned to go to the door.

"No, give her a couple of more minutes," Kerri said. Sheree loved riding that bike.

A few moments later there was a knock on the door. It was a local woman who lived in Parkmore Road and often kept an eye on Sheree. Sheree's bike was up against a tree, she said, but Sheree was nowhere to be found. Steve looked at her through the open doorway. Without turning his head he yelled to his de facto wife in the kitchen.

"KERRI!"

Kerri sensed the urgency in his voice and ran to his side.

The Murder of Sheree

"She's found Sheree's bike against a tree," Steve said. He ran wildly down the road towards the Nepean Highway, his heart thumping, the adrenalin surging. He saw the pink bike leaning against the giant pine tree. He sprinted across the Nepean Highway and into the foreshore scrub. He was almost blind with fear. Nothing.

As he ran, two or three lone walkers watched him with curiosity. He was obviously panicking. As he sprinted by them he yelled, "Have you seen a little girl in a tracksuit wearing a pink bike helmet? HAVE YA?"

One by one they shook their heads.

Steve ran back to the bike, still sitting at its resting place outside an empty holiday home. Steve bolted round the back of the house, then he checked the caravan park across the road. Maybe Sheree was in there looking at the birds in the aviary again. But there were no kids there at all. Oh God!

Steve dialled 000 from one of the phone booths in Parkmore Road and told the operator what had happened, before dashing home.

He walked quickly inside the house, but slowed as he approached the kitchen. He didn't want to tell Kerri what he thought had happened. For the first time he realised he was crying. He saw Kerri from behind, standing at the sink.

"She's nowhere," Steve said. "I've called the police."

Kerri didn't turn around but Steve saw her freeze. A year earlier, when Kerri knew her son was dead in his cot, she spent ages washing the dirty dishes in the kitchen, as if she could wash the heartache away. Now her arms furiously scrubbed the dishes and plates. The same feeling she felt when she saw Shane dead in his cot came back. She was numb.

"Yeah, I know," Kerri said flatly. "I know she's gone."

Kerri had been expecting something tragic to befall her. Shane junior, his dad, miscarriages. That was her lot in life. When you're down people kick you. If there's nobody around, life will do it for them. She knew then, with a certainty, that her lot in life was to have her will crushed. She didn't know why. Maybe she had done something wrong in a previous life. Maybe God was punishing her. Maybe He was testing her. But she knew there and then that Sheree was dead. She hoped it wasn't true and she fought to believe everything was all right, but deep down she knew.

The Murder of Sheree

That was the way it happened in her life.

Crystal looked up to Steve and said, "Sheree's been taken, hasn't she daddy?"

Steve wiped his eyes and lied. "No, she'll be all right, Crystal."

Within minutes the police arrived and offered to drive the couple back to the bike. Steve got in the back seat but Kerri refused. She wanted to walk the way Sheree had gone and headed off down Parkmore Road, half-expecting to find her daughter's body. When she reached the bike, she broke down and wept. She waited there, crying, for a full half hour. While the policemen wrote down every last detail Steve could tell them, Kerri stood alone, hugging herself, trying to keep out the cold, cold loneliness seeping into her. She tried to will Sheree back. She kept thinking, *She'll be back, she'll come out of nowhere*. Tears were running down her cheeks as a scattered crowd watched her from across the road. Over and over she said to herself aloud: "What's happened to Sheree?"

FRANKSTON DIVISIONAL Detective Inspector Laurie Ratz enjoys a reputation of being one of the wittiest and most optimistic officers in the Victoria Police. But he had had little to laugh about in the previous few weeks. A serial arsonist was torching high schools in the district and a prisoner had died in the Frankston lockup. Saturday, June 29 was Laurie's first day off for some time. He planned to make the most of it.

He and wife Merredea had a lively evening planned with other former staff from the Detective Training School where Laurie had spent several years as an instructor. He was shaving and Merredea was readying herself when the police communications centre, D24, called. DDIs are always notified when something serious - or potentially serious - happens in their district.

"There's a bit of a problem at Rosebud. We've got a missing person and it looks a bit unusual," Inspector Peter O'Neill told him. "She's a six-year-old girl and we don't know where she is."

Laurie was concerned but knew his local detectives would take charge. If they needed him, they would contact him. Laurie knew these sorts of things were usually resolved in an hour or two. And anyway, he owed it to his wife to make up for his recent work-related absences from home.

"Okay, (but) I'm going out," Laurie said. "I'm on the pager. Keep me posted. I'll ring the Super of the district and I'll still be at home for an hour or so."

Then Laurie told Merredea what had happened. Her reaction was immediate.

"Get out of the bath kids, dad's going back to work," she yelled to the bathroom.

"No, no, no," Laurie said. It sounded serious, he told her, but so do the hundreds of other missing children reports that come in each year - and 99.9 percent of them turn out to be nothing. He told his wife the kids were usually found at a friend's place, hiding in a cupboard; they take the long way home; they just get lost. Merredea didn't want to hear.

"If that was our own daughter," she said, "I'd want you to go down there."

A few minutes later the superintendent rang to direct Det. Insp Ratz to head to Rosebud and take command but he was already on his way.

THE FIVE o'clock radio news bulletin came on the car radio as Margaret Hobbs turned from Burwood Highway into Springvale Road, Vermont South. A six-year-old girl was missing, believed abducted, in Rosebud. As soon as she heard that, Margaret thought about her patients. In a flash she thought of Robert's escalating behaviour. She thought, *That's Robert Lowe.*

The thought shocked her. She suddenly realised she had been almost waiting for something like this to happen. Then she tempered her feelings. It would be no good jumping to conclusions. She didn't really know who had done it - and Robert could be at home or with some other people anyway. It was just that of all the patients she had, the only one who came to mind was Robert Arthur Selby Lowe.

IN THE 30 minutes it took to drive from Mt Eliza to Rosebud, Laurie Ratz was making mental notes of what he needed. Lighting, media help, an intense search. When he arrived at Parkmore Road he found the duty officer, Inspector Tim Knaggs, had already arranged the lighting. The crime scene would be examined for hours for any clues. The Search and Rescue officers were already on hand and extra detectives were on their way.

While the crime scene experts worked meticulously, uniformed police and detectives doorknocked every house in the vicinity. Cars were stopped and checked at roadblocks. As the light faded and Laurie Ratz was catching up with what had been done - and what needed to be done - Kerri sat in a detective's car, wrapped in a plainclothes policeman's jacket. It was cold outside but that wasn't all that was making her shiver. As she waited for her daughter, police and volunteer helicopters hovered overhead while uniform police, mounted police and trailbike riders busied themselves everywhere.

Sitting in the police car, Kerri could see an abductor but she couldn't make out the detail of his face. She could see Sheree crying and could hear her screaming. Kerri felt an anger but it couldn't quite take hold of her. Maybe she was trying to get inside his head. Why, why, why?

AS DARKNESS fell, Lorraine Lowe looked up from the medical reports she was typing in the back room and saw it was almost dark. Just then Benjamin rode past the window on his bike and she called to him to come inside. She was surprised when she heard Robert answer, "Yeah." She hadn't seen him all day.

"Oh, you're here," Lorraine said, and walked to the family room and stood by the sliding door that led to the patio outside. As Benjamin walked past her, Lorraine looked out and saw Robert.

"Rob, would you go and get some takeaway for dinner please? We've got a busy night tonight."

With that Robert turned and immediately walked out to the garage. Lorraine thought he must have just got home because he usually left his car keys on a hook in the kitchen and he didn't have to come inside to get them.

Half an hour later Robert returned. After dinner, Lorraine was tidying up when she heard the washing machine start up. She was surprised. Robert hadn't washed his own clothes once in 19 years of marriage. Lorraine had been washing all day but the weather had been unkind. The clothes-horse in the laundry was full of wet clothes. She walked to the laundry and nearly bumped into Robert as he made his way back into the living area.

"What are you washing?" Lorraine asked.

"Oh, just some casual clothes I need for the trip to Mildura," Robert said.

"Can't you use some other clothes?" she asked.

"No, I need these ones."

Oh well, Lorraine thought. Maybe after all this time he's becoming a little housetrained.

SHEREE'S RELATIVES rushed to Rosebud. Neil and Denise Greenhill, Jill and Anthony Mandile, Joy and Leslie Greenhill, and Steve's parents. Only Sheree's dad Anthony wasn't there. He was on a fishing trip with a few mates in Jamieson, in Victoria's north-east.

Ratz and his team grilled Kerri and Steve. Laurie knew that time was of the essence. It was essential to find out as much as possible and start a multi-pronged investigation. Tomorrow might be too late. Already police had searched Sheree's home, her friend's homes, the school, the beach, the shops, the parks. Now Laurie wanted to know everything he possibly could about Sheree. What was she wearing, where had she been, who had she played with, what's been happening on the domestic front? The questions went on and on. To Kerri they seemed almost irrelevant; for Laurie Ratz, they were vital. He wondered whether her father had taken her. Was she with him, or did the neighbours have her? Or was she playing with somebody?

Laurie set himself up in a command post - a commandeered booze bus - almost opposite Parkmore Road, where he co-ordinated the investigation. He had scores of tasks to attend to simultaneously. People were asking him questions, the phones didn't stop ringing. Someone wanted to know where should the police horses go. How were the search and rescue guys faring? Was the lighting adequate? One crew had finished a designated search area and wanted to know where they should look next. And Laurie was asking himself the most important question: 'What else should I do?' He was looking at maps, talking on the police radio, answering phones, giving briefings. Occasionally D24 would call him.

The Murder of Sheree

His district commander Chief Superintendent John (Jock) Balloch wanted to know what was going on. So did the media.

By early evening, police were armed with photos of Sheree as they continued doorknocking the area. All local surgeries were checked too, in case Sheree had been knocked off her bike and had been dropped off. Locals at the Rosebud pub knew her, not by name but by her face. The drinkers easily recalled what they had seen at 2pm. It was the Azumah Nelson/Jeff Fenech boxing bout and Fenech had been robbed of a win. The fight had been telecast in the pub. Nobody had seen the little girl today.

Sheree's home had been searched. Next, a line search with officers on foot, some with police dogs, was conducted for one kilometre east and west of Parkmore Road, taking in the foreshore bushland, the beach front, the toilet blocks and boatsheds. Police doorknocked every house in the area. Had anybody seen Sheree? Two helicopters hovered above, using nightsun equipment when night fell. Caravan parks were checked. Police cars crawled through the back streets. The shire duty foreman was called out to help the police search all the drains in the area in case Sheree had fallen down a drain.

While the police search continued, a group of eight local women and men walked slowly along the beach and the foreshore, poking and prodding with sticks. Everybody wanted to help. But there was no trace of Sheree at all.

IT WAS TO be a special Saturday night in the Lowe household. Benjamin was due to leave soon on a church mission to Papua New Guinea and he was to make a speech about his impending trip at church the following day. Robert took great pride in his sons' achievements and encouraged them to better themselves, particularly in public speaking. So this night, in addition to helping Lorraine prepare the following day's Sunday School lesson, he was expected to help draft Benjamin's speech. Perhaps he would pop in a little biblical analogy somewhere in the text, suggest a certain inflection at a certain point. Usually he would also remind the boys to stand tall and erect, and project their voice. Be confident, he told them.

The Murder of Sheree

But, for some reason, Robert wasn't himself. Lorraine noticed - she couldn't help but notice - that Robert was distant. He even seemed disinterested. His mind was wandering and he was talking about topics nobody cared about. He was distracting his wife and son. Lorraine tried several times to get Robert to become involved but eventually she took Benjamin with her to the bedroom where they worked on the speech alone.

AT 11PM, Kerri, numb with shock and anguish, faced a throng of reporters and photographers at the Rosebud Police Complex. She was dazzled by the lights but she was looking inward, not out. All she could see was her daughter trapped in a car, screaming for help. The gravity of what had happened was starting to sink in.

Kerri wept as she said, "Whoever has got her please take care of her. Let her come home."

"She's had a sad life. She lost her baby brother to cot death last year. She deserves to be at home. She loved to play, she's got lots of friends, she lives for her bike."

AT MIDNIGHT, Laurie Ratz adjourned the investigation. Everything he could think of had been done and there was still no Sheree. If the name of a suspect had bobbed up, the hunt would have continued through the night. But at day's end, all Laurie Ratz and his troops knew were that Sheree had been riding her bike, she'd been to the milk bar a couple of times, she was a streetwise little kid - and now she was missing. That was it. It looked like the investigators were in for the long haul. Knowing Sunday would be the start of stage two of the search for Sheree, Laurie wanted his people to be fresh for an early start. It was important that nobody worked to the point where they fell over.

At 2am, after finalising his arrangements and timetable for first light, the inspector slumped into his car and slowly drove home. Completely alone, this was the gut-grinding time. He didn't really see the road. In his mind he was recapping the afternoon and evening. Had he covered everything? What had he forgotten? He was fairly confident it wasn't a domestic-related abduction. That worried him. Even if it was a domestic it would have been of extreme concern. But having no idea who might be the offender opened the avenues of inquiry 360 degrees. Laurie was totally committed to doing everything in his power to find Sheree and felt he had the capabilities to do everything that could be done. Apart from Sheree's safety, one other thing scared him. He knew that if he found out later that he had forgotten to cover some base, forgotten to do something that resulted in the loss of a 6-year-old girl's life, he wouldn't be able to live with himself.

He arrived home, exhausted. He walked into his daughter's bedroom and checked the bedroom window was locked. Then he looked at the button nose, the closed eyes with the long eyelashes, the hair swept across the pillow. She looked so little and so vulnerable. He knew he would be checking on his daughter like this every night. As he walked from the room into the dark hallway he thought, *I'll bet I'm not the only father in Victoria that does that now*. At close to 3am he flopped into bed. He was so tired his body was aching. An hour later he was awake.

Where the hell was Sheree?

CHAPTER SEVEN

◆

KERRI sat red-eyed on the worn, brown, woollen couch, her legs folded beneath her, and drew on her umpteenth Winfield Red cigarette. Her throat was almost raw from chain smoking all night but she didn't notice. She stubbed the butt out on the overflowing ashtray next to the cold cup of coffee. All night Kerri had been wondering where her daughter was. Was she with a man, perhaps locked in a cupboard somewhere or tied to a bed, some sex plaything for a deviate? Was she already dead? Had she, quite innocently, been given a lift somewhere that Kerri hadn't thought of yet? Kerri looked out the window.

As the sun made its slow rise, she could just make out the scrubby tea-tree across the way that lined Parkmore Road. The dusty track trailed away from her into the darkness. She couldn't make out more than 20 or 30 metres into the gloom. Maybe when the sun rose fully, she would be able to see properly. Maybe whatever had been missed yesterday would be picked up today. It was Sunday, June 30, 1991. Day two of the search.

Laurie Ratz briefed his troops in Parkmore Road. By 7am, everybody knew what they had to do and the searching had resumed.

Laurie took a call mid-morning from Rape Squad Detective Inspector Dannye Moloney. Part of the Rape Squad's charter is to investigate all sexually related abductions. The men discussed how many of Dannye's staff would be rostered on to the investigation and how they should manage their resources. They agreed Dannye should spend his day off in Rosebud.

While the two inspectors were talking on the phone, Robert and Lorraine Lowe and their two sons were pulling into the car park of their Presbyterian church in Dandelion Road, Rowville, in Melbourne's outer-eastern suburbs. Benjamin, who had just passed his learner's permit test, was driving, with his mother seated beside him. Robert and Jonathan sat in the back. They were running a little late. As they turned into the car park, they heard a radio news bulletin about a 6-year-old girl who had been abducted in Rosebud. The four jumped out of the car and ran into the church. Nobody discussed the girl who had been kidnapped from near their holiday home.

It was a normal enough service, during which Benjamin gave his speech about his upcoming trip. Robert was delighted his son's speech was well-presented and very well-received. When the service finished and everyone gathered for a chat before heading home, one parishioner, Brian Lee, was fascinated as he watched Robert behave quite out of character. Normally Robert would briefly talk with a couple of young people but spend most of his time after the service with the other adults. Today Brian noticed Robert was keyed up and spending all his time with the children. He saw Robert sitting on a seat, eagerly cracking jokes. He was totally focussed on the children, his eyes alight and he had totally captured their attention.

As Robert continued talking, Brian noticed more hypnotised youngsters were drawn to him. At one stage it appeared all the kids, about a dozen of them, were standing around Robert, listening to what he had to say. Robert was leaning forward and sort of hunched over in an attempt to be at the same level as the children, to communicate better with them. Brian was intrigued. He couldn't quite hear what Robert was saying and he wondered what was so captivating. He assumed Robert's gregarious and boisterous manner was due to Benjamin's impending trip. Robert talked that way for 20 minutes.

THE INFORMATION Bureau at St Kilda Road Police Complex, which houses all records of convicted criminals, was checked for any likely child abductors, both on the peninsula and elsewhere. Laurie Ratz was looking for suspects, trying to find all the known sex offenders and known abductors. He was looking for anybody whose *modus operandi* was to pluck little girls from the street and place them in a car. There was a flood of names, aliases, addresses. Laurie also spoke to Detective Inspector David Sprague and Detective Senior Sergeant Steve Fontana of the Spectrum task force. Spectrum was principally looking at three abductions by an

The Murder of Sheree

offender dubbed Mr Cruel, the last - of murdered schoolgirl Karmein Chan - resulting in murder. Laurie wanted to see if the person who abducted Sheree might be Mr Cruel. The Spectrum experts were confident it was not.

IT WAS JUST after the social football match at Albert Park that Sunday between the Homicide Squad and the staff at State Forensic Science Laboratory that the two homicide detectives put their heads together. Detective Senior Sergeant Paul Hollowood and Detective Chief Inspector Peter Halloran spoke quietly and at length about Sheree Beasley's disappearance. Both men were concerned that this abduction might quickly turn into a murder investigation, yet the Homicide Squad had not been officially notified that Sheree was missing.

Peter Halloran had been the head of the squad for three years and Paul Hollowood had spent most of his seventeen years with the Victoria Police in the squad. They both knew that in investigations of this type, it was wise to plan on a 'worst case' scenario. That meant planning to investigate a murder. Both men were concerned that time was slipping away. If it was a murder, every hour put more space and time between the offender, any evidence left at the crime scene (if a crime scene could be located) and the police. Halloran said he would raise the matter with Force Command in William Street the next day.

AFTER CHURCH, Robert spent his afternoon in a very irritable mood. It seemed to Lorraine that no matter what he did or what she said to him, it made him grumpy. He washed his work car and then, begrudgingly, his wife's. Lorraine came out to help and saw that the whole car was unpacked. All the doors were open and Robert's work samples were on the ground. He was ready to vacuum but Lorraine noticed he was very agitated.

"I hope you're getting everything ready for the trip in there," he snapped.

"Yes. Do you want me to help you?" Lorraine asked.

He snarled at her. "Why didn't you place the ad in *New Life* (the church magazine) to rent out the unit for the school holidays?"

"I didn't have time," Lorraine said, peeved. He was being a real pain.

"If you wanted to rent out the unit, you could have placed the ad. I'm not particularly interested in renting it out over the winter," she said.

With that, Robert threw a tantrum.

"Why do I have to do everything? I have to do *everything*. I have to fix the tiles as well as go away on a business trip. It's all right for *you*!"

Lorraine was puzzled. "Didn't you fix the tiles yesterday?"

"I didn't get around to getting the grout at Kmart," he growled with a dismissive wave of the hand. "And don't you get in a scot."

Lorraine had had enough of this. He was being impossible. She couldn't work out what had upset him.

"Look Rob, I only came out to help you." She started walking towards him and bent towards the vacuum cleaner to grab the hose.

"Get right away!" he snapped and his hand motioned to her to leave. "Go back inside. Go and get the boys' bikes so I can put them on the back of the car."

Lorraine thought that was a bit stupid. If he did that, they'd only have to take them off again to load the back of the car. The family was due to go to church again that night so Lorraine suggested they put the bikes on when they got back. She was glad to go back inside and continue packing and just leave him alone. But she had barely gone inside when Robert dashed in and picked up a big brown plastic garden rubbish bag. Lorraine watched him as he stormed off out to the car again. She wondered why he needed the bag. She didn't dare ask him, though, the mood he was in.

DANNYE MOLONEY had been head of the Rape Squad since it was formed in April 1989. Dannye was the ideal man for the job, having spent nine months in 1988 investigating rape investigation methodology. In the process he had examined the international scene, perused the lauded FBI offender profiling system and become *au fait* with DNA profiling before it was commonplace. In short, he had studied everything that was tried and tested, and all that was new.

While Robert and Lorraine were arguing in Glen Waverley, Dannye was briefed by Laurie Ratz at Rosebud Police Complex on the state of the investigation. By 5.30pm, there was a management meeting. Laurie, Dannye, two of his men - Detective Sergeant Geoff Alway and Detective

The Murder of Sheree

Senior Constable Neil Merrick - and Rosebud CIB Detective Sergeant Ken Heggie discussed their next crucial steps. The investigation was already becoming cumbersome and they all knew they had to get on top of things before it became too wieldy. It was agreed Geoff Alway would co-ordinate the enquiries by reading the incoming Information Reports and dishing out tasks, while Laurie would take charge of the investigation.

Their first plan was to eliminate any suggestion the abduction was a Family Law Court matter. Another theory was Sheree had been taken hostage until Kerri and Steve repaid a drug debt. There was nothing concrete in that line of enquiry but some callers had planted the seed of doubt in the investigators' minds.

At the time the Rape Squad was investigating roughly 1300 rapes a year. Dannye knew if the squad took on the Sheree Beasley investigation, it would virtually close down the whole office. It was decided that Geoff and Lawrie would liaise with Dannye as frequently as necessary, thrashing out ideas and using each other as sounding boards. They all suspected this was an investigation that would not be over in a few days. And it looked like it was not going to be easy.

Seventy-five police, including mounted and off-road motorcycle officers, together with State Emergency Service personnel, the Southern Peninsula Rescue Squad and the Country Fire Authority were involved in the search that Sunday.

The water police checked Port Phillip Bay from Rosebud right through to Portsea and back towards Melbourne. Police trail bike riders, mounted police and officers on foot combed national parks and the rugged bushland. As the search went on, it panned out in wider and wider circles. They found T-shirts, underpants and sandshoes in various locations and then called in the investigators but each time the items were discounted. The door-to-door canvassing continued too while hourly radio bulletins broadcast the news, calling for witnesses to come forward. The phones were running hot with information flooding in. Somebody noticed a blue car next door that hadn't been there before. The man over the back fence was behaving strangely. Everybody wanted to help but the information was leading nowhere.

The Murder of Sheree

THE SEARCHING continued for three more days. The Southern Peninsula Rescue Squad used its helicopter to patrol the back beaches from Hastings to Somers and from Mt Martha to Portsea while the police chopper concentrated on the main area of Rosebud and McCrae. Local people came into the police station and offered to help with the searching. Several Rosebud Fire Brigade members joined police and SES in a foot patrol of the foreshore. It seemed the whole peninsula was swarming with police and volunteers trying to find Sheree. Local crime ground to a full stop. With police in nearly every street at one time or another, the local burglars and car thieves thought it would be prudent to stay inside or go elsewhere to commit their crimes.

DESPERATE FOR information about his granddaughter, Neil Greenhill started his own search of the Mornington Peninsula. Devastated by Sheree's disappearance, he searched everywhere. Neil's mum Joy tearfully told him that if anybody could find Sheree, he could. Neil believed those words, and took them to his broken heart. His frantic searching only exacerbated the pain and anxiety. Neil had never experienced pain like this in his life. Every fibre in his system felt as if it was stretched to breaking point. He couldn't sleep. He couldn't work. He cried all the time. He searched for Sheree in reserves and parks. He chastised himself. He stood in car parks by the bay, looking through his tears into binoculars, scanning the seascape before him. He looked in rock pools. He wondered what he was looking for. A body? Some clothing? Some teeth? An earring? What do you look for? Where do you start? Alone, he walked along foreshore dirt tracks. In public toilet blocks. Behind the shops. In dumpmasters. Under bushes. In holes. Nothing.

At 705 square kilometres, the Mornington Peninsula is about the same size as Queensland's Sunshine Coast. Neil hadn't realised how big the peninsula was and now he felt totally and utterly useless. Then the thought that Sheree might be dead entered his head and he called on his ex-wife's husband Bruce Doolan to help him. Neil wanted to check the backbeaches. He knew, like most Victorians, that the backbeaches were where bodies were occasionally found, like executed drug dealers Douglas and Isobel Wilson. Neil felt ill as he stumbled around the scrubby sandhills, his shoes full of sand and grit. With driftwood sticks the men poked around under the bushes. Neil's heart was in his mouth and he was shaking every time he pulled the foliage back to look. He wondered what he would do if he found Sheree's crumpled body stuffed under the tea-tree.

ROBERT LOWE set off for Mildura in his work car early on Monday morning, July 1, 1991. As he drove north across country Victoria, Detective Chief Inspector Peter Halloran called Det. Sen-Sgt Paul Hollowood into his office. Peter said Paul's crew would be assigned the case if Sheree's body turned up. In the meantime, a district task force was set up, based at Rosebud. Headed by Laurie Ratz, it was called "Zenith" - the vertical point of the heavens.

Geoff Alway brought Kerri to the Rosebud police station in an effort to determine if she had forgotten to tell the police anything - anything at all. She told the detective she had seen her ex-husband Anthony in his car near her home just a few days earlier. That was enough for Geoff. He took out a search warrant and at 9pm they searched Anthony's house in Station Street, Carrum. Anthony was home with his de facto wife and his cousin. He was helpful and said he understood why the police wanted to search the house. Anthony said he couldn't possibly have abducted his own daughter. He was fishing at Lake Eildon at the time she was taken. The police seized his car and took it away for forensic tests. But Geoff knew already they wouldn't find anything.

WHILE THE searching went on, Lorraine, Benjamin and Jonathan caught the train to Mildura to join Robert. They settled into their holiday unit and set about exploring the river town. The boys didn't get to ride their bikes that much because the weather was poor. It was a good break from home though. Lorraine thought Robert was better than he was on the Sunday but he was still distant.

On the Wednesday, to spare Lorraine the chore of cooking in the unfamiliar kitchen, Robert shouted dinner in a local restaurant. What began as a nice night out quickly turned into a nightmare. The restaurant advertised special low prices for luncheons. With his family standing around him, Robert asked the proprietor the cost of the meals. He was told the price, which was $2 more than the advertised luncheon price. When the proprietor tried to tell Robert the special price did not apply to dinners, Robert suggested he was being tricked. He caused a row, arguing long and loud. Robert was in the wrong but he was in his element. Every time the proprietor tried to explain, Robert cut him off. Lorraine and the boys shuffled their feet with their heads bowed while Robert became more abusive.

Everybody was looking. Lorraine and the boys fled quietly to the car while Robert continued arguing. He would never say he had made a mistake. It was a full 20 minutes before Robert came outside. He jumped in the rear passenger's seat and slammed the door before Benjamin drove off. Nobody spoke.

By now it was after 8.30pm. Instead of a relaxing night out, Lorraine got out the pots and pans and began cooking. She wondered what was troubling her husband.

LAURIE RATZ was resting at home. It had been weeks since he'd had a full day away from work. Not only was he heading the Zenith investigation but he also had to oversee all other major crimes being investigated in his subdistrict, which took in Parkdale, Dandenong and Springvale. Then the phone rang. It was Geoff Alway.

"We've got a witness!" Geoff told the inspector.

"Who?" Laurie was hanging on every word.

"It's a six-year-old boy," Geoff said.

Laurie looked at the ceiling. It wasn't getting any easier.

Geoff said Shane Park had been found after police spoke to children at Sheree's school. He had been with Sheree the day she disappeared. A man had picked Sheree up off her bike and put her in his small blue car. At least it was a start, Laurie thought. He and Geoff talked about how best to identify the car. Laurie didn't hold much hope but he knew he had to run with whatever the cards dished out. He knew from experience that once a breakthrough came along, you never knew where it could lead.

The Murder of Sheree

THE PHONES were running hot and several suspects were nominated as possible abductors. One suspect lived just around the corner from Kerri's home. He was a mentally impaired man who loved to creep around the foreshore toilets. A Frankston man who had once molested a child was also nominated. Another informer said Kerri and Sheree had been given a lift home one day by a man when they missed the bus. The police checked his background and saw he had just been released from jail. Some of the Zenith detectives worked hard on checking the three men's backgrounds. They found a connection between two of them and queried whether a paedophile ring was operating on the peninsula. On Thursday, July 4, the police raided three homes. The men were taken in for questioning and blood samples were taken. Two of them had alibis, one didn't. He was hard to eliminate but as the enquiry moved on, he slipped out of the frame.

As each precious minute ticked by, the chances of finding Sheree alive diminished. Through the media, Laurie Ratz asked all holiday-home owners to come forward so the police could check if Sheree was inside. That weekend there were so many calls that some people had to wait hours for the uniformed police or detectives to arrive. But it all became just another dead-end.

THE DETECTIVES took stock. They knew Sheree had been abducted - Shane Park verified that. It was now time to step up a notch. Anybody who lived on the Mornington Peninsula or in Melbourne's southern suburbs in the past 20 years who had been charged with any sex offence was now a potential candidate. Each one was tracked down, even if they had moved from the peninsula, and visited personally. Suspects' alibis were taken down in statements, then thoroughly checked out.

As more local suspects were being turned up, Laurie Ratz found he was often ringing a newly-promoted sergeant at the Transit Police in Melbourne for help.

When he was a detective senior constable at Rosebud CIB, Matthew Wood had interviewed and charged some of the men who were now Zenith suspects. Laurie was tapping into Matthew's knowledge of those suspects before they were spoken to. During one call, Matthew, who lived in

The Murder of Sheree

Rosebud and wanted to work near his home, asked Laurie if he needed a young, keen sergeant who was keen to catch a child abductor. The following Monday Matthew started work at the Rosebud CIB offices on Task Force Zenith. Several other officers, including Andrew Gustke from East Bentleigh CIB, also started that day.

Andrew thought the place looked a mess. There were people running everywhere and the desks were smothered in paper and Information Reports. He was a little annoyed there was virtually no elbow room at his desk. The place was crammed. On top of that, the local detectives who were not working on the case were in and out all the time, working on their unsolved cases. It was a shambles.

After the new detectives settled in and had a cup of coffee, they gathered with the rest of the Zenith crew in the CIB office downstairs. Geoff Alway and Laurie Ratz briefed the assembly on the state of play. There had been a number of theories floating around as to why Sheree had been abducted. They explained that a number of local drug abusers had rung in, naming Kerri as a prostitute, and a heroin and Rohypnol user. And Steve had been in jail. Maybe there was a connection in there somewhere. The favoured theory that day, which was later found to be completely false, was that Sheree had been taken until Kerri paid out an outstanding drug debt to persons unknown.

Andrew couldn't have been more disappointed. This was not what he had come for. He thought he was going to be involved in a straight-forward, sex-motivated child abduction. What he was hearing sounded like it would get very, very messy. He thought of his own paperwork piling up back at East Bentleigh. For Andrew, the saving grace was the theory might not be correct at all.

Later that morning, Matthew and Andrew, like all the other detectives, were independently allocated a fistful of Information Reports and told to check them out. Already 700 snippets of information had poured in and been transposed onto Information Reports. IRs detail information, received from any source, which is then classified from absolutely reliable at best to unclassifiable or totally unreliable at worst. Some of the information Zenith received was so scant it was almost impossible to work on. And as the police were to find out, a lot of the information coming in was a vehicle for people to launder their dirty washing.

Andrew teamed up with Detective Senior Constable Jeff Kyne, who had joined the task force from Elsternwick CIB. They sorted through their paperwork and realised they had about 10 houses to visit all over the southern suburbs. After mapping out a route for the day, which meant they would travel in a wide arc ending back at Rosebud, they headed off.

Their first port of call was an average-looking but tired weatherboard house. They parked their unmarked Commodore outside and stepped over the rusty black wrought iron gate with the one broken hinge. They walked along the curved concrete path to the front door. Andrew knocked. As he waited, he re-read the information report. It said the resident liked little girls. A check on the occupier had showed he had no prior convictions. And the initial information had been supplied anonymously.

Andrew was not impressed. He knew he would have to tread lightly here. He had nothing at all to go on. A man in his 40s answered the door.

"Yes?"

"I'm Senior Detective Andrew Gustke. This is Senior Detective Jeff Kyne. I'm from the Zenith task force and we are investigating the disappearance of Sheree Beasley from Rosebud."

He watched for a reaction. Would the guy flinch? Shuffle his feet? Avoid his eyes? Was he nervous?

The man's brow furrowed and then his expression changed from bewilderment to one of recognition. He spoke loudly, with an air of exasperation and anger.

"Oh yeah, I know who sent you. The ex-wife." He invited the detectives in.

For the next hour Andrew and Jeff heard the story of the messy divorce, who got the kids, who was paying maintenance and who was screwing who. It was a scenario that became very familiar. As the investigation went on, Andrew lost count of the number of times he went through this routine with blokes on the receiving end of a broadside from their ex. Eventually Andrew could tell, even before he got in the car to go and check it out, if the information was supplied by an ex-wife or ex-girlfriend. It meant hours and hours of wasted time.

THE INFORMATION Bureau printed a list of every person who had been convicted of a sex offence in the past 20 years who had lived on the Mornington Peninsula. Some of them were still offending but some were happily married and leading a normal life. To add to the investigators' problems, there was nothing *at all*, to implicate 99.9 percent of these "suspects". Sure, some were convicted rapists but some of them were snowdroppers, others were flashers, some had possessed child pornography in the past. How do you question them about a child abduction with nothing to go on?

Andrew Gustke expected a lot of them to slam the door in his face. But to his surprise, he found almost every suspect asked the police in. Even the really bad crooks would look at the detectives on the front porch and say, "All right, come in. It's got to be solved."

Sometimes Andrew looked at the men and felt he could read their minds.

"You're dragging up my past here. Just because I brushed a girl on the breast ten years ago in the bus stop you're now here thinking I've abducted a little girl."

It was usually very ginger when the police first went in, especially if the man had started a new life. If the suspect was with his wife, he would usually catch on immediately why the police were there. But the wife, who often didn't know about her husband's past, would ask, "Well, why are you here?"

Eventually the detectives perfected a style for this tricky time. After some eye contact with the man, they would make a gesturing motion to him and say to the wife, "Well, it's your husband I want to talk to." Then they would turn to the man and say, "Perhaps you would want to go outside?" Sometimes the suspect would say yes and they would spirit him outside. Other times it was like telepathy.

Occasionally the suspect would say, "No, she already knows about that stuff at the bus stop." That was the best response. Then the four of them would sit down and work out where the man was on June 29, 1991. It was during this side of the Sheree Beasley investigation that the calendars on the fridge or kitchen wall came into their own. Often it was just a simple check which revealed things like kinder duty, swimming sports, so-and-so's place for dinner or lunch. With the prompt, most people could remember what they had been doing. Then the detectives would speak to the people they had met on the day, corroborate their stories, and eliminate the suspects. But it all took so much time.

ONE OF Matthew Wood's tasks was to build a profile of Sheree by talking to every student and teacher at her school. The detectives were hoping to find something which would lead to a motive. With the principal and a child psychologist from the Education Department, Matthew drafted a questionnaire to go home with the pupils. The questionnaire asked that the children's parents sign an interview consent form. Over four days, Matthew spoke to nearly 300 pupils with a policewoman, a child psychologist and a teacher present.

Most of the littlies had no idea what was going on. Some of the children were very serious about it all. They would sit very straight in their chair and look intently at the policeman. Some kids thought the police needed to hear something. Matthew became accustomed to hearing make-believe stories about people with red hair and no teeth chasing children. Sometimes he wondered what they saw in their nightmares. Especially the kids in Sheree's class.

There were traffic jams outside the Rosebud Primary School each morning and afternoon. Parents wouldn't let their children walk or ride their bikes to school. As the mums and the occasional dad waited for the hometime bell outside the cyclone wire fence, they swapped stories of how Sheree's abduction was affecting their children. Some children got upset when they heard helicopters flying overhead. They thought it meant the police were chasing a bad man near their house. Other parents told of how they wouldn't let their kids play in the street. Most wouldn't even let their children ride their bikes beyond the front fence. One mum fretted about her little boy. He was too depressed to eat or talk. And the teachers had told her he had started hitting the other kids in his grade. He'd never done that before.

KERRI WAS inundated with letters of support, good wishes and love from complete strangers around Australia. One letter sent by 13-year-old Adelaide girl Sasha Hollens.

"I do not know how you feel but I do feel sorry for you and I hope you get her back soon and the man who took her sent to jail and kept there for good. I hope your family and friends are helping you. I hope you get her soon and I will pray for you and her day and night so she will be returned safely and unharmed."

ON JULY 12, Robert Lowe rang Margaret Hobbs at her clinic to query an account she had sent him for therapy. Margaret wasn't keen to talk to him. After all, she had thrown him out of therapy last year over the Flinders Street Station offences. After a strained conversation about the bill, Robert said, "Marg, I still need you." Margaret wanted to tell him to get lost but she couldn't bring herself to say it. And she had waited for years for the day Robert would treat therapy seriously. Without expression she said, "You know where I am."

AT FIRST LIGHT - about 6.30am - on July 15, Elizabeth Haworth was driving through Red Hill when she noticed a car parked on the grassy verge of Mornington-Flinders Road, just north of the driveway leading into a property named "Winthunga". Even though she saw nobody about, she thought the car looked as though it had only recently arrived there. The morning was frosty and cold but the windscreen on the small blue hatchback sedan was not misty. She continued on to her horse's stables without giving it another thought.

THE LOCAL PAPER - *The Southern Peninsula Gazette* - reported it on July 9 but the major Melbourne papers didn't break the news until July 14. Sheree's helmet was not found with her bike. She was wearing it when she was abducted. The news provided a breakthrough. On Wednesday, July 17, Sue Marx and her 11-year-old daughter Danielle came forward. They had seen a little girl in a blue car outside their motel in Nepean Highway the day Sheree went missing. But because the girl was wearing a pink helmet, they didn't ring the police. Only when the anomaly had been corrected in the press did they realise they had seen Sheree with her abductor. Sue Marx was extremely distressed by the circumstances. She was distraught because of what she'd seen but at the

The Murder of Sheree

time it hadn't really struck her as important. She realised she was now the best witness the police had. She felt terrible for not coming forward sooner but it wasn't her fault.

Shortly after 2.15pm on the day Sheree was kidnapped, Danielle was playing on the footpath with some friends outside the Copper Lantern Motel in Nepean Highway. Sue was sweeping the driveway and had worked her way up to the footpath. The traffic had been moving very slowly because of drainage works up the road at Chinaman's Creek. When the traffic came to a standstill, a small blue car had stopped directly opposite the mother and daughter, just three metres away.

Danielle saw Sheree first. Sheree's face was screwed up and she seemed to be screaming something at her. Danielle called out, "Hey mum, look at that girl!" Sue looked up from her sweeping and saw Sheree, looking petrified, in the front seat of the car. The car windows were up and Sheree's face was pushed up against the window. Sue was acutely aware the little girl was trying to attract her attention. Slowly, Sheree had silently mouthed the word 'HELP'. Sue thought the look on Sheree's face was a mixture of panic and anger. A few seconds later, the car moved off. Sheree's pleading eyes didn't leave Sue's face. As the car moved off slowly, Sheree's head turned, her face mutely imploring Sue to do something. Then, as suddenly as she had appeared, Sheree was gone.

NOW THE police knew which direction Sheree's abductor had headed. The searching started again, this time concentrating on the Nepean Highway. It continued into the next day but the doorknocks and minute examination of the roadway and surrounds again drew a blank. To add to the frustration, while 6-year-old Shane had said the driver was an older fellow, the Marx's felt he was a younger man.

Now that three people had seen a blue car, Laurie Ratz called in John Bradbury, a detective senior constable from the Stolen Motor Vehicle Squad. John Bradbury had been at the SMVS for 10 years and was regarded as an expert in his field. He begged and borrowed 7 cars that roughly fitted the description of the car the Marx's had seen. He lined them up in Parkmore Road, right beside the spot where Shane said a man had picked up Sheree. Independently, Sue and Danielle picked the same car. A 1985-88 blue Toyota Corolla. And they both picked the same colour blue - described by the manufacturers as 'Azure Blue'. A fly-sheet with a profile picture of the car model was quickly compiled and circulated among police and distributed to the public. It asked people to list the registration number of any similar car sighted, where it was seen and at what time. Local postmen were asked to use the form on their rounds.

The detectives headed to Toyota Australia for a list of all vehicles that matched the description. There were 775. But the car company only had Vehicle Identification Numbers for the cars, not registration numbers. The police had to cross-check every VIN with the Road Traffic Authority to ascertain the cars' registration particulars.

Blue Toyotas were being stopped by police all over Melbourne and the owners asked for their movements on the day of Sheree's disappearance. Those alibis also had to be checked out. The work went on and on and on.

THE TASK FORCE, which comprised only a core of 22 officers, was stretched to the limit. Already 100s of 'suspects' had been interviewed. The task force was trying to eliminate suspects as quickly as possible to see who was left.

Andrew Gustke continued interrogating people in their homes and workplaces, unearthing both the lighter and darker sides of human nature.

"Where were you on Saturday, June 29?" he asked the 'suspect'.

"Where was I? I was on an interstate trip," the man said.

His wife confirmed it but there was no airline ticket to check. The detective took it in his stride but his mind ticked over. *This bloke's lying.* The look on his face and his body language gave him away.

The man then named a Brisbane hotel he had stayed in.

Yeah, like hell, Andrew thought. "Well, I'll go and check it out. Thanks for your time," he said. He left and dropped in on a few more blokes with prior convictions for sex crimes before driving back to the station. He walked to his desk and noticed there were five phone messages, all from the man who had lied to him just a few hours earlier. Andrew flopped in his chair. He wanted to light up a cigarette but he was too tired to go outside. Then the phone rang. Andrew pushed some of the paper out of the way and grabbed the phone. It was the same bloke.

The Murder of Sheree

"What I said to you before - that was all lies," the man gasped. "I need to see you, can I come and see you? I was really with this woman."

Andrew smiled. *So that's why he was lying.*

"That's fine," Andrew said. "I'm not going to interfere with your marriage but I just want to know where you were on the 29th."

He told the detective the whole story.

Andrew was not the only detective who then had to go and check with the 'other woman'. But on the way to eliminating the husbands as suspects, the wives often found out where they really were the day Sheree disappeared. Most of the guys felt that being charged with murder would have been easier to handle.

The detectives also uncovered other sex offenders. Detective Senior Constable Harry Simpson from Mornington CIB uncovered two paedophiles who operated their own private peep show at home. The initial information came from an Information Report which said the pair, who worked together in a factory, rang in sick on June 29 and again on July 1. They had been acting strangely, the anonymous caller said. When Harry went to their home and checked around, he found a two way mirror between two bedrooms. In the second bedroom, the police found a video camera hidden in a wardrobe. The camera was pointing through a hole cut in the back of the wardrobe, which looked straight onto the bed in the first room. The men had been luring boys to their home and making child pornography home movies. Harry was only too happy to take both men into custody. Both men were tried for child sex offences and jailed.

ANOTHER DAY. More door knocks. More "suspects". Andrew and Jeff walked through the overgrown front lawn and stepped onto the front porch. The flywire door, full of torn holes, was wide open. The spring had broken off long ago. Andrew knocked on the door and waited. He noticed a musty, bitter kind of smell. A few seconds went by, then the men heard the muffled sound of footsteps in the hallway approaching the door. It opened slowly. Standing before them, partially obscured by the door, was a small, shabby man with a frightened look on his face.

"Yes?" he asked timidly. He looked nervously back and forwards from face to face.

"We're from the Zenith task force," Jeff said. "We're investigating the disappearance of a 6-year-old schoolgirl, Sheree Beasley, who was abducted in June. Do you mind if we come in?"

Instantly the man relaxed and smiled. He opened the door and invited the detectives inside. Andrew saw the length of the hallway was lined with piles of newspapers that stretched up almost to the roof. As they walked along the hallway, the men were hit with an overpowering smell of stale air. Andrew asked if he could smoke inside.

"Yes, yes. By all means," the man said and walked to the kitchen. Andrew followed him and stood in the doorway. He could see dust everywhere he looked. He felt dirty just being inside this house.

The owner collected a chipped, pale yellow saucer.

"There you are," he said, handing over the makeshift ashtray, and walked to the loungeroom. The man sat in a big club lounge chair that Andrew estimated was about 60 years old. The fabric on it was so thin it was almost see through. The two detectives sat on the couch. Andrew put the saucer on the arm of the chair and lit up a smoke to cover the shocking smell. He saw a raggedy cat scoot behind the man's chair.

Andrew got out his paperwork and started talking about Sheree. He showed the man photos of her in her tracksuit, a photo of her bike, a photo of the type of car the police were looking for. He noticed the man was nodding eagerly and had a smile on his face. Andrew was aware something unusual was happening but he couldn't put his finger on what it was. Then he noticed the man had his hands inside his trouser pockets and appeared to be fondling himself. Andrew tried not to notice. He kept talking and occasionally asked the man a few questions about himself. The hands began moving more vigorously in the pockets. The eyes glazed, the smile became more distant.

"Look, would you mind not doing that?" Andrew said. He pointed to the man's erection in his trousers.

The man wriggled in his chair. "Oh, but I find this very titillating," he said.

"Yeah? Well just cut it out while we're here," Andrew said. He was getting fed up with the number of sex offenders he was dealing with. He was talking to them every damn day. As a child, Andrew had holidayed with his family in Fifth Avenue, Rosebud. He remembered the carnival, the kids on the beach, the fairs, the parks. He had already decided he would not be taking his kids down there for a holiday.

ON SATURDAY July 20, the Lowe family was at the Rosebud unit. Benjamin was bored. His mum was knitting, nothing much was happening. He asked his dad to take him for a driving lesson and was pleased when Robert agreed. As Benjamin was reversing the car up the driveway, he heard the newsreader on the car radio call for all blue hatchback drivers to check their cars in with the police.

He said to his dad, "Would you like to check the car in?"

"No don't worry about it," Robert said.

"What happens if a policeman pulls us over?"

"I'll get some identification."

"Won't mum worry?"

"I won't tell her." Robert went inside, got some identification, and returned. They drove off to Portsea, stopping at some back beaches along the way.

A FEW DAYS later Geoff Alway was in Canberra with biologist Nigel Hall and crime scene expert Brian Gamble, following up a promising lead. An Australian Federal Police officer, Peter Kuhnke, had an informer who told about him a man who had sexually molested his own children in Victoria. The informer said the man had recently moved to the nation's capital and he drove the type of car being sought by the Zenith detectives. And he had been in Rosebud, where his family had holiday-homes, the weekend Sheree was abducted.

When Geoff and his AFP counterparts raided the man's home, simultaneously eight houses in Victoria connected to him in some way were also raided. But it turned out this was not the man the police were looking for. He had been in Rosebud the weekend *before* Sheree was abducted but he was nowhere near the area on June 29.

ANDREW WALKED into the CIB office and went through the usual morning routine. He picked up another bundle of Information Reports, split them with Jeff Kyne and hit the road. One Information Report in particular caught Andrew's eye. It was from Sergeant David Crosbie from Croydon police. Zenith analyst Senior Constable Maree Kepert had filled in the details he had provided which took up just three lines in her handwriting. Andrew noticed it had been written out that day - July 24.

"Suspect male approaching children at the Croydon pool in a blue hatchback DLT 771. 1/3/91."

That was all it said. Andrew stood there looking at the IR. Had he missed something? Croydon and Rosebud? What's the connection? The only match he could see was the car. A blue hatchback. He checked with Maree who told him Sgt Crosbie had rung in and said a teacher had reported that a man had approached three of her male students at a swimming carnival. Andrew did a registration check on the police computer. DLT 771 was owned by Maria George of 179 Flinders Lane, Melbourne.

Andrew had perfected his own system. If he felt the information provided warranted a personal visit, then those IRs were reasonably high priority. Some could be written off without doing anything at all because they obviously didn't have any connection. And if he didn't think they required a personal visit, well, they were a reasonably low priority. But this one! It was one of those he felt almost embarrassed to ring up about. He put it off for a while. He went on to more important tasks.

The next day he rang Maria George. Andrew had been in the rag trade for five years up until he was 24 - he was production manager for Perri Cutten - and knew Maria George enjoyed a good reputation in the industry. She had been running her company for decades. Andrew had been to her office many times years before, although he was certain she would not remember him. Her company was one of many haberdashery places that supply lace and other odds and ends for clothing manufacturers. He decided against mentioning his background.

Maria George told him the car was driven by a family man who was a good worker. But Mrs George wasn't too forthcoming with much more information. She was used to police harassing her man. She had had a number of calls in the past 6 months about that car, and her rep had told her police had always picked the wrong man. She said she doubted that Andrew was a police officer. Andrew got so annoyed he told her he would get a uniformed policeman to come around from Russell Street to prove he was a cop. He told her he was making enquiries in relation to the Sheree Beasley investigation.

"My sales rep would not be involved in anything of this nature because he is a married man with two children and he is a good family man," Mrs George said in her heavy European accent.

Andrew kept pressing for the name until she relented.

"Robert Lowe," she said but she refused to give out his address or phone number. "I will get him to call you," she said.

Andrew hung up and hung his head. *Will this ever end?* It wasn't an important IR. He was trying to get rid of it but he still didn't have Robert Lowe's address or date of birth. He did a quick mental recap, comparing the two sets of circumstances.

Croydon, swimming pool, boys involved, no girls, back in March.

Rosebud, Parkmore Road, a little girl, in June.

The only connection was the car - and there were plenty of others around. Some IRs took months to clear up, and some took a minute. This one felt like it was going to hang around.

At 1pm the same day, Robert Lowe stormed into Margaret Hobbs's clinic in Victoria Parade. He was very agitated and acting strangely. It was a controlled anger but it seemed to Margaret he was very close to going over the edge into violence. As he paced back and forth in the small room, Margaret became increasingly concerned.

"What's wrong, what's wrong?"

"Nothing." His teeth were clenched and he couldn't stand still. Margaret had never seen this side of him before and she was surprised. Normally a twitch in his nose was the only sign he was distressed or angry.

"Where have you been? What have you been doing?" Margaret was trying to get a handle on the anger.

"Nothing."

"Nothing?"

He mumbled something about Sydney as he paced quickly.

"Robert, what is it?"

"I want to see Tony," he said in a raised voice. Margaret's son-in-law, lawyer Tony Nicholson, had an office in another part of the building.

"Why Robert?" Margaret was frowning.

Robert kept pacing. Then he turned quickly and viciously threw some paper money notes into her face.

"Here, keep it," he barked. His face was set firmly but his nose began twitching.

The colour came to Margaret's face. She gathered up the money, crumpled it and threw it back at him. Angrily she said, "I don't want it Robert. You don't owe it to me." She was angry with him but she couldn't work out why he was behaving so oddly. Robert was usually very much in control. Finally Margaret learnt he wanted to see Tony over a bill about a court case.

What had upset Robert was that Lorraine had opened it. What puzzled Margaret was the amount of anger Robert displayed. And it had nothing to do with Margaret, who had patients booked that afternoon. Tony was busy, so Robert had to wait. He waited downstairs for four hours, sitting, pacing, muttering. About 5.20pm Margaret walked downstairs and learnt from the receptionist that Robert had gone.

"Did you see what sort of car he was driving?" Margaret asked. She had Rosebud on her mind.

"Oh, no, he went about 20 minutes ago."

Margaret walked to the front of the building and looked out onto Victoria Parade. There was no traffic, which was unusual for late afternoon on a weekday. Then she saw a little blue Toyota Corolla hatchback drive past and she saw Robert was driving. She turned and walked slowly back up the steps. She felt ill.

IT WAS JULY 30. Andrew arrived at work at 8am as usual. And, as usual, it would be at least twelve hours before he would head home to his wife and children. Matthew Wood was still compiling the Sheree profile and Andrew was to help him. Andrew was looking forward to that. He was sick of all these nowhere enquiries. But for now he was still bogged down with the Information Reports and other work.

Just before 9.45am he was still sitting at his desk, absorbed in his files, when someone said: "Andy, there's a Mr Lowe on the phone for you."

Andrew thought for a moment.

Lowe, Lowe, Lowe.

"Oh yeah, I know the one," Andrew said. "Good, good, good."

Get rid of this now, he thought. He picked up the phone.

"Mr Lowe is it?"

"Yes, that's right."

"Thanks for calling back," Andrew said. "I need to speak to you about your company car."

"Yes?"

"What is the registration number of your car?" Andrew's left hand searched about his desk frantically trying to locate the IR. *Ah yeah, here it is.*

"D something, I can't remember." The caller spoke perfect English, in a clipped, smooth voice. There was a trace of an English accent and he sounded a little irritated. But Andrew pressed on. He read from the Information Report.

"Is it DLT 771?"

"Yes, I think so."

"Does anyone else drive the car?"

Mr Lowe was getting annoyed. He was speaking a little louder, a little quicker.

"No. It is mine. What is this all about?"

"I am investigating all blue hatchback cars in relation to the disappearance of Sheree Beasley from down here at Rosebud," Gustke said.

"Yes?"

"I would like to get some details from you first. What is your date of birth?"

"January 29, 1937."

Good, thought Andrew, *Now I can do a criminal history check.*

"Your address, Mr Lowe?"

"13 Mannering Drive, Glen Waverley."

"Have you ever been in trouble with the police?"

"No."

"Can you remember where you were at the weekend of the 29th June this year? That's a Saturday."

"Yes, I was at home with my wife and kids."

"Do you have any connection with the Mornington Peninsula or the Rosebud area?"

"No."

Andrew was starting to feel uneasy. *Gee, he's very sure of himself. Very adamant about what he wants to say. And very condescending.*

"Do you ever come down this way at all?"

"No."

He's lying. Well, he sounds like he's lying. But why?

"What is your phone number at home, Mr Lowe?"

"It is a silent number."

I want to ring your wife. You said you were at home with your wife. I could come to Glen Waverley but it's not that important an IR that it merits a visit to your home.

"That's all right. I only need it just in case I have to get back to you."

"It is a silent number and I don't want to give it out."

"It isn't going anywhere," Gustke persisted. "I'll just need it if I need to ring you back and after that it will be destroyed."

"No. It is a silent number and I don't want to give it out to anyone," Mr Lowe said.

"All right then."

"Is that all?"

Andrew said: "Thank you Mr Lowe" and hung up. At first he felt resigned to visiting Mannering Drive but when he replayed the conversation in his mind, it felt all wrong.

That was a 'plastic' conversation, Andrew thought. *It wasn't real. It was like he planned it all. Robert Lowe lied to me. I know it. But why? And what about?*

Andrew had never had this feeling with anybody else he had spoken to during the enquiry. People got angry when he spoke to them, or they wouldn't talk to him, or they got peeved, or they avoided him. But nothing like this.

Andrew immediately made notes of the conversation. It might mean something later on down the track. Then he went straight to the police computer and punched in Mr Lowe's details. A number of prior convictions came out. Wilful and obscene exposure. Offensive behaviour. Indecent assault. Andrew's hair stood up on the back of his neck.

Why is this bloke lying to me? He must have known I would check.

As he tore the print-out from the computer, Andrew realised the IR he was trying to write off was now something he was going to work on. He was excited. He wondered where this was heading.

Andrew looked at the prior convictions again, then he rang the Information Bureau in Melbourne and asked them to fax through more details on Mr Lowe's history. While he was waiting for a response, he walked towards the CIB office and passed John Bradbury in the corridor. Andrew showed him a printout on the registration details of the blue Toyota DLT 771. John Bradbury was the car expert. He would know just by looking at the printout.

"Is this in the ballpark range that you're looking at?" Andrew asked.

John looked at the identification and chassis numbers and said, "Yeah. Why?"

Andrew didn't answer. He was lost in thought. *He's got priors, he's lied to me, now the car.*

A glint came to his eyes as he moved quickly through the office. He went to Geoff Alway's desk but the sergeant had just come back from Canberra and he was telling some other detectives how it had gone. Andrew tried to tell him about Lowe and how he lied on the phone but Geoff was only half-listening. There had been other good suspects before.

"This bloke looks good," Andrew said excitedly. "He's got to be a good suspect. We've got to check out any connections with Rosebud." Geoff was still only half listening. He was opening up the internal mail and absently reading file after file. Suddenly he looked up.

"What did you say this bloke's name was?"

"Lowe. Robert Lowe."

Geoff looked down at the Information Report he was reading. Then he handed it to Andrew and said, "Have a look at this."

Andrew read the document. It was from Crime Stoppers, a service which takes tape recorded messages from the public, mostly anonymously. He quickly looked down at the text and read:

The Murder of Sheree

```
I know a guy through therapeutic dealings who has
a history of sexual offences. He has been charged
for indecent exposure and also for chatting up
young kids. He has a holiday house in Rosebud and
owns a blue hatchback. He has only just returned
from Sydney where he was on business as a salesman.
He is a commercial traveller. He is married with
two kids and lives in a house in Mannering Drive,
Glen Waverley. His name is Robert Lowe. He is in
his 50s, about 5,10, and thin with darkish hair.
He often wears a hat.
```

Andrew read it twice more. He could feel the hairs on the back of his neck again. He wondered who had rung up. *Therapeutic dealings.* Andrew thought it might be a doctor, or possibly a prostitute. He fairly flew to his desk and rang the Shire of Flinders. He asked them to check the index of names of property owners in the shire. Bingo. Mr Lowe owned a holiday flat in Florence Avenue, Rosebud West.

By 1pm, all the available task force members were assembled. Andrew briefed a captivated audience. Morale was suddenly skyhigh.

THE FOLLOWING day Detective Senior Sergeant Dale Johnson was seconded to the task force. He was to be in control of the investigation while Laurie Ratz took some well-earned recreational leave. Dale spent the first two days reading through folder after folder of IRs. While he was reading, and the other detectives were working on a plan of how best to put their chief suspect under the magnifying glass, Robert Lowe drove to the Yarraville bus terminus. He leered at several schoolgirls while rubbing his crotch through his trousers. He was spotted by several women who called the police and he was arrested.

At the police station, it was the same old story. Lowe would not tell them anything about himself and was overjoyed when the police could not work out how he had got to Yarraville from Glen Waverley. He had parked his car hundreds of metres away from the bus terminus and had taken care to have nothing in his possession to link him to the car. He was charged with wilful and obscene exposure and offensive behaviour. He was released on bail. Then he went home for dinner with his wife and boys.

The Murder of Sheree

THE DETECTIVES decided to examine every minute detail of Mr Lowe's life. There were door to door enquiries in and around Florence Avenue. Andrew Gustke checked out all the haberdashery shops on the Peninsula to see if Lowe had visited them. He learnt Mr Lowe had visited some shops on business but that was months ago. The detectives checked Lowe's bankcard and bank accounts. He might have accessed his accounts in Rosebud on June 29, but he hadn't. They checked service stations to see if the car had been seen. It hadn't. His previous employers were spoken to. Most had no complaints about him, yet most of them had to "let him go" after only a few years service.

All the football clubs on the peninsula were checked to see if Lowe was a member. He might have gone to a local game that fateful Saturday. But he didn't belong to any club. Police officers who had charged Lowe with his various crimes were spoken to. Most couldn't remember *him*, rather they remembered his attitude. He was overbearing, arrogant and very argumentative. Some even thought they had got the wrong man. Zenith investigators learned from these officers that Mr Lowe would always deny being involved in any offences. He would lie.

When Geoff Alway and Dale Johnson checked through Lowe's criminal history, they noticed it referred to a Dr Hobbs way back in 1984. They checked the court records and found a report from Mrs Margaret Hobbs, psychotherapist. She had to be the next port of call.

NEIL GREENHILL had been unable to sleep, unable to work, almost unable to function. He couldn't concentrate. In general conversation, he stopped talking mid-sentence, unable to remember what he was saying. Nothing seemed to make sense any more. He wept uncontrollably as he drove along the highways in his work car. Once he found himself driving on the wrong side of the road, heading for a truck. Sometimes he drove aimlessly, trying to come to terms with what had happened. A car accident, he could understand. But this.... If only he knew for certain what had happened to his darling granddaughter. Rain drummed on the car. He thought of Sheree huddled under a tree trying to seek shelter.

It was midnight and he found himself sitting in his car outside a church. He stared for a minute or maybe an hour at the mute building. His mother's face flashed into his mind.

If anybody can find her, you will. The words were etched in his mind.

He heard himself screaming at the church yet the words seemed to be coming from somewhere and someone else.

"How can you let this happen?" he yelled at the silent building. Was it welcoming him, or mocking him. Then he opened his car door, leant out and was ill.

THE DETECTIVES were granted a search warrant for the Florence Avenue unit. On August 2, 1991, when they knew nobody was home, they entered and found a well-appointed two bedroom home. It looked as though it might be used on a regular or semi-regular basis. A *Herald Sun* newspaper on the table dated July 20 showed someone had been there at least since that day. The police left after a cursory look around.

Four days later, Zenith learnt Lowe had flown to Sydney on business on August 4. Geoff McLean and Dale Johnson found Lowe's work car in the Tullamarine airport long-term car park and looked for anything distinctive like stickers or scratches - anything that might prick a witness's memory. But while the car certainly matched the description of the one that was seen in Parkmore Road, there was nothing out of the ordinary about it.

Dale was very happy Lowe was in Sydney. This could help the investigators. If Lowe spoke to his wife while he was away, it would have to be on the telephone. Dale sought and was granted a warrant to tape all phone calls made from or to Lowe's home phone. The police also installed several listening devices in the house.

JUST AFTER 5pm on Thursday, August 8, Geoff Alway and Dale Johnson knocked on the door of 139 Victoria Parade, Fitzroy. It was a two-storey terrace house, converted into consultation rooms for several specialists. One of the rooms, up the steep, carpeted stairs at the back on the second floor, was used by psychotherapist Margaret Hobbs. She invited the detectives in.

Geoff opened the door, with its yellow frosted glass, and walked into the room. He guessed it was about eight metres long and only about three metres wide. To his right, he saw one window which faced a faded white brick wall. Another window at the far end of the room overlooked a dingy lane which ended in a cul-de-sac.

On their immediate right, the detectives saw a brown leather chair, facing the rear of the room, and Margaret's chair just two metres away. Against the wall to the left was a beige two-seater couch. Beyond it was a table housing some letters and a thriving butterfly plant camouflaged an untidy scramble of books threatening to topple off an overflowing book shelf. Several beautiful watercolour landscapes, painted by a patient, adorned one wall, next to some pencil portrait sketches. In the other corner was Margaret's working desk, on which sat a computer, a telephone and an answering machine.

After they introduced themselves properly and explained why they were there, Geoff told Mrs Hobbs they were investigating Sheree's disappearance. The police could immediately see she wanted to help them but she appeared to be in a jam. She spoke about ethics and confidentiality. She told the policemen she hadn't seen Robert as a patient for seven or eight months. She had seen him recently when he caused a kerfuffle over an old account. Geoff and Dale both thought the same thing. It sounded like Mr Lowe was under some sort of pressure.

They asked Mrs Hobbs to describe her job. She explained that as a psychotherapist, she could not dispense medication, so she was confined to counselling. She said psychotherapists usually didn't have formal psychological training, although many have been trained in psychiatric social work and have colleagues who are youth officers or psychiatric nurses. Her training had allowed her to work in the parole and probation department as a psychotherapist.

The detectives asked more questions about Lowe, and Margaret was clearly uncomfortable in talking to them, although she did tell them a few things. In their short conversation the police learnt that Margaret thought Lowe was not an honest man. He was a man who played games. She said religion was a very important part of his life but it was all a charade. He hid behind his religion. He was a regular shoplifter, just for the thrill. He usually stole things he wouldn't need.

Margaret told them he used obscene and vulgar language when he spoke to his victims. He was reliant on pornography and known to approach boys. He was always trying to shock his victims, she said, although children going through puberty would laugh at him. He was an opportunistic offender, who would masturbate or expose himself four or five times in a day. Margaret noted Robert was taking many risks and seemed to be reaching the stage where he couldn't control himself. And she told the detectives he had been fired from several jobs because of his behaviour.

The men were a little surprised when Margaret told them she doubted he would ever show any remorse or guilt. They didn't expect this sort of talk from a woman who had spent all her working life speaking up on behalf of these types of men. But she explained he was a very difficult man to deal with because of his arrogance. In fact, Margaret had stopped treating him because he was playing cat and mouse with her. And she told them Lorraine Lowe didn't know her husband had been to court apart from the first appearance at Springvale.

The policemen's interest in Lowe escalated as Margaret continued talking. Geoff was frantically taking notes as Margaret detailed more information. She described Lowe's car, and said he had a house in Rosebud. He didn't drink alcohol, and he wasn't on medication. To Geoff, who had had more experience with sex offenders than Dale, that was important information and it set off alarm bells in his mind. Lowe was out there, flashing, making sexual comments to kids - or maybe abducting them and killing them - just because they're out there. No other reason. He was a predator.

As they drove away from Victoria Parade, both men wondered what it was about Lowe that prompted Mrs Hobbs go against her ethics and talk to them. Then they thought aloud as they mulled over the exciting new information. They both agreed that what they had learned didn't make Lowe the offender but it certainly made him a pretty probable suspect.

They checked to see if he could have been at Preston when Kylie Maybury was abducted and murdered. They felt certain that if they found Lowe had been near the abduction site around the time of Kylie's disappearance, he would be a prime suspect. But try as they might, they couldn't take the matter any further. It was too long ago.

The Murder of Sheree

AT 7AM the next morning - Friday, August 9, 1991 - Dale Johnson and Matthew Wood met at Rosebud police complex. It was the last planning stage of their new tack.

Dale and Matthew arrived at Mannering Drive at 12.15pm. It was a pleasant neighbourhood, full of well-tended gardens and two storey homes. The street was immediately to the west of the Police Training Academy. The Academy, a former Christian Brothers training college, is sometimes known as Coppers Christi, a play on words as its first name was Corpus Christi. It occurred to both men that Lowe would have loved living beneath the spire where the religious and police connotations intertwined. On the one hand, the sight of the spire would have reminded him of his role in the church, while on the other, he probably would have snuck home night after night, after terrorising children, to go to bed right under the noses of hundreds of trainee cops.

Matthew and Dale walked through the arched front gate, past the small cypresses and green bushes next to the two car garage, and up the steps onto the front porch, where they stood next to several pot plants. Dale had a tape recorder strapped to his body so he could secretly record any conversations. He knocked on the door and looked around while he waited, taking in his surrounds. Just beyond the camellia bush at the front door, he saw a large tree fern next to the front window, surrounded by small daisies and snowdrops. The lawn was cut short, with neat, curved edges. In the centre of the front lawn sat a cream coloured bird bath. Dale thought the front yard looked peaceful, almost serene. Almost too serene.

After the officers introduced themselves, Lorraine invited them inside, where they stood near the dining room table. While they spoke and listened, they quietly took in everything they saw.

The home was well-appointed and smelled clean. The beige semi-shag pile carpet was obviously regularly vacuumed. The men walked into the loungeroom, past the piano and the club-style lounge suite, with its cream and brown conservative paisley covering. In between the seats sat a glass topped circular table, where a cluster of lavender stood in a crystal vase. Lorraine led Matthew and Dale past the feature wood wall, against which was a book case full of encyclopedias, dictionaries and bibles. Dale

The Murder of Sheree

noticed the red velvet curtains and then spied a wind-up wooden clock hanging on the wall. He looked at it closely and saw it was made in Korea. A number of family photographs adorned walls and furniture. Everything was neat, clean, tidy.

As they stood in the dining room, the detectives also watched Mrs Lowe's body language. Lorraine was nervous - she knew from Robert that the police like to stir up trouble. But at the same time, she was glad they had come. She had heard about the blue car involved in the Sheree Beasley abduction and was pleased the police were being thorough.

"Where was the family on that weekend?" Matthew Wood asked.

Lorraine quickly racked her brain. She hadn't thought of that. What would this have to do with her family?

"I think we were home," she said.

"What about your husband?"

Lorraine thought quickly. The family never went to Rosebud unless they stayed the night there. She had only done that once in the past couple of months and that was two weeks ago - July 20.

"I'm sure he was at home," she said. "I think he was at home with me. He'd been to a church meeting in the morning." Even though Lorraine's attitude bordered on indignation, both policemen felt they were dealing with a very timid housewife. She was at least helpful, if a little overawed. They asked when Mr Lowe would be home. Mrs Lowe said it would be in a few days' time. They left the task force phone number and asked Lorraine to get her husband to ring as soon as he got home, no matter what the time.

That night Robert rang Lorraine from Sydney. She told him what had happened. He told her not to talk to the police.

"Oh you didn't ask them in? Oh don't ever do that," Robert said. "What did you tell them?"

Lorraine told Robert what had happened. Since the police had left, she had been thinking about their visit. Now she wasn't so sure Robert was home on June 29 but she couldn't remember.

"I can't remember exactly what we did," she told her husband.

"I was home with you all weekend," he said. He was angry she had let the police in. He rang her on the Friday and Saturday nights too, each time asking about the police visit. Robert had stayed in Sydney for an extra couple of days so he could see a rugby league match with his brother Rick, who was in Australia on business with National Mutual. When the brothers met on the Sunday, Rick thought his brother looked agitated and not himself. Rick felt Robert was very depressed but couldn't find out why. Rick had been unable to secure an extra ticket for Robert to go to the game.

When Rick went off with some friends to watch the match, Robert sat in Rick's apartment. He rang Lorraine several times. He talked about the police each time but Lorraine couldn't really understand what he was on about. She thought it was very peculiar. He rang her every hour, asking if the police had been back.

Robert arrived home late and tired on Sunday night. But Lorraine still went at him about ringing the police. She remembered they had said he was to ring as soon as he got home.

"It's too late," Robert said in an exasperated tone. "I'll ring them in the morning. Now tell me again just exactly what did they ask you and what they said."

Lorraine went through the story again. Then Robert grilled her further. He wanted to know what they looked like, how old they were, how long they stayed for, whether they sat down, whether they'd gone into any room. Lorraine told him but she was getting annoyed. She just wanted the whole thing cleared up. But instead, Robert complained he was tired and went straight to bed.

First thing Monday morning Lorraine pestered Robert again. She didn't want him going to work and getting involved in business meetings and forgetting to ring the police. She didn't want them coming round again. Robert reluctantly acquiesced and went into the bedroom. As he walked in he said it was probably too early to ring. It was almost 7.45am. Lorraine waited outside the bedroom door, out of sight, listening. She heard Robert dial a number and then almost immediately hang up. Lorraine thought it was unlikely the phone rang at all at the other end. She silently ran down the hallway and into the kitchen just before Robert came out. She asked him what had happened.

"There was no-one there," Robert said with a "told-you-so" expression

The Murder of Sheree

on his face. She asked him to try again at 8 o'clock but he said he would ring when he got to work.

"I want to contact my solicitor first," he said.

"Why do you need to do that?"

"Well, I'd be stupid not to," he said. Then he left for work. As soon as he left the driveway, Lowe was under surveillance. The surveillance police - or 'dogs' in police vernacular - had been tasked to follow and watch Lowe 24 hours a day. There were more surveillance police working on Lowe than would normally be used. If Lowe approached any "targets", one crew would stay behind and take particulars of his intended victims, and pass that information onto the investigating detectives to follow up. The thinking was Lowe might say or do something that could link him to Sheree's abduction. And the task force wanted to see just what this bloke was like. It's one thing to read about a suspect on police forms - it's another altogether to see him in action.

Lowe didn't disappoint. By lunchtime he was back to his old tricks. At 1.25pm the police saw him park his blue hatchback near Windsor Primary School. While sitting in the front seat, like a seasoned contortionist he changed from his suit into white shorts and a navy blue jumper. Then he crept away towards the school. Ten minutes later he was chased away by a teacher. He jumped into his car and sped off.

Half an hour later, he parked his car in Fitzroy Street, outside the St Kilda Bowling Club and walked to the St Kilda light rail station platform. He approached three teenage schoolgirls and pulled down the front of his shorts. Then he scuttled off, while the girls flagged a passing police divisional van. Lowe walked through the parkland next to the bowling club before kneeling down and masturbating in full view of Aughtie Drive traffic. Sated, he walked to his car, changed back into his suit, and drove off. A little while later the surveillance police watched him step into a public phone box. In Glen Waverley, Lorraine picked up the phone.

"Hello?"

"Hi love, it's me."

"Have you rung the police?" Lorraine said quickly.

"Yes. I'm just ringing so you won't worry. I rang them just now. "

"Yes?"

"It's nothing to worry about. It was just a routine enquiry. We don't have to do anything else and they won't be bothering us any more."

Lorraine let out a sigh of relief. She had been thinking of ringing the police herself but now Robert had called them it was all over. Still, she couldn't help concentrating on June 29. Her memories of that day were vague and she didn't like that feeling. She wanted to be crystal clear as to where Robert had been. She brought up the topic again.

"Can you remember where you were on that day?"

"What day?"

"Robert! The day that girl was abducted."

"We were all at home. Don't you remember that? You must remember. I was with you and the boys."

"Mmm," Lorraine said. She wasn't so sure but he might be right. She just couldn't remember. Each Saturday was pretty much like the one before.

WHILE ROBERT Lowe was getting his kicks frightening other people's children and lying to his wife about the police, Dale Johnson was sitting at Rosebud police complex planning the following day's interview. He wrote down all the questions he wanted answered. Dale had heard the taped telephone conversation when Robert rang Lorraine from Sydney. He thought Lowe was trying to manipulate his wife into changing her thinking. He felt Lowe was encouraging her to remember something she couldn't recall because it didn't happen. Dale recalled hearing Lowe telling Lorraine on the phone he was at home with her on June 29. He had kept asking her, "Don't you remember?"

The detective had a definite plan. If Lowe went off on a tangent in the interview, Dale would listen but then go back to the original questions. And, initially at least, whatever Lowe said, even if was an obvious lie, Dale would accept it.

But even though Lowe looked good as a suspect, Dale wasn't all that hopeful that he would 'roll over' and talk. And given Lowe's church background, and the fact he had been at a church meeting the day of the abduction, he wasn't even sure Zenith was on the right track.

The interview was to take place at the Homicide Squad office in St

Kilda Road so that it could be video taped. At that time Homicide was one of the few offices in Victoria that had video taping facilities for interviews.

Laurie Ratz was fairly convinced his troops were on track. They had tried but were unable to eliminate Lowe from the inquiry. And nobody else had popped up who looked like knocking Lowe off the top of the suspect list. That was even more significant.

THE NEXT DAY - Tuesday, August 13, 1991 - was not a day Lorraine was looking forward to. Several X-Rays she was to take to the specialist lay on the dining room table. She had an appointment with a specialist about some pain she was experiencing in her chest. Lorraine had had a history of breast lumps. Professor Bennett had removed two lumps from her breasts when she was working for him years ago and she had to keep an eye on any lumps that might appear.

She was concerned about her blood pressure. She had been a bit dizzy at times, too. She was given the all clear when she went to a 24 hour clinic - except for the lump in her right breast. The doctor ordered a mammogram, although she thought it was just a cyst, and referred Lorraine to a specialist. But Lorraine was terrified she might have cancer.

Like most couples, the Lowe's had their own morning routine. Lorraine would shower while Robert put on the kettle. Then they would swap over before waking the boys. Lorraine was showering at 7.05am when Dale Johnson knocked on the door. He had quite a crowd with him. Matthew Wood and Tony Jacobs stood behind him. So did Detective Senior Constables Geoff McLean and Kate Foley, forensic photographer Mick Hradek, Crime Scene expert Senior Constable Steve Drummond, biologist Alice Orlat, a Transport Branch driver, and Detective Sergeant Greg Bowd and Detective Senior Constable Geoff Branch from Spectrum. The fingerprints expert arrived a little later.

Robert Lowe opened the front door and then walked outside in his flannelette pyjamas, slippers and a blue dressing gown.

"Yes?"

Dale could see Lowe wasn't fazed. He thought Lowe knew why they were there.

The Murder of Sheree

"Mr Lowe is it?"

"Yes?"

Dale introduced himself and told Lowe why they were there. As he spoke, he watched for any giveaway sign in Lowe's face, or in his actions. The detective was in no doubt Lowe had been expecting them. He wasn't shocked or surprised at all - in fact, he was haughty. He looked down his nose at the policemen. Matthew Wood thought Mr Lowe was very confident. Almost arrogant.

Dale showed Lowe the search warrant and brushed past him into the house. As the other officers filed in, Lowe sidled up to Dale as if to say, "Here I am. Don't go near anyone else." Then he pointed to the bedroom. "My wife's in there," he said. "My sons are down the back, don't go down there." Dale just looked at him.

As the police swarmed about the house, Lowe started issuing orders. "Don't disturb that," he commanded. He was pushing the boundaries to see how far he could go with the police. Dale had been expecting this. Lowe's previous police informants had told him Lowe would try to take charge and dominate the police.

"Sorry, we've got a warrant," Dale said sternly. He wasn't going to take any crap. "This...," he waved his hand around indicating the police searching through cupboards, desks, files, photo albums, "is going to happen. Your house is going to be searched. The way *we* want to do it."

The autocrat in Lowe died. He silently acknowledged it was useless to resist. Realising he couldn't say much anyway with his family present, he no longer spoke unless the police prompted him. And Dale largely ignored him. He wanted to speak to Lowe at the police station, on his home turf.

Now the detectives wanted to see Lowe's clothes and shoes. Lowe meekly yet still defiantly led them to his bedroom. He stuck his head into the bedroom en suite.

"You'd better get out of the shower, Lorri. The place is full of police," he said.

Lorraine laughed. She thought there might have been a burglary - but Robert was probably joking. She dried herself and stepped out of the bathroom. She couldn't believe her eyes. There were police everywhere.

The Murder of Sheree

The police told the family to have their breakfast so the boys could go to school. Robert assembled the family in the kitchen round the table and asked Dale Johnson, "Do you mind if I say a prayer?"

"No, go ahead."

The Lowe family held hands round the table and gave thanks to the Lord as was their daily custom, while police officers stood around looking on. Lorraine watched her husband's face as he led the family in prayer. She saw he was preoccupied, mouthing the words without conviction. His mind was somewhere else. Then the police walked him to the en suite where he showered. Lorraine cooked the boys a breakfast of eggs and sausage, while she told the police what they could and couldn't search. They listened to her politely but just went about their business. That made her angry but she was petrified as well. *What was going on?* She carried the cooked eggs across the kitchen towards the table but her hands were shaking so much she dropped one - splat! - on the floor. Lorraine muttered to herself as she wiped up the mess. Finally Robert walked back into the kitchen, dressed and ready to go. There were tears welling in his eyes. A tear ran down his cheek.

"I'm sorry, that's all I can say," he sobbed to his sons. Benjamin and Jonathan didn't move, nor did they speak. They just looked at their father and then at the police officers around the house. Then they stared at their meals.

Robert turned to Lorraine and repeated the words, over and over.

"I'm sorry, that's all I can say."

Lorraine was stunned. Her feet were rivetted to the floor. *Oh my goodness*, she thought. *You seem to be taking responsibility for Sheree.*

Neighbours started to gather outside, watching as Robert's car was winched onto a police truck, to be taken away for forensic examination. While Dale and Matthew stood with Robert and Lorraine, the searching went on throughout the house, both inside and out. Lorraine stormed over to Matthew Wood, who was standing near her X-Rays in the dining room. She demanded to know what was going on.

"It's just part of an enquiry and your husband is a suspect for the Sheree Beasley abduction and we want to know what he was doing on that day," Matthew told her. "We're trying to eliminate him from the inquiry."

"Oh, you picked a fine day for this". She picked up the X-Rays and then flung them down again. "I've got to go to the hospital."

Matthew was apologetic. "Well, we didn't know that."

As Lorraine looked at him her attitude changed instantly from anger to fear, or curiosity - or maybe it was a sense of loss. It was just the way Matthew looked at her. When he said quietly, "I think we better have a little talk," she stopped dead in her tracks. She linked what Matthew had said with Robert's strange apologies. In that split-second, Lorraine knew her marriage was over. The police had brought with them Robert's criminal past, a slow-working quicksand which would eventually drag his family down. But it was to be a long, slow torturous process.

As Dale and Geoff McLean led Robert to the front door, Lorraine handed the police a letter from Ross Brightwell which confirmed Robert had been at a church meeting on the morning of June 29. Lorraine had organised that letter. She wanted to know if Robert had gone to the prayer meeting after the police had first visited her home.

The police escorted Lowe from the front door of his home into the secluded courtyard next to the carport/garage. Dale told him his car would be taken to the Forensic Science Laboratories for examination.

"Oh, my tools of trade, my suitcases that I use for work. Can I take them out of the car so that when you take the car, those suitcases won't be gone?" Lowe asked politely. "They're my employer's samples."

Dale let him remove them. He knew they'd be searched by other police anyway. Lowe took the four suitcases out and put them in the carport before the trio headed off to Melbourne. Dale thought Lowe looked very sheepish. There was scarcely any conversation in the car between Glen Waverley and the Homicide Squad office.

The policemen sat opposite Lowe in the interview room. Dale had his prepared notes in his police folder and was ready to begin. Lowe sat down, looking bored. The raid on his home had temporarily thrown him. He had never had the police raid his home like that before. But in an interview room, he was in familiar territory.

Dale kept to his plan. When, after a series of questions, Lowe denied owning any properties in Rosebud, Dale accepted it and moved on, sticking to his prepared questions. Then came the time to ask the hard questions.

Dale wanted to know why Lowe had lied to Andrew Gustke on the telephone. While Dale asked his questions, Lowe sat with his head resting on his hand, looking almost disinterested across the pale green laminex table.

"You were very hesitant to make available to the police the information that you had premises down there in Rosebud," Johnson said.

"Yeah."

"Why was that?"

Lowe looked Dale in the eye and spoke with total conviction.

"I think my wife and I spoke about it. Two reasons. My wife and I spoke about it very briefly. I think you had been in touch with, well the people from Rosebud had contacted her on the phone and she said at the time - I don't know if she was asked the question - but she said at the time 'I didn't tell them about the property at Rosebud'."

"She said what?"

"I think she said she didn't tell whoever asked her on the phone, I believe, that she didn't tell them that we had a property at Rosebud."

"All right."

"Now I don't know if she was asked, probably she wasn't even asked the question but she said she wasn't - she didn't tell them that we had a property at Rosebud. Now we haven't discussed it much but I was sort of under the impression I said, 'Oh, well, there's probably no need to,' you know..." Lowe leant forward as he spoke, to make his point.

"Well, what about today when I asked you whether you had any other properties and you gave me a negative answer?" Dale said.

"Well, properties...That one is one that has been sort of handed over to us. I also did say about Rosebud. I think there was a question 'Have I got properties?'. Now I've forgotten exactly what I answered there but..."

Johnson could see Lowe's mind ticking over. He could see him thinking, *Oh, so they know about the flat.*

"- Well before you said -"

"-I said I didn't want to reveal the name of it or something did I?"

"No, no, earlier on in the interview I was asking questions about your home address."

"Yeah."

"At Glen Waverley."

"Yeah."

"When we were doing that particular line of questioning I asked at the end of that whether you had any properties."

"Yeah, well I know, yeah, I recognise that and I thought there was, you know, in relation to what my wife had sort of said, I sort of thought 'Well, look there's probably no need to'."

Dale's dislike for Lowe was beginning to show. "Well don't you think it's pertinent? We're investigating the disappearance of a -"

"- Yeah, I know, I know." Lowe's tone was that of a schoolboy who was sick of being told off by his mum one time too many.

"- of a girl from Rosebud."

"Yeah."

"Don't you think that would be a pertinent thing to let us know?"

"Yeah, I guess so, yeah."

"Was there any motive behind not disclosing that?"

"No, only that, and the fact that the people that look after the unit. He's very, very sick with cancer and he's you know I just didn't really want to, they would..."

"We're talking about the disappearance of a 6-year-old girl." Dale felt Lowe needed reminding. "I want to ask you some questions in relation to your prior history."

"Hmm, all right, hmm."

"Have you ever been treated or analysed for any sexual problems or fetishes?"

"Yes I have."

"What was the problem?"

"The problem was sometimes passing the odd comment to a girl or way back, this is going 10, 12 years or something back - but there was a problem for obscene exposure, or classified as that, that was 12 years ago I think that particular one. That was in Melbourne, but I was told at that particular time to plead guilty and I'd get a bond - I don't know whether this is relevant - and my name would be scrubbed off the records and things like that but it actually wasn't scrubbed off the record."

"Is that the only time that problems arose, is it?

"As far as obscene exposure I've probably had some problems. I've had problems relating to that but not obscene exposure but things that are classified as maybe offensive behaviour, put it like that."

"Have you ever been spoken to by police or anything like that in relation to approaching children?" Dale asked.

"Well, what age do you call children?"

Dale started moving a little in his chair. "Children! I'd say 14 and under."

"Well, around say, around the 14 age group, but not 6 or 10 or anything like that," Lowe countered.

Dale wondered why Lowe differentiated between 6-year-olds and 14-year-olds. They were all kids anyway.

"Have you ever been spoken to by police in relation to 6-year-olds?"

"No."

"At all?"

"No."

"Period? Full stop?"

"As far as 6-year-olds are concerned, no, no, I haven't, no, no." Lowe looked a little shocked, as if he was surprised anybody would make such an accusation.

"What about schools, primary schools. Have you been known to frequent primary schools?"

"No."

"Swimming pools?"

"No."

"All right."

"Not for a mighty long, long time."

Well, that's a contradiction, Dale thought.

"How long?"

"Fifteen years."

"Fifteen years you've never been contacted by the police?"

"As far as...In fact, that wasn't anything to do with a 6-year-old girl."

"I'm talking about primary school age children. Do you frequent primary schools?" Dale knew he did. He had read the dogs running sheets from the day before.

"No, no."
"Not at all?"
"No."
"Swimming pools?"
"No."
"Have you ever been to Springvale Court?"
"Yes."
"How long ago was that?"
"Ten years."
"How about December 1984?"
"Well, that's what I'm talking about. Ten years."
"Well, it's not quite 10 years yet is it?"
"Well, I don't know how long ago it was but..." Lowe started to shift a little in his chair.

"Did you appear there for wilful and obscene exposure?"

"Yep." He sat up straight, then moved back, leaning away from Dale. Suddenly the refined, intimate mood Lowe had tried to cultivate was gone.

"Offensive behaviour?"

"Yeah."

"Yeah, that's where there were two doctors reports tendered to the court."

"I don't know, if you say it affects... if you say so, probably was."

"Yeah, there's a couple of reports here that I've taken from the court records in relation to the evidence given on your behalf in the courts at the time. One was from a Gwen Astin. Does that ring a bell? Were you being treated by Astin?"

"Yes".

(Lowe had stopped going to see Astin shortly after.)

"Did you go with the doctor's blessing or not?"

"Yeah."

"'Cos you moved on. Would it interest you that the doctor's been contacted and the information that I have is that you left of your own accord and against her recommendations?"

"Well, I did leave of my own accord yes."

"Stated: 'He didn't want to help himself.'"

"No it wasn't. I went to another, I was going to another person and that other person did not like me going to two psychiatrists or doctors."

This bloke's unbelievable, Dale thought. *He looks you in the eye, lies, and then lies again when you pick him up on the first one.*

"Would it be true to say, or from what I'm reading here, that you were treated for a compulsive behavioural order termed 'exhibitionism'?"

"Yep, yeah."

"Does it still exist today?"

"I think so. Honestly, yeah."

"You think you still suffer from it?"

"Yeah."

"Have you still been getting the urge to expose yourself?"

"Well, I don't expose myself because I know it's against the law and you can't, you know, do that."

After further questioning, Dale turned the conversation to Sheree.

"All right. I have here a photograph of a 6-year-old child. That child is Sheree Beasley."

"Mmm." Robert didn't want to look at his interrogator. He was looking a little flustered.

"Would you have a look at that? There's a blow up of her. A small one. Have you ever seen that girl before?"

Robert looked at the photo. "No, I, I don't know. I've never seen her."

"She look familiar at all?"

"Any 6-year-old." He shrugged his shoulders and looked at Dale, then Geoff and back to Dale as if to say, 'See it wasn't me'. Then he said, "I've never seen her. It's just like any, probably 6-year-old, who's..."

"Have you ever seen the clothing before?"

"No. No, it's quite adequately striking I suppose, isn't it? Or the pants are, you know."

"Made out of a type of parachute type material?"

"Yeah."

"Have you ever seen that child?"

"I've never seen her or the clothing, no."

Questioned, Lowe went on to say his exhibitionism was under control.

Dale then detailed the Croydon pool incident and Lowe's arrest in Yarraville for offensive behaviour.

"See the fact is, Mr Lowe, I think you have got a problem and I don't think you have it under control and I think that you're continuing to commit these types of offences. What do you say to that?"

"Well, I made a comment before and I've forgotten what it is but you've got it recorded and I just, you know, accept what was said. What can I say?"

"You accept what you said, or what I said?"

"What I say." Lowe was getting angry but it was controlled anger. He didn't like being confronted with the bad side of his personality. He only wanted to talk about, or have people see, what he regarded as his good side.

"Well, in Preston in January 1985 you were interviewed for an indecent assault on a 6-year-old girl on the 6.11.85 (sic). Was that you Mr Lowe that was interviewed?"

"No, no."

"Present address then was (deleted) Mannering Drive, Glen Waverley. The vehicle used was a Honda 75, blue, IDL 658, registered to Lorraine Lowe, (deleted) Mannering Drive, Glen Waverley. Were you in fact interviewed over that Mr Lowe?"

"I don't remember. I can't remember that."

"Were you also charged at Mt Waverley on the 5th of the 11th, 85 with wilful and obscene exposure at Bateswood Reserve Ashwood. Do you recall that incident?"

"I recall something like that."

"You can. What are all these?" Dale pointed at the list of prior convictions he had in his hand. "All these police ringing you up and interviewing you out of the blue just, or do you think there's a reason for it?"

"Oh, it's not for me to comment."

Well who should comment on your sick behaviour? Dale thought.

"All right. In actual fact you've got a prior history that goes back beyond Australia haven't you? You've got a prior history that goes into New Zealand. Is that correct?"

"No."

"You've never been convicted of anything in New Zealand?"

"No."

"'Cos my information Mr Lowe is that you've actually done terms of imprisonment in New Zealand. Is that correct?"

Mr Lowe did not answer. He looked away with a look of defiant disgust. He did not want to talk anymore. He didn't like being caught out.

"Well, would you like to comment on that Mr Lowe or not?"

"No."

"You don't?" Dale was clearly now enjoying himself. He could see Lowe squirming. "Can you remember whether you did imprisonment in..."

"I don't want to comment."

"You just don't want to comment." Dale was sitting erect and almost had a grin on his face. "Bear with me for a minute. I might be able to enlighten you. No, I don't seem to have the particular paper here." He shuffled some papers on the desk. "No, I've found it. Could you state your full name?"

"I've given my full name."

"Yeah, and how many christian names have you got?"

"Robert Arthur Lowe."

"Do you also have the name of Selby?"

"Not now, no."

"Did you?"

Lowe did not reply.

"Mr Lowe, did you ever have the name of Selby in your name?"

"No comment."

"All right, well, the information I have is that you have the following criminal history.

1959, in Wellington, indecent assault on a male. Fined 100 pounds.

10.3.61, in Auckland, obscene exposure, imprisonment for six months, rogue and vagabond, imprisonment for six months, obscene exposure, imprisonment for three months;

65 in, in Wellington, theft." Dale looked up for a moment and stared at the suspect.

"Is that you Mr Lowe?"

The Murder of Sheree

Lowe looked away. His eyes were dreamily half closed with an affectation of boredom but he was clearly peeved.

"No comment," he said, again feigning disinterest.

Dale looked at him and felt his stomach turn.

"What about in Victoria? You've been to court a number of times. The same sort of offences. Is that correct?"

"No comment."

"Richmond in 69, wilful and obscene exposure, you were interviewed, put before the court, it was dismissed;

Moonee Ponds 1970, loiter for homosexual purposes, put before the court, it was dismissed; Richmond 1974, wilful and obscene exposure, put before the court, again dismissed;

Prahran, 1984, theft from a shop, $200 as Robert Arthur Lowe;

Springvale, 12.12.84, offensive behaviour, wilful and obscene exposure, $500 good behaviour bond, undergo treatment from Dr Hobbs as Robert Arthur Lowe, that's the report we referred to earlier.

Oakleigh 7.3.86, wilful and obscene exposure, offensive behaviour, put before the court, both charges dismissed;

Broadmeadows 22.7.86, offensive behaviour fined $1000;

Prahran theft from a shop, fined $500 as Robert Arthur Lowe;

Melbourne, 9.9.90, offensive behaviour, insulting words, fined $750.

Would this be a true summary of your prior court appearances, Mr Lowe?"

"I have no comment," Robert said grandly. It sounded like a regal command.

"No comment?" Dale said incredulously. "There are a lot of things I think that haven't been to court as well. 1984, a female was approached down the beach, a young female, three months pregnant. You approached her and had a conversation with her and asked her to get into the car. The car was a metallic blue Mitsubishi Sigma sedan registered number BMI 548. It was a Chrysler station wagon to Invicta group of industries of 38 South Road, Braybrook. Did you ever work for Invicta Mr Lowe?"

"I make no comment."

The interview had reached a stalemate. Dale could see he was not getting anywhere with Lowe. As the interview ended, Dale asked if he

The Murder of Sheree

could take Lowe's fingerprints. Lowe refused. When Dale asked for a blood sample, Lowe vacillated for several minutes. Then he spoke to a solicitor before he finally said no. That threw Dale. A guilty man probably wouldn't behave like that. But an innocent man might. Dale couldn't work out where Lowe was coming from. As he walked out of the interview room, he had no idea if Lowe was Sheree's abductor. Sure, he had lied his head off but that didn't mean he was the abductor. And curiously, Lowe had been cocky when the interview started. He was quite happy to be interviewed, just like an innocent man would. Lowe wasn't fussed. It was almost as if he was saying, "I'm here and I'm playing the game".

Dale had been able to strictly control the questioning, as he had planned, but he was acutely aware all the way through that Lowe was trying to manipulate him. He was surprised Lowe had stuck to his tale that Selby - his mother's maiden name - wasn't in his name. Yet Dale knew for a fact that it was. He wondered what that was all about. Many times Dale thought he was about to pin Lowe down with some smart questioning. But Lowe simply told barefaced lies and then bent the facts around to try to fit the lies. Dale could see he was an amazing liar who thought quickly on his feet. He just kept twisting things around.

While Dale pondered what had just happened, it occurred to him that, at least as far as he was concerned, Lowe was unique. Dale had interviewed many armed robbers, arsonists and druggies but Lowe was the first paedophile he'd ever had to question. An armed robber might say nothing when he was interrogated. If the police got all the evidence he would be arrested and locked up. Most of the robbers Dale had arrested accepted that as the way things were. An occupational hazard. But Lowe was different. He seemed to treat the interview process as a game. To Dale it seemed as though Lowe wanted to tell as many lies as he could. Usually after 10 or 15 minutes Dale could get a handle on what his suspect was like and what was the best way to talk to him. With Lowe, he couldn't understand him at all. Lowe was articulate but he seemed to not have a personality. That was weird. And he rubbed Dale the wrong way. He was infuriating with his lies and half truths - and after all this work, he was still a suspect. Dale couldn't remember feeling so frustrated before.

WHILE LOWE was being interviewed, searchers found a *Herald Sun* newspaper article hidden in his work car. It was a front page story on missing schoolgirl Karmein Chan. The words "Solved by going elsewhere", "Has to be resolved", "Unresolved" and "Murder" were scribbled in biro across the top of the article. They also found fibres and hairs in Lowe's car and vacuum cleaner. More police were searching the Rosebud unit. There they seized several fibres and hairs found in different parts of the home.

Fingerprint expert Sergeant Wayne Salt found a small partial palmprint and fingerprint on the inside of the back bedroom door in the unit, 80cm from the ground. Sheree was 110cm tall.

AT GLEN WAVERLEY police station, Lorraine's situation went from bad to worse. She sat in an interview room with Matthew Wood. He was thumbing through a large file on the desk in front of him. Matthew turned the file so that Lorraine could read it. As she bent slowly forward to look at the documents, Matthew said, "You say he's done nothing wrong...read that - and that and that." Lorraine read the long list of Robert's previous convictions. Lorraine felt the colour drain out of her face.

"That's why he's a suspect," Matthew said.

Lorraine read on. Her head was spinning.

Wilful and obscene exposure?! And Robert had been in jail! For homosexual offences!? How could this be the same man she was married to?

Matthew then asked what Robert had been doing on June 29.

Shaking, and in shock, Lorraine made a statement that she was at home with Robert that day. But her recollection was hazy. Her main concern wasn't June 29. She was trying to work out how her world had caved in since she got out of the shower. Dazed, she sat in the back seat of the police car while they drove her home.

DALE AND GEOFF drove Lowe home. It was a sunny mid-afternoon but Dale was far from feeling bright and happy. The officers couldn't keep Lowe quiet. He was talkative and sickeningly cheery. They dropped him at his home and drove off. Lorraine noticed the change in Robert, too. He was very pleased with himself. But now that she knew about his past, she was steaming. Looking him straight in the eye, she asked: "Is there anything that I didn't know about that you have done that had brought this all on?"

He looked her right back in the eye and said: "Absolutely nothing. The police are just trying to stir up trouble." He was smiling. On top of the world.

Lorraine asked why he hadn't told her about his previous convictions. Robert was furious.

"If you're stupid enough to listen to the police, I'll have nothing to say to you."

He stormed out of the kitchen, grabbed Lorraine's car keys and walked into the carport. The surveillance police watched as Robert opened up one of his workcases and removed several pornographic magazines, some speedo bathers, shorts and some cloths before hiding them in his wife's car. They followed him to the local shopping centre where they saw him drop the items in a dumpmaster. And when he drove off, the dogs retrieved them and took them back to Dale Johnson, who was waiting at the Police Academy. Dale was angry the searchers had missed them when the house was raided but now his mood had picked up. He dubbed the items Lowe's Wanker Kit. The speedos, shorts and cloths were sent off for analysis.

That night, Lorraine sent the boys off to bed early. She badly wanted to quiz her husband about what was going on. By 10.30pm they were in bed. But Robert simply turned away from his wife and went straight to sleep. Lorraine looked at him agog, then thumped him furiously across the back. He jumped and rolled over.

"What?" he said annoyed.

"What's going on Robert?"

"I've got an early start tomorrow and I need my sleep," he said. He rolled over and went back to sleep. Lorraine thought about waking him up again. But she knew that Robert had deemed this episode over. And once it was over, she knew she could never talk about it with him again.

The task force detectives sat around the Rosebud office watching the video recording of the interview between Dale Johnson and Robert Arthur Selby Lowe. After all these weeks, it was a buzz to have something tangible.

But was this the offender? The officers ran the tape forward, freeze-framed, checked for body language. They watched for hours for some chink. They could see Lowe was lying but that didn't prove anything. It chilled Geoff Alway to watch Lowe's performance. Some offenders might joke during an interview like that but not this bloke. He wasn't uncooperative with the police. He just lied his head off. He seemed to be a compulsive liar who got his thrills running rings around the police. Geoff knew they had a hard job ahead of them. But they had to find the body. Everybody had given up a long time ago of ever finding Sheree alive.

Laurie Ratz felt flat. He had been reasonably optimistic before the interview but when it was over he knew they had not progressed at all. Lowe had been pretty calm for the most part and very, very cool. In fact, what surprised Laurie was that Lowe was very cold. He was a very difficult person to interview because he didn't leave many chinks in his armour for the police to tackle. When police interview a person like that they've got to look at their ego and what their motivation is. Robert Lowe's motivation wasn't staying out of jail. A lot of crooks in a similar situation might want to strike up a deal to avoid jail. But nobody could work out what Lowe's motivation was. It was easy to see he was a liar. He was lying all over the place. But just because he was a liar didn't mean he was a murderer. Laurie sensed what Dale Johnson had sensed in the interview room. Lowe had thrown out the challenge. He was almost saying, 'Catch me if you can'. Now Laurie was very concerned that his men had given it their best shot, without result. He knew that the next time they interviewed Lowe - if they ever got to have another crack at him - would probably be their last chance.

MEANWHILE THE dogs continued tailing the prime suspect. As his work car was still being examined by the police, Lowe was now driving a rental car at work, a 1982 green Commodore sedan. Just before 1pm the next day the dogs watched him park and walk into Flaircrafts in Glenhuntly Road, Elsternwick, where he stayed for just two minutes. Ten minutes later he parked his car in Shelley Street, Elsternwick, near Goldsmith Street. Then he walked very slowly along a laneway off Shelley Street towards Elwood High School. He prowled the lane several times and then got back into his car 20 minutes later. After a three minute drive he parked in Dalgety Street, St Kilda, and spoke to a prostitute who had approached his car. She got in the car for a few minutes before getting out again and walking away. Lowe continued gutter crawling but did not see any other women. Then he parked his car in a nearby side street and sat with the seat fully reclined. Half an hour later he drove off. No matter what his employer Maria George was paying him, she wasn't getting her money's worth.

Dale Johnson was later handed the surveillance crews' running sheets. He was amazed. The day after he had been interviewed over the abduction of a 6-year-old girl, he goes out and offends almost non-stop! Any normal thinking man would have to think, "the coppers are around".

On Monday August 19, 1991 - now seven weeks since Sheree disappeared - the dogs followed Lowe to Camberwell. Just before 1.30pm he was sitting in the McDonalds store in Burke Road at a table, next to six or seven teenage girls in school uniform who were chatting and laughing. Lowe opened his newspaper on the table and started eating a hamburger while he gradually leant towards the girl closest to him, straining to hear their conversation. When he finished eating, he continued reading his newspaper while he eavesdropped. When the girls left, Lowe walked towards the rear of the store. One of the dogs, Detective Senior Constable Duncan Merrillees, followed at a distance but lost him. As Duncan walked back to the front of the store, he saw Lowe stroll out of the men's toilets. His face and forehead were dripping with water. Then Lowe went to his car, pulled a briefcase from the boot and walked to another business premises to sell some wares.

Twenty minutes later he was back in McDonalds where he returned to the toilets. Another dog, Detective Senior Constable Shane Hillas, walked in to see Lowe sitting in a cubicle, with the door wide open. Lowe's pants and underwear were bunched around his ankles. He was masturbating wildly with a glazed look on his face, totally oblivious of his surroundings. Shane left the room and a few minutes later Lowe fled the restaurant, jumped into his car and drove off. An hour later he was in High Street, Ashwood. Slowly he drove past Ashwood Primary School as he leant forward and ogled several young school girls who were standing outside the school. He patrolled the street several times at a very slow pace. But he was out of luck. The girls went back inside the school. Lowe drove off.

LORRAINE KEPT trying to talk to Robert but he just kept railing against the police, saying they were trying to stir up trouble. And he wouldn't discuss his past at all. Whenever Lorraine brought it up he would say, "Oh well, what's past is past". There was nothing to worry about, he said.

But, of course, there was. Lorraine and the boys didn't know how to feel. They were devastated their husband and father was a suspect in the Sheree Beasley investigation. Lorraine was shattered by the revelations about Robert's past. And Robert was persisting in ignoring the whole issue. He simply kept saying he was at home that day. Occasionally he detailed some things he had done around the house - fixed Benjamin's aviary, fixed the fence, pruned some trees. Otherwise he refused to talk about it.

One night he sat in the family room with his sons watching a TV sitcom while Lorraine looked on, unseen, from the kitchen. Her husband was trying to act like a child and lighten the atmosphere but the mood was heavy. Robert was trying to be funny while his sons were obviously worried and irritated. The show was mildly amusing at best but Robert was roaring with laughter. He slapped his knee and carried on like an adolescent. He was over-acting and to Lorraine, it showed. Both boys quietly got up and walked to their rooms. Lorraine waited a little while before she checked on them. She found them both sobbing on their beds. In the background she heard the false laughter from the other room. Her husband's strange behaviour, coupled with the new knowledge of his prior convictions, forced her to think of June 29, and Sheree.

A FEW DAYS later, in the late afternoon, Geoff Alway and Matthew Wood called into Mannering Drive. They dropped in to hand over a copy of Robert's video taped interview with Dale Johnson. By law, a suspect in Victoria must receive a copy of his or her videoed interview with police. Lorraine answered the door and Geoff told her why he was there.

"But I also came here to tell you that I want you to have a look at it somehow before Robert gives it to his lawyer," he said. "Let me know what you think about it."

He was still holding the video in his hand when Robert walked in. He had just finished work. A look of anger crossed his face when he saw Geoff. When Geoff explained why he was there, Lowe snatched the video tape from the policeman. Lorraine saw Robert was rattled and preoccupied with Geoff. She gently prised the video from Robert's grasp.

"I'll put it somewhere safe," she said.

Normally Robert would never let Lorraine see something like that but he was concentrating on the police. Lorraine winked at Geoff over her husband's shoulder and hid the video in the bedroom.

The green LED numbers showed 2.57am. Silently Lorraine peeled back the bedclothes and slid from her husband's side. Tiptoeing, she picked up the video from the bottom of the wardrobe and crept along the hall, past the kitchen and into the family room. She plugged an earplug into the TV, pushed the video into the VCR and sat in the dark, watching. There he was, her husband, sitting across the table from Dale Johnson. It looked strange. She could never have pictured him in such an environment. While she watched Lorraine was acutely aware Robert could walk in behind her at any moment. But when she heard the dialogue, she was more worried about what was on the television. She was numb with shock at Robert's obvious lies. He even seemed to lie about unnecessary things, like his name! She was horrified. What surprised her more than anything was the ease with which he lied. She had always thought it was fairly obvious when a person lied. They either seemed nervous or blushed or didn't look someone in the eye. But to look a policeman in the eye and lie was something she had not seen before.

A long-forgotten incident flashed into her mind. Suddenly she was 29 again, sitting in her father's kitchen, late at night. Her dad was smiling. She was knitting a special shirt for Robert's birthday. It was funny how she remembered it so clearly. His birthday was on October 26. With a start she realised Robert's birthday was really on January 29. Why did he lie about that? The video finished and Lorraine switched off the set. She sat, alone, in the dark. She could not bring herself to get back into bed again.

The next morning Robert took the video to his solicitors. Robert's lawyer Peter Ward rang Lorraine and told her not to speak to anyone about the investigation, especially the police. Lorraine agreed. She finally got to meet the specialist whose appointment she missed the day the police came to the house. The specialist removed the lump and told her the tumour was benign. What a relief! But that blasted video tape was preying on her mind. For days Lorraine agonised over what to do. Should she ring Geoff Alway or should she just let it be? For help and guidance she turned to Pastor Ross Brightwell. He told her she should never be afraid of the truth.

"If you know there are lies on the tape you should let the police know, otherwise it is just as bad as lying," he counselled her.

Still, Lorraine struggled with herself for several more days. She knew Robert had lied about some things on the video. Her pastor had told her she should tell the police. Yet she was terrified. She had started a new life at 29 - she didn't want to have to start again. She knew if she called the police and told them of Robert's lies, it would impact on her life so badly that things could change forever. It would probably mean stepping into the unknown again, possibly even living alone. Just one phone call might destroy the one thing she had always wanted. Her thoughts were swirling. The Robert she knew - the dad who encouraged his kids in sport, the man who loved her and cared for her, the caring church elder. The Robert Lowe she didn't know at all but whom the police knew so well - wilful and obscene exposure!, psychotherapists, medication, and the lies, lies, lies.

She thought of her sons and how depressed and upset they had been recently, yet Robert just didn't seem to care. He wouldn't even talk to her about what was going on. Then, in her mind's eye, she could see Robert smiling. Funny how she hadn't realised how often she had seen that smile before. It wasn't the smile of a man having a good time. It was more the look of a man remembering something. But while it was obviously an enjoyable memory, it was something that didn't bear speaking about. That much Lorraine knew. She closed her eyes tightly, said a quick prayer, and then picked up the telephone. She told Geoff Alway that Robert had said some things which "weren't accurate" in his interview with Dale. In what seemed like five minutes, Matthew Wood and Detective Senior Constable Tony Jacobs were at Lorraine's front door with their notebooks and pens. Within minutes they were taking down Lorraine's statement.

THE POLICE SPOKE to Robert's church associates. Although Brian Lee told the detectives about Robert's strange behaviour the day after Sheree's disappearance, most of the church folk felt the police had targetted the wrong man. But secretly the wheels were turning inside the church hierarchy. Pastor Ross Brightwell called a meeting of the senior church people on August 21. There he tearfully told the gathering that Elder Lowe was under investigation for 'crimes against the State of Victoria'. He didn't elaborate but it wasn't long before everybody knew what he was talking about. They took a vote, and Robert was excommunicated.

AS THE DAYS rolled on, the enquiry became incredibly frustrating. The task force couldn't eliminate Lowe but they couldn't firm him up as a suspect either. There was talk from some police outside the task force that the surveillance police should now be allocated to other crime squads who needed their services. Zenith had already had the dogs much longer than usual. Force command was concerned that if the dogs were taken away, Lowe might abduct another child. They decided it would be foolish to leave him alone. The directive came down - firm him up as a suspect or eliminate him. Dale Johnson knew that was easier said than done.

Some of the forensic test results started to come back. There were no unidentified fingerprints in Lowe's car or home. Apart from lying about his Rosebud holiday home and having prior convictions for being a pervert, there was nothing to suggest Robert Lowe was involved in Sheree's disappearance.

THE FOLLOWING week Lowe rang the Zenith task force, looking for Dale Johnson.

"It's Robert Lowe here, can I please speak to Jonno?" he asked.

He had heard other police use Dale's nickname. Lowe wanted to pick his car up. He didn't mention to Johnson he had written to the

The courting couple. Lorraine Sangster and Robert Lowe.

October 10, 1972. Lorraine and Robert marry at Camberwell Baptist Church.

Psychotherapist Margaret Hobbs in her clinic in Victoria Parade, Fitzroy.

Kerri and Steve Ludlow.

Sheree - (clockwise) polishing off an ice-cream, playing with sister Crystal and granddad Neil Greenhill, being cheeky with Aunty Adele, not camera shy.

Detective Inspector Laurie Ratz.

Detective Inspector Dannye Moloney.

Detective Sergeant Geoff Alway.

Detective Senior Sergeant Dale Johnson.

Robert Lowe teaching youngsters the fine art of cricket.

Robert Lowe enjoying Christmas dinner with his family at Glen Waverley.

Our Little Angel - Sheree's family compiled this board after her murder. The photo at top right was taken just two hours before her abduction.

Sergeant Matthew Wood and his wife Donna.

The Murder of Sheree

Ombudsman, complaining about police harassment. Dale told him he would organise something and get back to him.

But Dale had another plan. He decided to make the most of giving Lowe his car back. He rang the Lowe's late in the day and spoke to Lorraine. He told her the forensic tests on Robert's car had been completed and it was now ready to pick up at Rosebud. That night Robert caught trains and buses to get to the Rosebud unit. Bright and early the next morning he strode confidently into the police station. As Dale handed over the car keys and talked briefly with Lowe in the car park, the dogs readied themselves. Dale suspected that Lowe, elated at getting his car back, might check whether Sheree's body had been found - if he was the offender.

Lowe smiled and got into his blue Corolla. He drove into Boneo Road and the dogs, who had been in position for some time, took off after him. But as often happens during surveillance, they lost him. They checked the freeway, the side streets, the Nepean Highway but he'd disappeared in the traffic. Dale cursed and threw his folder on the ground.

But somehow the dogs found Lowe that afternoon. This time he was in the Dandenong area. At 3.20pm he parked the hatchback in Doveton Avenue, Eumemmering. He took off his suit jacket and put on a dark coloured baseball cap before walking to a cluster of shops, continually looking around as he did so. At the end of the shops, he entered a laneway, opened his fly, pulled out his penis and masturbated while he faced the roadway. Then he walked back to his car, took off his hat and drove to the Doveton Technical School. Very slowly he cruised past, peering intently into the schoolgrounds. Then he took off, driving straight to Edward Avenue, Dandenong. He got out of his vehicle, again with his baseball hat on, and walked along Woodlee Street next to Dandenong North Primary School, Dandenong High School and Cleeland Secondary College. He walked through the schoolgrounds before suddenly breaking into a sprint. He dashed from the grounds to his car and sped off. Five minutes later he was seen driving very slowly round and round the block bordered by Mollison Street, Gardiner Street, Koonalda Street and Dunearn Road in Dandenong. Then the dogs lost him again, only to find him 45 minutes later driving slowly round the car park of Waverley

The Murder of Sheree

Gardens shopping centre. A little later he went home for dinner with Lorraine and the boys.

The dogs weren't amazed solely by the amount of Lowe's criminal activity. What really surprised and upset them was he didn't just wait for an opportunity to occur. He surrounded himself with opportunities. If it was school lunchtime, he would be lurking around the gates. If it was a hot day, he would frequent swimming pools. Large takeaway food stores which attracted a lot of schoolkids were favourites with him, too.

He gave a lift to three teenage girls who were hitchhiking in Rosebud. He tried to chat up a woman on the beach one day but she told him to get lost. The police estimated he spent more than half his work time scouring the streets for targets. And he knew greater Melbourne like the back of his hand, especially the parks and areas where kids played. The dogs saw he had an encyclopedic knowledge of schools, toilet blocks and reserves where kids played, from the Dandenong Ranges in the east, to Rosebud in the south, Preston and Northcote in the north and Yarraville, Footscray and Williamstown in the west. Very occasionally he would pop in to the Barrel Cinema, a theatre which shows explicit pornographic movies, in Melbourne.

AT 7AM ON Friday August 23, 1991, Dale Johnson started work at Rosebud. He was poring over more paperwork, searching for a breakthrough.

At 8 o'clock Ross Brightwell rang him.

"I'm ringing because I believe Robert went down to Rosebud on that Saturday," Ross said.

"Why do you believe that?" Dale asked. He sounded calm on the phone but he was gesticulating wildly to the other detectives in the office. Johnson covered the mouthpiece and quietly called to the other detectives in the room.

"Hey, someone here's saying he *did* come down here that weekend!"

Time stood still in the office as the churchman detailed his story. He said in the weeks leading up to that weekend Mrs Lowe had said there were tenants expected in the unit and something had to be fixed. A bath tile or something.

The Murder of Sheree

Robert had told Ross he had to go to Rosebud before his Mildura trip. It was vital he had to fix this tile.

Then Ross's wife Ruby got on the phone and told Dale she remembered it vividly. She even had mention of Robert's trip to Rosebud in her diary.

This was the first time the police had ever heard of a trip to Rosebud on June 29. Dale and his troops were over the moon. Their luck was starting to turn. Three days later Maria George sacked Robert.

THE SPECIALIST removed the lump in Lorraine's breast and told her it was benign. He kept an eye on her thereafter, sometimes aspirating little cysts with a needle. It was a worry and it was troublesome too, but Lorraine was relieved to know that with everything else going on, at least she didn't have cancer.

THE POLICE were very interested in their physical exhibits. Without a body, or even knowing what might have happened to Sheree, they relied heavily on their forensic finds. The hair and fibres were still being tested at the Forensic Science Laboratories in MacLeod but most of the Zenith team wanted to know about that palmprint found in the Rosebud unit. It was a left palmprint and was obviously a child's.

The police found 27 children had stayed in that unit with their families at one time or another. Every child was tracked down and fingerprinted. Even two kids who had shifted to Zambia with their parents had their prints taken for comparison. But none of them matched the print on the back of the bedroom door.

The biggest problem was finding some of Sheree's fingerprints and palmprints for examination. There were none on record, so the police had to try to find some she had left somewhere. The experts examined her home, her classroom, her relatives' homes - anywhere she might have been and touched something. They didn't find one print. Andrew Gustke went to see Kerri's grandmother Joy at home. Kerri told him Sheree had given her gran plenty of presents. Andrew was looking for anything Sheree had drawn or made, or even just touched. He walked into the modest brick home and stood in the small loungeroom. He couldn't help notice the room was set up as a shrine for Sheree. Photos of Joy and Leslie's great-granddaughter were along the wall and all over the mantelpiece.

Joy couldn't stop crying. She no longer bothered to stop talking when she wept, for she cried all the time. Andrew watched her at first but when he thought of his own grandmother, he didn't know where to look. As his eyes moved round, all he could see were pictures of Sheree. Joy left the room and came back with an old Easter card. She held it out to Andrew. He read the words, scrawled in large childish writing: "I love you Granny". Joy sobbed uncontrollably. For the first time in the investigation, the emotion hit Andrew hard. With tears in his eyes he said, "Here, give it all to me and I'll take off." He put the card, and some toys and paintings in a bag and left the house. He sat heavily in his police car and put Sheree's things on the seat next to him before he started to cry.

AGAIN DALE got the police chopper down to the Mornington Peninsula. He flew from Cape Schanck to Red Hill, sweeping backwards and forwards. He felt Sheree had to be on the peninsula. But all he saw were masses of trees, hill after hill, park after park, beaches, gullies, tracks, and homes on huge properties. To search the whole thing properly would take more than a decade, he thought. Dejected, he made his way back to the office and opened his mail. There was a letter from a lawyer who represented Robert Lowe, saying his client would be very happy to be interviewed again. It didn't mention Lowe's complaint of police harassment to the Ombudsman.

The detectives decided they would bring Lowe in and talk to him at length. They hoped to gain his confidence which might lead to a confession. He might lead them to a body. They felt they had no other option, other than to do nothing.

LORRAINE COULDN'T stand it any longer but she didn't know what to do. She and Robert rang Graeme Lowe in New Zealand for some advice - Robert idolised his older brother and would do whatever he suggested. After Lorraine and Robert put their cases, Graeme suggested Robert leave for two weeks so Lorraine could work out her feelings. They both needed breathing space to sort themselves out, Graeme said.

The Murder of Sheree

On September 4 Robert left home and moved into the Rosebud unit. The police installed a hidden listening device in the unit before he moved in.

Benjamin had suspected his home phone was tapped ever since the police raid. Now his dad had gone, Benjamin scrawled a crude sign and stuck it near the phone.

"This phone is a tap," it read. "Don't be a Wally with water." He wasn't trying to foil the investigation. Black humour was his way of trying to deal with an impossible situation. Benjamin loved his father but the more he saw and the more he heard, the more he felt his father might have abducted Sheree. And at a time in a young man's life when he talks to his peers about his father's achievements or position in life, Benjamin was growing more introverted by the day. Already the other kids were talking behind his back about his dad.

Robert was now living right in the middle of the investigation, virtually under the noses of the police. For an exhibitionist, it was a wonderful situation. Almost everywhere he went in and around Rosebud, he saw police trying to get evidence against him. Sometimes he even went over to the cops and spoke to them. He was feeling omnipotent now he had been interviewed and the police couldn't prove a thing. What he didn't realise was all the ropes that anchored him in the real world - father, husband, respectable salesman, elder, lay preacher, church choralist - and provided a mask for his double life, had been cut forever. He was now adrift, out of control, heading inexorably downhill, to depths almost as unimaginable as the crime he was suspected of committing.

POLICEMEN LEARN pretty early in their careers that if they let investigations affect them, they're not much use to anybody. It's important to switch off sometimes and try to think of something else.

Laurie Ratz walked inside and realised that nobody was home. He poured himself a scotch, grabbed the TV remote and sat down. It was time to give the mind a rest. He stared at the screen, and took an occasional sip from the glass. Ten minutes later he sat upright with a start. Lost in thought, he hadn't realised the television was still turned off. He was miles away - in Rosebud, watching a blue car, on a dirt road, near a pink bike.

The Murder of Sheree

ON SEPTEMBER 11 Assistant Commissioner (Operations) Gavin Brown went to Rosebud to commend the task force on their good work. He assured them force command and the people of Victoria had faith in what they were doing and wished them every bit of luck and success. As soon as he left, the detectives went back to work. Now they were checking travel agents and taxation records, in the hope some minuscule clue would lead somewhere. They checked everything they could think of. There were still about 100 blue hatchback cars to be checked.

ON SEPTEMBER 12, Lorraine was visited by Matthew Wood and Tony Jacobs. The men, especially Matthew, dropped in often, speaking to Lorraine about Robert. They were trying to find that extra little bit of information that might help the enquiry. While they were sitting at the dining room table chatting, Lorraine asked them who this fellow Ratz was.

"Why do you want to know?" Matthew asked.

Lorraine told him she had found one article about Sheree's abduction that mentioned the inspector's name in a pile of old newspapers in the garage. It was now in a pile that was soon to be picked up. Tony went outside and rummaged around until he found the article. Tony noticed that the word 'Ratz' had been underlined. The men seized the paper as an exhibit and left. Lorraine sat down and tried to recall what had really happened on June 29. The next day she made another statement. This time she said she could not recall seeing Robert at home during that day.

ELEVEN WEEKS after Sheree's abduction, Lorraine phoned Robert's brother Rick in New Zealand, telling him of the shocking turn of events. Rick flew to Melbourne and was met at Tullamarine airport by Lorraine - and several detectives. They were driven to the St Kilda Road Police Complex where they spoke to Dannye Moloney in his office on the 11th floor, which commands sweeping views of the city skyline and surrounds. Dannye told Lorraine and Rick that Robert Lowe was not the only suspect but he was a strong suspect. He roughly outlined the case against Robert, without going into detail, and then asked Lorraine to leave the room.

The two men spoke alone for some time. Later, Rick went to Rosebud and stayed at the unit with Robert. Lorraine was driven home by the police. Half way home she burst into tears. The gravity of the situation was starting to really hit home.

Rick spent the night with his brother. Rick wanted to know what was going on, while Robert denied any involvement in Sheree's disappearance. But his answers were annoying. He was being evasive, pedantic, obstructive, vague. Rick's temper finally flared and he belted his brother in the head. Robert still maintained his innocence.

AT 12.20PM the following day - September 21, 1991 - the police raided the Rosebud unit and took Robert in for questioning. Lorraine and Ross Brightwell were taken to the Rosebud Police Complex, too, where they waited in the mess room. Dannye Moloney assured them that by the end of the day, the police would know whether or not Robert was involved. In one of the rooms sat Rick Lowe, who had gone to the police station earlier that day at Moloney's request to watch the video of Robert's interview with Dale Johnson.

Geoff Alway was with Lowe for hours just to get his confidence in the hope he would talk - and then crack. Dannye tried too and then Rick went in.

Andrew Gustke was watching from a monitor in one of the task force offices. He couldn't believe how strong-willed Lowe was. He was undoubtedly the strongest suspect he had ever seen in an interview room. He went for hour after hour after hour - answering questions, chatting, smiling. He was obviously tired but he just kept going. Andrew couldn't believe it. He wondered where Lowe got the strength to carry on. And it was obvious he was enjoying himself! Most suspects might go for three or four or five hours and by then they have had a gutful. That was what really annoyed all the police that night. An innocent man might say, "Look I've had enough, I'm going."

Not Robert Lowe. He was with the police all the way. He was tiring out investigators. Andrew was tired. He wanted to have a nap on one of the bunks in the spare room. Tongue-in-cheek he asked Dale Johnson to wake him when Lowe was about to confess.

Lorraine and Ross sat in the police mess room. Rick was in there from time to time too, pacing up an down. Ross joined him occasionally.

The Murder of Sheree

Lorraine hardly moved from her seat. Rick disappeared from time to time with the detectives, usually coming back in and talking in an agitated fashion. The police took it in turns to inform them that nothing had happened. Dannye Moloney came in and sat beside Lorraine.

"What's happening?" she asked.

"Don't worry," he said. "It's going well."

For who?, she wondered.

About 6 pm the police brought in some Chinese takeaway food and set it out on the long table. Lorraine could only stomach a bowl of soup but an hour later she brought it up. At one stage Ross burst into tears. He made a joke about Paul and Silas in prison singing hymns, and suggested they should try singing but they quickly abandoned that idea. Lorraine winced each time she heard a banging of metal gates, thinking her husband had been locked up, but Ross thought it was probably the local drunks being looked after for the night. They cried together and they laughed but mostly they stared into space. They drowned in cups of coffee. Ross rang his wife a few times and occasionally he talked to the cops who came in for a coffee. Every time they came in though, Lorraine jumped. She expected one of them to tell her that Robert had confessed.

After dinner Lorraine and Ross washed the plates and cleaned up. It was a welcome relief to be busy. After wandering aimlessly round the mess room table, Lorraine went outside for some fresh air. It was a balmy night and as Lorraine walked round the outskirts of the station, the pungent scent of lavender overwhelmed her. For a moment or two she drank in the wonderful smell. Lavender was her favourite flower. She enjoyed simple things like the smell of flowers, the smell of roast chicken coming out of the oven, surrounded by baked potatoes and pumpkin, the smell of clean washing straight off the line. She turned and looked at the police station, the lights inside shining brightly. She wondered how on earth she had arrived where she was standing now. She had buried her past when she left the Exclusive Brethren. She wondered now if she was staring at her future. Reluctantly, she plodded wearily back to the messroom. Matthew Wood brought out a bible and asked Ross where he should start. Ross suggested he start at the Gospel of Mark. He thought that would appeal to Matthew.

The Murder of Sheree

Matthew offered to take Lorraine for a walk along the beach, or to show her Parkmore Road but Lorraine didn't feel like going in case something happened. Matthew walked out and Rick came in. Lorraine and he talked again about the events of June 29. As they spoke, Ross informed Rick that Robert had told some church people he intended going down to Rosebud that day.

"*Now* you're telling me!" Rick said, and left the room.

Geoff Alway had finished talking to Robert. Rick was allowed in to sit with his brother for a while. The interview had been going for more than 11 hours. Rick was tired, Robert was flushed. The police had thrown everything at him and he was still going strong. Then Rick told Robert the police knew he had been to Rosebud on June 29. The church people had told them. The colour drained from Robert's face.

Thirteen hours into the interrogation, Andrew roused. He could hear Dale's excited voice.

"He's gonna roll, he's gonna roll, he's gonna roll!"

The pair ran into the monitor room, and stared at the television, sitting next to the whiteboard. Dannye Moloney was inching through a scenario of what might have happened with Sheree in the car. On the monitor, the officers could see Robert was mentally vacillating.

Then he said: "Oh, yes, I was. I forgot. I *was* in Rosebud." Andrew and Dale looked at each other briefly, then back at the screen. Lowe was physically shaken. This would be a moment they would never forget. Then Lowe, who had slumped a fraction in his chair, stopped, shook himself a little and sat up in his chair, erect and strong. The policemen knew then that if he had thought about confessing, even for just a moment or two, that thought was now gone.

Dannye came out feeling drained. Geoff McLean spoke to Lowe too. But it was to no avail. Geoff Alway interviewed Lowe for five or six hours. It was one of the hardest interviews he had ever done. Lowe was cocky and arrogant yet he was pretending he was trying to help. Geoff saw he was dealing with a bloke who was always trying to out-think him. A couple of times Geoff thought he nearly had Lowe confessing. But then Lowe would draw on some inner strength and continue playing his game. Whenever any of the investigators talked of Sheree, Lowe would let them talk, then he would get very angry and become aggressive. All the detectives noted Lowe had a short fuse. Several times he snapped in the interview, leaning across the table at his interrogators, snarling back at them. While he was talking to Lowe in that tiny room, Geoff realised Zenith had made a mistake. They assumed Lowe had a conscience. It was clear he had none whatsoever.

Building rapport with an offender might work in some circumstances but not with Robert Lowe, Dale thought. When it was his turn, he wanted to play like a West Indian fast bowler. Blow this rapport stuff. The bloke killed a little girl.

With Rick in the room, Dale spoke to Lowe of all the things Robert would not want to hear. Exhibitionism, sex offences, pornographic magazines, masturbation. The interview deteriorated into a screaming match.

"No, no you're destroying all the rapport that's been developed," Rick said loudly.

But Dale continued. He talked about the boys at the Croydon swimming pool, of Lowe's prior convictions. Now Lowe didn't want to talk. Dale thought he was hiding behind his brother. As things warmed up in the interview room, Dannye intervened to quieten things down. Dale would continue to ask confronting questions, he told Lowe. The effervescent, smiling, obliging Lowe had vanished. Deadpan, and in monotone, he answered every question with "No comment". Dale realised the night was over. He wanted to put Lowe through the wall.

It was a little after 3am when Dannye Moloney called Lorraine and Ross into an office downstairs. Dannye was sitting behind a big desk and he asked them to sit opposite him. Lorraine thought he looked crestfallen. Dannye told them they had reached the worst possible outcome. The police had achieved very little and it would now be a 'long haul', he said. Lorraine was devastated. Dannye asked her if she had any questions but she was too tired to take in fully what he was saying. Then without knowing why, Lorraine asked to see Robert. She was still in love with him yet she felt she did not know him anymore. She just had to take another look at him. Matthew escorted her to the interview room but before he opened the door, he told her that all she had to do was glance at the policeman and he would take her straight out again. She was afraid to meet her husband.

Matthew opened the interview room door, and in the spartan room, empty but for two chairs, a table and a tape deck, she saw Robert. He was sitting at the table, a little flushed, looking excited. Lorraine felt and looked haggard. She and Matthew were exhausted but Robert wasn't at all tired. He looked a little smug; rather pleased with himself and all the attention. He stood and welcomed them into the room. It occurred to Lorraine he was acting like a bank manager welcoming a couple desperate for a loan. She realised he was actually very happy, as happy as the day he had come home from the first interview with Dale Johnson. She had never seen him higher than that day and this.

"Lorri, you look awful!" Robert said, and then smiled.

Lorraine frowned. She asked Robert if he had been telling the truth; he vowed he had. Lorraine was loath to believe him, even though she wanted to. He asked how she was, she told him. Then she got up to leave. As she and Matthew walked to the door, Robert leant in front of her and asked coyly: "Don't I get a kiss?"

She gave him a peck on the cheek. Matthew looked like he was about to be sick. Then they left the room, and shut the door.

The night was over. Robert was free to go back to his flat. Lorraine could return to her misery.

Geoff Alway drove Lowe and his brother back to the Rosebud unit. Robert was effusive and jolly. He made a joke to Rick and then started laughing. Rick seemed to be convinced that Robert was innocent. Geoff Alway was steaming. He stopped the unmarked car and turned around, with his left arm cocked on the back of the passenger seat.

"Look, Robert," he said. "It's not over. Don't think for a minute that the pressure's off."

Indignant, Lowe snarled back.

"What do you mean by that?"

"I'm convinced that you killed Sheree Beasley," Alway said. "I know you did it and I'll prove it."

Lowe's face dropped as Geoff finished with: "This is only the beginning."

Lowe just looked at the detective. The three men then got out of the car and stood on the naturestrip beneath the stars. There was a bite to the early morning air and the smell of ozone rolling in from the beach across the road. The street was deathly quiet except for the hum of the power lines overhead.

Rick stepped forward and shook hands with Geoff. Robert went to emulate his brother but Geoff ignored the hand.

"You'll see me again, Mr Lowe," Geoff said. It was the first time he could remember Lowe being lost for words. Geoff got back into his car and as he drove off, he saw the two men walk down the driveway towards the unit. Geoff knew they had the right man. Lowe was in Rosebud that day and he had told a web of lies to cover himself. It had to be him. The blue car, the lies, the propensity for Lowe to offend, the prior convictions. *People don't lie to you for no reason*, Geoff thought. *It doesn't mean they're the offender, but there's always a reason for it.* He yawned and started the long drive home. He had to be back at work in the morning.

Tony Jacobs drove Ross and Lorraine home. For most of the trip, Lorraine and Ross sat in a daze. Lorraine arrived home just before 5am and flopped into bed, where she lay, staring at the ceiling.

The police were as disappointed as they were exhausted. While they couldn't confirm or eliminate Robert, he had at least admitted he was in Rosebud on June 29. The question for Laurie, Dale, Geoff and Co. was - Where to from here?

CHAPTER EIGHT

◆

KERRI was an automaton. She couldn't concentrate on what people were saying to her. The doctor had prescribed some relaxants and anti-depressants but she didn't notice any difference. She wept often and hardly slept. When she did, it was curled up on the couch or the loungeroom floor with Steve. For some reason she couldn't fathom, she could not bring herself to sleep in her bed. Maybe subconsciously she thought it would be better to sleep in the lounge and wait for the phone to ring with some news.

Occasionally she made her way to the local shopping centre. Everywhere she went, people stared at her. She had been on the television news, her face had been in the papers. People stopped her on the footpath, in the mall, in shops; they wished her the best, and gave her kisses and hugs. Everybody hoped she would get her little girl back; they all hoped the police would catch the mongrel. They asked her how the case was going. They were trying to be kind but she relived the horror every time she talked about it. She was very grateful for everyone's concern but she wished everyone would just leave her alone. All she wanted was her daughter back.

WHILE MATTHEW Wood, like all the Zenith detectives, was working a minimum 14 hours a day, six days a week, his wife Donna was caring for their new baby. Everywhere Donna went in Rosebud, people were talking about Sheree's abduction. Nobody could believe such a crime could happen in their sleepy holiday town, in the middle of winter, when usually nothing happens. A small minority believed there was something fishy about the abduction. Spotfires of gossip and rumours sprang up.

"It had to be the mother. You could tell just by looking at her on the

TV and in the papers."

"She looks rough. Yes. Probably a pro. Yes, those sorts of people just bring trouble on themselves. We don't need those sorts of people coming down here from Melbourne, do we?"

Just bring trouble with them."

"I'll bet it was the father."

"A friend of mine has a friend whose brother is a copper. They reckon it was somebody in the family. You're not going to have a little girl taken by a stranger in the middle of the day, now are you?" It was all unfounded and untrue.

DONNA HEARD them all. As a former detective and now the wife of a Zenith investigator, she became something of a celebrity on the playgroup/health centre circuit. All the young mums wanted to know how the investigation was going. Some were concerned the abductor might be a local man. But although Donna had a good idea of what was happening at Zenith, she couldn't talk about it. She knew if she said anything at all it could compromise the investigation, especially as Lowe was living so close by. And while Donna had seen her fair share of rapists and other sex offenders as a policewoman, Lowe scared her. Her local playgroup was in a secluded street two streets away from his unit. Donna went to playgroup every Wednesday with a mobile phone at the ready and her senses on full alert. Even if Robert Lowe hadn't abducted Sheree Beasley, she already knew enough about him to worry about what he might do.

KERRI WAS always crying, always upset, always had a faraway look about her. She was constantly on sedatives. Steve was always angry. Just sitting and waiting was destroying them.

In desperation they went to a clairvoyant who said Sheree was playing in a house. The psychic saw Kerri's 6-year-old sitting in a bedroom, drawing pictures, in a house surrounded by a white picket fence. Sheree had been abducted by a couple who couldn't conceive a child. That gave Kerri some hope.

Independently Neil Greenhill rang a clairvoyant in Coburg eight days after Sheree disappeared. She told him on the phone she could "see" a small blue Toyota sedan. Neil didn't tell her about Sheree on the phone. The woman asked him to bring some photos of the loved one he was concerned about when he visited later that day. He grabbed the first photo of Sheree he could find. When he handed it to the clairvoyant, he saw it was partially blurred.

The psychic said she knew by the tone of his voice he was going through something. Neil told her he was Sheree's granddad. The woman had seen the news, she knew what he was talking about. She told him she got "bad vibes" because of the ghosting on the photograph. That's all she could say. She said she had been thinking about Sheree and all she could see was a blue car. She brought out her writing pad and showed Neil she had written "small blue Toyota" on it before he came. It might have been interesting but it didn't tell Neil where Sheree was.

He went to another fortune-teller who told him Sheree was in or near a national park. Kangaroos "meant something", she said. Neil drove and walked around the Mornington Peninsula's national parks. At 11 o'clock one night, Neil thought of the Melbourne suburb of Kangaroo Ground, about 30km north-east of Melbourne. He spent hours there, searching blindly in the dark.

Throughout his searching, Neil's eyes were open but all he could see was an unending fog. Nothing was clear. His head felt like it was in a vice. He didn't know what to do next, where to go, what to say to his wife or teenage daughters. He had closed himself off from Denise when he needed her most. He was barely sleeping. He tried to switch off by throwing himself into his work but his heart wasn't in it. His workload fell away. He tried hard to concentrate but found he couldn't. Then as he drove home, at night, he would hit the wall again - the all-consuming fear for Sheree and what might have happened to her.

One of Neil's neighbours said she had a friend who occasionally had visions. Neil went to see the young woman, who worked in a day care centre. She said Sheree had been taken by a man, a man who had come into Australia via New Zealand, although she did not know which country he originated from. The man had wavy hair; he might have a beard. As she continued, Neil noticed the woman became worried, then frightened.

THE MURDER OF SHEREE

The name St Clair came to her mind. She didn't know what that meant. Then she saw a house, with Sheree in the back room sitting on a kind of mattress. It was afternoon and the sun was shining through the window. Sheree was playing with some toys. And there was a woman there....

Neil spent days looking at maps. He found St Clair in the NSW Hunter Valley near Singleton. Denise didn't want him to go alone but the following weekend Neil did just that. He said he was going with an open mind but Denise could see he had pinned his hopes on the trip. He found the town and drove around it all night, and all the next day, checking anything that might match a vague description of the house Sheree could be in. Nothing matched. Shattered, he cried all the way back to Melbourne. He hadn't slept for more than 50 hours. That was the only weekend Neil didn't spend searching the Mornington Peninsula.

NEIL RETURNED home from another frantic, blind search of the peninsula. He walked into the bedroom and slowly undressed, then got into his pyjamas and slipped into bed. At first, the pain was like a little stab in the chest, then it spread out, partly paralysing him. Quietly he said to Denise, "Look, I've got to get up, there's something going on here. I'm having a heart attack."

Denise helped him up and raced him to the local doctor. The good news was it wasn't a cardiac arrest. It was an intense muscle spasm brought on by stress. The bad news was the stress wasn't about to go away.

LAURIE RATZ was getting used to the letters and phone calls from psychics and clairvoyants. The higher the public profile of a police investigation, particularly where a child is involved, the more often the police are inundated with information from soothsayers wanting to help. One woman captured his interest more than any other. Not because what she said was so accurate, rather it was so oblique. Laurie was never into cryptic crosswords, which was a pity, because he spent hours trying to work out what Madame Starfish was on about.

He read the first question: "Would the Yogi sue me?" but he just couldn't figure that one out. In another letter, Madame Starfish posed the question: "If the PM eats brussel sprouts, what does he think of

Melbourne's spring beans?" Laurie felt like a bit of a dill but he knew he had to cover every aspect of the investigation. Maybe she was related to the offender, maybe she knew who he was. She could have been the offender herself. So were they cryptic clues? Laurie read all the scribblings in great detail and other detectives spent hours hypothesising. But it led nowhere.

THE DIRTY undercurrent of baseless rumours continued. *It was the father. It was the stepfather. It was Kerri. It was a payback for an unpaid drug debt.* They were all wrong and Kerri had heard them all. She wasn't keen on going out but she wasn't going to sit inside forever. Kerri felt she had to get out of the house. She decided to take her grandmother Joy out for dinner at a club on the peninsula.

Given their circumstances - Joy and Kerri were aware that wherever they went, people would point and start whispering - they had a reasonable night out. Naturally when people saw Kerri the discussion in various parts of the club turned to Sheree's disappearance. When Joy was on her own for a few moments, a woman she didn't know sidled up to her, and in a knowing tone, said she had heard who took Sheree.

"It was the grandparents," the stranger confided.

CHAPTER NINE

◆

THE MORNINGTON Peninsula boasts some of Victoria's finest and most diverse scenery with green rolling hills, seaside aspects, bushy retreats and panoramic views of Port Phillip Bay from Arthur's Seat. Cattle graze in lush paddocks just a few kilometres from the bay, while kangaroos gather and bound across golf courses and in national parks. Holiday properties range from ramshackle shanties to million dollar mansions. Visitors can relax in a country Devonshire tea house while admiring the views, or perhaps idly watch young ladies riding their horses along the well-worn bush tracks. Three young horse-riders, Joanne Tyrell, Angela Chambers and Kellie Reardon, were riding along the eastern side of Mornington-Flinders Road, Red Hill, at 10am on September 24, 1991. The surrounding properties were blanketed in a thick green carpet after the heavy winter rain. As the trio rode on, along the property line of Winthunga, they inhaled the rich scent of damp, fertile soil and the distinctive smell of pinetrees. Then they smelt something rotten. They looked around and spied the remains of what they believed was a dead kangaroo. It was lying on a thick bed of grass near a circular drain that ran underneath the driveway leading into the property. The girls rode on, talking about the "animal" carcase.

DALE JOHNSON had just got home when the phone rang. A body had been found at Sorrento back beach. Some kids, playing in the sand, had uncovered what looked like forearms stripped of flesh. That would be unusual if the body was only three months old but the sea lice could have done that. All the crime scene services were called. State Coroner Hal Hallenstein turned up, so did the media. TV network helicopters were buzzing everywhere. Working under special lighting, the experts toiled away. At 11pm they finally told Dale: "Nothing human here." They were dog's bones. They dug the hole up and found somebody had buried a pet. But in the meantime, the newsflashes went out. Some bones had been found and Zenith was investigating.

Kerri heard the news and thought it was the end of all hope. She sat by the phone and waited for the call but it didn't come. As one day ended and another began, Kerri heard the radio news that the police had not found anything at all that related to Sheree's disappearance. First thing next morning she rang Dale Johnson.

"What's going on?" she demanded. "Why didn't you ring me?"

Johnson apologised and explained what had happened.

"I didn't call because I didn't want to upset you," he said.

I made a bad blue there, he thought. *I won't make the same mistake again.*

The next day, Kellie Reardon's sister Dorothy rode to Winthunga. It was 7.30pm, just on dusk. Dorothy rode close to the dead kangaroo and became certain it was not a kangaroo at all. To her it looked like a badly decomposed, small, human body. Within the hour there were police everywhere. Detective Senior Sergeant Paul Hollowood and his team from Homicide were called in. The area was cordoned off and closed to all traffic for one kilometre each side of the site while forensic experts pored over the crime scene and the body.

Eucalyptus trees spread above the drain like protective umbrellas. Pine needles lay scattered amongst the thick layers of the long, green grass. A jonquil or two blossomed near a drain. Matthew Wood was focused on the job at hand but he thought of his own daughter too. He found it very hard to look at the "body", exposed on the thick, soft grass mat. The toes had been eaten from the feet, the rib cage lay exposed, the back of one knee was eaten away. The skull was still jammed up a 30inch diameter drain pipe, about six metres away.

Matthew took notes, marking down the position of the body, the injuries, and anything else of note.

DALE JOHNSON was called out too. It was the second time in three nights. He arrived at the Red Hill scene at 10.05pm and shone his torch on the legs and lower torso, laying on its bed of grass. Twenty minutes later he and Chief Inspector Ken Blay were at Kerri's home. She wasn't going to suffer unnecessarily again.

Kerri knew by the knock and the time of night who it would be - and what news they would bring. The policemen walked in slowly, carrying their clipboards. Dale thought of his own daughters and wondered just exactly what he would say. Kerri motioned to the policemen to sit down opposite her at the kitchen table. She steeled herself as they took their seats and stared them in the eyes. One of the cops had a tear rolling down his face. Steve stood away from the table, behind Kerri. She looked up from her battered tissue and cocked her head a little. Her eyes met theirs defiantly.

Flatly, she said: "She's dead, isn't she?'"

Dale paused for a minute and took a deep breath. "We think so," he said. "We're not sure, but there's definitely what appears to be a child's body."

Kerri hugged herself and rocked backwards and forwards on the chair, crying. She felt she was being pulled apart.

"Why don't you know?" she demanded angrily. "Why not a yes or a no?"

"We're not sure, but there's definitely what appears to be a child's body located. The body's badly decomposed," Dale said. He had given plenty of death messages before but this was the worst. He thought of his own kids again.

Kerri wondered what she had done wrong. Broken relationships, drug overdoses, cot death, child abduction, media attention, no clues, then the scare earlier about the dog's bones. When would this all end? She wanted to believe the police had made a mistake.

"I thought the body was the other night," she said sarcastically. She hoped they would say they might be wrong. But they didn't. Then she broke down completely. Steve started crying too. The officers stayed for a while but there was nothing they could do and nothing they could say. Kerri wanted to see the remains. She wanted to see how anybody could kill her daughter and dump her on the dirty ground but the officers wouldn't let her go. Then they left, promising to come back later with an update.

Dale busied himself at the scene and surrounds, helping the Homicide team while they co-ordinated the crime scene search. Then he drove back to Kerri's place with Geoff Alway just before 1am. As they walked slowly up the driveway, figures approached him out of the night.

"What is it?" a silhouette asked. It was a man's voice. "Is it true? Is it her?"

"We still can't be sure," Dale answered to the darkness. Then he heard the collective wail of disappointment and devastation. "Ooohhhhhhh."

Dale hadn't realised there were so many people outside. The voices invited the detectives into the house but as soon as he went inside, Dale regretted the move. He felt like an intruder - he wasn't prepared for so many people. The small house was full. The detectives had never seen such misery and anguish before. Kerri was howling; some of the relatives, stunned, just stood still, staring. Others walked around sobbing. Some hugged. Red, puffy eyes. Somebody, glad to be busy, made coffee for the detectives. Then they all gathered round the detectives and the questions started.

"Tell us. What's happened?" somebody asked.

How do you break this sort of news gently?

"We can't be sure but it is a little girl's body and on the balance of probabilities, and it's a child about the right age, it would have fitted," Johnson said.

The room erupted with crying, sobbing, moaning.

"How long do you think she's been there?" Neil asked.

"She's been there for quite a while."

Neil had always clung to the hope Sheree was alive. Now he walked around dazed, repeating to himself: "All those clairvoyants, all those people..." He had prayed Sheree would not be left out in the elements during one of the wettest winters in years. Now these policemen were telling him she was not only dead, but she had been rotting in the wind and rain for months. At first, nobody knew what to say. Then everybody was talking at once. People stood staring, others paced. God Almighty. How can this be?

By 2am, Kerri was so distraught she hyperventilated and collapsed. A doctor was called but he refused to come. He said it was too late. Neil

The Murder of Sheree

told him she was Sheree's mum and it was believed her body had just been found. The doctor was unmoved. They called a second doctor who, just before he went back to bed, told them to give Kerri a paper bag to breathe into. A third doctor agreed to come and he gave Kerri an injection. She felt no improvement at all.

While the doctor was attending to Kerri, Lorraine Lowe lay awake in her bed. That wasn't unusual - she hadn't slept more than three hours a night since Robert's interview at Homicide. But now she was shaking with fright. Through her bedroom window she could see a shadow at the front door. With her eyes fixed on the dark form, she very slowly reached through the darkness, across the bed, to pick up the phone. As her hand went for the handpiece, the phone rang. The noise jolted every fibre in her body. It was Matthew Wood. He was in Glen Waverley, and was ringing to tell her he was on his way over. He was going to explain that Sheree Beasley's body had been found but he didn't get a chance.

"There's somebody at the front door, there's a shadow there," Lorraine whispered. "I don't know what he's doing."

Within minutes Lorraine heard a car roar up the street and stop outside. The officers searched around the house and found nothing, save for the word "pedofile" misspelt on the front door step in black texta. Rugged up in big black overcoats against the cold night, Lorraine thought the men looked like undertakers as they slowly walked into the house. Then Matthew told her what had happened at Rosebud. There was nothing more the police could do for her at the moment. The detectives left.

Lorraine felt a strange feeling of relief flood through her. It was terrible what had happened to Sheree but she knew now that Robert was in the clear. He might, have a problem - a disgusting, incomprehensible problem - but he was not a murderer. At least that was a weight off her mind. She spoke to her sons for a while, then they went back to their rooms and lay in their beds. But nobody slept.

Lorraine had just finished another toss and turn when her metal garden sprinkler crashed through the bedroom window, showering her with glass. She screamed hysterically and dashed barefoot from the room, crunching over the shards of glass and reaching for the light switch. Flick, flick, flick. The power was off. Someone had taken the fuses out of the fusebox

The Murder of Sheree

and thrown them over the front lawn. She panicked. What if somebody was in the house? Terrified, she ran to her boys and then rang the police again. The local uniform guys were there in a few minutes but there were no prowlers anymore. Lorraine sat with her boys, wide-eyed and shaking, until the sun rose.

Down in Rosebud, the police were monitoring the listening device in Robert Lowe's unit as they had done since he moved out of Glen Waverley. On this night there was nothing much to hear. Of all the people involved - Sheree's parents, her family, Lorraine, Benjamin and Jonathan Lowe and the police - on this night, only Robert Lowe had a peaceful, uninterrupted sleep.

AT FIRST light the next day, Zenith and Homicide were still searching. Andrew Gustke was one of the few detectives who didn't go to the crime scene the night before. He arrived at Winthunga just after first light and started doorknocking, taking notes and asking questions. Around lunchtime, he took a quick break and sat in his police car eating a sandwich. As he ate, he saw Paul Hollowood and Paul O'Halloran talking to Detective Senior Constable Mick Flanagan, who through the night had looked at Sheree's remains laid out on a trolley at the coroner's court. Andrew got out of his unmarked car and joined the other men, who were standing at the boot of another police car. As they stood to the side of the road, Mick sketched out what he had seen. Bits and pieces of bones and head. But some parts were missing. Sheree's tracksuit and shoes were missing too. So were her panties. Andrew waited until the discussion ended and then he walked back to his car and got in. Throughout the enquiry, he had kept two photos of a smiling Sheree in his folder. He showed them to everybody he spoke to, using them as memory prompts. Now he opened the folder and stared at her image but the remains on the sterile trolley pushed into his mind. Tears welled in his eyes. He felt sorrow, but also anger, even rage.

How could you shove her in a drain, of all places. What are you?

Bastard, there's got to be something here at this drain that links you, whoever you are if you're not Robert Lowe, to what you did to this child.

The Murder of Sheree

NIGHT FELL quickly on the Friday. A uniformed policeman was placed at the scene to guard it. There would be more searching tomorrow. The young cop had a look around and then he took a quick walk. What he saw next prompted him to make a call on the police radio. Soon Dale Johnson was back in Red Hill. After talking to the uniformed guy, he headed off across the road to the property opposite the drain. He walked under the huge dark trees and in the dirt he found a badly decomposed child's left forearm.

It was a grisly find but Dale was filled with hope. The hand was shaped as if the non-existent fingers were outstretched and the thumb was stretched across to the little finger. For the first time in a long time, Dale was happy. The palmprint in Robert Lowe's Rosebud unit was from a left hand. Carefully, the exhibit was labelled, bagged and later shipped off to the forensic science laboratory in Macleod. But it was too badly damaged. There were no prints left.

The road was blocked off to keep the media and motorists away. About twenty Protective Security Group police, on their hands and knees and armed with sticks to part the grass, leaves and bush, moved through the undergrowth. Horseriders patrolled the nearby bush. Somebody found a long thin razor blade in a blue plastic case lying on some gravel near the side of the road. The blade was a little rusted. It didn't seem to fit the scene at all.

Local contractors flushed the drain. They found some teeth and other particles of human remains. Now the intense initial crime scene searching was over, the investigation was handed back to the Zenith detectives, for the time being.

WHILE THE search for clues continued, Professor Stephen Cordner conducted a postmortem at the Victorian Institute of Forensic Pathology in Kavanagh Street, South Melbourne. Dressed in blue surgical pants and top covered by a white plastic apron, the specialist turned on his tape recorder and began the autopsy of "the skeletal remains of an unknown child". Case number 3189/91. Four homicide detectives watched the autopsy through a long window, sitting in high, blue swivel chairs from an elevated platform in the narrow viewing room. Professor Cordner's assistant, Jodie Leditschke, took X-Rays and samples from the body. Steve Cordner had four things in mind as he performed the autopsy - identification, cause of death, how long the victim had been dead and any clues that might help reconstruct the circumstances of death. The first two hours were spent observing the remains before disturbing them. Then he methodically dissected the body, looking for the relevant abnormalities and looking for signs, and disease and injuries that would help the questions asked, such as why and in what circumstances the child died. The post mortem took about eight hours spread over three days as the evidence was compiled and analysed.

Professor Cordner concluded the skeleton of the child's body was complete, except for the right 12th rib, the right forearm and hand, left hand, toes, some teeth, the hyoid bone (at the base of the tongue) and part of the thyroid cartilage or Adam's apple. The pelvic bones and length of the hair on the scalp indicated it was a girl who was probably about 110cm tall.

He did notice one peculiar injury. The top vertebrae in the neck was fractured. The professor knew that was an extremely unusual site for an isolated fracture. It was possible the fracture had been sustained after death, although it showed no animal teeth marks.

And there was something else. The Adam's apple, which had been found next to the skull in the drain, had a curved edge to it. Steve Cordner thought it looked like it had been sliced by a knife. If DNA testing could prove the cartilage was human, it would probably indicate the victim had been severely injured by a knife, or a pair of scissors. But due to the advanced state of decomposition, the experts were unable to conclude whether the cartilage was human or animal. But there were other clues that this child, suspected but not yet proved to be Sheree Joy Beasley, had been strangled to death. A portion of the thyroid cartilage and the hyoid bone were not found with the body. These were often injured in cases of strangulation. But despite the conjecture, due to the poor condition of the body, and the absence of many of the major organs, the cause of death was unascertainable. That upset the professor, there was nothing more he could do.

Steve deals with facts and issues when he examines corpses. It's afterwards that the emotions swell up within. He had followed the Sheree Beasley case closely in the media and he had a daughter the same age as Sheree. He knew, as he drove home, that of the 6000 post mortems he had performed, this was one of the most difficult. He would never forget it.

THE DOORKNOCKING went on. Andrew was impressed with some of the houses he got to see inside in Red Hill. Many of them were holiday homes for wealthy professionals from Melbourne. Homes with breathtaking views, some with pools that overlooked the Bay. What failed to impress Andrew was the attitude of some of the residents. Some were very unhelpful. Some were quite insulting. Some just wanted to ignore the investigation but that was the last thing Andrew and the others were going to do. Andrew was tired after three long months and was still plugging away for a breakthrough. He walked into one home where the husband and wife were both professionals.

"Look, I can't see how this can happen here," the husband said of Sheree's body being found. "Would you like a glass of wine?"

"No thank you," Andrew said. "Can you tell me who lives here and if you have any boarders or friends that might stop over?"

"I really don't see that it's any of your business, but…"

"But we have found Sheree Beasley's body and we're just trying to establish who might have been in the area."

"Oh, no, no, no. Nothing like that would have happened here," the husband said. Then he motioned to a chair by moving his head and said in a soothing, annoying tone, "Sit down and have a glass of wine."

"No thanks," said Andrew. "We're looking at all the properties in the area and checking to see if someone may have stayed here that weekend."

"You're a detective are you?" The man smiled at his wife, then turned to Andrew. "You're the shortest detective I've ever seen."

Andrew saw red. *These people can't even take the murder of a little girl seriously*, he thought. "Yeah, well, it's the old saying," he said. "It's not how much dog is in the fight, it's how much fight is in the dog."

The rest of the questioning went quickly, without any formalities. Nobody smiled either.

The Murder of Sheree

Melbourne and most of Victoria stood still on Saturday, September 28, 1991. It was the Australian Football League's Grand Final Day. If people couldn't get tickets and be part of the huge crowd at the Melbourne Cricket Ground, then they were usually glued to the television screens watching the direct telecast. This year the game was played at AFL Park, the AFL's second largest stadium, in Mulgrave, due to ground works at the MCG. Dale Johnson was an avid football follower and normally he wouldn't miss watching the Grand Final, but he was back at Red Hill, co-ordinating a line search near the drain area.

Matthew Wood had the day off for a change. Matthew is never very emotional, which is why Donna took particular notice when she walked past the loungeroom. She saw him clutching his daughter, just a few months old, to his chest. He looked like he would never let her go. Donna heard her husband speaking quietly into his daughter's ear.

"No-one will ever touch you," he kept saying, over and over.

The Hollowood family was spending the weekend on the peninsula, just a couple of kilometres from Rosebud. Paul spent the weekend reading all the information reports and witnesses statements. Now that the body had turned up, he knew it was just a matter of time before it became a homicide squad investigation. By lunchtime on Monday it was, although there was a little grumbling from his crew. They had previously been handed a number of difficult investigations to clean up. They were getting a bit of a reputation for being handed the hard jobs. Hollowood pointed out to his men that was because they were thought of as being very competent.

Kerri held a brief press conference at the police station on September 30. Sitting perfectly still and looking completely broken, she spoke in flat, unemotional monotones.

"I hope he suffers; I hope he rots in hell," she said. There was a plea for information from the public, and it kept coming in. The State Government posted a $100,000 reward to try to prompt the vital breakthrough.

The Murder of Sheree

ON TUESDAY, October 1, with the crime scene searching over, Chief Inspector Peter Halloran went to Rosebud with Paul Hollowood's crew. The homicide squad chief spoke to the Zenith team. This was now a Homicide Squad investigation, he told them, and Paul Hollowood was in charge. Some of the Zenith troops would stay on. Dale Johnson wanted to stay but his boss wanted him back at Frankston. There was nothing Dale could say or do. He had worked his guts out for three months, and he reckoned he had the right man in the gun. But now, even if Lowe was the offender, somebody else would be locking him up. It was a dreadful wrench.

Paul Hollowood spent the day reading all the reports concerning the crime and the investigation. The next day he addressed the assembled task force in the Rosebud Police Complex. He walked to a whiteboard which was filled with a list of things that pointed to Robert Lowe. But Hollowood wanted hard evidence, not innuendo. He ruffled a few feathers when he rubbed out almost everything on the board. All we have, he told the assembly, are four hard pieces of evidence. All that was left was Blue Car, Abduction, Rosebud, Body. That was it. Not a lot to go on. Paul didn't win over a lot of hearts and minds when he said: "There is a tonne of suspicion and very little evidence. Just because we have one good suspect doesn't mean we stop working on every other suspect."

Many others agreed with that sentiment but manpower shortages had prevented other leads being followed up. It was clear from this meeting that despite a lack of resources, the workload was about to increase.

Later that day Detective Senior Constable Tony Jacobs took Benjamin and Lorraine Lowe for a drive around the Mornington Peninsula. The police were aware Robert had hidden much of his personal and criminal life from Lorraine and the boys. And not only did Robert lie about his past crimes, he was always very vague about any aspect of his life. The police were trying to find out if Lorraine knew of certain areas on the peninsula that Robert frequented that could somehow link him to the murder. She directed Tony along the family's usual route to Rosebud from Glen Waverley. Down the freeway, past the Frankston Hospital, up Olivers Hill, then along the Nepean Highway to Rosebud. She showed them various back roads they had "explored" in the past. There was Browns

The Murder of Sheree

Road and Truemans Road in Rosebud. She told Tony they went to Sorrento backbeach fairly often too. Then she mentioned Robert and they sometimes drove around pineconing, taking the best ones home as ornaments. Tony wanted to know where. Lorraine remembered one spot particularly because it was the most recent time she had gone looking for pinecones with her husband. She directed Tony along the back roads around Arthur's Seat, pointing out various spots they had stopped that wet January day. Then she showed him the site where they had stopped and had raced to see who could collect the most. Tony pulled to a stop but the car was still running. He turned to Lorraine.

"Are you sure this is the spot?" he asked her.

"Yes, I am," she replied. They were sitting outside Winthunga, on the road just above Sheree's makeshift grave. What Tony told her next took her breath away.

AT 1.25PM on Wednesday, October 2, 1991, Matthew Wood returned a suitcase to Robert Lowe at the Rosebud unit. Lowe invited Matthew in for a cup of coffee and a chat, despite his lawyer telling him not to talk to the police. Lowe brought up the topic of Sheree. Matthew told him the current situation was devastating for Lorraine and the boys. As they spoke, Matthew saw that Lowe was enjoying himself. He was very affable and smiling - he was quite confident he was playing the police on a break. Matthew thought he would play the game Lowe's way. Maybe if he was friendly to him it might make it easier for Lowe to come in and confess - if the thought ever crossed his mind.

After Lowe told Matthew he couldn't confess to Sheree's murder because he hadn't committed the crime, Matthew told him Lorraine was shattered. While Lowe continued talking about his alibi, Matthew talked about Lorraine's smashed window and how she was showered with glass.

"Those are the sorts of things she's going through, you know? She had glass in her hand," Matthew said.

"I don't suppose you know who did it?" Robert showed concern.

"No. They live in torment, mental torment, and you are the one that's putting them through it." He hoped he could make Robert feel guilty.

"What can I do?"

"Tell the truth. That's what I say, you know. Tell the truth to me and I'll tell her and she can come down and talk to you."

"Well, I can't tell her the truth while I'm..." Lowe's voice trailed off. "Can I?" Then he wanted to know where he stood in the investigation. "And I - as far as I know - am probably the number one suspect. Would that be right?"

"Yep," said Matthew. The two sat opposite each other at the kitchen table.

"Yeah, so obviously I would turn to a solicitor because you've got to get some protection, haven't you?"

"If you're saying you've got nothing to hide, why do you need a solicitor?"

"Because you'd be stupid not to," Lowe said. He smiled.

Matthew returned to the guilt tack. He continued talking about Lorraine.

"They've had eggs thrown, they've had, ah, paedophile written on the front steps, on the front steps."

"A step of the house?"

"Yes, they've had 'Rot in Hell' written. They're the ones that are copping the brunt for you. It's not you."

"I know, I know." Robert didn't want to hear that.

"All I'm saying to you is -"

"- How could someone write on the front steps? Was this at night-time?" As the police often found with Robert Lowe, the conversation was now off on a tangent.

"Yeah."

"Is Lorraine still using the front room as far as you know?"

"As far as I know. Trying to sleep. The woman's getting no sleep." Matthew was redirecting the conversation. "All I'm saying to you is, I'm trying to appeal to you for Lorraine's sake, and Benjamin and Jonathan's sake. Tell the truth, I ask no more than that...if you've done this."

"How can I cover it?"

"If you've done this, fine, tell the truth. If you haven't done it, fine, tell the truth."

"I will."

"But tell the truth and I mean the whole truth. There's no justification for lying and no reason for lying. Tell the truth. Do you, do you admit you've lied at all?"

"Mmm, might have." Lowe looked coyly at the table. Matthew thought he was suddenly behaving like a shy young woman trying to attract the attention of a man she fancied.

"You have lied?"

"Mmm." Lowe continued to look down, nodding. A smile hadn't quite formed.

"Have you lied to the police? Do you, do you think you've lied to us in the past?"

"What, since the beginning of the investigation?"

"Yes."

"Ah, yes, there have been lies but put it like this, it was more dodging the openness of the truth, put it like that."

"But sometimes the truth hurts," Matthew counselled.

"I know."

Matthew didn't hold much hope for a confession. But at least he had established some form of rapport with the chief suspect. He continued.

"No-one's going to crucify you, no-one's going to hang you, but the whole thing starts with you."

"But I'll get a fair, fair few number of years in jail, won't I?"

"Well, that's a realistic proposition but I can't, I can't determine that." The conversation floundered a little. Then Matthew went back to the topic of Lorraine, the suffering wife.

"But one thing I want though," Matthew said. "I want you to tell the truth to her. I don't want you to lie to her just to get back to her..."

"I've finished with lying," Robert said flatly. "In fact, when I've lied, I hadn't really considered it lying...I won't lie to her. I will not lie. Now you've got to accept that," he said with finality. To Matthew it sounded like a heap of crap.

THE GRIND went on. To alleviate the frustration and tension, sometimes the task force cops joked that in a decade they would be the subject of a *Sixty Minutes* program, for still working full-time on the Sheree

The Murder of Sheree

Beasley investigation. Occasionally they commented on a movie being made about the investigation and then they dagged each other over which actor would play them. Nobody could see an end in sight.

The results of the forensic tests started coming in. Hairs found in Lowe's car and unit, while similar, could not be positively matched with any of the 117 scalp hairs taken from the body. None of Lowe's tyre marks or shoe prints matched those found at the abduction site. Try as they might, the police could not link Robert Lowe scientifically with Sheree's body, or her abduction.

The electronic surveillance stayed in place, hoping that Lowe might say something to implicate himself. And surveillance teams continued secretly dogging Lowe. Initially the police were disappointed but they were never bored. At 6pm on October 5, they watched Lowe walk along the foreshore in Rosebud West. The beach was bathed in golden sunlight. It is a popular beach with families due to its shallowness, especially when the tide was out, like it was now. Robert took off his glasses and shirt. A number of strollers and joggers passed by. Two or three people sat about on the sand, enjoying the warm evening. Wearing only shorts, Robert did a series of pressups and short sprints along the water's edge, close to two women and a man walking by. Twenty minutes later he was standing at the water's edge with both his hands inside his pants, fondling himself. Then he walked through the shallows for about 200metres to a sandbank. He crouched in the shallows and took off his shorts and bathers underneath. Sitting in the tepid, shallow water he splashed himself before walking onto the sandbar and stretching down on his stomach, where he simulated intercourse with the sand. Then he sat and put a plastic bag in front of his genitals. Once it was in place, he stood up and masturbated while facing the water's edge. He then walked back to his unit.

On his 19th wedding anniversary - October 10, 1991 - Lowe visited Margaret Hobbs at her clinic in Fitzroy. He was the same Robert - reasonably outgoing and chatty, sitting in the leather chair, very much in control of himself. Margaret was sometimes aware that while she was talking Robert wasn't listening. He would respond and answer questions but Margaret had found long ago he would tell a story, but not the truth.

He told her he was a suspect in the Sheree Beasley case. She thought

The Murder of Sheree

Robert was there to seek treatment for his "problem" of exhibitionism but she had other concerns. Ever since she saw Robert driving the blue Toyota, she had a strong suspicion he had something to do with Sheree's disappearance. If she could draw him on the subject, that was what she would do. She saw it as legitimate therapeutic endeavour.

Robert Lowe wasn't interested in stopping his behaviour. If Lorraine would only say he was home that day, he would be okay. But Lorraine wasn't interested in talking.

Lowe needed a good alibi. It was essential he get back with his wife. Maybe while he worked on his alibi and kept visiting Margaret, the therapist could act as a go-between. They spent the session talking about how Robert thought his behaviour had been recently. He didn't think it was too bad at all but he did have a court case coming up at Williamstown after his arrest in Yarraville. As usual, Robert was vague on what had happened, or even what the police alleged he had done.

Five days later, DNA testing positively identified the body from Red Hill - until then known in the forensic laboratories as case 3189/91 - as Sheree Joy Mandile @ Beasley. Crowds flocked to her funeral held at Our Lady of Fatima Church in Rosebud on Friday, October 18. A white draped tiny coffin bearing three long stemmed roses from Sheree's sisters and a coloured photograph of Sheree stood alone at the front of the altar. Father Peter Conroy, who had also conducted the services of Sheree's brother Shane and stepfather Shane, referred to the smile that characterised Sheree. He told the mourners that when Sheree was baptised, she was dressed in white, a sign of her new inner Christian dignity. The white draped coffin symbolised her baptism to God and the innocence so badly abused.

"We feel so much anger, outrage and sadness," he said. "What can be said about the travesty that has brought us round this body today?"

"We see some of Christ's anger that something built for reverence and respect has been taken, abused and distorted. Here are the remains of a life that was young and innocent, to be respected and enjoyed - typified by the smile of her photo - taken, abused and thrown away. God shares our anger and is angry with us that we can take our human freedom and abuse it, take the gifts God has given us and mistreat them; in his Son, he cries with us. We ask why. Courage and faith are asked of us. Sheree is one with Christ, not only in baptism, but in innocence that suffered. God brought life out of the death of his son. Don't cease to cry out for justice, and let the cry be sincere."

The priest said the evil of the abduction was compounded by the evil of unfounded rumour and gossip endured by Kerri and other family members.

"Evil on evil," he called it. "Cry out for justice and protection of the innocent. Pledge support for Kerri and all who feel the pain, and ask for forgiveness for the part of society that violates the innocent," he prayed.

"A life which was beautiful but abused and thrown away. Let there be justice because we have been badly maltreated."

On behalf of his distraught daughter, Neil Greenhill tearfully thanked all who attended and the police force for its help and comfort, "though no amount of words will bring what we really want. Everyone who knew Sheree should think of something funny she did and smile on the inside, while crying on the outside. "

One of Sheree's favourite songs, 'When I See You Smile' was played, and then Kerri spoke briefly. She was barely audible. She thanked the police, and those who attended the funeral. She recalled Sheree's eyes and smile. "You're not dead, just away..." Kerri said to her absent daughter. As incense wafted through the church, the coffin was carried down the aisle to the flower laden hearse to the accompaniment of Phil Collins' *'I Wish It Would Rain Down On Me'*, Steve was one of the bearers. Nearly everyone broke down outside the church.

Rosebud Primary School also held a memorial service which broke Kerri's heart even more than the funeral. She cried to see all those little children so upset. The funeral and the memorial service touched the entire Melbourne community, and far beyond.

Herald Sun columnist Barry Dickins captured the mood in an article printed in the *Herald Sun* on October 22, 1991 entitled: 'A Heart Must Have Gone Out'.

The Murder of Sheree

DNA tests prove Sheree Beasley was the child discovered in a drain at Red Hill: the young corpse was released to her family last week.

She was six years old and full of beans. How could it happen? Children are meant for arms, not drains.

Just a little article in the paper, is that all they are? These kids. Someone's personal angel. Surely there must be a mistake? Science shows us who it was. The positive identification of grief is fool-proof.

Who is the infant-assassin? Who is the murderer of the meek and mild? Who can do these things?

They are abducted like flowers and tossed aside like weeds. They suffocate all of our hopes and stifle all of our wishes. Whose hands did it? Whose heart went out?

The heart must have gone out like a light, to do something like that. Nothing was going on inside the soul of the killer. Except sickness and destruction and madness.

It's very hard not to hate them, these creatures capable of lining our drains with childish ghosts. They fill our hearts with anguish and terror, then depart.

Is it a conspiracy or a curse? Our young people must be wondering whether life has value, the way things are in our society.

Whom can they trust? Whom can they believe in? What do the children feel when they read the little articles in the paper? She was Sheree Beasley. Only six years old. Her poor Mum.

The rain cries in its fashion. And so do drains and gutters. Sometimes sadness is not enough, and you get that way that lamp posts and telephone wires cry more human than you do.

It's like a giant sob, in a way. The whole city quietly sobbing. People sob in their fashion, even if they seem strangely still and unmoved and silent.

The family stare and no one knows where to look. Here is the drain. Here is the body of the little child. Adorning a drain. Is this her proper resting place?

Heaven is; and heaven was the mother's arms.

The police don't know who did it, or how anyone could do it. They curse under their breath and sip cold coffee in the car. They work on the case for weeks. They cry, in their fashion.

In the end it's just a murder. Another one. So many lately. So many children taken from arms and placed in gutters, as if that's their proper home.

From perfectly healthy baby girl to joyous child running in sun and racing through rain. Protected from all elements, except this: white devils just keep on doing it, don't they? Who are they?

The mother cries in the bed until it sinks like a ship. A vessel of tears. Wrath at six o'clock. More crying, madness and cursing.

Every single thing in Melbourne is crying for Sheree Beasley. People and churches. Police stations and brick walls. Prisoners in Pentridge. Birds and telephone wires. The wind and all the little children.

ROBERT WAS enjoying himself. He had not been charged with any crime, yet he realised the police knew he was in Rosebud on the day Sheree was kidnapped. He also knew it would certainly be in his best interests if Lorraine would have him home where he could continue to tell her he was home that day. But she wasn't talking to him, not even on the phone. He started writing to his family to try to get back home. He first wrote to his younger son Jonathan.

It was posted on October 25, 1991 - almost four months since Sheree's disappearance. (All letters are reproduced verbatim.)

Dear Jonnans,

This is your Dad writing. I hope you are doing OK. I haven't written before now because so much has been going on at home there I didn't know if I should or shouldn't. But your Uncle Graeme said, "Yes, write" so here goes.

Congratulations by the way to your Hawks on their brilliant win. I hear you got a seat - well done. I hear your cricket is going alright although I don't hear much. Just remember how Michael Mossey told you how to attack the ball - hard.

Jonnans, I'm very sorry for much of the things I have done wrong. There have not been as many as you may have been lead to believe and certainly they weren't as bad as some people might say. But they have been wrong and I'm sorry for that.

Concerning the case why the house has been turned upside down - namely the death of the young girl I want to assure you I had nothing whatsoever to do with that. I had never seen her or where the body was found. The first I heard about it was on Channel 7s 5.30 news when I was in the kitchen and you and Benji were near the T.V. and I said "Thank goodness I was home when it happened" although with the sound of the TV you may not have heard me say it.

Jonno, I don't know what is going to happen about our family. I may be around, I may not - I'm talking say after Christmas and more when things may settle down. I don't know what Mum's thoughts are at this stage but YOU do have a say. You can tell Mum or me in a letter if you want what you want best for each one of us. Mum will probably have the greatest part of the say, but you must tell her or me or some other adult if you want me home or not for example or if you want to see me or not etc.

I miss the cricket at La(r)Pent with you and I miss a lot of things I've always enjoyed with you. Things like seeing you play footy or taking you to tennis, golf, Gunnamatta, MCG, VFL Park, etc. As a family we've enjoyed some wonderful times together like Fiji, Sydney, Mildura, Apollo Bay, Golf. I've always liked playing basketball in the back garden and in your younger days cricket before the house extension. We've been lucky as a family with an excellent home, school and church, plus health and happiness. For this you have a lot to thank Mum for. It is her birthday on the 26th of next month, November so you and Benji will have to work things out together just what you can get her. Ask her if you like, or just listen for tips from her.

Now I had better finish. I still hope to see something of you because I love you very much and whatever happens in the future I promise you I always will love and continue to pray for you.

All the very best.
Love to Mum and Benjamin too.
Yours
Dad.

PS As you probably know it was your Mum's decision I should leave. She told me it would be for 2 weeks only. Some day later I'd like to be invited home again, but that decision comes from Mum and you two boys. Love D. PTO

PS. Congratulations on your 38 not out last week. I wish I'd seen it. Keep that left foot over to the right when you bowl!

My solicitor told me the law encouraged fathers to see their sons as often as they want while Mum and I are going through our seperation. I am your Dad - the same person you've always known. I'm proud of you and I hope you will not be ashamed of me. I've made mistakes but who hasn't, and mine are all minor according to the law.

You can talk to me or do anything with me, the Law says. I won't force you - that's your decision, but the quick you get used to it the better for you. I will never harm you nor Mum. I have never harmed anybody. Also I am not fighting Mum. I LOVE HER and want to keep her as my wife but that is largely her decision and yours if you still want me as your Dad.

If I come to the cricket again soon or not, I will probably say "Hi" to you. It's stupid not to say

anything. I would not want to embarrass you. Mr
Buzza said for me to come as often as I can, but
I'll see.

Now having just seen you, I'm at Frankston and the
bus is due. So...

Love Dad.

PAUL HOLLOWOOD wanted to talk to Robert Lowe again. Paul knew a fair bit about Lowe's past but he wanted to learn more. Despite interviewing Lowe twice, surprisingly Zenith had never asked for Lowe's full account of what he had been doing on the day of the abduction. The most the police knew was what he had said during his Rosebud interview. He had been to Rosebud but was home by 2pm. Hollowood put out the word that he wanted Lowe brought in for questioning. Finding him was easy, with the surveillance police still watching his every move. He was picked up at 8.25am on October 30, loitering around the Frankston railway station. The police already knew by now that Frankston was a favourite spot for Robert to ogle young girls. And from what they'd seen him do already, there was no doubt he was a danger. The surveillance police were convinced they were on the right man.

Sitting in the Homicide Squad offices, Lowe asked to use the phone to ring a solicitor. When he was brought back to the interview room, he refused to be interviewed. The formalities took nine minutes.

In his years of dealing with the police, Lowe had learnt the ropes. He'd learnt how to exploit the law and run rings around the more inexperienced police. But now he was playing with the heavies.

Like an actor who worked his way up from bit parts to starring roles in B grade movies, Robert Lowe knew the ropes in interview rooms too. But it had only served to teach him the fundamentals. Now he had stepped up a league. He was now the star of the biggest show of his life and he needed some coaching if he was going to pull it off. And now that he was being asked for an alibi, he needed a pretty good script. Later that day he rang Margaret Hobbs. He told her he was being pursued by the police.

"And, ah, I've got a confession to make Marg," he said. "I'm enjoying all this. I like the excitement." Margaret didn't say anything. Then he remarked: "Isn't that sad?"

When he got home to the Rosebud unit, Lowe put pen to paper.

Robert's next letter was to Lorraine on 30 October 1991, posted just after he was interviewed by Paul Hollowood.

> Lorri,
>
> I don't know if you're in Soc Sec or not but when I joined no-one told me the benefits apart from getting a Health Care Card. I hope you have it and use it. That card as I later found out entitles you to concessions - or at the HCC listed on the enclosed sheet. eg Transport I can travel on my train, tram or bus for $3.00 per day from Frankston (Zone 3) or 2.85 from Glen Waverley (Zone 2) - even all day and return. SEC is 15% off and others. So any accounts for this unit you receive please send here and if you're on Soc Sec you are entitled for same in Glen W.
>
> Sorry about my signing as seperated. I hated it too but because I couldn't get to Knox <u>with you</u> for appointment at 10.30 because of Transport from me and because we'd agreed not to communicate after I left. I had to tell them you were living in GW and I was temporarily living in Rosebud and I would therefore deal via Frankston office. Apparently it is not binding but just for their method of payment. The price difference of 12 approx doesn't matter. We could change it if you want I could go out to Knox every 2 weeks. I'd even like to do it if it helps eliminate that "seperation" word. The Chamberlains are "estranged husband and wife" - not seperated.
>
> Margaret has raised these points with me. I comment where I want to reinforce or correct something because I sometimes wonder if she details all the info back to you. She takes virtually no notes for security protection of her clients.
>
> On the question of Red Hill I still cannot remember anything about the town and certainly the road where the drain went underneath.
>
> Before the elders came down I phoned both Ross and Bert and they said the elders want to see me for me

and show then any cause I had for them not to dismiss me. I looked forward to their coming, prepared a nice supper, offered them to stay the night although I told Ross I'd like Bert and Richard to come - not him here and I'd tell him why if he agreed to meet with me in town. He never arranged a meeting but while he continued to stubbornly insist I did do that to the girl "I know you did etc" I couldn't have him holding forth with that comment disrupting the meeting and further persuading the others of this point. However when Bert and Richard came, after I'd prepared a whole list of things to tell them and show them why I should not be dismissed they told me <u>I had already been dismissed and name removed from membership.</u> This I thought was grossly unfair

1) because they had broken the promise of both Ross and Bert and

2) I was pronounced guilty without even being asked and

3) on the grounds of all my former sins (which they didn't know what they were - going back 20 years or more). That sounds like Exclusive Brethrenism to me - judgements made without opportunity being given to speak or defend and promises of theirs broken. They apparently had a quick meeting on Wednesday night and the decision was made then by themselves only - not me and that decision was irrevocable.

After that they really didn't believe anything I said and I thought you'd be told I lied 20-30 times instead of the one only about the court case coming up. I told them there was no court case coming up in November now because it had been adjourned until sometime in the new year and the date had not been fixed yet. And that is fact. They weren't in a listening mood at all but at the end I read out to them a letter I had drafted to you. I enclose that letter for your info. It is only in draft form but I don't know that I'll ever get round to wording it as well as you write letters. However I think Bert was slightly impressed with what I had to say.

I asked Bert why he hadn't visited me as an elder to check up on my spiritual or other life before I was excommunicated. He said, "I didn't have your address."!! When I asked him by phone the night before they came did he have my address he said "I can get it from Ross". So the excommunication act was far more important and worth coming to Rosebud for than nurturing one in need.

Lorri you ask Margaret "why won't he tell the CIB the truth etc." You may have said that to her before but today was the 1st day I'd heard it. I'm glad you're asking. Keep asking Margaret things you don't understand. While we're not in direct contact there's going to be questions and misunderstandings so let me have the chance to clear them all up for you. It might take long lett(er)s such as this but communication and understanding are vitally important.

Now back to the question why don't I tell the CIB etc. Apart from the 1st meeting when we were raided and invaded and I did honestly think I was in Melbourne it was only in the early hours of the Sunday morning at Rosebud - that I have been interviewed again. In that interview the CIB never asked me what I was doing on the Sat the girl went missing. It was all recorded about 14-15 hours of my telling the truth because that's when I first started the truth. But they never asked me the question. I did tell them all they asked and I don't think either the CIB or I realised they had eliminated to ask me that.

Apart from Matthew Woods calling in late one night with a brief message from Ross the CIB have not spoken to me again.

Today however they picked me up in Frankston on my way with seeing (psychiatrist) David Clarke and Margaret Hobbs because the Homicide Squad who have now taken over the case find they have no record of what I was doing that day. Peter Ward's instructions have always been "Don't talk to the Police". As a top Criminal lawyer for 20 years he knows his business. Peter was in court today but I have booked a late meeting with him tomorrow

(Thursday) to tell him "If I've nothing to hide why not tell them". Hiding makes me look more guilty. I want to tell because I have nothing to hide but I must at least listen to his reasons. I want to do the best for you too. It was very important I had that question from you via Margaret "Why won't he tell" because otherwise I would have accepted Peter Wards advise for my own protection without knowing this was really worrying you. So keep asking please .

Sorry about the cricket. I was nervous too. I was told I should go - the law encouraged that. I wasn't going to talk or pinhole J. just let him know I cared - the question you asked me in this unit recently. I thought you'd drop J at 2 and pick him up at 5 and did not expect you to be there. Sorry I so frightened you. I was nervous myself but I'd never hurt you. I'd hoped I might catch a glimpse of you at 2 or 5pm because it's been 4 weeks so I was pleased. But I'm sorry I "got Jonno out" and I will not go again unless you ask me, or I ask you and you say "Yes". I'd love to go just to see J or even you or even Benji somewhere from a distance - but I won't. So that you will feel comfortable.

On rereading the letter I'm enclosing I read to the elders. I am not happy with paragraph 2) I'm not saying it is wrong. I know in many many cases it is right. But it would be unfair to say that about each and everyone. For instance, I don't think that would apply to Matthew. He has been very good to you I know and I appreciate that. What put me off him originally was his request to me to own up and come clean. But he doesn't say that now. I have difficulty trusting the Police because of past experiences and because Peter Ward is so adamant in not telling them - therefore distrusting them. When I asked Matthew today did he think I'd done it he replied "I can't comment" It wasn't a yes or certainly. I thought he was genuine and sensible. I just wish Ross was as genuine and sensible instead of this "I know you did" business. Such an attitude can't help you make up your mind. I should have had Matthew bring you down that day as he offered although Peter Ward would not have allowed it.

Is there anybody you could get to take a photo of you B & J . Most of those we have you took if you could maybe ask anybody or (indecipherable). For quickness that may now partially solve my longing to see you all.

Lorri this letter just covers facts to clarify. I trust there is no emotion in it for you. Now to lighten things off a bit - since my services are not needed at La(r) pent Cricket I had a session with Darren Berry (Vic wicket keeper) and Scoop, you can rightly tell Jonnas, and they were seeking assistance concerning the Vic Sheffield Shield Squad. I spent some time with them today going over the finer points of winning the Shield again. I'm certain they appreciated my input. They recognise good advice when they hear it and they looked towards me for experience and wisdom! Needless to say Darren Berry and "Scoop" were in Myers - but I was there 'keeping. Now must go. L. Rob.

PS "Scoop" is Simon O'Donnell.!

The public outrage continued, with people writing letters to newspapers.

> To whoever caused the fate of Sheree Beasley. You are a human mistake, a young life is silent, there is no escape for you.
>
> Awesome forces that govern our planet and the universe must reject you.
>
> Nature will hunt you down. A furnace awaits you.
>
> - Colin Beaton, Keysborough,
> Letter to the editor, *Herald Sun* November 6, 1991.

LORRAINE'S health was deteriorating rapidly. More lumps in her chest had been found, she was losing weight and was still getting only three hours sleep a night. She tried to busy herself with domestic chores - her own and the ones that had fallen to her now her husband was living in Rosebud. It was dark when she remembered she had to put out the rubbish bin. She walked through the archway in the front garden wall and onto the driveway. Instantly she froze. The black figure of a tall, heavy-set man stood in the shadows about three metres away. She gasped and then flinched as she felt a sharp pain on the side of her forehead. She heard the crash as the bottle broke on the ground next to her. Terrified, she raced inside and called the police before walking to the bathroom and washing off the blood. She was surprised when she saw herself sobbing in the mirror. She thought she had run out of tears long ago.

LOWE TOOK to riding a small red bike Benjamin had when he was five. He cut a ridiculous figure in his shorts and baseball cap, hunched over the tiny machine. Lowe loved wheeling along the Nepean Highway, through the Rosebud shopping centre, occasionally stopping to talk to anybody he cared to. He meandered along the foreshore tracks, stopping to lean against the brick wall of the women's toilets for a while before moving off again. He felt already he was part of the town. He had joined the local church and took bible classes. The congregation loved him. He indignantly told anybody who would listen he was a suspect in the Sheree Beasley case but the police had done their homework all wrong. Word had spread that Robert Lowe was the man - the police were doorknocking in town and asking about him. One morning Lowe was out bike-riding when some locals told him he was being watched by the police. One of them had spotted one of the surveillance police sitting in a car, watching. Lowe tried to catch the police out. Sometimes he would jump off the bike and hide in the bushes for a few minutes before mounting it again and speeding off. He took circuitous routes to get from one point to another. But the shadowers stayed with him all the time.

When he was in his unit, Lowe would often take his pants off and walk around talking to himself while masturbating. Occasionally he would make gestures or speak to himself. He would walk across the room and say, for example: "Oh, they don't know what they're talking about." Often as he was walking across the room, he would stop suddenly and say, "But I loved her, but I loved her." Much of the time he was at home was spent writing. He would sit at the desk in the loungeroom and make notes. The police who were watching on a television monitor in a secret hiding place thought he looked like he was studying for an exam. He was very busy. But what surprised the police most was that, for an unemployed man under investigation for one of the worst murders imaginable, he was very happy. In fact he was ecstatic. He loved it.

MARGARET WAS shaken every time she saw Robert. No matter how each session unfolded, the room seemed to be charged with some sort of energy while he was there. It wasn't so much that he was a suspect for Sheree's murder. It was more the fact that he showed no remorse at all. He talked about Sheree as if she was some inanimate object. The only time he showed any real emotion was when he talked about being the prime suspect. It was then that he disgusted Margaret even more. He enjoyed the attention from her and from the police. If he was innocent, she thought he should be outraged and frightened. If he was the offender, she thought at least he would show some concern, and anxiety. But he was calm, and, it seemed, almost fulfilled. To Margaret, a parent herself, it was impossible to comprehend how a father in his position could be so disinterested in a little girl's death.

Each time he left her clinic, Margaret would clean up, to try to make the place feel clean again.

Margaret came to see the sessions as a battle. She was dealing with a hidden persona that only gave glimpses of itself. It hid behind mood changes which were often so rapid they drained her. One minute he would cry and Margaret would try to soothe him. Suddenly he would be angry. As she tried to calm him down, he would move up a notch to vicious. Then he would be vitriolic. Then he would change topic and talk calmly about something totally unrelated. At times it was surreal.

On November 12, Robert again visited his psychotherapist. Margaret was getting angry.

"Come on Robert, tell the truth, perhaps you did go down to do the tiles but when you left you went cruising around Rosebud looking for a target," Mrs Hobbs said.

"No, not Rosebud, I'm known there," Robert said.

"Sorrento then."

"No, not there."

"Wherever then." She knew he was playing a game with her but she was not in the mood.

"I may have been looking for a target but around Mornington and Frankston. I'll have to think about it."

Margaret told him his "target" age was inappropriate and getting regressive.

"You know why I do that. If I approach an 18-year-old I might fall in love with her and get hurt," he explained.

"I don't approach boys and girls because the boys get jealous."

KERRI AND STEVE went on a heartbreaking trip to the Rosebud Kmart store. Sheree's Christmas presents were still on lay-by and the couple went to settle the account. They had decided they would pay off the presents and take them home, where they would sit under the tree with the other kids presents. Walking down the aisle where children's bicycle stackhats were sold, they spied a grubby looking old man. They had seen him before, walking along the Rosebud streets, loitering round the shops, sitting on bench seats. He always had a superior air. Every time Kerri saw him she thought he looked like a lord surveying his manor.

Lowe had gone to the shop to look at bike helmets after the local police had seen him riding his bike without one. He didn't really intend buying one but it gave him something to do. He fondled the helmets absently. As Kerri got closer, she noticed the vagrant looking at something on the shelves when he turned and bumped into her. Kerri thought he had done it intentionally. The three stopped in their tracks. The vagrant looked down at Sheree's mum. Kerri thought the way he looked at her was peculiar. He looked cocky, with a sort of a wry smile. She thought he looked like he had something over her yet she had never met him. She was frightened of him and recoiled a little. Nobody spoke.

The parties went their separate ways. Steve looked back and muttered. "Fuckin' dickhead." Lowe walked out to his son's red pushbike and pedalled down the street with a smile, and a carefree attitude. Steve and Kerri walked to the lay-by section to pick up the presents Sheree would never receive.

The Murder of Sheree

ON NOVEMBER 16, Robert rang Margaret Hobbs. He wanted to arrange a meeting between his wife, his sons, and himself, with Margaret as mediator. He wanted to discuss the current situation. Margaret asked Lorraine whether she was interested. Lorraine wanted nothing to do with him.

Robert was turning up to therapy with a notepad and pen. He had always done that but now he was asking numerous questions about the murder investigation and jotting down notes. What would the police be looking for? Would they have found any forensic evidence? Did they think the body was put there the day of the murder, or later? Margaret would hypothesise, Robert would listen intently and then take notes.

ROBERT WROTE another letter to Benjamin in November 1991. The tone of his writings had changed .

```
Dear Benjamin
I write to tell you how really sorry I am about all
the trouble I have caused you Benji. I will be
writing to Mum and Jonnans seperately. I know I
have sinned in times past and although I have
confessed these to God I have not to you at this
stage. So the Bible tells us in James 5v16 "Confess
your sins one to another so that you may be healed".
So that is my confession and my prayer that you
will be healed and strengthened. God promises in 1
John 1v9 "If we confess our sin He is faithful and
just and will forgive us our sin and purify us
from all unrighteousness." That is His assurance
to me and in fact all of us - He will forgive us
all our sin.

Benjamin, when I'm talking about my sin I am Not
talking about what happened to Sheree Beasley. I
assure you I had nothing to do with it and therefore
have no confession to make on that matter. That's
for somebody else to confess - if he ever would. I
trust you understand.

Now, next subject - next Tuesday is Mum's birthday.
I suggest you get a spongecake from Safeway filled
with cream. Get 6 candles from the pantry. Put one
```

The Murder of Sheree

on one side of the cake and 5 round the other side. Sing up loud when you light it and do it together with Jonnans. OK?

Normally I would give mum 2 bunches of flowers as this is a sign of loving and something precious we have for each other. However because of my sin I have spoilt this somewhat and I don't think I will this time in case I upset Mum who could even feel like tossing them in the bin - probably not, but rather than risk that it might be a better idea if you gave a bunch or two of carnations or whatever a florist at Wheelers Hill recommends. Mum does love flowers. Ask the florist which last the longest. Check the leaves aren't browning and buy whatever you can afford for the vase at home. If you've already got her a present just a small bunch from Safeway or the florist would be fine. It's the thought that counts - not how much it costs. Graeme might be over then. He can afford a lot more so don't worry if he gives even more flowers, because Mum needs a lot of flowers and a lot of good food.

Next subject. You might have been upset when my Church membership was cancelled. I was told by my doctor (a Christian) and a top person at the Presbyterian College "not to worry - because I was still a member of God's Church". The man in the College and another in the Presbytery thought the way it was done might not be right anyway. Anyway don't be ashamed of me for that. No one else seems to be that I know of other than the elders. I certainly am not ashamed of the Gospel of Christ. It is the power of God unto salvation. The Bible in Eph 4v32 tells us "to be kind and compassionate to one another, forgiving each other just as in Christ God forgave you fella".

There is a principle in all this for when you're a leader. When 2 or more parties are in dispute the leader must meet with both or all representatives of each party to ascertain the problem. He must check the facts, listen to their hurts, then take these to the Lord in prayer and await His answer. God's decision is your decision to be conveyed again to each disputing party. Some won't like it, but ALWAYS leave the door open for all parties for prayer and fellowship support as brothers in Christ. In this way you do not Judge. Mat Ch7v1 says "Do not Judge others or you too will be judged" (also Rom 2v1) God alone is the Judge (James 4v12).

So in this way Judgement in our hearts is replaced by Gods LOVE COMPASSION JOY PEACE PATIENCE KINDNESS GOODNESS FAITHFULNESS GENTLENESS and SELF CONTROL. (Fruits of the spirit Gal 5v22,23).

Jesus was always like this - even to those caught in a sin (or more) like me. I have truly and completely repented and God forgave all my many sins (Ps 103v3) The bible tells us in Gal 6v1 "Brothers if someone (Robert/Dad) is caught in a sin, you who are spiritual should RESTORE HIM GENTLY". Then 1st Peter 4v8 adds "Above all, LOVE EACH OTHER DEEPLY BECAUSE LOVE COVERS A MULTITUDE OF (DAD'S) SINS.

Billy Graham the evangelist whose ministry brought me to the Lord in 1969 - Mum knows, has probably been used by God to bring more souls to the Lord than anyone in History. I'm told Billy Graham reads 1 Cor 13 - the chapter on LOVE every day. It is the MOST EXCELLENT WAY (CH12V31) Love is patient kind etc IT KEEPS NO RECORD OF PAST WRONGS. LOVE protects, trusts, hopes perserveres, LOVE never fails (I hope our marriage never fails)(v4-8) LOVE is the greatest (v13) Read this often especially when you're away. Love covers all sins (Pr 17v9).

Simon Peter asked Jesus "How many times shall I forgive my brother in Christ when he sins against me? Up to 7 times?"

Jesus answered "I tell you NOT 7 times but seventy times seven ie 77. That command is in Mat 18v21,22.

God has a special message for you Benji in 2 Cor 2v5-9. "If Dad has caused grief Dad has not so much caused grief with the writer Paul, as with you Mum and Jonnons to some extent - not to put it too severly (or hard). The punishment inflicted on Dad by you lot eg seperation and not seeing you Jonnons or Mum, rejection almost by each of you, put out of the family home, heartache and loveloss pains, can't sleep, church dismissal, loneliness intensely, court cases, trials, shame etc (some of which you have also suffered but at least you have each other). How desperate would you feel if the situations were reversed and this happened to you?

Anyway, the bible says "the punishment by you is sufficient for Dad" verse 7 <u>"Now instead you ought to forgive and comfort Dad</u> so he will not be overwhelmed by excessive sorrow." (I can take only so much).

Verse 8 <u>"I URGE YOU THEREFORE TO REAFFIRM YOU LOVE FOR HIM - DAD."</u>

Verse 9 <u>"The reason I (Paul) ask you is to see if you will stand the test and BE OBEDIENT IN EVERYTHING."</u>

Please Benjamin certainly before you go to PNG please forgive me, reaffirm your love for me and comfort me so that all our consciences are clear and at peace and one with God. Don't go anyway haveing anything against anyone. Replace hatred or lack of love with Gods full love in your heart for me. It's not easy to do but you must try. But Jn 14v15 says If you love me you will obey my command JN 13v35 People in PNG will know you're a missionary if you love everyone (even Dad).

JN 15v12 Jesus says "MY COMMAND is this:- LOVE each other (even Dad) and I have loved you."

I would love a prayer card or personal letter or phone talk if and only "If" you feel you can. I have been walking cleanly and honestly with God for fully 8 weeks now. I need your encouragement and Mums to keep going. The above is not intended as a sermon. It's just what God says and obviously wants you and all of us to do. I'm doing my part. We are still a family and I only want the very best in God's eyes for each one of you (Why - because I love each of you <u>FULLY</u>). My love to Mum Jonathan and yourself.

Dad.

```
PS. If you have any doubts, check the scriptures
thoroughly. The decision is between you and God
alone. However let Mum read the letter as I don't
want to do or say anything wrong or misleading.
```

THE FOLLOWING day, at another session with Margaret, Robert asked if the police thought Sheree's death might be the result of manslaughter, not murder. Margaret told him the police thought it might be accidental as the body appeared to be hurriedly disposed. Robert was delighted with that. He scribbled down some quick notes.

"I never put my hands on her and dragged her into the car," Lowe said. Then he asked if he could be charged with manslaughter.

"Only if you were to tell them what happened. Otherwise it would be murder," Margaret said. Jotting down Margaret's words, he said, "Well, if I pleaded guilty it would have to be guaranteed that Lorraine would not divorce me."

Margaret just stared at him.

THE NIGHTMARE was always the same. Lorraine found herself crawling along a tunnel that narrowed the further she went. For some inexplicable reason, she had to get to the other end, to see what the tiny ray of light was. The claustrophobic feeling was unbearable. It was hot and sticky and close. Then, as she inched forward on her elbows and knees, she would get jammed. The more Lorraine tried to extricate herself, the more she became entwined in the clinging, viscous tunnel. Then she would panic, and wake to find herself wrapped tightly in a twisted cocoon of bedsheets. The police officers waiting in the garage outside, hoping to catch the people who had been vandalising her home and attacking her, would call out, asking if she was all right. Yes, she'd be okay, she would call with a sense of resignation. Drenched in sweat, Lorraine would pull herself from her trap and change the dripping sheets. After a glass of water and some reflective time, she would eventually go back to bed - and have the same nightmare again. Sometimes she would have it three times a night.

Crystal's nightmare was always the same too. A man was coming in the window to take her away. But each time he grabbed her, she woke up screaming, waking her little sisters. Kerri would be awake anyway but what could she say to calm her daughters? How could she tell a 4-year-old there's nothing to worry about, when she knew damn well there was?

ROBERT HAD made a commitment to Margaret he would continue to seek therapy. And anyway, he needed a report from her for his court appearance in December for his escapades in Yarraville in July. Margaret had a reputation for being an outstanding court performer. In her 25 years of dealing with prisoners and treating offenders, she had never once given evidence for the prosecution. Robert knew he could trust her with anything he said or did.

Knowing Robert, and harbouring a suspicion he had abducted Sheree, Margaret was not looking forward to seeing him. She knew Robert only played at therapy. But she had an overriding curiosity. She had to know whether he was involved in Sheree's disappearance. What followed over the next 18 months was a twisted game of chess, with no rules and no prize at the end. Margaret sought the truth about Robert's involvement in Sheree's murder and tried to get Robert to be honest so she could help him. But she wrestled with her conscience all the time. Was she doing the right thing trying to find out about Sheree, or should she just try to modify Robert's current behaviour? While Margaret chased a true version of Robert's involvement, Robert began compiling an alibi.

On 25 November, 1991 - four days after police technicians secretly installed a legal listening device in Margaret's clinic - Robert met with his therapist, and his millionaire brother Graeme, who had flown in from his New Zealand home to try to help. Before they began the session properly, Margaret spelled out Robert's behaviour to his older brother.

"He just has not been motivated to change at all. And the reason why he hasn't been motivated to change is that he's been getting a fair deal of precarious enjoyment out of his behaviour," she explained. "I can't deal with it without full co-operation and motivation. I've thrown Robert almost literally out of the door and I've confronted him with his family and what he's doing to his family. I've appealed to him on moral grounds, I've appealed to him on spiritual grounds and none of those have worked," she explained.

"He's been assured (Lorraine) never would (leave him) and that's allowed him to carry on so that his behaviour has been escalating, Graeme, over the years."

Robert sat quietly and listened.

"The fright is...," he piped in, "frankly, not so much about Sheree Beasley, but I may lose my wife and family. That is the fright to me and that is the biggest fright I've had in my life."

Later in the conversation Lowe told his older brother how he operated, defending his actions as harmless. As an example, Lowe talked of schoolgirls going home after school that he "might have followed".

"I parked my car a fair way, always from where the girls are and I parked my car way down here in a side street. I go back to where the girls are coming on and I just look at them and um, see if there are any sorts of prospects that you want to follow. When they're in a whole bunch you don't do anything with them. You, when they're in by their singles, you don't do anything with them because it scares them. I never approach a girl by herself. I never approach a girl by herself. Never, ever. Otherwise they get frightened, they run away. There's always two. They bounce each other. Their, their comments, or they joke. Now, on that occasion, I - there were no girls. The girls were all coming out. There were far too many together. So I went back to the car and got in the car and next to where the car was parked there was a little girl. I paid virtually no attention to her. She may have said something to me. As far as I know her mother was inside, I don't know. And I just - she said something, I, I would have just, I may not have reacted, then I might have gone like that and I went straight to my car."

"I find that very hard to accept, Robert," Margaret said.

He then admitted he approaches targets "five times a week at the very most".

"Graeme, I'm fairly disciplined in what I do. I look at girls. I can sum them up. I am, I consider myself pretty disciplined in what I do, in this, and that's why I got away with a lot. I'm pretty disciplined at that and I'm no, never. I know girls which are dangerous that you can't ever, well... I've never, ever got them into the car. Never even touched a girl, nor have I ever wanted to touch a girl."

"You're dreaming," Graeme said.

Lowe then confessed he had approached hundreds of 'targets' over the past twenty years.

"Look, I would love to aim at the 18, 20, 22-year-olds," he said.

"Why don't you then?" Margaret asked.

"Because- I told you the answer to that. Because I'm scared I will get an attachment and that you, you form a relationship. I'm scared of that and I'm scared that I'll fall in love and fall out of love with Lorraine, that's the reason."

Margaret pointed out she could see Robert's behaviour was getting more out of control since 1990.

"Yes, I have, you're quite right, you know. Yeah, but not to the extent of killing or murdering or whatever you like to call it to this girl here," he said.

"We aren't talking about killing or murdering," Margaret pointed out.

"Well, even panicking Margaret. Panicking or even getting a girl into a car or even touching a girl. I have never done it. I've never done it. Never touched a girl. I, I must confess, I've put it to, as far as I can remember..."

"As far as I can remember," Margaret mocked. "That's not a normal catch."

"Margaret, I'm talking of going back to 30 years."

```
Dear Fella Benji

I wrote you a letter a few weeks ago. I hope you
got it. I'm just waiting for your reply because
the postie hasn't delivered it yet. Perhaps he
will tomorrow. No! don't worry! I don't expect any
letters back from you Jonnons or even Mum at this
stage. I just want to write to each of you
occasionally just to tell you know I'm really
thinking of you because I love you all - no matter
what.

Rosebud and the area is a lovely place although it
hasn't all been easy this time. I usually walk
along the beach from West Rosebud to Rosebud or
Rye daily. But I also enjoy immensely riding your
```

old red bike - the nearest I have to a car! I got a flatty the other day, but with a new tyre, seat right up, oiled and greased I can go miles. Mum and I (or was it Father Christmas) gave you that when you were about 5 - check with Mum - and it's still going great.

A couple of days ago I rode up to Rosebud early then back and had breakfast at Rye, morning tea at Blairgowrie and on to Sorrento on your Red Peril bike. As I entered Sorrento I stopped at the big Pine trees where we used to spend those 40 degree days near the beach. I was going to draw a love heart on the table near where we'd sit but God said, "Don't" - least I become a vandal. So I didn't.

Up to the top of the hill I pushed the bike and headed straight for the newsagency where Mum would usually buy a Womens Weekly to read at home or on the back beach. The "Weekly" wasn't due in till Thursday. I'd thought there was to be an article in it about Lindy Chamberlain (Mum will tell you who the Chamberlains are) - they are still married - not divorsed. The shop was displaying Lindy Chamberlains book. One chapter was entitled "Raided and Invaided" and I thought of the similarities of them as Christian people and ourselves and what we're going through because of me.

Once up to the back beach at Sorrento I tied the bike to the bench the seagulls usually occupy in front of the car watching Mum settle down with much contentment to read her book. The day was fine and quite warm - about 26 degrees. The tide was out, the waves flat because of the northerly breeze. I walked down passed the swimming pool and along the slightly green rocks, round the corner to the smallish flat rock on which you Jonnans and I have played since you were small. No waves around it with the tide out but there was still water in the rock pools that run one into another. I just sat there and enjoyed all the memories we've shared for many years. I looked up the sand slide round the corner but it would have been too energetic for me. So I walked along the beach to Sphinx Rock

The Murder of Sheree

and from a little way up I could see London Bridge at Portsea. Again all the memories poured back as I remember Mum Grandma and Jonathan as a baby in one area and you making a dash from one rock to the cliff face when this huge wave came up. The Ranger grabbed you and picked you up under his arm as if a lamb but you're a lot bigger than that now and I'm proud of you for it. It was a frightening experience. Life gives us frightening experiences even those from God. He didn't allow that wave to hit us that day more than we could stand. But he does give us such experiences to test us and to make us put our faith more and more in him. Even in these difficult times which I regret God still seems to be in control if we draw close to Him.

When I returned to the car park the car had gone. So I unhitched my bike and wheeled it up the hill past the tracks that lead to the lookout where you and Jonnas used to play in abundance in younger days. Down past Mum's house I headed for the ice cream shop we always do. I ordered Mum a cassatta ice cream she likes but when I took it out she wasn't there. So I had to eat it myself!

On the way to the Rescue Helicopter pad I called in at the hotel at the top of the hill where a busload of Scottish (mainly) tourists were coming out after lunch. I parked my bike and went in and saw all the beautiful pictures of Sorrento early days - the trains in Sorrento main street, the paddle steamers at the wharf. Then I came out only to find that the whole busload of tourists had been held up because of the way I'd parked my bicycle in the narrow street! Freewheeling down the hill I then watched the huge tourist bus with passengers board the car ferry en route to Queenscliffe. Last to go on though was a medium to smallish caravan and that reminded me immediately of plans Mum and I have talked about many times in our retirement that we could get around and tour Australia. I was saddened at that because we might never do it - just because of the stupidity of myself trying to enjoy a season of sin. I've wasted opportunities and thrown so much away. But I still do pray that may be God will allow us to do this.

The Murder of Sheree

There are so many other things I reminisced about as I peddled back through Rye and Toot(garook) and to this temporary home. I thank you for the use of this God given bike and to all of you for these great memories. I hope we can put it into action again one day.

You'll be off to PNG and Qld in 3-4-5 weeks. I'd love to see you before you go. Talk to Mum about it if you want to in the same way as you talked to her about divorce or seperation. If you don't want to see me I will understand. But the decision is one which you may be with Mum's help will have to make - to meet with me or don't do anything and meet with me. Don't do something if you do not want to do it. Don't be ashamed of me. 1Cor. because all my sins which were many are all washed away Since Jesus made clear in my heart as the chorus goes.

You'll probably have exams this week or next. I'll be praying specially for you. I am with you in Spirit and am not far away anyway so just believe I'm with you and right behind you supporting you if that's what you want me to do.

One thing I promise that may still worry you is that I had nothing to do with that girls death. Some people in Melbourne still think I did.

But God knows the name of the person who did do it and He knows I did NOT. Those who believe or think I did put themselves on a pedestal as knowing more than God. I'm talking about Christians. The police just want to pin the death on anyone they can. They aren't even looking for the real person and the motive I think could be behind it all.

An article on the front page of the Gazette (Waverley) 30th Oct states "The police believe Sheree was killed on the evening of her abduction or the next day". I was home soon after lunchtime and I certainly did see the 5.30 news report on Ch 7 when you, standing behind the swivel chairs, Jonno between the TV and the fireplace me at the kitchen bench - the three of us watching - Mum didn't stop typing then.

```
Show this letter to Mum if you wish. I like her to
see what I write to you fellas. I will not write
often, I don't want to annoy anyone.
God Bless. Love Dad.
(PS) Benji - I wrote this quite a few days ago and
I now have a clearer understanding that you probably
don't want to see me before you go. That's ok.
When I wrote it I didn't know how you'd feel.
Speaking on the phone is a possibility but no
worries if you don't want to.
```

DECEMBER 10 brought Margaret Hobbs another black surprise. She was asking for some background material from Robert concerning his early life. She had to submit a report to his lawyers about his criminal behaviour and his criminal past. Robert spoke to her in a manner he had never done before. He talked to her, openly, about his dark past.

Talking about his deviance, he protested he didn't do too much that was all that bad. He stood up to show Margaret what he did when he approached little girls.

"I don't expose myself Marg, this is what I do," he said and put his hands down the front of his trousers.

Margaret cut in quickly, holding her hand up to tell him to stop.

"No thanks, Robert, you don't have to give me a demonstration," she said.

He appeared quite dissociated and titillated as he talked about the offence with which he had been charged. He was obviously sexually excited just talking about it. He talked about it freely and was a little disappointed when Margaret didn't want to continue the discussion further. Then the talk of his past began.

He told Margaret he had gone to a boarding school in Melrose, Scotland, when he was 8-years-old. When he was 12, he was interfered with by one of the masters in the dormitory. By the time he was 14, he and another boy would masturbate each other regularly. That developed into full sex with another older boy two years his senior in the toilets while other boys were playing sport. Robert told Margaret he was a little fearful of the older youth.

The Murder of Sheree

With a proud smile, he recounted how he was the tennis champion at primary school three years running, he had set the high jump record at school, and he was a good cricketer.

When he left school at 18, he spent a few months working on a farm. His life of crime began at 19 when he stole a car.

"And I just got into the car and drove it. I was just heading home when the village policeman noticed it," Robert explained. "He came and jumped on - came to the side window and said, 'Look, whose car is it?' and I've panicked I guess and drove off and he was on the running board, had running boards in those days, and I drove off and he clung on a bit and then he eventually fell off and then I was charged. And that was, you know, my parents were deeply shocked because my father, my stepfather...was the police surgeon."

Margaret was amazed. For years this man had not given any hint at all that anything like this had happened to him. Now Robert was actually explaining things about himself that painted him in a bad light. She didn't realise it at the time, but his mask was slipping. She sat transfixed while the story continued.

Robert passed all the air force entrance tests but he spent one year in the army instead and he hated it. He served in the local garrison in Hale, near Bradley. Then he told of how the family moved to New Zealand in 1957, settling in the capital, Wellington. His stepfather Peter MacKinlay bought a practice in Levin, about 60 kilometres north of the city.

Robert boarded in Wellington with a university teacher.

"I was immensely lonely," Robert said. "Shocked with, I don't know, shocked, gazing, just killing time. Immensely lonely."

He said that he wasn't good at making girlfriends or picking up girls. But then, according to Robert, he was picked up by men for sex.

"I got picked up I guess, near a toilet by someone wanting homosexual...I don't know if I was looking for it or not but I was half, you know, I just wanted someone who you can talk to and someone you can relate to. And you know I got into a homosexual toilet type thing. No permanent relationships or anything like that. If it was a question of masturbation, that, that I could probably accept but some of the people wanted extra things. I didn't like that. I couldn't accept it and so on the whole things became dirty, grubby. I just didn't like this thing at all. So it wasn't really satisfactory. I did then get into a job I quite enjoyed which is actually with an airline in reservations and I enjoyed that but then I did get into um, I was charged with a homosexual relationship. The magistrates were very tough."

Robert told Margaret how he was jailed for six months for loitering for homosexual purposes. Then, after he was charged with stealing a pair of shoes from a Wellington shop, his parents sent him to a psychiatrist. Robert told Margaret, who hadn't moved the whole time her patient was speaking, that the psych told him to move away from the family to Auckland.

"And from there I also did get into trouble and I got a jail term for something but I've forgotten what it was but I think it'd be about the same thing. It's called a rogue and a vagabond. If you commit an offence, a second or third offence, you're considered a rogue and a vagabond. It's the old Street Offences Act."

Robert started mixing with girls in Auckland and took up with a merchant sailor's wife. Robert fell in love with her and moved in with her and her little boy. But his love was unrequited and he moved out six months later.

In the 1960s, he moved to Melbourne and got a job in Waltons. He lived in run down places and went to Scots Church for worship.

Margaret knew this was as close to the truth as she would ever get with Robert. He had spoken quietly, almost apologetically. This would be as far down as he would ever let his guard drop with her. Then, as the conversation moved on, Robert protested his innocence in relation to offending against little girls.

"I don't touch girls. The enjoyment I get out of them is their reaction. If I talk to them about big boobs or, or, whatever, then they would react to it. That's what I would..." his voice trailed off. "Look, Marg. Not only have I not done this, the Beasley one, but I have - there is no other girl anywhere around the state, Australia, or anywhere, even New Zealand, going back there, who I've done this to or even had in my presence. They will not find anything. They might find some areas of suspicion, like this one. I, I, I know I've done, I know I've done a lot of things that are wrong

Marg, a lot of things, but nothing at all like the Beasley thing. They are things that are wrong but they are things which are borderline because I've tried to do my bit of behaviour which is questionably whether it is an offence or not."

ON DECEMBER 11, at 11.25am, Paul Hollowood and Detective Sergeant Jeff Calderbank of the Homicide Squad visited Lowe at his Rosebud unit. Hollowood still wanted to talk to Lowe and was trying to get him to come in to participate in an interview. What Paul desperately wanted was some sort of alibi, so he could pick away at it. If he got an alibi and could destroy it, he could be well on the way to building a case of murder.

Paul knocked on the door and both policemen stood on the porch, waiting. Lowe answered and looked down his nose at both men.

"Mr Lowe," Paul said. "I thought I'd take the opportunity to come down and see you since our last interview as you wished time to be able to talk with your own personal solicitor."

"Yes?" Lowe was a little puzzled.

"You've seen Peter Ward?"

Lowe agreed he had spoken to his solicitor. Paul explained he was only interested in the abduction and murder of Sheree Beasley, nothing else. Lowe cheered up considerably. He wasn't in trouble again. It was just the police asking about the little girl.

"I feel that I wish to say something to, ah, what's the word?"

Paul helped him out. "You mean to eliminate yourself - exonerate yourself from being involved in her death."

"Yes, eliminate myself, so I've been here working on my statement. I have it here and once I've finished, I'll provide you with a copy. You do not have anything from me, do you, from the other interviews, about what I was doing?" He was trying to sound helpful but both policemen thought he sounded smarmy.

"Well, I'm at the Rosebud police station so if you want to come in and see me just do so. Okay?"

"Well, yes, I'll do that because I want to help myself out of all this."

"All right, we'll wait to hear from you then."

"Now I have couple of questions, if I may, to ask. I've written them down." Lowe then searched through a pile of papers on his writing desk. He found what he was looking for. "Yes, now." He held the paper high in front of his face and read loudly. "If I provide the statement, will I eliminate myself?"

"I'm not able to say anything until I've read what you've prepared," Paul said.

"Yes, I understand but if I can prove that I wasn't involved in Sheree's death, do I eliminate myself?" Lowe could have been speaking to a small child who questioned his authority.

Paul chuckled a little as he said, "I'm afraid you're putting the cart before the horse at the moment but if we find you are not involved in the death of Sheree then you are eliminated."

"Right." Lowe sounded emphatic, as if he had just won a point in a game of cards.

"Are you prepared if necessary to also participate in the identification parade that we spoke of in an earlier interview?"

"Well, if it will eliminate me, certainly I am willing to take part but I have some reservations as I know your people have been showing my photo around and these people may recognise me from that."

"No, the people that would take part in the viewing of the identification parade haven't been shown your photograph at all."

"Well, I can't be sure of that but I'll think about that and discuss it with Peter Ward."

"Well, I think that's best to do. Discuss it with Peter Ward and tell us what you're prepared to do, okay?"

"Yes." Lowe looked at his scribblings again. Then he looked up and said loudly, "Another thing I wish to ask. What would I get if I was unable to show I didn't kill her?"

Paul was nonplussed; that one was from left field.

"Sorry, what do you mean?"

Lowe spoke impatiently. He thought he was asking the most obvious of questions. "Well, what type of sentence? How many years? Peter Ward tells me 23 years."

"Well, I can't comment on what penalty the courts can give. I'm sure

Peter Ward can tell you all about that," Paul said.

"Yes, he has but he said if I talked to you, that's what I'll get."

"Look, I think that's all up to yourself and Peter Ward to discuss."

"Well, I haven't been 100 percent happy with him. He's never even asked me if I killed Sheree Beasley," Lowe said, with incredulity. Paul and Jeff thought Peter Ward had made a smart move.

The policemen said their goodbyes and left. The plan had worked well. Through the listening devices at Margaret's clinic and the Rosebud unit, Paul knew Lowe was building an alibi. He even knew roughly what it was going to say. It would say that he had been at home on the day Sheree had disappeared, spending the afternoon doing various chores in the backyard and round the house. Paul Hollowood's men had been out taking statements from people they knew Lowe would rely on for alibi testimony. Knowing Lowe's alibi was almost ready, Paul knew that if he told him he was keen to see it, an exhibitionist like Lowe would not be able to resist the temptation to come in and flaunt it. If Lowe had a weakness in this sick game he was playing, it was his arrogance and overconfidence, Paul thought. He liked it when the crooks thought they were smarter than the police.

ROBERT APPEARED in Williamstown Magistrates Court on December 16. On the offensive behaviour charge he was sentenced to three months imprisonment but it was suspended for 12 months. If he stayed out of trouble there would be no penalty at all. The wilful and obscene exposure charge was withdrawn and he was ordered to pay $317.47 costs. Robert was pleased with the outcome, and he was excited that he had finally finished his written alibi. The following day he dropped in to the Rosebud Police Complex and handed Paul Hollowood a copy of his three page alibi statement. They set a time for an interview at the Homicide Squad offices in Melbourne for 3pm on Thursday, December 19.

Robert refused to see the connection between Sheree's murder and his wife not having him back. He thought that because he denied the offence, she should welcome him with open arms. His word should be enough. He didn't even consider that he had told so many lies that nobody could believe a word he said. Margaret was trying to tell him to sort out the Sheree mire first, then he could sort out his marriage. He wanted to do it the other way round. He exasperated Margaret. She couldn't get him to understand. One short exchange between patient and therapist, just before he was due to go and meet with Paul Hollowood showed how far apart their goals were.

Margaret had gone back to basics, yet again, to try to explain what he was doing wrong.

"See, you've got (different) types of exhibitionism. Simple exposure, simple exposure and masturbation as to some form of communication such as speaking, shouting or whistling so that, that's you. So you fall into this particular category here, which personally Robert I feel is worse than a plain wilful and obscene," Margaret said.

In monotone, Lowe asked: "Are we going to spend long on this or what?"

ROBERT WAS due in 15 minutes. Margaret had been awake half the night with worry. Now she was standing in her clinic and her stomach was in a knot. That poor little girl. Was it Robert? It was very much sounding like it. But then again, if anybody could make up a story for the sake of gaining attention, Robert Arthur Selby Lowe could. Margaret sat down, just before he strode in. Impeccably dressed in a white striped business shirt, neat tie and grey suit trousers, he looked every bit the middle-aged professional man about town. Margaret told him he should not take his statement to the police unless it was the truth. Lowe politely thanked her for her concern but said he was confident and had made up his mind. Then he confessed he was quite enjoying the drama of it all. The subject turned to Sheree's missing clothes.

"They'll never find them," Lowe said. "The person would have them in his car and took them to Queensland or something."

Margaret suggested he was fascinated by Sheree's abduction and those carried out by Mr Cruel. The enormous buzz for the abductor was no-one knowing who it was, she said. Lowe said he paid scant attention to the abductions of the other girls.

"Weren't two of them released?" he asked, referring to Sharon Wills and Nicola Lynas. Then he told Margaret he had never had a girl in his car or "done anything like this before". Before Margaret could speak, he cut in with "There's always a first time, isn't there? The person who did this wouldn't live in Red Hill or still be driving a blue car around."

Again Margaret drew breath to speak but Robert cut in again. "They could though, couldn't they? But they would have to know the area of the drain. Which I don't."

When the session ended, Robert smiled and confidently strode out into busy Victoria Parade and caught the tram to the Homicide Squad in St Kilda Road. He pointed out to Det. Sen-Sgt Paul Hollowood and Detective Senior Constable Harry Simpson that he was right on time - it was exactly 3pm, as arranged. Robert smiled at that. He was off on the right foot.

Paul Hollowood thought he was fairly fortunate for he had had the opportunity to speak to Lowe a couple of times before. He was able to build up a profile on the man and have a good think about how to tackle him. An interviewer is always happiest when he has the upper hand and Paul felt he was already in that position. Sometimes when Paul had conducted interviews in the past he had hardly any evidence or information to work with. In those cases he would hope the suspect would trip up and come out with something. But with Lowe they had done their homework and they knew enough about Robert's alibi to see immediately what was a lie and what was not. From the brief interview on October 30 Paul knew Lowe was very smooth and confident - confident to the point of being cocky. Lowe reinforced Paul's view when he arrived on this day in businessman's attire.

After a few preliminaries in the main office, the three men walked to the interview room, which contained three chairs and a table on which sat a three tiered tape recorder. A video camera was mounted on the wall, aimed at the suspect's chair. Outside, in the main homicide office, sat Paul Hollowood's crew, wondering which way the case would turn. Robert placed his three-page masterpiece, and a couple of pens he had brought - just in case any last minute adjustments were needed - on the table.

Paul Hollowood had spent much of his 17 years as a policeman at the Homicide Squad. He had interviewed scores of suspects and offenders

The Murder of Sheree

who had killed accidentally, or out of rage, jealousy, passion, revenge. In rooms like this one, vagrants, businessmen, housewives, pimps, prostitutes, burglars, thieves and gangsters had sat terrified while the detective had asked penetrating question after question. Today it was a pervert's turn.

Robert Lowe, too, was well-prepared - or as prepared as he could be. He had spent the best part of 30 years or more terrifying little girls and boys which had led him to interview rooms much like this one. Today he knew he would run rings around another cop.

They sat opposite each other, like two chess grandmasters, ready to commence an epic battle. Much rode on what would happen in the next few hours. Hollowood could crack a difficult murder investigation, and bring some sense of justice to Sheree's family - and to a degree, a large part of the populace who lived in fear that some man might snatch their daughter next. If Lowe was the winner, he could walk free, untainted, eliminated. He knew he had done his homework well. He knew from past experience that the police don't go into these sorts of things too much. He just knew his alibi would carry the day. He leant forward, with his arms folded on the desk. He was calm and relaxed but eager to begin. The video camera, behind the Paul Hollowood's right shoulder, caught the drama with its unblinking eye.

Paul looked at Lowe. It was as if the suspect was in a personnel interview, applying for a job. He was very cool and so sure of himself. Paul turned on the tape recorder and video camera. It was 3.45pm. Lowe smiled smarmily, then, with an air of authority, leaned further forward. His right hand cradled his chin and cheek as he began reading, in his most perfect, precise English. He could have been undergoing an elocution exam.

"This statement is made by Robert Arthur Lowe of Rosebud West, Victoria, to the police," Lowe began. "This statement is about the whereabouts of Robert Lowe on the weekend of Saturday the 29th of June, and Sunday the 30th of June, 1991. It is made entirely voluntarily by Mr Lowe on his own initiative, even without a solicitor being present," he read.

He paused for effect. He looked across at Paul, then at Harry Simpson. Then he looked down again.

"It is made as his further contribution to assist the police in solving a

The Murder of Sheree

crime allegedly committed on that weekend. On Saturday the 29th of June, 1991, Mr Lowe left his Melbourne metropolitan family home at 7.25am to attend a church meeting in Nunawading at 7.45am. He remained there in the presence of several others until 10.30am.

From there he returned to his wife briefly at the same family home before saying goodbye and heading off on a pre-planned and pre-advertised trip to Rosebud at 11am.

Mr Lowe arrived at the family holiday unit at Rosebud about 12 noon to carry out repairs in the bathroom. This was completed as far as was able to be done about 12.50pm.

Mr Lowe then returned to the family home, arriving about 1.50 to 2pm. He talked with his wife and planned the afternoon activities which were carried out in and around the property until dusk at 5pm. From that time, Mr Lowe spent the rest of the evening at home, spending the night there.

On Sunday the 30th June, 1991, Mr Lowe left the home with his family, his wife and two children, at 8.45am to go to church at Rowville. The family remained there until approximately 11.45 to 12 noon.

They returned home and would have been in and around the family home until 5.35pm when they had returned to the Rowville location arriving at about 5.55pm. They would have remained there with Mr Lowe until approximately 7.50pm, returning home at 8.15pm, collected some take away food at 8.30 and home again by 8.45pm on Sunday the 30th of June.

I trust this is of help to the police and the inquiries they are making.

In the Toyota Corolla DLT 771 Mr Lowe drove, females from approximately seven years to 77 years have been in that vehicle at different times, sometimes with Mr Lowe driving and other times when no adults have been in the car."

Paul and Harry sat impassively, listening to every word. Paul read his own copy of Lowe's statement as the suspect read it out. The video tape kept rolling. Lowe continued reading an addendum he had written.

"THIS NEXT statement is made on the whereabouts on Saturday, the 29th of June, 1991, to be included together with the report on the 29th and 30th, 1991."

Curiously his writings then switched from the third person to the first.

"After leaving the meeting at Nunawading about 10.30am, I bought an Age and returned home at 10.45am. Before leaving for West Rosebud, I asked my wife if she could get out the children's clothes and her own together with suitcases I was to take to Mildura to make sure they could all fit in and to ascertain how much still available space we might have left. I also checked with her if there was any linen etcetera to go to the West Rosebud unit from the spare room. Two tea towels. After a cup of coffee together, I left about 11am.

I arrived without stopping at the West Rosebud unit near Tootgarook at 12 noon approximately. I went straight to fix the ten to 12 bathroom tiles. I took off those that were loose and reglued them but I was not able to grout them as I had left the grout gun behind but the work done was secure enough should we let the unit over the holidays. I believe the Rosebud neighbours were somewhat aware of this.

I left West Rosebud at about 12.50 to 1pm returning via the Mornington Freeway via Frankston, arriving home about 1.50 to 2pm. I went straight to my wife who was typing in her office. She asked me how I got on, I replied 'Okay, I'm back a bit early because I left the grout gun behind and I couldn't complete the work. I'll finish it another time but if we were to let the unit over the July holidays, the tiles were quite safe.'

I asked her if she had got out the children's clothes but she replied she hadn't had time. She's got a lot of work to do that has to be done today and anyway the boys weren't home. I made her and myself a cup of coffee. I then set about tidying up the mess in the garden because I was going to be away two weeks. Benjamin and I had cut an old apple tree down some weeks earlier and each week were trying to dispose of the numerous branches and couplings into the rubbish bin. Many were strewn all over the back lawn in the hope that the thin ones could be picked up by the mower as I cut the grass.

Benjamin rode in on his bike about 2.30 to 2.45pm and asked if he could go and get a friend to go to the basketball game another friend was playing in at the Glen.

I said 'Yes, but go and tell mum in case she has something else she wants you to do.' So he went and I stacked the branches, chopping many and then cut the grass. I then planned to plant two to three new fruit trees which were still in the pots and I asked my wife exactly where she wanted them planted. She showed me and they were planted and fertilised.

I may then, not certain, have completed nailing the palings on the fence. The neighbour and I had been repairing a few weeks or more earlier and probably completed building a window frame for Benjamin's bird aviary. I then brought up some logs to the back door for the fire place. I went straight inside at dusk about 4.45pm.

When Channel Seven's 5.30pm news came on the abduction was headlined. Benjamin and Jonathan were both nearby. Benjamin said, 'You were in Rosebud dad' to which I replied, 'Thank goodness I was back in time.' There was no mention of the blue car so I did not make issue of my being back with the boys and my wife who was typing.

I was home at the time and as with the other missing girls, it could have been anyone. Lorraine did not get up and watch the news until the abduction portion was just finishing. She didn't really see any of it and returned engrossed in her typing."

IN A WAY, Lowe's statement was a brilliant piece of work which showed how cunning he was. He had mixed fact - left home at 7.25am, stayed at a church meeting til 10.30am - with lies - he had not checked for linen; in fact, he had not gone home before going to Rosebud. Plus he had included a variety of events - fixed the aviary, chopped and stacked branches, planted trees - no doubt relying on other faulty memories. Those things had happened but they had happened either before or after June 29. Lowe was banking on people remembering those events, and surmising it must have been that day. It was now nearly five months ago. He had also been clever enough to not be too specific in certain areas, just as an innocent man would. *I may then, not certain, have completed nailing the palings on the fence.*

When he finished reading, he sat back and relaxed, with one arm draped across the back of the chair. He had a "any questions?" look on his face. Cop that copper. He had thrown out the challenge. Paul Hollowood was pretty happy too. It had been a while since he had planned an interview that had gone exactly as he wished. With this statement,

Lowe had locked himself into an alibi that was no alibi at all. Lorraine had been spoken to, as had Benjamin and Jonathan, and the next door neighbours about fixing the fence. Lorraine had remembered the trees were planted after the trip to Mildura. Benjamin was adamant no work was done on the aviary. The neighbours were doing Tai Chi next door in the back yard on June 29 - there was no banging on the fence that day. Paul politely asked Mr Lowe to sign the statement and initial a few typing errors. Robert was engrossed in what he was doing. He would be on his way home soon. It was all he could do to stop himself from grinning.

Paul Hollowood started innocuously enough. He told Lowe he just wanted to ask a few minor questions about the statement. Lowe was keen to assist. Over the next six and three quarter hours, Hollowood asked deliberate, specific questions on each section of Robert Lowe's version of events. One by one, each section was knocked out as an alibi. The fixing of the fence, the planting of the trees, the work on the aviary, the cup of coffee with his wife. At first, Lowe spoke in a patronising and condescending manner, as if Paul was too stupid to realise what Lowe was saying. But Paul ground on. He sensed Lowe was coming apart under the pressure.

Over the hours, the crisp-looking Mr Lowe slowly slumped, and sat crumpled in his chair. His masterpiece was reduced to tatters. Fidgeting in his seat, he leaned away from Hollowood and occasionally his face twitched nervously. But he had to stay and tough it out. To do otherwise would be to lose face.

In the end, all that was left of Lowe's account that could be believed was that he had left home, by his own account he had gone to Rosebud, and he had then come home.

The cop and the suspect were still sitting opposite each other over the brown table top, bare except for Lowe's three page alibi spread out like a hand of cards, a cup of coffee in a paper cup and Hollowood's black folder. Lowe sat with his right elbow and forearm resting on the table top as he reclined back in his chair. His left forearm rested on the back of his chair. Hollowood sat casually with his left leg draped across his right knee. What amazed him was how Lowe kept trying to cover a lie with a lie. In fact, instead of being vague with his lies, he was then trying to give further detail and the lies just grew and grew and grew. Paul couldn't understand that. It occurred to him that Lowe hadn't even realised that basically there was no alibi story left. Paul went on.

"I put it to you that you are well aware of these events. You were well aware of the events when you were questioned by Mr Gustke, you were well aware of events when you were first questioned here at the Homicide Squad office."

Lowe looked peeved. He spoke almost as if he was stuttering. It was clear he was flustered now and was searching for the right things to say. But he got it all wrong.

"That...is...a...great...presentation...for...the...video...Mr...Hollowood," he said indignantly, while he peeked uncertainly at the camera.

"Mr Lowe, this is a fabrication isn't it?" Paul pointed at the three pages on the table.

"No! I'm telling you the truth. And if you won't believe it, I see no point in continuing with this interview." Lowe tried to outstare Paul. Then, annoyed, he said loudly and slowly, "I'm telling you the truth. You've done this for a great big media beatup, or something like that."

"Mr Lowe, you're here for no beatup." The pleasant tones prevalent at the beginning of the interrogation were now gone.

"I'm telling you-"

"We're here to get to the truth actually."

"Well, why not get to it?" Lowe snapped.

"That's why we're asking you the questions."

"But you won't *believe*."

"Well, how can we believe what's been discounted?"

"What are you talking about being discounted?" Lowe appeared genuinely confused.

"Your alibi."

Lowe shuffled in his seat and looked miffed. "You can discount it if you like."

"Nobody can corroborate it. Nobody can confirm it."

Lowe sat very erect in his chair and looked down his nose across the table. Loudly, in a high voice, feigning indifference, he said: "I'm not in, I'm not interested in it."

Paul sighed. "Are you back to not caring about it?"

Lowe was now sitting forward with both arms folded, resting on the table.

"I don't care too much about it, no. I didn't do it, it's not my problem. I've never seen the girl. I have no complex about it. What I'm trying to do is - you made certain promises to me Mr Hollowood."

"What promises are those?"

"Which I expect you to…"

"Mr Lowe." Paul was losing his patience.

"The promise is that if I come and see you - in fact the promise is if you put me through an ID parade and if I'm not picked out, that I will be eliminated."

"I think the only promises - and I say that we don't make promises - the other thing I've told you is that you still haven't given us a - an account-"

"No, you said…"

"-Which can be corroborated in relation to this event."

"Mr, Mr Holloway…"

"Hollowood."

Lowe leant further forward and spoke a little quicker. He thought he was picking up the initiative.

"Mr Hollowood, you stated if I can be eliminated from, from the ID parade, not picked out, I will be eliminated, correct?"

"Well are you prepared to take part in that ID parade?"

"Yes." Suddenly Lowe was speaking quietly.

"Right, well, we'll organise that identification parade then."

"Yeah." The confidence was gone.

"In the meantime, Mr Lowe, I still put this to you as being just a fabrication."

Lowe eyed Hollowood like a hawk. For a second it appeared as though Lowe was investigating a murder and interrogating a suspect.

"But that is a statement that you made, isn't it?" Lowe nodded to himself as he asked the question. He spoke as if he was about to break the case wide open. Paul wasn't fazed. Let him play his games, he thought.

"That's a fabrication, isn't it?"

"No. That I will be eliminated."

The Murder of Sheree

Hollowood had had enough of this crap. He raised his voice.

"Mr Lowe, how about answering one of my questions?"

"The answer..."

"That," Hollowood pointed at the alibi again, "is a fabrication."

"I did ask you a question first," Lowe said in a corrective tone.

"You're not here to ask questions, remember?"

"But you made that statement that I would be eliminated if I went through an ID parade."

"I've never made that statement that you would be eliminated."

The reaction was immediate. Lowe's mouth opened and, in disgust, he dropped the pen he had been fingering. He leant back quickly on his chair. Then he stood up. He got to his feet uncertainly, like a man who was trying to adopt a strong stance yet with no real conviction.

"Mr Holloway (sic) you are...you've said it to me several times." Lowe was trying to sound outraged but wasn't quite succeeding. He had to pursue this line of indignation to deflect the intense focus of Hollowood's questioning. After hours of questioning, Paul had stripped away all the lies, half-truths and blurry information. Now he was targetting the alibi itself and Lowe knew he had nowhere to manoeuvre. He persisted in trying to put the pressure back on Paul. He was trying to embarrass him on camera.

As Lowe stood, his fingers flicked into his trouser pockets then out quickly, settling on his hips. One knee bent outward a little. There was controlled anger on his face, which didn't seem real. He looked a little effeminate. Paul Hollowood looked up at Lowe across the table from his seat.

"Sit down Mr Lowe," he said quietly.

"You tell me the truth Mr Holloway (sic)." Lowe was simulating anger but his lips were shaking from nervousness, not outrage.

"Sit down, Mr Lowe, please," Hollowood said firmly.

"Can I ring up please?"

Harry Simpson intervened: "Mr Lowe, if you do settle down-"

Paul continued: "Mr Lowe?"

"I, I would like to make a phone call." Lowe was shuffling around on his feet, the hands flicking into the trouser pockets again. It was time for as much help as he could get. He needed to retreat. He was losing badly.

The Murder of Sheree

"Mr Lowe, we'll interrupt this interview so you can make a phone call, okay?"

"Thank you."

"Hang on a moment. Do you agree that the time is now 9.34pm?"

"Yes." Lowe grabbed the cup of coffee and with a superior affect, one hand on hip, tilted his head back and drank from the cup. He tried to give the appearance of a man who had just finished an important business meeting and was getting ready to meet some new clients. But he was shaken. He looked at his watch. Paul continued.

"Right, we'll interrupt this interview right now."

Paul and Harry picked up their collection of witnesses' statements and other paperwork. As they readied themselves to leave the room, Lowe took several nervous swigs from the coffee cup. As he did, he watched the detectives from the corner of his eye. As Paul approached the door, which was behind Lowe, he pointed to the chair.

"Just grab a seat back there thanks."

But Lowe unsteadily raised himself to his full size and threw out his chest. Then he thrust his face forward and stepped between the policeman and the door.

He said with sarcastic cheek: "Why don't you look me in the - me in the eye Mr Holloway, Mr Holloway." He had never been so far on the back foot in an interview before. Nor had any policeman done his homework so thoroughly. Lowe was desperately trying to gain the ascendancy and show he had Paul Hollowood's measure but his nervousness shone through. And anyway, he was way too late.

"Get the name right," Hollowood said angrily as he leaned forward and stared back into Lowe's face before leaving the room.

"Mr Hollowood," Lowe corrected himself pathetically as the detectives walked out. Lowe sat down immediately and slumped in his chair. He wasn't happy with his performance. Shaken, he shuffled his papers together and then sat with his head resting on his hand. He wasn't broken. Rather he was just a little tired. And desperate for another tack to take. Being caught out lying had never really been a problem, even if it was the police. The solution had always been to tell more barefaced lies until everybody gave up. For some reason, it wasn't working anymore.

The police took Lowe from the room and gave him access to a phone. He rang Margaret at home.

"They've tricked me, they've tricked me," he hissed.

"Is that you Robert?" Margaret said. Robert sounded very angry.

"They've tricked me Marg. It was an ambush," he said. Margaret asked him if the interview was over. Robert told her it soon would be. He promised to visit her as soon as possible to discuss what had happened. Then he rang off.

Half an hour later the interview recommenced. Lowe leant as far forward as he could, his head resting in his right hand, looking down at his alibi, occasionally looking up at Hollowood for split second glances. Lowe spoke in a very calm, matter-of-fact manner, with his voice as soft and smooth as could be. There was an almost apologetic tone, but not quite. He was trying to make Paul feel guilty.

"I guess I just wanted to apologise, in a way, that I had got a little bit uptight towards the end of that conversation and uh, you know, I guess I have been here seven hours already, or over, seven and a quarter, and I guess I'm a bit hungry, I would have loved something to eat, but um, I'm worried there's no transport in getting home, it's dark. I can usually hitchhike but you can't hitchhike after dark. And ah, I've already given you 32 hours of my time, available for you people to question me and investigate me and I've given that. So I don't know how much more you wanted to go."

He sat back a little and looked down, like a weak and defenceless spurned woman angling at getting her lover to come back to her. He shuffled with his alibi again, then he turned his head slightly and resumed his attack on Paul. He said coyly: "I guess I was a little disappointed when you said you hadn't made a promise to me about the..."

Hollowood had heard enough.

"- Well, the problem we have at the moment is, we spoke about this statement to begin with, is that we're not happy that it can be corroborated in any form."

"Okay, it can't. I accept that." Lowe blinked several times, then looked down. He was conscious of the video camera. He needed to sound conciliatory, in case it was ever used in court.

Paul told him he could still go into an ID parade if he wanted but it would have to be held another time because of the late hour. Paul said he would be in touch about that. He invited Lowe to go over his alibi in the interim and recheck it if he wished. Quietly Lowe told both men he didn't have anything to add. Then Paul asked Lowe if he had anything further to say.

"Yes." Lowe glanced quickly at the video camera several times. "Has what I've said actually been....just now, what I've - my apology to you been recorded?" Appearance, not substance meant everything.

For criminal investigators it's often said they have to be able to think like a criminal to catch them. Paul knew it was important to be able to empathise with the suspect and see where the person was coming from. He had always been able to do that before but he was sure he wouldn't want to be sitting in an interview room with someone like Robert Lowe saying, "Oh, yeah, I know where you're coming from. I can understand why you did this."

Still, short of Lowe coming out with a confession, the interview was everything Paul had ever hoped for. Now that Lowe had been interviewed on tape and was still sticking to his story which had been proved to be untrue, the police had false denials they could use in evidence against him. In evidentiary terms it was Zenith's first big break. It was strong evidence - but it wasn't enough to lay charges. Lowe was allowed to leave.

ROBERT GAVE Margaret a copy of the video to peruse. At their next session on December 23, they discussed the case again and reviewed Robert's performance. Amazingly, Robert was pleased - he thought he had done very well. Margaret was horrified. She felt certain he would soon be charged with murder. After Margaret spent an age trying to convince Robert he had not done well at all, he talked about the investigation itself, and the pivotal role he was playing.

"I don't - I must say," Margaret said, "I haven't had any tips or anything about this Robert, it's just my own feeling that you have somehow backed yourself into quite - I am furious with myself for letting you make that statement, Robert. I said to you before you left this office, I said, 'If you've got anything to hide, don't make it'."

"I haven't said anything Marg." Robert told her he had nothing to worry about. He had a clear conscience.

"Well, you may have a clear conscience," Margaret said, "but it looks like it might get you charged. You're going to end up in one of those terrible situations like Lindy Chamberlain did."

"If it is, well, so be it."

"But how can you say that? I mean, how can you be so complacent about your future?"

With resignation he said: "Yeah, I know, I know."

"'So be it' indeed," Margaret admonished him, like a head mistress.

"I know," said Robert, like a schoolboy.

"You're almost modelling Lindy Chamberlain, Robert. It's going along the same path. I've had an horrendous thought about it the other day. I thought, 'My God, this case is modelling the Azaria Chamberlain case!' It's got the whole thing going, you know. You've got missing child, missing clothes, it's just weird. What's it about?"

"Except Michael and Lindy stuck together."

"Yes, well..."

"Here we've got-"

"- It could happen to you Robert. Perhaps you're going to model it right the way..."

"Yeah."

"I just can't get over the way this is going along the same path, you know? With you playing, you know, this innocent, what's it, victim, been persecuting you. Almost playing a game with it. Why are you doing that? This is the worst thing that bothers me with you Robert."

"What, my complacency?"

"Well, it's not so much your complacency, it's almost as if you, you, you're trying to get yourself convicted. It's like, it's like," Margaret groped around for the right words. "I don't know, it's a strange sort of a situation as if you-"

"- look-"

"- if you're setting yourself up as a suspect and playing up to it. I mean, if you - you really Robert could not have done a better job than if you were guilty. You've played up to the hilt. Right the way from the word go.

You've played suspect number one; still playing it now. What are you trying to do?"

"I, I somehow have that little bit of streak in me I suppose and I've often felt this - I don't know if this is relevant - but I've often felt that."

"It's all relevant."

"I've, I've often felt that you know, you've got this all in front you, wouldn't it be a bit better just to..." Robert was enjoying teasing Margaret with this oblique talk.

"Bloody well admit it Robert and get it over with."

"Oh, yeah, I can't admit the murder or anything to do with that girl. I cannot admit it but I think it goes back and I don't know if this is right Marg but the lack of love in my life. Now when you get chased by the police and that or whatever, it, it sort of circumspects into a something that is missing in your life. And Lorraine's filled that gap. There's a huge gap there now so I guess some of the excitement of the police or whatever it is, is filling a little bit of that gap. Look I know it's lousy, but I'm not meaning to, I'm honestly not meaning to, but it, it just..."

"You do mean to do it Robert. You play it to the hilt. I've seen you playing it to the hilt. Look Robert, you're talking to me."

"I know."

"You know how well I know you Robert, so don't do it to me."

"I'm not trying to Marg, it's just, it's, it's, in the same way that sometimes I feel guilty about things." Another teaser.

"About what?"

"Well, I don't know."

"I mean this is the insatiable appetite that you've got for attention and concern, or something like that."

A psychiatrist Robert had been seeing on an occasional basis had prescribed Androcur to suppress his high libido. Margaret wanted to know if he was still taking it.

"Yes, yes but I had problems last week," Robert told her. "When you said I was lying to you I thought it might have been, I might have been picked up by some security person following me or something like that. I promised last week because um and I meant to tell you but every day, you must ask me or I must tell you first off, what have you been doing, have you misbehaved this week cos last week I nearly did and I thought that's what you were asking about on Wednesday that I haven't been trusting you or something, you know, telling the truth. It's just that I pretty well ran out of my tablets last week or the week before. Yeah, the week before and I went to get another script and he told me, 'Look I've given you five scripts'. I said, 'I'm sure you haven't'. He said I didn't think I had. Couldn't find them at home so I went home and searched everywhere for them and I still couldn't find them. I don't know, wouldn't think so. Well, I must have thrown them out by mistake. And he said he cannot get me a repeat because you have to go through hell or huge order type thing and they are very restricted and all that. So this worried me and I had hardly any left so I was beginning to take them about once every - only when I was coming up (to Melbourne). I was taking off every second, third day. I phoned him. I couldn't find them and it wasn't until I went back to him Tuesday or Thursday that he - on Thursday - that he finally said, 'Look I can get you another thing',...I didn't know. He was going away for a month's holiday. He was away so I was going to be a month without them so I was worried and um last Wednesday I had to go to the dentist at Waverley, Glen Waverley, in the afternoon I went out to Glen Waverley, one's Mt Waverley and other's Glen Waverley, or sometimes, if I go to Mt Waverley I just go. I only look around the supermarkets I don't go anywhere near home because I like the area and sometimes I thought I might see someone. I went around the supermarket but all the girls came out of school then and they've got a new bus-stop totally new as far as I was concerned and they came and just sat up in the bus-stop and I walked up and down there perving with - I was on a tightrope. Then I came back and got on a train and got off at Richmond. I didn't even come to the city. I got on the train at Richmond, the train was packed and in my compartment, when I got in there, was a whole lot of kids who were coming back from a camp and their buckets and everything, single one of them was just so tight and all these kids were jammed up against me. I just felt so uncomfortable. You could only stand. They were all standing too. But I just felt it was uncomfortable so I must confess but I didn't do anything wrong, no. But I just thought suddenly, 'Oh, look I might have been followed and Lorraine had phoned you and said this'."

No, he wasn't taking his medication. And yes, he was still approaching kids. But soon Robert was back to talking about confessing to Sheree's manslaughter on the condition Lorraine would state, in writing, that she'd come back to him in eight to ten years. Margaret was more interested in talking about the interview Robert had had with the police.

"I actually was, had tears in my eyes at the end of that interview," Margaret said. "I'll be quite honest with you Robert, I sat and watched it and I started out watching it like this, " - and she showed Robert how she was sitting upright, wide-eyed, waiting for the video to begin - "and at the end of the interview I sat with my head down with tears in my eyes because I thought, 'Robert, what have you done, what have you done?' You can't see things the way that other people see them. You're not looking at police procedures."

Robert didn't understand what she was talking about.

"You're a Jekyll and Hyde, Robert," she said. "There's a lovely part of you and there's a very secret deviant part of you as well."

Robert leant forward in his brown leather chair and answered in a half-whisper.

"That secret part is over me," he said. Not in a frightened tone. It was obviously a pleasurable experience.

THEIR LAST session for 1991 was on New Year's Eve. After talking about trying to get his marriage working, Robert began asking Margaret about Sheree's death. He said he wanted to know exactly what was known about the little girl.

"But what clothes were taken off? The jacket, wasn't it?" Robert asked.

"There's a..."

"Was everything else taken off or not?"

"Helmet, and, and a shirt, pink thing, tracksuit." Margaret wanted to know why he was asking this sort of thing but thought if she just continued, he might say something to implicate himself.

"Well, her helmet, it was, was, I don't know, would probably still remain in the car by the person who had done it," Robert said.

"Hum," Margaret said. Where was this conversation going?

"He's not going to throw it out on the road or something. It would be found by now."

"Hum, yes, but it wouldn't still be in the car." The realisation hit her like a brick. She hoped he hadn't noticed her jolt. He was enjoying talking about Sheree's death. If he was involved, Margaret thought, he is now reliving it.

"No, it wouldn't now."

"You know. There'd be nobody carrying a pink helmet in a blue car." Maybe he will tell, Margaret thought.

"No, but the fellow's probably driven up to Sydney or something."

"Yes, yes."

"He's not going to be sitting around Rosebud."

"No, of course not."

"And why am I sitting around Rosebud?"

"Well, Robert, you can't say that. It's one of those..."

Now Robert was opening up about Sheree, Margaret started talking hypothetically about the abductor.

"Perhaps he intended to sexually assault her and drop her off or just pick her up and drop her off. Perhaps it was somebody who just wanted to pick the kid up and drop her off a mile further on and cause a big furore and get a kick out of that, you know?"

"Yeah."

"Who knows, and something went radically wrong."

"Mmm." Totally noncommittal.

"Another reason you see because people who are interested - and I mean you - that don't really know Robert, it could have been somebody who is involved with the other abductions. It's a big buzz, it's a big buzz."

"Yeah, they kept (inaudible) on top of that."

"Yes, but it's a big buzz," Margaret said. "If you could imagine -"

" - Oh, when it hit the headlines and all that, for the person who's done it?"

"Yeah."

"Of course it is -"

"Yes."

" - a huge buzz."

Margaret thought she was getting somewhere. "Oh yes, I would think -"

"That buzz doesn't appeal to me."

"Well, buzzes do appeal to you, don't they, Robert?"

"Yeah. Buzzes do appeal to me but I never gave that one any thought Marg." He had gone so far, then shut off the conversation. The conversation meandered for a few minutes before heading back to "buzzes".

"I was saying, whoever did it got a big buzz out of it." Margaret tried again.

"Yeah, yeah."

"It's a big buzz to do something like that. It's a buzz just to pick a kid up and then take her a couple of kilometres down the road and then drop her off."

"Well, that's right," Robert said.

There was a feeling of menace in the room yet again. Margaret wondered if this would ever end. More importantly, she wondered how much longer she could stand the strain.

CHAPTER TEN

LEFT TO his own devices, without a wife and family, or a job, Robert's personal hygiene deteriorated. Now he looked like a vagrant. He was not shaving regularly, he was turning up for sessions with Margaret Hobbs in dirty clothes - usually a crumpled shirt and sometimes he wore no socks. He took to scavenging for food in rubbish bins. His freedom told him he had beaten Paul Hollowood, the best man the Victoria Police could throw at him. For a few days after his clash with Paul Hollowood he was shaken but he quickly reverted to his old self. His interview performance had been poor but he no longer remembered that. He was enamoured with his own importance whenever he replayed the video of the interview with Hollowood. Within the space of a few days, Lowe was feeling omnipotent again.

Margaret was disappointed and bewildered that Robert was such an abject failure in therapy. Every other man she had counselled had either reformed completely or had made tentative steps on the road back to 'normal' behaviour. Something in her turned her interest in Robert into a well-meaning crusade. She needed to know why he wouldn't respond to therapy and was fascinated at his inability and reluctance to alter his behaviour. She saw Robert's lack of insight every time she saw him. He could not - would not - acknowledge anything that disrupted his view of the world, and more importantly, himself. Appearance to others meant everything to Robert; it was crucial he kept his behaviour absolutely secret. He had been doing it for so long, he was keeping most of his behaviour secret from his therapist - and Margaret wondered whether he even kept it from himself by switching off. He was living with one foot in a fantasy world and the other stuck in reality. Margaret repeatedly told him the only way to resolve his marriage was to finalise the Sheree Beasley matter.

Margaret kept telling him that if he didn't resolve the murder case with Lorraine, he should at least resolve it with the police. But still he refused to see the connection between the two issues. Margaret could handle patients who wept or screamed but the strain of Robert's behaviour was driving her mad. Often she didn't know who she was talking to because of Robert's emotional switches. He would get angry and then he would start to cry. Then he would stare at Margaret while he was talking, with a totally flat gaze, looking detached and disinterested. Sometimes as she drove home, or prepared dinner for her husband, or sat in the armchair watching TV, she would think, "Margaret, why are you shaking? You should be used to this sort of thing?" Day after day, night after night, she sought the answer to her concern. Gradually she came to see what concerned her. She realised Robert was working to a very threatening, very aggressive, very calculated plan. He was trying to subdue or subvert her, to get her on-side, either as a co-conspirator or at least a supporter. Now that she saw that, every time he came in, a wave of nausea swept over her. He talked about Sheree, the murder, the abduction, the clothes, the police investigation, and being interviewed, as if he was describing a very ordinary, say, stamp collection. Margaret kept the thought that she could be talking to a child murderer in the recesses of her mind. She couldn't let that feeling blossom. If she did, she knew she wouldn't have the strength to dealt with him.

Only her motivation to get to the truth prevented her from telling Robert to leave therapy for good. If she didn't follow through, she knew she would have a failure on her hands for all time. It frustrated her and it angered her. She was angry with the police. Here she was, trying to help Robert overcome his compulsive behaviour, while trying to find out whether he was Sheree's killer. And the police were doing nothing. They visited infrequently, to offer support and to find out what Robert had told her. What she didn't know was they were playing a game, too, for through the listening device, they knew every word of every conversation. But they had to pretend they were relying on Margaret. To them, there was a danger the therapist could have a change of heart and tell her patient the police were interested in him. If he stopped talking, they might never find out what happened.

Margaret was being torn apart. She had betrayed her client by talking to the police, something she had never contemplated in 25 years of counselling. But this case was different. Margaret was thinking of Sheree and the effect her death had had on her family and on the community. Another little girl might be abducted. And she was concerned, now that Robert was taking notes for alibis and "confessions", that he might try to implicate her as an accessory after the fact.

Guilt-inspired nightmares haunted her. Sometimes the police were coming to see her once a week, sometimes she wouldn't see them for a month. But talking to them - even if she didn't tell them everything they wanted to know - made her feel uneasy when she sat opposite Robert in the next therapy session. Whenever he looked at her for more than a few seconds, she felt like a Judas. She was in an impossible jam - trying to help Robert, trying to help the police, trying to help Sheree's family, trying to help Lorraine. Though she had guided many men on their way to a better life, now she was finding it hard to read the map herself.

She agonised over tricking Robert. Sometimes he would ask her, "Is this confidential?" and she would say it was, while thinking to herself, "It's confidential at the moment, Robert but tomorrow it might not be." And she'd sought legal advice about being present with Robert while he compiled his alibi. She knew Robert was trusting her to either conceal a major crime or collude with her in the manufacture of a confession. She knew she was in dangerous territory.

ABOUT 100 police conducted another fruitless search on the peninsula, from Arthur's Seat to Red Hill and back to the Nepean Highway. The police also went back along the routes from Rosebud to Red Hill, doing more door knocks. They canvassed Florence Avenue again and line-searched along the backblocks around Eastbourne Road. They had been hoping to find somebody who could identify Robert Lowe in the car with Sheree. While some witnesses had seen Sheree in a blue car, nobody had identified her abductor. Things could be lot easier if that happened. But not too many coppers held much hope of an identification now. It was January 1992, seven months after Sheree had vanished.

The Murder of Sheree

ON JANUARY 7, 1992, Margaret had a phone call from Michael Chamberlain, the former pastor who was charged, convicted and later pardoned over the death of his daughter Azaria at Ayers Rock. Mr Chamberlain told Margaret he had received a very disturbing letter from a Mr Robert Lowe who had mentioned her name in his writings. The letter described how Mr Lowe had been accused of a crime he had not committed and his wife had forced him to make a statement. The former churchman also told Mrs Hobbs to tell her patient not to write any more. It seemed to Margaret that Mr Chamberlain had a good handle on Robert Lowe and wanted nothing more to do with him. Later that day Robert came in for another session.

"I think you should keep a low profile at the moment," Margaret said. "That also means really behaving yourself. That's worrying me as well. Are you taking your medication?"

"Yesterday and today."

"Why only yesterday and today?"

"Ah, I guess I must take it more. I haven't seen any, um, danger areas but there are danger areas."

Margaret was trying to confront Robert more often these days. Some days she succeeded, others were bleak.

"You're the danger."

"Yeah."

"Never mind about the areas, Robert. You're going to find it very difficult to stop doing this after the number of years you've been doing it."

"I just wanted a little bit of um, I suppose, you know, titillation in my life."

Margaret was aware that every time she became a little short or curt with Robert, she became uncomfortable. For a few minutes she would lose her apparent self-confidence. Tentatively, she continued.

"Well, what's happening with your sexual-sexuality? Is it still around?"

"Well, though it is still around, yeah, but oh, not much at the moment, Marg. I'm just a little bit frightened of the - you know, the situation. When I go out - um, it just worries me a little bit. It's, um, where I've always walked and always taken my bike, Benjamin's bike, um, it's not on the roads, it's along the - through the foreshore tracks and things there. 'Cos there's nobody been there for donkey's years, you know, but now there's all caravanners and things and campers, you know?"

"Yes, yes."

"So it worries me just a little bit but um..."

"What worries you?"

"Ahh, you know, I go along there. Nothing is - it's a problem for me, 'cos, see I like, I like girls around..."

"Yes."

"There are a lot of girls and they're fairly, um, they're oh, they're all right. I don't see anybody, you know, but they're not fully under their parents' control, I guess."

"Mmm."

"And um, you know, many times, I go along the beach. There's not so many on the beach at the moment."

"Too cold, yeah." Margaret wanted him to see she was on the same wavelength.

"Yes, I go along the beach and, but, um, sometimes I just walk along, you know, go along, always been along..."

"Are you getting any sort of temptations at all?"

"There are temptations there."

"Yes?"

"Yeah, there are."

"Good. I mean, good you are telling me, yes. I would expect you to say that, though."

"There are temptations. The girls - um, the beach is too cold. All, you know, around the camps."

"Mmm."

"And around the, um, you know, the, hiding around the toilet blocks and things like that which is about the only place they can go, you know."

"Yeah."

"Play cricket up against it or chasing around and things like that."

"Mmm."

"But I haven't been round there much, but I've been round enough to know that it spells, it spells danger."

"What - yes, do listen to your own warning signs because Robert, you're under my care at the moment."

"Mmm."

"I feel a bit responsible for that."

"Mmm."

Later Margaret went back to basics to try to penetrate Robert's stubborn mental state.

"You've got, you've got a terrible problem, Robert. When I sit down and look at it objectively....."

"I know."

"...it encapsulates you in the profile."

"Hum."

"And I scream. It's grim, Robert, because there's some, what we call psychopathology there which is very worrying and that's-"

" -I'm not with you, really."

"Well psychopathology, really Robert, means that you've got a behavioural pattern that continues unabated. There are some personality traits there, like you continue on doing it in the face of all sorts of consequences. You don't learn from experience. You know, you go to court yet it doesn't stop you doing it. There's not a lot of remorse there."

"There is to my wife and family."

"Now."

"An enormous amount."

"Now, but not before."

Robert sighed. "Yeah, I agree, yeah, I agree."

Later...

"At one stage, Robert, some years ago, I did a big profile on you and it's a bit worrying."

"Why is that?" Robert was interested. He was fascinated that he should be the subject of a profile.

"Because it's, it's, it suggests that you've got a personality that goes along a certain tack and everything that you do and everything you've done is fitted in with it. That's a big worry, Robert, because even now you've got some blocks that I can't penetrate."

"Hmm."

"You don't seem to realise, for one, where you are at the moment and you're not focussing on what should be the main problem."

Later Margaret continued...

"You - There's, there's something missing, Robert. I'm sorry I have to say this to you-"

"- I know, I'm not-"

"- because you're not insane, you're not mad, but you can't grasp reality. You, you have problems with reality. You're not reality based. You don't think the way other men do in this situation and I've got other men in this situation Robert, or similar. You don't behave like they do. You do not behave like an innocent man."

"As far as the Beasley thing is concerned?" Robert asked. Margaret sensed the shutters had come down. He was not going to tell her anything just now.

"Yes."

"Yeah."

Margaret tried to push from her mind the intrusive visions of a little girl, dressed in a pink and purple tracksuit, wearing a pink stackhat, riding a pink bike. She had never met Sheree but she had seen her chubby face smiling at her from the newspapers and the TV news. To stay clinical and detached, she tried to talk about Sheree as if she was an object, rather than someone's daughter. Despite trying to rid her consciousness of the pretty images of Sheree, whenever Margaret sat with Robert Lowe, there were always three people in the room. To Robert, there was always only one.

"You do not behave like an innocent man. You're throwing guilt on yourself."

"Hum."

"Right from the word go..."

"Hum."

"...you've implicated yourself with lies..."

"Hum."

"...and with deception."

"Hum."

Robert didn't want to hear about his failings. Better to concentrate on something else. He played the sorry victim instead.

"I've got nothing in my life at the moment," he whined.

Margaret was at him straight away.

"...Manufacturing excitement, you're manufacturing adrenalin. You know you're getting off on it. If you, if you have some encounter with some girl as you've said, and I've heard you say, that it keeps you going for a couple of days. It's like a drug for you, isn't it?

"Hum."

"And all the encounters with the police. That's all fine, excitement, you know. I wonder how far you go to manufacture excitement in your life."

"It counters loneliness and depression."

"But there is no need for you to be lonely and depressed in your marriage, Robert. You could have made more of it. You had a family, two lovely boys, terrific wife, nice house. You had no reason to be lonely and depressed, did you?"

"No."

Then...

"You've got some, some thinking which is very clever. You've, you've, you've out-done police over the years. You've out-thought them, you've out-manoeuvred them, you've run rings around a lot of them. It starts to pall a bit you know. You begin to think to yourself, 'I need to get more excitement than this'..."

"Yeah, but I don't know where I'm going to get it from."

"...and people are saying constantly, you know, you've got to behave like an innocent man and you're not. You haven't - right from the word go - have you behaved like a man who is totally innocent of these charges."

"I'm enjoying it a little bit, that's the stupidity of it." Feigning remorse, he looked at the floor, then up to Margaret. A smirk slowly grew.

"I know you are. Isn't that awful? Robert will you answer me? An honest question?"

"Uh huh."

"If you're enjoying it, are you in any way deliberately creating situations?"

The rich, beautiful voice came alive in self-defence. "I'm not Marg. No, I'm definitely not."

"But if you - What do you mean you're enjoying it?"

"But it worries me. It honestly worries me that, that the thingummyjig that gets me going, motivates me and excites me a little bit, is the only thing in this life at the moment that .... I haven't got Lorraine, I haven't got the kids, I haven't got any sex - what else can you?..."

"What else can you do?"

"What else can I do? I haven't got a job to enjoy."

"But if you're enjoying it, Robert, and you keep going on implicating yourself, you're going to get - you're going to, you see, well, you're in too deep now..."

"I know."

"...I honestly believe to get out of it. I just wonder to myself - and you can jump on me and shout at me if you like Robert because I know your personality and I know the way you are - I just wonder whether you've created the situation yourself of getting attention that's got out of hand." This was not a trick question. This was at the very core of what was troubling Margaret.

"Yes, I thought you were going to say that. I enjoyed that interview (with Hollowood) damn it. Peter Ward always said you know, don't do anything and I, I was obedient to that but then Lorri said, you know, if you don't go to the police she won't have me back or words to that effect."

Later...

"Why don't you go and ask for an ID parade and get off on that?" Margaret was talking sex drive.

"No, no, it won't get me off on it. They told me." Robert was talking exculpation. Cross purposes yet again.

"What?"

"They won't let me go on that. They won't let, they won't eliminate me if I got through. It doesn't eliminate me, they said, which is different to what they said in the first place."

"No, I mean excitement if that's what you're looking for, Robert."

"No, no."

"You've, you've created excitement by going on."

"I did a little, even got a little bit of excitement initially on that because I knew I could beat them."

"You haven't beaten them though Robert."

"No, I know."

"What are you going to do when they come and arrest you? What are you going to get out of that? This is murder, remember? Abduction and murder. Not just murder." Her eyes fixed on Robert's but he didn't notice. He was somewhere else.

"Almost a little bit of excitement," he said wistfully. "I almost got a little bit excited."

"Hum."

"I shouldn't tell you this because you'll hold it against me." Robert had quickly sensed long ago, by Margaret's total devotion to him and persistent attempts to get to the inner man, that she was vulnerable. He liked that. He knew he was her total focus of attention. Nothing could be more appealing to a manipulative exhibitionist. Robert knew he could toy with her by holding back, lying and twisting facts, or simply changing the topic when he didn't like it. He enjoyed the feeling of power in frustrating someone who wanted to help him. Yet Margaret was probably one of the very few people Robert had ever encountered in his life who felt that way about him. Robert could gauge how much power he held over Margaret by her response to his questions, or titbits. She was always interested in what he had to say. That was how it should be. If she played the right way, he might throw her some snippets that could let her know what really happened. Or rather, what could have happened. But not too much. Robert never liked to give too much away.

"Robert I won't. Please Robert. I've, I'm, look please be honest with me Robert. That's all I'm asking you to do. It's not…"

"You'll tell Lorraine. I'm not telling you anything." Yes, he had her. He was in control. It was a wonderful feeling. She dealt with people like him all the time, yet she was totally powerless against him.

"Give me a bible and let me swear on the bible that I will not tell Lorraine. Robert, please. I haven't told Lorraine anything in seven years."

"Yeah, I know."

"Why am I going to tell her now?"

"I know."

"Just tell her the truth. Share it."

"I just got almost a little bit excited. This is one of the worst crimes you could ever commit." He smirked.

"Hum." Margaret was disgusted but tried not to show it.

"And I can beat them at it."

"Yes, why do you think you can beat them at it?"

"Because I didn't do it Marg. They can't unless it's the Lindy Chamberlain thing, they can't... and even she beat them."

Margaret felt him slip through her fingers yet again. Disappointment queued up behind fear, bewilderment, anxiety. Her head was spinning. Now she was running on pure adrenalin.

"*Eventually* she beat them," she said.

Robert sighed. "I know that, I know."

Margaret tried again.

"But you can still go along, leading them along, you know."

"I don't want this life, I hate it but at the moment there's only one thing better and that's being with Lorraine."

Robert then flirted with the idea of going away to live and ringing Margaret weekly but then discounted the idea. Then he said:

"Well on the Beasley thing, I have no shame or remorse."

Margaret hypothesised that Robert might have decided to kidnap Sheree to create a drama before going to Mildura. The 'buzz' would sustain him while he could not 'perform' with his family present. Margaret suggested he could have snatched Sheree 'just to talk dirty to' and then drop her off further along the road. Margaret was leaving every way open for Robert to talk about what he had done. And he picked up the thread.

"I might do that to a 12 or 13 year old or even 11 or 12," he confessed.

Again Margaret was filled with hope.

"That might not be likely because someone that age would be difficult to snatch and would resist too much," she pointed out.

In a corrective tone, Robert said, "But not for sexual purposes..."

"- No, not for sexual purposes, for -"

"...but for a prank," he said. But he deflected any further questioning. He only wanted to talk about Lorraine and how she was faring.

The Murder of Sheree

WHENEVER KERRI was missing for more than a few hours, Steve usually knew where she was. Still unable to accept her daughter's death, Kerri would find herself drawn to Sheree's grave at the Mornington Cemetery. Sometimes she couldn't remember how or when she got to the gravesite. Other times it was a deliberate visit, before which she would buy red roses and sometimes a little gift at special times. Some weeks she went three times, other weeks only once. Sometimes it was during the day, sometimes it would be late at night. She would stand over the plaque on Sheree's grave and talk silently to her little girl.

"I miss you. I want to be with you," Kerri would tell her.

She fought the urge to suicide, reminding herself that she had other children to care for.

THE NEXT THERAPY session was on January 13. Again Margaret sat opposite Robert as he settled comfortably into his leather seat. They were talking about Sheree again.

"Do you think I could do something like that?" he asked. He had a curious look. His head was tilted slightly and he had a smile on his face. He was the professor, asking the brilliant but still slightly naive student for an answer to see if she was on the right track.

"Yes, I've already gone through that last week when I said how I thought it could have happened," Margaret explained. "I said it could not be proven that the child had been sexually molested and that I could say truthfully that I did not think that he would have gone that far but that he only picked her up -"

"- For a ride," Robert interrupted. "Tell me what you think I did then," he said. Clearly he was enjoying himself. He had an evil glint in his eye. Margaret continued to meet his gaze but felt as if she was under a magnifying glass. Robert's eyes never left her face. She felt he was studying her to see if he could shock a reaction out of her.

Margaret said she thought he could pick a 6-year-old child up.

"A 6-year-old child?" he teased.

The therapist said she thought he could. She told him he had shown he was not good at ages and he was aware now that older girls could identify him or his vehicle.

The Murder of Sheree

"All right. Go on," he commanded. He settled back in his chair a little.

Margaret guessed at what Robert could have asked Sheree.

"Would you like to come for a ride and see something?" or "What have you got under that pretty pink suit?"

This was not what Robert wanted to hear. Perhaps Margaret was getting too close for comfort. His face set and he shut off immediately. Then he leant down and whipped a piece of paper from his shoulderbag. As he unfolded the paper on his lap he said, "I want to ask you something." His actions spoke louder than the words. *I am in control here. These sessions will be run the way I want to run them.*

He read from his notes.

"Would you tell Lorraine and (brother) Graeme that I did not get her in the car for immoral purposes?"

Margaret felt her heart skip. She said she would.

"Would you tell them I'm not a paedophile?"

"Yes, I would." Anything to get further down the road towards the truth.

Robert quickly consigned his notes back to his bag. He was covering all his bases, very carefully, before he drafted this next statement. It might be his only chance. And he had successfully changed the topic, bamboozling Margaret. When he was gone, Margaret wondered why he even bothered coming.

The next day Robert rang.

"What we were talking about yesterday, about those things I could have said..."

Margaret was listening intently. "Yes....?"

"I could have said them but it's hypothetical," Robert said.

He needed to cover up a little more. Therapy was all right as long as it was fun, and it didn't reveal too much.

BRIAN LEE hadn't seen Robert since the day Robert was talking animatedly to all the children at church. Yet on January 9, 1992, Robert rang Brian at his Wantirna South home.

"Hello?"

"This is Rob Lowe. How do you feel about talking to me?"

The call caught Brian off guard.

"To be honest, I feel uncomfortable," he said.

"Well in that case I won't bother you," Robert sighed. "I was just going to ask a couple of questions concerning Benjamin but because you feel uncomfortable I'll go." He hung up. Brian looked at the phone, then walked away. Two minutes later, the phone rang. It was Robert again.

"I know you feel uncomfortable and I'm not sure why, but anyway, I was wondering if you had heard any news of Benjamin."

Brian was a little annoyed.

"It should be easy to understand why I feel uncomfortable. All of the drama, police visits, attacks on the house, Lorraine being hit with a bottle, paint daubed on the car."

Robert loudly protested his innocence. Brian knew it was useless to have an argument with Robert. He wore everyone into the ground. Brian changed the topic and told Robert all he knew of Benjamin. When he finished, Robert expressed his surprise at the attitude of the church members who felt uncomfortable with him. Again he talked of his complete innocence of any wrongdoing, how he had co-operated with the police and how he hadn't been charged. For those reasons, he couldn't understand why the church members felt and acted any differently towards him than they had before. Brian said he was in no position to know the truth.

"Only God and you know that," Brian said.

Robert agreed and said God was totally aware of his innocence and that God also knew who and where the offender was.

Instinctively Brian picked up a pen and asked Robert how he filled his days. Robert told him he was running between five and 10 kilometres a day, riding his son's bike around, visiting hospitals and calling on the infirm, doing voluntary work, attending church at Rosebud, reading his bible, going shopping and keeping fit. But his life was boring and unrewarding now that he was unemployed.

Brian kept listening as Robert switched the conversation back to the Sheree Beasley investigation. Brian started taking notes. He only wrote what he thought were the key words Robert was saying because he couldn't write as quickly as Robert spoke. As the conversation progressed, Brian wrote: "Car", "car colour", then "a girl", "a little girl", "Sheree", "Sheree Beasley", "taken", "murdered", "the day". Then Robert told Brian he was at home by 1.50pm to 2.00pm.

"In this country you're innocent until proven guilty," Robert reminded him.

Brian thought Robert was placing a great weight on this principle. But Brian saw things very differently. He told Robert that if anybody was guilty of something, then they were guilty. The possibility that someone may not be found out or not convicted doesn't make them innocent, he said. They discussed this at length although Brian had no success in pushing his argument. It appeared to him Robert believed that if you are not found out, no matter the crime, then you are innocent.

Unprompted, Robert explained his prior police convictions were minor. They were "in the category of offensive behaviour," he said. Then he told Brian he had a "thorn in the flesh that I have had to bear with for years and I admit that this is a weakness". Robert steered the curious conversation back to the police. He said he was being persecuted. Brian was interested in Robert's statements to the police before September 1991. Stories had begun circulating in the church.

"Prior to that date I didn't tell any lies but I may have told half-truths," Robert said.

Brian didn't understand. Robert told him it meant telling the truth but not telling everything.

The phone call finished at 4.24pm - 85 minutes after it began.

MATTHEW WOOD was door knocking again in Florence Avenue, Rosebud. Robert Lowe rode into the street on his son's red bike and approached Wood.

"Hello, how are you going?" Lowe said, cheerily.

"Good thank you."

"Have you got time to talk?"

"Sure."

"How is Lorraine and the boys?"

"Very unwell, thank you. Are you ready to come down and tell us the truth yet?" It was worth a shot.

"I've already told you the truth. You don't seem to want to believe me."

"It's not a matter of not believing you." Matthew smiled. "It's just that we've disproven your story."

"I'd rather not talk about that," Lowe said dismissively. "Tell me, how are the boys and Lorraine?"

"I was talking to her the other day. She's fine," Matthew said.

"Is she still looking well? I've been told she's lost a lot of weight."

"With what she's gone through, it's no wonder. She told me you are going on a holiday. When are you going?"

"Oh, I don't know, maybe the weekend." Robert was enjoying the conversation. He smiled.

"Where are you going to go?"

"I'll probably go up north to the border, have a look around."

"How will you get there?"

"Probably hitchhike. I might get the bus."

"How long are you going for?"

"I don't know. It depends on how it goes. I might go for a week or two. Why are you so interested?"

"I'm just interested, that's all. I've no doubt that Lorraine will ask me what you're doing."

Lowe prepared to ride off on the child's bike. "Give my love to Lorraine and the boys," he said cheerfully. "No doubt I'll see them around." He rode off with a wave and not a care in the world.

"I'll pass it on," Matthew said. "See you around." The policeman shook his head as he watched him ride off. Matthew turned and walked up another driveway.

THE FOLLOWING day the surveillance police saw Lowe leave the Rosebud unit at 10.30am on his son's red bike. He wore his shorts, shirt and green cap as he slowly rode the tiny bicycle to the Rosebud post office and stepped inside. Ten minutes later he rode east along the foreshore tracks towards McCrae. Robert had tried doing anti-surveillance since he had suspected he was being followed. The police had laughed as they watched him hide in bushes or under trees, looking around for the invisible police. But today, Detective Senior Constable Graham Jones and the other police noticed Lowe was not riding around in circles. Graham lost sight of his target about 100m west of Parkmore Road but other police could still see him riding. Instead of trying to find Lowe in the scrubby foreshore, Graham backed a hunch. He drove his unmarked police car to Parkmore Road and parked near the two phone boxes Steve Ludlow had used to ring the police seven months earlier to alert them to Sheree's disappearance. Then he stepped into one of the booths and pretended he was making a phone call. He had a clear view of the Nepean Highway and the foreshore area to the north, and right along Parkmore Road to the south, almost all the way to Sheree's former home.

Lowe dropped his bike in scrub, then jogged south along the track to the Nepean Highway. Then he hid behind some bushes. He popped his head out and looked west along the Nepean Highway, checking to see if he was being followed. Then he came from behind the bush and briskly stepped on to the Nepean Highway and looked up and down the road. Just to ensure he was safe, he quickly walked about 10m back onto the foreshore track – and then turned his attention to Parkmore Road. With a set face he strode across the Nepean Highway and continued up Parkmore Road, past Graham Jones talking to himself on the phone. Lowe walked south directly down the very centre of Parkmore Road for approximately 30m before he stopped abruptly and looked quickly up and down the street. He was standing on the spot where Sheree had been kidnapped. Graham watched as Lowe stood there for a full minute before he turned around and walked back to the highway.

He was walking very swiftly but daren't break into a run. He crossed the highway, reached the foreshore track and then sprinted at full speed. He dived onto another, smaller track and then the surveillance police lost him in the undergrowth. Having relived the excitement of a little girl's terror, Lowe was now hiding in the bushes. At 11.38am, the police spied a relaxed Robert Lowe, riding west along the Nepean Highway. After doing some shopping amongst the young mums and their little charges at Safeway in Jetty Road, Lowe returned home, smiling, shortly after 2pm.

Joy Greenhill had seen Robert Lowe in the Safeway store. A local newspaper employee had told her Robert Lowe was the suspect and had pointed him out to her one day as he was walking down the street. She followed him around the aisles, watching him from a distance, with a morbid fascination. Even if he wasn't the man who killed Sheree, she thought he was a little weird. He walked with his chest pushed out and surveyed the area around him as if he owned it. He was full of his own importance. Joy wondered if he could have murdered Sheree. It was too bizarre to think the killer would be walking around, large as life, in the area where the investigation was at its most intense. Surely the culprit would be a long way away by now.

MARGARET WAS attacked in Kingsbury Lodge at Larundel while counselling two criminally insane inmates. That attack, coupled with the stress of dealing with Robert Lowe, the ethics issue and 25 years of dealing with sex offenders was taking its toll. Feeling the strain, she sought help. The psychologist became her full time therapist. The other was a Christian psychiatrist who thought Margaret was dealing with something that others had seen before. She told the doctor she couldn't understand Robert Lowe and how she couldn't get to the man underneath. She told him of Robert's polite behaviour, of how he was quite charming, yet he was incorrigible when it came to offending with children. The doctor told her to read the book *People of the Lie* by M. Scott Peck, subtitled *Towards the Psychology of Evil*. She did and she cried. She read it again and she cried again. She showed it to a few other professional people who knew Robert and they all said the same thing.

"This book should be called the autobiography of Robert Lowe."

Margaret was never into Evil versus Good, Satan versus God thinking but what she read stunned her. Peck talked of Evil as a noun. As she read through the book again, she thought of all the terrible criminals she had met in her life. None of them ever came close to Robert Lowe. In his book, Peck told her that a diagnostic tool *par excellence* for recognising evil was revulsion. She recalled she felt a little revolted the first time he ever came into her office. She realised now she had overcompensated because it was too unscientific. She remembered chastising herself. *You can't feel like this Margaret, you've been dealing with men like this for 20 odd years.*

Peck's book told her that when evil people 'get into' killing people, particularly children, they are so insensitive they literally don't see their victim. Margaret recalled the same phrase Robert had been telling her for the past few months. *I didn't see her Margaret, I didn't see the little girl.* On one occasion, when he was 'fabricating' a confessional statement that wasn't quite clear, Margaret asked him, "Why did you do that?"

She shivered as she remembered his answer. "Oh, insensitive, I suppose."

She could see that he followed the dialogue set out in a book he had never read.

Therapists fly away from the term evil. It wasn't until she read the book that Margaret started to believe in its existence. And she had met it, and would meet it at the next session with Robert Lowe. In his book Peck says people are drawn to the light but some people are consumed by it and some people try to destroy it. And he says it is very dangerous to battle with evil. It can make you very sick. But if you battle with evil and you win, there's a small shift of power in the world. Margaret thought of Robert, talking about Sheree in the 'as if' mode. His eyes, particularly when he talked about what he had done, never left her face.

Every other patient Margaret had dealt with was bad but Robert was something different again. Peter Reid had been a bad lad. Everybody she had dealt with had good reason for turning out the way they did or for behaving the way they did. But the Peter Reids put their hands up and said 'I did it, I deserve what I get'. Everybody that Margaret had ever known in therapy had been like that. Robert was the only one who did not come clean about his personal behaviour.

Gradually the truth hit home. Margaret didn't tell many people at first because she was concerned they would think she had lost her marbles. Even to her it sounded horrendous, sort of fantastic. Margaret Hobbs, professional therapist and atheist, acknowledged to herself that she had met true Evil.

Meanwhile, Robert decided to go on a holiday. In his absence, the maelstrom abated, at least temporarily, and Margaret reflected more objectively on his behaviour. She read through some of her notes she had made in the past three months. She realised clearer than ever before how hard it would be to ever get Robert to admit the truth about Sheree Beasley, if he had killed her. She knew he was lying about something - the police had smashed his alibi. But he was the sort of bloke who could make up a story just to revel in the attention. So was he a killer or not? Probably yes, possibly no. Possibly yes, probably no. Margaret wavered from day to day and hour to hour. She reassessed Robert's thinking to see if she could see a way in, a way to get to the truth. But she saw formidable walls in front of her. Robert had explained to her that if a person apologised for some crime or event, it means that person is seeking a pardon by signalling that the crime or event should not be considered a fair representation of what the person is really like. Bizarre, she thought, but that is how he thinks. He believed also that such an apology separates the good self from the bad self and promises more acceptable behaviour in the future. She read through some notes of Robert's homilies she had taken down.

"When apologising, an individual is attempting to say 'I have repented and should be forgiven,'" thus making it appear that no further rehabilitation is required," Margaret read. The only problem with that, Margaret thought - and it was a big problem - was that he kept reoffending almost immediately. But Robert never really wanted to talk about that side of his 'problem'.

The last three months of 1991 had given Margaret her most informative insight into Robert in the seven years she had known him. His implicitly threatening behaviour and illogical thought processes, together with his consistent lies about June 29, were scary enough for Margaret. She felt revulsion when she was near him as well as fear. But he saddened her too. He was an emotional desert. Margaret saw a man who could only adopt roles, not live them. Certainly, he gave the outward appearance of believing in those roles but they were simply brilliant but empty performances. He strutted emotion in her clinic. He cried, he got angry, he was remorseful, feigned conscience, talked of remorse, then denied or ignored morality. Margaret finally realised he was just playing a game - with the police, with her, with Lorraine and the boys, with Sheree's memory. What really brought it home to her was his total lack of joy or contentment in his life. He understood anger, frustration, envy, hate, rage - the negative emotions were his strong points. He was never happy, except when he was attacking youngsters. Margaret realised that when she noticed she had never witnessed any mention, or comprehension, by Robert of the feelings of joy, contentment or happiness. When he tried to portray those emotions, Margaret could actually see straight through him. That's when she saw there was nothing inside. What a terrifying way to live a life, Margaret thought.

LOWE NO LONGER dyed his hair, which had now turned its natural colour of grey, with brown tinges. Often he didn't comb it properly, or at all. A beard was flourishing, and he continually wore the same clothes. Any witnesses back in Melbourne would have difficulty reconciling the grey wavy hair and whiskers with the younger-looking, dark-haired, clean-shaven man who had taken a little girl from Rosebud back in June.

ROBERT CONTINUED on to Sydney, then to the country home of Michael Chamberlain. But the former Seventh Day Adventist pastor wasn't home. Then he continued north to Brisbane, calling in to visit his best man from 20 years earlier, Pastor Graeme Smith at his home in The Gap. The cleric was amazed. He remembered Robert as an attentive, immaculate man when he was with Lorraine. Now he looked like a vagrant. He smelt bad and he was unkempt and unshaven. Graeme thought he looked under a bit of stress. Robert sat in his old friend's home and told the pastor about the Sheree Beasley case. He protested his innocence. He had been wrongly accused and was totally innocent. The churchman thought it was a peculiar visit. He hadn't seen Robert in more than a decade yet he had popped in for only an hour and left. What was that all about?

Robert continued north, staying at cheap accommodation houses and occasionally with people who gave him a lift when he hitchhiked. Then he stayed at Daintree for a while, swimming and sunning himself. It became a very relaxing and replenishing holiday.

The Murder of Sheree

WHILE ROBERT was taking time out from script writing and trying to dodge police interest, Lorraine was doing a bit of cleaning up at home. She was still in shock over the turn of events and found she was functioning like a robot. Cleaning might give her something to do to take her mind off things. Her husband a murderer? It couldn't be, could it?

She started on the toilets, then moved to the kitchen, the family room, the bedrooms. In her typing room, she started tossing out magazines to make way for the boys' school magazine. There she found some notes Robert had taken during a bible course years before. She held the folder and again the good memories flooded into her mind. She could only see the good man she had known for all those years. The kind, caring husband, the man she was to spend her life with, the man who had been so good to his boys. The memories overwhelmed her and the tears welled up again.

Stop it, she told herself. *Be strong.*

She opened the folder. Hidden behind Robert's handwritten notes she found a *Women's Weekly* magazine dated April 1989. She opened the magazine and almost fainted. The feature article was about the parents of young children who had been abducted or disappeared. She hadn't put it in the folder and she knew darn well the boys wouldn't have, either. Why would Robert want to keep that? And why hide it? Why in the bible notes? She ran to the phone, and called the police. She knew they would want to know.

NEIL GREENHILL was home alone, sitting on his bed. The house was silent. Slanted sunlight pierced the still room. The day outside was warm and it would normally be called a 'nice' day. But Neil didn't see it. He was wracked by inner turmoil. He had been talking to a psychologist in an effort to overcome his grief, which helped a bit, but everything in his life seemed upside down. Nothing made sense anymore. He shut himself off from the world he no longer understood. He had built a wall between himself and his own family. Laughter had died in his home. Wife Denise and their two daughters were too scared to show any signs of joy for fear of upsetting him.

Neil had always been a happy-go-lucky guy. Denise was the disciplinarian at home, Neil was the funster. But now he was angry, grumpy, weepy, snappy. His grief consumed him. Sheree was dead and now she had been properly buried but the mongrel who did it was still free.

His feeling of powerlessness was all-consuming. He wanted to help find the killer, but couldn't. And he didn't know how to deal with the pain. Dazed, he stared at the carpet, then at his feet. In his mind a befuddling mix of death, Satan, Sheree, pain, grief and confusion blended with an overpowering sense of hopelessness. *I can't deal with this*, he thought. He wondered if Kylie Maybury's grandfather felt like this just before he killed himself.

Neil weighed up his options. On one side he had a lovely family, a good job, good friends. On the other there was the sense that life was not worth living. When life loses meaning, death holds no fear. It was only the realisation his death would cause his family more pain that stopped him taking his own life.

CHAPTER ELEVEN

◆

THE ZENITH crew searched for more clues yet again, this time from Arthur's Seat to Red Hill and back to the Nepean Highway. There were more doorknocks in and around Florence Avenue, Parkmore Road and Winthunga, just in case anything had been missed. And something had been. They found a witness who hadn't been home during the other doorknocks. Janine Kent told them she found Sheree's bike, its front wheel still spinning, lying on the road on June 29 shortly after 2pm. Janine had picked up the bike and put it against the tree. That information was kept secret from the public. Only Janine and the abductor knew the bike hadn't been put against the tree by Sheree's abductor.

The task force also worked hard trying to eliminate every other reasonable suspect. They hoped that, in the end, only Robert Lowe would be left. The police dared to get hopeful as it was really starting to look like they were on the right track. Lowe was worried enough to consult Margaret Hobbs and even though he hadn't said anything concrete about Sheree, he was getting better in the suspect-stakes all the time.

Detective Senior Constable Alex Bartsch knocked on the door. A slim, short man answered. He was another suspect who had prior convictions involving children and he had only recently moved into the area. Alex asked for his name. Mark Bensen, the man Robert Lowe spent so much time with years before when he left Caulfield Grammar, gave the detective his particulars. Then he proceeded to give an alibi for June 29. Alex knew he could check that alibi out easily. But he couldn't work out why this man was so reluctant to provide any further details about himself. Alex asked him if he knew Robert Arthur Selby Lowe. After all, Lowe's kids had gone to the same school where Bensen had been teaching physical education. But Mr Bensen said he had never heard of the man.

Alex felt he was lying, but he couldn't work out why. It wasn't until after the investigation was over Alex learned Mr Bensen had spent all those nights at Lowe's house, talking about unfair dismissal. He never did find out what they were talking about.

WITH THE JOB completed in Rosebud, Zenith moved back to the Homicide Squad offices in the St Kilda Road Police Complex on February 7. Apart from the Homicide crew of Paul Hollowood, Alex Bartsch, Paul O'Halloran and Murray Gregor, only Matthew Wood, Andrew Gustke, Dave Noonan and Gavin Wallace were kept on. Paul Hollowood resisted pressure to make an arrest. He knew that - apart from being totally unprofessional - if he arrested Lowe too soon and waited for the extra evidence, it might not be forthcoming. And traditionally in most Australian police forces, once a task force makes an arrest, it loses its resources. Hollowood would need them just to put the brief of evidence together.

In March, Paul instructed Detective Senior Constable Murray Gregor to collect and compile all the evidence to see if there was enough to build a circumstantial case. Not only did Murray have to chase witnesses and other police officers (who are notoriously slow at providing statements for other officers briefs of evidence) but he had to nut out what was going to be included and what wasn't. And that meant reading and re-reading transcripts of hundreds of hours of tape recordings.

Meanwhile, snippets of information were still coming in from the listening device in Margaret Hobbs' room. That didn't raise Paul's spirits at all. He knew they would wait forever for Robert Lowe to come and confess. Because of that, extra duties fell to the already work-weary detectives. Paul knew that if all other avenues in the investigation weren't covered, a smart lawyer could use that unfinished work to create an element of doubt in a Supreme Court trial. For Paul, it was much better for the police to say, "We eliminated all other suspects except Mr Robert Lowe", rather than, "I don't know who else we didn't check."

Paul knew that if Lowe did confess, a clever barrister would make much of his propensity to lie. Along this vein, Paul sent his men out to speak to people Lowe had merely mentioned in passing in his dealings with Margaret Hobbs. Hollowood instructed them to speak to those people without having them realise they were being questioned. The detectives were trying to corroborate whether some things Lowe was telling Margaret were true, even if they were just about a car, a visit to a park, or a chat with a friend about a typewriter. They found most of what he was saying was pretty spot on.

KERRI AND STEVE married on March 14, 1992 at the Frankston Botanical Gardens. They didn't ask any of Kerri's family to attend. The couple had to borrow money for the service, conducted by a celebrant, and only their daughters were part of the bridal party. It was a quiet, simple affair, carried out not far from children playing happily on playground equipment while their parents picnicked nearby. It was Kerri and Steve's one happy occasion amid all the misery and despair. Then they went home and waited for the next disaster to hit them. They didn't know what it would be but as sure as eggs it would come. There was no money, or reason, for a honeymoon.

ON MARCH 17, 1992, Robert was back in Melbourne. He visited Margaret at her Fitzroy clinic where they started talking about guilt.

"What does God tell you to do about guilt?" Margaret asked.

"He tells you if you confess it - and I always heed this because it's entirely true and Lorraine knows that - if you confess it and turn your back on it and, um, He wipes it away and actually He forgets about it Himself."

"Yes, but you have to stop, don't you?"

"Yes."

"You've got to stop, you've got to truly repent. You've got to make amends."

"Yeah."

"What amends are you making for what you have done?"

"Well, from the Christian point of view you don't have to actually make amends, um, and, and I believe in the Catholics, you do, but in Protestants, you don't."

"You just have to confess and you're forgiven?" Margaret tried not to sound incredulous. After all, she was talking to a 55-year-old man.

"Well if you gotta...confessed then you have to got to be, um, totally repentant and promise not to do it again. God knows that you will make a mistake but..."

"Well, where have you done this before? Have you repented before and asked God for help before?"

"Yes."

"All the years you've been doing it?"

"Yes, yes."

"It hasn't worked has it?"

"No."

"Why?" Margaret looked at him for a few seconds. "'Cos you've never truly repented?"

"Because I'm...it could be, it could be, I've never been shocked into my system that I am now."

Margaret pointed out things weren't going all that well for him.

"You've got a wife and kids who are frightened of you."

"Only because of the Sheree Beasley thing," Robert said matter-of-factly. It was of no concern.

As the session progressed, Margaret nudged closer to the heart of the matter.

"I just think you're involved."

"Okay."

"You know, I don't think you needed the child. I know you didn't sexually assault her but I think you were involved," Margaret said.

"Okay."

Margaret could feel her heart thumping against her clothing.

"Then you have to be honest with me, Robert."

"I will. You've got all the weight against you Marg and against me. I don't blame you thinking I'm involved. From time to time you've stood up immensely well, remarkably well, but there must always be doubts but you have promised to support me and I appreciate that."

"Yes, I do. I've gone -"

" - Of course, there must be doubts." Robert said, nodding. He looked very sure of himself. Again it seemed like a conversation in academia.

The Murder of Sheree

Margaret thought a good starting point would be to talk about girls in general. Robert picked up the thread.

"I could, I have a, almost a block if you like, when I go backwards and try to remember. It's not necessarily purposely a block. It's two things. One is if I've done it I probably want to block it out of my mind and the second thing is, from the Christian point of view, that is supposed to be how I should behave."

"What is?" *What on earth was he talking about?*

"In that, if I am, if I am, if I have something against somebody, if I've something against yourself for instance, like that."

"...you mean?"

"No, if you forgive, if you come to me and say 'Robert, I'm sorry I blamed you, I've blamed you for that', or, 'I did tell a lie' or said something like that, I'd forgive you because you've admitted it and become repentant and at that stage of that transaction I, you've asked for my forgiveness. I've given you my forgiveness. At that stage it is forgiven and forgotten."

"I understand that." She didn't agree but she could see it made sense to him.

"And that's what God does and I literally sort of carry that principle out 'cos I don't like people digging it up two years later again. It's finished and forgotten and this is the same principle that I work on, my previous convictions that I have difficulty remembering them, 'cos as far as Lorraine and I am concerned they are forgiven and forgotten and I'm sure Lorraine even puts them out of her mind. It's just the police have brought them all up and it's the shock of it. If Lorraine hadn't put them out of her mind she probably wouldn't be nearly as shocked but she's - the police have brought them up and put them back into her mind when she probably doesn't even remember and therefore probably thinks that I've done this and haven't even told her about it."

"You haven't told me this."

"About what? No, I'm talking about the offensive behaviour cases."

There was 'hypothethical' talk about the murder, then Robert talked about his beliefs.

"I believe there are two spirits," he told Margaret. "A Holy Spirit of God and a spirit of the Devil - "

" - Yes, so do I," Margaret said. "The greater propensity for good - "

"- And I believe because of my misdeeds of the past that the Devil has attacked our family...And the fact of the Sheree Beasley thing is just another thing on top intended to keep Lorraine and I apart. I believe it is a spirit that has attacked us and I've dabbled in sin, dabbled in lying and other things and God has - and, and that has enabled the Devil to get into our family."

"Through you?"

"Through me. I now think that the Devil is actually using Lorraine. I don't want to blame her 'cos she doesn't recognise it but the Devil is using Lorraine to tear the marriage apart and that is contrary to God's will. He doesn't want any families broken up or marriages split."

"So the Devil's been working through you for quite a while, hasn't he?"

"Yes, he has."

"You've given him access to the family?"

"Yes, yes. I admit that but I think the Devil has got off my back now 'cos I've behaved myself for six months and he's jumped onto Lorraine. She doesn't recognise him."

The talk only served to remind Margaret what she had read in *People of the Lie*. This was really very evil stuff. The man's expression never changed when he talked about Sheree. Perhaps he showed a little boredom, because he didn't really want to talk about it, but there was not even a hint of remorse, or guilt. Maybe he was innocent, Margaret thought.

Robert was worried he might be called before an inquest. It was his second major concern. His first was always getting Lorraine back. He started to write a letter while Margaret looked on. He read aloud as he wrote:

```
So what do we do? It isn't easy but once we've got
over the initial problem, we should, I believe,
have an even better marriage. Eventually if we
learn from our own mistakes. If you require honesty,
humility, courage and assistance, we also have on
our side excellent peer group support, and just
before that I've got, (inaudible) Trust will emerge,
the safeguard and for any inquest, we, we commit
ourselves to God for victory and protection.
```

He put his pen down and he started to cry. He was in a bind. He left with his letter half finished.

DETECTIVE SENIOR Constable Alex Bartsch first met Margaret on March 27, after sitting in a flat nearby, listening to her talk to Lowe for several hours. Alex had heard her talking with Lowe many times before he met her. It seemed to him Margaret felt she couldn't quite control Lowe, that she wasn't getting anywhere with him. Alex thought Lowe was controlling the conversations, pushing them any way he wanted. Whenever Margaret got to the heart of the Sheree Beasley case, Lowe would divert her to another topic.

Initially Alex thought Margaret was playing games with the police. Whenever any of the officers asked her what had been said in a session (usually after they had just listened to it), she would tell them very little, if anything at all. Before Alex met Margaret he was determined that was going to stop. At the same time he thought she was a long way towards having Robert confess, without really knowing it herself. He planned to simply ask Margaret outright if she thought Lowe was Sheree's killer. Alex wanted to ask her if this situation of verbal game playing was going to go on *ad infinitum*.

His first impression surprised him. He saw immediately that Margaret was trapped. She didn't know whether she was doing the right thing by continuing to see Lowe, or by asking him about Sheree, trying to get concrete answers. Alex felt for her. He could see she was frightened of Robert. He wanted to tell her that every time Robert was in for therapy, there were two policemen within thirty seconds of her rooms. But he couldn't say a thing that might compromise the investigation. She might tell her patient.

The first thing Margaret said to Alex when they met was, "Do you know I am not a doctor?" She was being defensive.

"Yes, I know you're not a doctor." Alex said.

"Right, got that cleared up," she said, looking the detective in the eye.

Margaret was reluctant to go into detail about her sessions with Robert. Alex felt Margaret wasn't on Lowe's side but she wasn't on the side of the

The Murder of Sheree

police either. And the police felt things were going too slowly. The listening device had been in Margaret's clinic for six months. Zenith felt the occasional visits to Margaret would lift her spirits and induce her to persevere with Lowe. If she didn't - if it all became too much and she refused to see him anymore - that would probably be the end of the evidence-gathering for the police. And Murray Gregor's assessment after sifting through all the available material, was that there wasn't enough evidence to sustain a murder charge. There was very little that would stand up in court.

As they talked, Alex was very impressed by Margaret. She was obviously a formidable woman, with a powerful intellect. It was equally clear, though, that her nerve was tested to the limit. She looked drawn, and Alex thought she was a little jumpy. He suspected if he was a therapist in the same situation he would feel the same. He thought it must be like getting stuck in a huge maze, with no map to help you out, while different people with different interests were continually advising you to go in opposite directions.

They started talking about Robert Lowe. Margaret obliquely told Alex some of the things Robert had said. Alex nodded and took some notes. Then he cut to the chase.

"Did he say he did it?"

"No, he says he didn't do it," Margaret said. "I don't know whether he's done it or not. That's just the way he is. He's a persistent liar and he's pretty good at it."

Alex and Margaret were to become good friends.

Robert occasionally called into the house in Mannering Drive and rang Lorraine, but she refused to speak to him. He started calling or writing to other people, asking them to pop in to his home and speak to Lorraine for him. They did so until Lorraine told them how upsetting it was. Thwarted, Robert turned to Margaret, gently pushing her towards Lorraine. He told Margaret he was now behaving himself, that he was innocent and misunderstood by the police. Then he would ask Margaret to pass on his love to Lorraine. Margaret had told him countless times that Lorraine would think more highly of him if he spoke the truth. Finally he asked Margaret to ask Lorraine to come to therapy. Margaret could act as chair. Specifically, he said he was going to ask Lorraine not to divorce him if he pleaded guilty to the manslaughter of Sheree Beasley. Margaret consulted a lawyer. Robert was about to admit to killing a little girl and now he wanted to talk about it further. Margaret didn't know where she stood legally but the lawyer reassured her. He told her it was perfectly all right for her to chair the meeting. It was a legitimate form of therapy.

Margaret could see the end of the nightmare in sight. She spoke to Lorraine and told her Robert had been behaving himself. Now he wanted to talk to Lorraine about Sheree and their marriage. Lorraine held out for a few weeks, demanding to know precisely what Robert's involvement was in Sheree's abduction and death. When, via Margaret, Robert pledged to tell her, she reluctantly agreed to go. She didn't know what to expect but she hoped the meeting might at least get to the bottom of all the mess. A meeting was arranged at Margaret's clinic on March 30, 1992.

ROBERT ARRIVED half an hour early. Margaret noticed how he had tidied himself up. He had shaved and he had changed his shirt - he was wearing Lorraine's favourite. He was a little apprehensive - appropriately so, Margaret thought. Robert recognised this as a grave situation. His only consideration was the marriage. Margaret was apprehensive yet for the first time in a long while, she felt there was some hope.

Robert reached down to the floor and pulled some notes from his shoulder bag, and started reading. He was doing his homework on what he had to say. Margaret saw his lips silently mouthing the words.

Lorraine arrived wearing a bright floral dress. It was the first time she had worn it. As she entered the room, she saw Robert, on her right, stand quickly. She was very nervous and very frail. She didn't know what to expect. Margaret thought she looked a little frightened of Robert.

Robert sat in his usual brown leather chair, his back to the southern wall. He was sitting directly opposite Margaret. Lorraine sat on a two seater couch on his left, making up the triangle.

Not far away, in the cramped loungeroom of a small flat, Alex Bartsch and Andrew Gustke were listening to the conversation on their radio/tape recorder. Both men expected the case could be blown wide open

The Murder of Sheree

because of the brinkmanship. They knew Lowe had to tell Lorraine something or he risked not seeing her again. He would have to stand, completely alone against the police, without an alibi and possibly with his wife testifying against him. Alex and Andrew thought if ever there was going to be a confession, this would be the day. Robert had pushed everything to the absolute edge.

Robert tentatively started talking.

"As far as Sheree is concerned, as I said, I wanted to save our marriage at all costs and I would consider...spending whatever number of years in jail. Everybody's giving me different figures on that, even on a manslaughter thing. I mean, you've even got to get it to that point. I mean, if I'm going to be charged with murder, I might get 24 years."

Lorraine stared at him wide-eyed. She could not believe the words were coming out of his mouth. She had had immense difficulty in trying to visualise Robert putting a little girl into the car. All she could see was the good side of Robert she had been exposed to over the years. This talk of murder was so foreign. She just couldn't picture him doing anything like that at all.

Robert continued to profess his innocence, yet Alex and Andrew were happy. Things had started off okay. They looked at each other with raised eyebrows.

Margaret was keen to work to an agenda. She wanted to gradually get to the talk of the confession of manslaughter. But Lorraine only wanted to get to the crux of the whole issue. She'd been mucked about long enough.

"Have you got something to tell me that you haven't told anyone else?" She looked at her husband. He was staring coldly back at her. Lorraine was aware she was shaking visibly. "Have you?" she pressed.

"If I said yes, what would it do to my marriage? And if I said no, what would it do to my marriage?" He was very calm.

Margaret looked at Lorraine and saw she was terribly agitated. Margaret thought it was probably the first time Lorraine had confronted Robert like this.

"You're answering my questions with another question," Lorraine said.

"Sorry," he said. He went on. "Lorri, if I just tell you every single thing

The Murder of Sheree

and you come back to me and say, 'Look, it makes no difference to the marriage', it's still not going to do anything. I see no benefit in - I need some incentive and you know... I don't know. I know the truth but if the marriage is going to fall apart - and I don't believe it's God's will it should - I know it's a huge thing and I don't believe anybody should tamper with it, other than you know..."

Lorraine was sitting on the edge of the couch.

"Look, I'm not interested Rob in playing games today." Her eyes flicked up and met his for a millisecond.

"Okay, I'm sorry."

"You know, I mean, it's like promising a kid a cake if you do something."

"Lorri, what do you want me to say?" Transparent sincerity was oozing out of him.

"I just want you to tell me what you did on the 29th of June. You must have been asked that question more than any other question in your life."

Robert repeated that he had already told her. He then obliquely raised the issue of pleading guilty to manslaughter.

"What do you say?" Lorraine screeched. "If you pleaded guilty to manslaughter?" *He must have killed Sheree if he was going to plead to manslaughter*, she thought.

"Well, if I pleaded to manslaughter," Robert said, "I would have your approval and our marriage would be saved." He still needed an out. He had planned that Lorraine would have to take the blame for forcing him into writing a fake confession if the police became involved again. Lorraine was exasperated.

"You're tying strings on again, aren't you?" *Or was he just doing this to get the marriage back together?*

"Yes, I know I am, yeah."

Margaret blinked as the thought hit her. The whole reason Robert had used to get Lorraine there was probably a trick. He would not directly ask Lorraine to stand by him, if and when he pleaded guilty to manslaughter. He could not ask the question directly. It occurred to Margaret that he simply could not tell the truth. It was as if he had been programmed somewhere way, way back in his life to never tell the truth, no matter what the topic.

The Murder of Sheree

Lorraine continued to grill her husband, while he deflected anything that threatened his plans on how the session should run.

"What are you going to say if you plead to manslaughter? Just tell them? You can't just walk in like any old goat off the street!" Lorraine was still shaking but now she was shaking with anger, too.

"If they're going to charge me with murder then they're going to want to know exactly what I did that day."

"If they charge you with murder?"

"Well, they will, won't they?"

"Well, no they won't...," Lorraine said. She was getting confused. This talk of charges, courts, murders, was something she had never encountered before. The conversation stalled for a while. All the policemen could hear was the tick, tick, tick of the clock on the wall near the door. After some thought, Lorraine said:

"If you go in and plead manslaughter, you'll have to provide them with the proof." As she slumped a little more at the shoulders, sitting with her hands clasped tightly in her lap, Robert was sitting higher in his chair. He had perked up considerably. Things were going his way. Margaret wanted the talk to go another way. She piped in.

"Nobody knows Robert, except you, what happened." She could see Robert was enjoying every minute of this. He was enjoying talking to Lorraine, he never lost his tone all the way through. There were times he was even laughing.

"Well, I don't know what happened," he said. "I know what I did but I don't know what happened."

"Well, if they charge you with murder," Margaret said, "they'll say, you know, they present all the evidence, the child was picked up, somebody comes and says one thing, they saw this, this, this, and this. She was strangled, suffocated, beaten to death."

"Dropped out of the car," offered Lorraine, horrified.

"Jumped out of the car," Margaret suggested. *We might be getting somewhere here,* she thought. As she watched Robert, she could see the wheels turning.

"I'm considering saying to them 'I did it'," Robert said pensively, "if our marriage stays together and you and I-"

"- Can you substantiate that you did it?" Lorraine said. "To them?"

Robert talked around in circles and didn't give an answer. A few houseblocks away, Alex was listening and shaking his head. He couldn't see the room, the faces, the body language, the smirks. He was just concentrating on what he could hear. He heard two women working together to get this man to tell the truth. He also heard Robert Lowe fishing his way around for the best possible scenario, not just for the Sheree Beasley murder investigation, but in order to get his wife back. Alex could hear him take the conversation and push it a certain way, almost feeling for answers, like the salesman he was. He was looking for selling signs, and when they weren't accepting his stories, he would be frustrated and take a different tack. Alex felt he could almost hear him thinking, *I have to come to something that is believable because they certainly don't believe what I'm telling them.* Alex thought this day was very much like the day Paul Hollowood interviewed Robert at the Homicide Squad office. Here, Robert was lying his head off, and the interrogators weren't copping what he was saying. And like Paul, both the women were standing up to him, which was something Robert couldn't stand. Like all liars, he didn't like it when people challenged him.

Margaret tried to take control again.

"If we can leave it at that Robert. If it was left at that and then you said the police aren't going to say if you went to them, 'well, that's terrific Robert, great'. You know...The proof of the matter is, is that you can't just say that you've..."

"They've got crazies off the street doing that all the time," Lorraine said.

Robert defended himself. He was innocent, he said.

"You spit out lies like alcoholics drink beer," Lorraine said.

To ease some of the tension, Margaret left the room to make some percolated coffees. She was gone for just a minute but when she came back Lorraine was sitting bolt upright on the edge of her seat. She looked as though a spider had crawled up her back. Robert was sitting on the edge of his leather chair, leaning forward to get as close to her as possible. The tension was incredible. Lorraine calmed down a little when Margaret came back into the room. There was an unstated bond between the two women. Neither of them were going to take no for an answer today.

"Why don't you treat yourself like a man and do what you know you have to do?" Lorraine said. She was getting frustrated and very angry. Robert ignored her and turned to the therapist.

"I'll consider that option, Margaret," he said quietly. "It's the first time it's been raised. And let me consider it."

Alex and Andrew swore.

Robert mentioned a friend was praying for him.

Margaret: "He would be praying for the, the-"

"He's not asking that I be found innocent. He's praying that the person that did this will be found," Robert said.

"Well, that could be you,"Lorraine said.

"Yes," said Margaret.

"Yes, yes, yes, it could be," Robert said. Margaret thought the situation was becoming impossible.

Later the trio started talking about Robert's prior convictions and Lorraine's lack of knowledge about the full extent of them.

"Ignorance might be bliss but it's hell when you find out," she said. She was close to tears. She launched into Robert.

"I told you about eight years ago. I warned you when, although you declared although the court found you guilty, you weren't guilty. I've forgotten how many years ago. It was the last thing you declared to me that you were innocent. I said, 'Yeah, look, you know, you fool around like this you'll get into something up to your ears and you won't get out of it'. One of those, I was thinking more that one of the girls would say 'He raped me', or - I wasn't thinking of the Sheree scenario but it happens to be the Sheree scenario that's come up. Do you remember me saying that?"

Lorraine could have been talking to an 8-year-old boy. Robert was behaving like one.

"Yeah, I think so," Robert said.

"Yeah, well, it's happened, hasn't it? I'm not crowing about that but I could see you were heading that way. Now you're in the hole." There was a brief silence apart from the clock ticking. "You know, if you were sincere, you would be honest right through the 20 years of our marriage and you would be honest right now and what's been happening. You wouldn't have to..." Her voice trailed off. Then she said what she had wanted to say for a long time.

"You've manipulated me all your life. You even - you're even trying to do it today. I speak the truth while you - you're manipulating me. You're manipulating everybody to the ends of your satisfaction. Your satisfaction is wanting your wife back and a happy way of life but you won't-"

"-I think it is *our* satisfaction but however, maybe, maybe I'm wrong." Robert was working on making Lorraine feel guilty.

She didn't know how to get the point across. Yet it was so simple.

"Do you see?" Lorraine said.

"I'm wrong." He didn't want to see. He was infuriating.

"You're manipulating, " Lorraine said. "You won't tread the truthful road, or whatever you want to call it, and settle things and get in the clear without pulling along all these manipulations along after you."

Already Margaret was feeling drained. This was like trying to pin down a snake. Robert couldn't be pinned down to anything specific.

Lorraine said she had been thinking about her marriage.

"I've thought about it a lot. It's like a little single-fronted shop. Probably selling flowers or something. Smells lovely and looks lovely and out the back you're running a brothel. That's what our marriage seems like. And you've got the key to the door in the middle and that's why you want to get it together again, so you can open up for business at the back."

"No, absolutely!" Robert jumped forward. He hadn't realised Lorraine could see him so well.

Suddenly Lorraine felt very alone in this strange room, where men with deviant behaviour sat and told Margaret about their latest escapades. What the hell was she doing here? When would the nightmare end?

"I don't think I know what love is," Lorraine thought aloud. "I'm looking forward to experiencing it one day." Then she turned to Robert and said, "You couldn't have hurt me more if you put arsenic in my coffee."

The conversation drifted back to Robert going to the police. He said that was one of the things he had considered doing. Lorraine lost her temper.

"Well, go and do it now! Right now! Come on!"

Robert turned to Margaret. "With you showing me what to say and do?" he asked plaintively.

"Yes, I'll help you. Yes," Margaret said flatly.

Lorraine wasn't listening any more. She was issuing orders.

"Right now! I think we've waffled it out enough. Would you stand up this instant and do it?"

"I said that's *one* of the things," Robert said. "I haven't made up my - it was a consideration. There may be others..."

Lorraine turned to Margaret with a look of disgust on her face.

"See, now we start to waffle. See?"

"No Lorri, I asked - the very first question was telling the truth and it's counter to that," Robert said correctively.

"So you, you, you, if you stood up and went off, it would be telling lies?"

"As far as Sheree Beasley is concerned," Robert said confidently.

He skilfully turned the conversation away from Sheree and onto other matters both Lorraine and Margaret weren't interested in. After another lull, Lorraine expressed her dismay at Robert's anti-police attitude.

"Those men were decent men looking into an horrific crime which they're - they took on as 'I've got a little girl out there'. They weren't interested in who they were nabbing. They were interested in finding that little girl. She could have been alive at that stage and they wanted to find out as fast as they could."

"Yeah, I know," Robert said contritely.

"If you haven't done this and some man owns up to this or if they find another man - as you say, people are praying. That's all you want. The lying to the cops is almost as horrific in my mind and in their mind as if you'd done it. And I really mean that Margaret."

"Mmm, I agree actually," Margaret said.

Robert sat still, looking at the floor. The storm would pass soon.

"The money spent, the time spent....on Sheree's people which I know a little of. Honestly, the scenario of this last nine months is almost worse to a lot of people and I'm not just saying me - a lot of people. But if you've just been up and got your whatever is - charged and done with, it's been worse and as long as you've dillydallied around here, if you haven't done it, there's a man out there laughing."

"I know." Robert's face showed concern for what Lorraine was saying. That's what was required.

"And you're to blame for his non-arrest and for the anguish that everyone else has gone through because you won't acquit yourself like a man and do what you have to do," Lorraine said.

"I didn't anyway. That's right. I don't know what else I've got to do from now but I didn't. I know..."

"Whatever you do from now," Lorraine prophesied, "you're in hot water." Then she tried to explain to her estranged husband the effect events had had on their sons.

"I don't know how to put it into words. The heartbreaks...," she paused for a moment and checked herself. *Tick tick tick.* She didn't want to cry.

"...They don't deserve to have their lives shattered at that age. Fifteen. Benji's 17, just going through HSC, a 15-year-old, you know Margaret, I've been told from the psychiatrists. They've had to see these sorts of people when the most important thing to a child, a boy of 15, is his peer group. How do you think he feels? Silent (phone) number, police calling all the time and at one stage, not now, terrified his friends will find out, terrified of when they'll find out, not *if* they will. There's no doubt about it. They're all going to know. Whatever scenario you like to look at in the future. Those that don't already know are too embarrassed to say anything. How do you think they feel? How do you think I feel in bed when I hear them tossing, awake all night? And one of them comes into the bedroom and hops in the bed near me and just holds me and I could go on and on, Margaret. I don't want to cause big sob stories. You don't know what we've been going through."

Robert sounded like an anguished young lover. "Tell me."

"Had them off to the doctor this week."

"Who?"

"Both of them."

"Why?"

"Stress related things. I mean, this is, this is what we're going through. I've lost 20 kilograms. We haven't got all the Margaret Hobbs and the (psychiatrist) David Clarkes and the this and that dancing around us. It's just the three of us. And I tell you what. The Bible said - if you want to

The Murder of Sheree

quote the Bible - the threefold cord is not easily broken. We've clung to that, we're a threefold cord, whatever that might mean and we're not easily broken. You're not going - you're not going to cripple us..."

Robert gushed. "..I don't want to Lorri, that's the last..."

"...discard us."

"That would be the last thing."

"My life is absolutely in tatters. I had to start my life again when I was 29 through nothing to do with you. You know what I'm referring to. It's very hard to pick it up at my age now and start it again and I haven't really come to terms with trying yet. The only thing I do is just for the boys. You know, be sort of the mainstay. You have to do it. And the last thing I want in the home," she shook and paused for a moment, "is some further problem of waffling around the truth."

Lorraine turned to Margaret.

"I had to sit the boys down. I've had to point out to them all the time not so much recently Margaret, but a direct question needs a direct answer."

She looked back to Robert.

"They've, they've copied you. If I say, 'Did you do this?' - 'could have'. And I've had to absolutely say, 'Look here, yes or no?'. They've had to unlearn. It's like a debriefing for them. It's been dreadful, Margaret. I'll tell you an example of it. I, I died inside Margaret when this happened. When the police took your car," she pointed at Robert, "and you hired one and we went to church on Sunday morning, Benji thought it was a bit of a joke, you know kids, and 'What will they say when we've got a new car?' and 'What will they say when they say where's our blue car,' and you said, 'Oh, we don't have to say anything to them, it's none of their business' and Benji said, 'Oh, we'll just say the old car's being looked over'. You know, he thought that was funny and you were thrilled."

Robert remembered. A smirk came over his face.

"Yes, you're laughing now." Lorraine was raising her voice. "You said, 'Well done Benjamin, that's the way to do it' - and I died inside."

Robert wasn't overly concerned. "Mmm, fair enough."

"We're not having that emptiness back in the home. We have truth in our home."

Robert sat listening. He hadn't seen her this upset before. If he could get through this onslaught, he knew he would get her back. He knew it was against the bible's teaching and Lorraine's beliefs for their separation to last. Then he would be back home, and very possibly, safe from the police. He kept his head down as the tirade continued.

"Have you any conception of the families that have been involved, even in the Sheree thing? Have you any conception of what you, yourself have caused? I'm not saying whether you're guilty or not. Any conception of the families that have been called out at all hours of the night, all because you were evading the truth. You've probably got no idea. It would run into hundreds of people that for - maybe they haven't had their lives wrecked, but they've had their year wrecked and I mean that. Every area of our life that we touch, there are people in anguish over this. Hours and hours of manhours spent while you've sat down there in Rosebud enjoying your game with the cops. When you had that 15 hours down at Rosebud in the interrogation by the police and you lied and waffled and turned and did everything round and round and said, 'Listen we never got anywhere'. Didn't get to the truth whichever the truth was. We were all exhausted. The cops were too. They've all got families. The ripples go further and further out. They're under stress. All these men with young families and as we were going home, as I said goodbye to some of them and went home at four o'clock in the morning, you know, two or three or four, Rick had to be taken back the next day - I think it was the next morning - and he said, 'Oh well, but everyone will be exhausted,' and I turned around and I said, 'Robert won't be. He'll be on cloud nine. He won that round'. They said, 'Oh don't be stupid, he must be tired out.' Not a bit of it. You got into the car and you were absolutely elated. It's a real game, Rob, and I think you need to stand back and look at yourself. I was right. They rang me up and they said, 'I don't know you how you did it but you were spot on.' Taking Rick up to Frankston like a Cook's Tour, even had the cheek to hop in the cop's car and go with them. Isn't that right?"

"Yeah, yeah, probably right." He was pleased. After all these months, Lorraine was sitting with him, talking to him. Soon it would be his turn.

Margaret cut in.

"Robert how many times have I said to you, 'You're enjoying this, aren't you?'"

"I do enjoy it. I'm sorry but I did enjoy it," he said. A little smile crossed his face.

Lorraine was shocked.

"You know we've got life and death things that, that are at stake here and you even laughed then," she said.

"Hmm."

Now it was Lorraine's turn to shock Robert.

"See Margaret, Robert has always made - all this time it's been, I know I've been...naive but as you said, probably why he was attracted to me in the first place is somebody he can manipulate, get his shop front window happening. And even when he lost his job and I thought it was just through the - it wasn't recession then but whatever, it wasn't half the time, it was because of his past behaviour and he never told me this and he wouldn't even let me tell my parents he was out of work. They would've - you know what parents are like - I mean, you need their help. Not financially but for support and everything. I was not allowed to tell them anything. I've had to cover for him the whole time."

Lorraine was really wound up. She stopped, gripping the handkerchief in both hands on her lap. She thought for a second and continued.

"The urgent business appointment was with the dumpmaster. He knows what I'm referring to..." The day of his first interview with Dale Johnson. "...Fortunately he was under surveillance and they caught him."

Margaret looked at Robert. "I'm just seeing the suspicion of a smirk on your face Robert," she said sternly.

"Yes, so do I," Lorraine said.

Robert then spat out that he had nothing to do with Sheree Beasley. He spoke pleadingly, as if he wanted to help but had no way of doing so. He could not believe how Lorraine had changed in the short time they had been separated. No, he could not believe how the coppers had changed her. It was their fault.

"What do you want to achieve? What can I do?" he asked his wife.

"To make something of the shreds of the rest of my life, that's all. Just to survive to the end of my life. To give the boys some sort of a home that they...Oh, for God's sake, they need...that's all that's left in my life. I haven't got any big plans in my life. Just to survive to be there to give the kids a chance because they're the innocent victims. They don't deserve this, that's all. I'm not out after another man, I'm not out after a glamorous life or anything. I couldn't care if I lived in a tent. But I'm going to do the best for my boys. That's the only thing I've got to do. I mean, that's my obligation left in life. I don't know why I've been placed through this. I guess eternity will know, I don't know why. Some people have told me it will make me strong, it'll make the boys strong and I think it will. I think they'll be mature, they've lost their boyhood unfortunately. There's not much laughter in them sometimes. They've grown up. They used to love their fun, their young ways. They've lost that."

"I used to love it with them," Robert said.

"You tried to have two sides of it though. You can't have your cake and eat it. You can't have both." Lorraine looked at him. Nothing was going to change, she thought. *I might as well be talking to a brick wall. He asked me to come here and I'm doing all the talking.*

She realised she was losing her temper.

"The rest of my life is going to be made up of trying to earn a bit of money to survive. I thought by this stage I would look forward to retirement with the man I thought I loved and I thought loved me."

"I *do* love you," Robert said.

"I did love him and I thought he loved me," Lorraine told Margaret. "Might be a better way to do it. I *did* love him. I thought this stage of my life would be - in a couple of years anyhow - the boys would be through school and I was looking forward to life. I'll be working til I'm 70 now to get those boys - I'm not exaggerating Margaret - to get those boys on their feet. I mean, that's the truth, that the...As I've said, I'm not worried. I'll survive. I'm a survivor. I'll survive somehow. I hope I will. Now and then I feel as though I'm going under but I'll survive probably because that's the sort of person I am. And I'll dig in deeper because I'm a determined person."

She turned back to Robert. There was blood in her cheeks. She looked at her husband and really saw him for the first time.

"You've had your fun, now those things have to be paid for. There's a cost to entertainment. You've had your entertainment and this is the price you've got to pay."

Robert just looked at her. He was close to smiling again. He didn't mind when Lorraine got upset with him. It showed she cared. As he watched, he saw Lorraine put her left hand to her mouth. It looked like she was biting the side of her finger. Then she started wrenching at one finger with her other hand.

"This ring's never been off my finger," she said. "The first time it's been off since the 10th of October, 1972. I'm going." She leaned over and put her wedding ring on Robert's knee before she dashed from the room in tears. She was almost hysterical. Robert looked down at the band of gold on his left knee. He was absolutely stunned. He didn't know what to do. This wasn't part of the script! Lorraine had taken total control in one gesture and he had no lines. He hadn't even considered this scenario. Suddenly the game was over - the control was gone.

He leaned forward, white with rage and pointed menacingly at Margaret.

"This...is...your...fault. This...is...your...FAULT," he said through gritted teeth. His eyes were blazing. Margaret cowered a little in her seat, feeling powerless. Robert stumbled quickly to the door and looked down the empty stairs. "Lorri, come back - don't be silly," he called out, half commanding, half pleading.

"Where's she gone?" he asked nobody and went to run down the stairs.

"Just a minute Robert, leave her alone," Margaret said quietly. She was trying to sound firm but the words didn't sound very forceful as they left her lips. She could see something building up in Robert. Then he started shouting as he towered over Margaret.

"This is your fault!" he shouted. "You go after her and give it back!"

His grim face, drained of colour, was set firm. Margaret sensed danger. She had never seen him like this before. She wondered what he was capable of doing. He raced down the stairs into the front office. Margaret heard him shouting "Where is she? Where's she gone?"

If he finds Lorri, Margaret thought, *something will happen*. He had gone completely mad, totally out of control. Margaret saw Sheree, frightened, in a small blue car, sitting next to this uncontrollable anger.

The office girl told Robert Lorraine had gone but in fact she had been spirited into another office and had locked herself in. She was waiting for Ross Brightwell to take her home. Petrified, Lorraine stood in the small, empty room listening to the commotion. She was holding her breath for fear Robert would hear her and rip the door off its hinges.

Margaret stood in the open doorway at the top of the stairs. Somehow what was supposed to be discussed behind closed doors had exploded out into the real world. Suddenly, Robert appeared again at the bottom of the stairs, breathing heavily and staring at Margaret up the stairway. He stomped up towards her. Margaret had put her coat on - she was starting to feel very cold - and put her hands in the pockets. She walked half sideways, half backwards back into her office and stood next to the chair she had been sitting in. Robert burst in and picked up his shoulder bag. He turned to go to the door again but stopped for a split second, then spun towards Margaret. His mouth was twisted downwards into a scowling snarl. He bared his teeth momentarily and Margaret could see a tiny rod of spittle joining his open lips.

"This is your fault!" he shouted again as he leant forward menacingly. He was only two metres away. "You've done this. Now you go out after her and you give her this ring and tell her to stop this," he demanded. He left the room only to return seconds later.

While Robert's anger continued to rise, Margaret was trying to maintain her composure. To look frightened might egg him on. She watched him closely, while trying not to stare. She had seen snippets of anger in him but it was always controlled. This was the first time she felt for her own safety. She looked closer at the contorted face. He was somebody else - this wasn't the person she knew. Imperceptibly she moved behind her chair and stood stock still, wondering what to do next. To her surprise, Robert turned and shot out the door, and ran down the stairs into Victoria Parade.

The office girls ran up and told Margaret where Lorraine was hiding. Seconds later, Robert was back in building. He pushed open the front door of the building and called up the stairs, "Come out here, you, and find her." Margaret did no such thing.

Alex was at the ready. He could hear things were going haywire. He waited until he thought Lowe had gone and then ran from his secret listening place towards the psychotherapist's office. He got the shock of his life. As he ran to the front of the building, he almost bumped into the murder suspect storming out onto the street. *He must have gone and come back again*, Alex thought. Lowe was fumbling around in his knapsack as he walked and then he stopped and stared at Alex. They gave each other a start. Then Alex saw a look he had never seen before. There was fear but there was also anger. The eyes stood out. They looked like two steady pinpoints, focused directly on Alex. This was the rage of some cornered beast - afraid, but ready to fight. Alex's body steeled and he took a step back. He was ready. He had seen frightened crooks and he'd seen angry crooks but this was a mixture. He was genuinely taken aback by it. The look spooked him completely.

The two beads were still fixed on him. Alex knew instinctively what Lowe was thinking. *Get the hell out of here. What are you doing to me?*

It was a moment that for Alex is suspended in time. It took an hour and it was all over in one second. Lowe's look showed how desperate he could be. Then the facial expression changed slightly, and Alex watched as the frightened animal transformed into a desperate one. Cornered - not helpless but with that last look before inevitability. Defiant but hopeless. *I'm gone, but I'll fight you.*

Alex realised Robert was in such a state that he didn't know what he was doing. *The man who thinks he's so much in control, has lost control.*

He thought of Sheree. He could imagine the moment when Lowe realised she was dead and he had to take a certain course of action.

She's dying, or dead, I've got to cover my tracks.

There's that same inevitability, Alex thought. Fear and uncontrollable rage, they meet at one point - and that's the look.

But instead of fighting, Lowe simply turned and walked quickly away down Victoria Parade towards Richmond. As he walked off, Alex realised Lowe hadn't even seen him. He had seen a threat, not a person, and now that the threat was gone, he was already starting to calm down. Alex doubted Robert would even recognise him again.

Margaret was standing in her clinic as the busy traffic in Victoria Parade droned on, like big Doppler blowflies careering around a room. She clutched her giddy head in her hands. The threat had passed. Just as she sat down, and sighed loudly, shaking her head, the phone rang. It was Robert, calling from a public phone box.

"I'm sorry, Marg, I got a bit upset," he said. "I've calmed down now."

As soon as Margaret heard the voice, she froze. She was nodding but no words were spoken.

Calmly Robert inquired, "See you on the first?"

"All right, Robert," Margaret whispered and hung up. She wondered how much longer this would last.

Alex walked quickly up the stairs and sat with her. As he debriefed her about the day's events, his mind was racing. He was evaluating the conversation Lowe had had with his wife. And he was trying to appear interested in what Margaret was saying but he was deflated. Everything had fizzled out. If Robert wouldn't confess with all the pressure from Lorraine, then they might never get him. Today had been their best chance - and now it was gone.

Lorraine had gone to the clinic to hear what Robert had to say. She had hoped she would be able to learn finally what his involvement in Sheree's death was. She had no intention of handing back her wedding ring when she first entered the room. Now she was at home, still angry and upset. Robert didn't want to talk about what had gone on. He had simply teased her. She still couldn't believe how he smirked all the time. The more she thought about the meeting, the more repulsed she felt. She felt dirty. It occurred to her that her husband was possessed by something evil. It was beyond belief, yet there it was.

She wearily took off her new dress. Somehow she knew every time she wore it from now on she'd feel dirty, no matter how often she washed it. She rolled it into a ball and threw it in the bin, before washing her hands in the bathroom.

Robert realised he was in deep trouble now. The woman who would never divorce him, the woman who believed the bible's teachings on marriage, had done the unthinkable. He knew now he had to concoct something special if he was to salvage his bond with his wife. He hit on the idea of manufacturing a "confession" which would minimise his criminality in Sheree's death. It was a big gamble but he felt it was worth it if he could get Lorraine to believe his "true" version of events. She might even stand by him if he was charged with some involvement with Sheree.

THE CAR PARK of Waverley Park, formerly VFL Park, was one of Jill Mandile's favourite spots for walking her dog. She looked forward to the walks where she could be alone with her thoughts and sometimes cry while nobody was around to see. What she couldn't understand was, Why? Why did it have to happen? She didn't understand and she knew she never would.

The dog retrieved the stick, and ran up to her, its tail wagging wildly as it panted for breath. Jill picked up the slimy stick and threw it again as she turned and started to walk back home. She was thinking of how she could no longer go to Red Hill. One time she had driven there with friends to inspect a friend's new home. But just as they neared the spot where her granddaughter's remains had been found, Jill felt a horrible, claustrophobic sensation take hold of her, suffocating her from within. Her friends had no option but to turn the car around and drive off.

Jill had her hand to her mouth as she remembered. As she continued walking she looked down. To her left she spied a small concrete drain. The sight of it and the shocking recollection it triggered caused her to gasp for breath. Her knees began to shake and she thought for a split second she might faint. Instead she started a frightened run, back towards her home. She knew she couldn't ever go back there again. She realised too, that the faith in God she had carried all her life, had died.

ON APRIL Fools Day, 1992, there was another counselling session. Margaret picked up where the last session ended.

"How dare you speak to me like that!" she said, referring to his outrageous outburst.

There was a silence for a few seconds, punctuated only by the ticking of the white clock on the wall. Then they recapped the last session with Lorraine. Robert could not believe his wife wanted to remain separated from him. He thought, despite her giving back the wedding ring, that there was a ray of hope for his marriage. Margaret begged to differ. Then

Robert talked about how things were always happening to him. That morning he was approached by a stranger in Frankston as he got off the bus. The stranger told him God said Robert needed a New Testament bible. Despite his protestations that he had one, the man gave Robert the bible. Margaret wondered if Robert had stolen it.

As the session progressed, he started to lose control, but in a different manner. He was at a loss as to what to do next. He threw adolescent tantrums - "Why is she doing this to me? She's lying about me not being home!" Margaret sensed there were cracks emerging in his emotional makeup. She wondered whether he was finally comprehending that Lorraine was serious in what she said.

Then, clearly agitated, Robert leapt up and left the office, shouting at Margaret as he left.

"You better tell Lorraine to watch herself or something might happen to her!"

He went out into the street. Margaret followed at a distance and yelled to him in much the same manner as she would to a naughty boy.

"Come back here! You explain what you mean."

Robert walked back in and trudged up the stairs.

"What did you say?" Margaret said. "What did you mean by that about Lorraine?"

Robert looked as if he was amazed Margaret was even quizzing him.

"Oh, she could have a car accident," he said.

Margaret felt like shaking her head. She wanted to get back on track. She was getting angry with this ridiculous behaviour.

"Anyway, look, back to the subject, is why do you think the relationship's broken up then? Do you think it would still have been going-"

"- Because the Devil's got her, Marg."

"Mmm, very convenient."

"I know you don't believe that."

"I do believe the Devil's got her, I have no troubles with that. But who is the Devil?"

"Yeah, me, I know."

Robert talked about pleading guilty to manslaughter and then said he wasn't worried about a court case. He said he had nothing to fear because he hadn't done anything. The room went quiet for a few seconds. *Tick, tick, tick.* Then Robert drew a deep breath and said very quietly:

"Literally, if you want me to tell the truth, I can tell you how I was involved. Yes. I could tell you how I was involved...."

The hairs stood up on the back of Margaret's neck. She felt sick. "Mmm," was all she could say. She swallowed hard. It took her breath away. Was there no end to the surprises this man could come out with? She struggled to maintain her composure.

"Yes, I will help you Robert. Yes, of course." Margaret was talking in the general sense of his welfare. She was fearful of what might now be said but she also felt a rush of relief. Perhaps they were now getting somewhere.

"...and we can work along that line," he said.

"All right, well let's work along that line then," Margaret said. But still Robert could not do anything without applying conditions. To him Sheree's murder and the problems he was encountering because of it were inextricably linked to his marriage woes. Sheree was a bargaining tool. To Robert, she still had her uses.

"All right, you tell me that all this is, is, on the condition of not just a divorce thing being stopped, but that we are going to get together in courting..."

"All right."

"...and the marriage, we're still going to be legally married..."

"Mmm."

"I will be back in the home. I'm not asking for a bed or whatever but, it's all on that, Marg."

"All right, all right."

"Okay, right."

"Now, you will tell me you're involved and we'll work on it together? What do we work on? You said something the other night about, ah, having your memories triggered or something, didn't you?"

Robert nodded. "Mmm, mmm."

"Now what do you want me to do there? Did you want to go down to Red Hill and have your memories triggered or something?"

"What I want to do first is to see if Lorraine agrees to this commitment. Is that possible or not?"

"I don't - I'm not sort of terribly optimistic about that Robert because umm…"

"-No."

"…You, you know what'll she say?"

"(That I'm) bargaining."

"Yeah, I'm not going to be in that again and she said that and I think umm…"

"Well, I wouldn't do it without her knowing."

"Well."

"I'm not, I'm not interested in…"

"Mmm, well, we can't, we can't be stuck then."

"Well, there's always ways around." Robert looked like the desperate salesman trying to come up with different ways of clinching the deal. Margaret knew he didn't want the marriage back because of love or commitment or even for fulfilling responsibilities. The only reason Robert Lowe wanted to be back home was because of appearances. As long as his life looked 'normal' to outsiders and those in the church, well, that was all that mattered.

Robert talked of what he might say about Sheree's abduction and death.

"I might give you some thoughts."

"All right, you give me some thoughts. That's fine," Margaret said. She expected him to change tack again. She wasn't getting overly confident.

"Yeah."

"And you said to me about umm, if you want me to take you down to Red Hill so's…. you can have a look around and it might jog some thoughts," Margaret ventured.

"No I might. I'm not adjusted to it yet. But I might, I'm open to it."

"Yeah. Could - Robert, could we keep this between you and I for, for a few, for a while?"

"Mmm. Mmm."

"Right."

"Yeah, because it's, it's dangerous isn't it?" he said in a low, conspiratorial, excited voice.

"Bec - Yes and it's you and me."

"Yeah, I won't say anything. "

Robert packed his notebook and pen into his bag, as if he was leaving a university lecture. This had not been a session to try to modify his behaviour, or to try to get to the root cause of his absurd and twisted manner. It had been a damage control exercise, where he was trying to manipulate Margaret to manipulate Lorraine into accepting him home again. It was bizarre and it was never likely to work. But to Robert Lowe, it made perfect sense. He had examined his options carefully. The only way out for him was to talk of an accidental death. That was the only thing his wife might accept. There was really no other way out now that he had talked himself into a corner.

THE SONGS that had brought so much joy to the Greenhills were now songs that brought tears. Kylie Minogue's *Locomotion* would prompt delightful memories of Sheree with her plastic microphone and clumsy but quick dancesteps. Then the memories would quickly wither and turn black. Sometimes family members would start arguing over silly things and not know why. Sometimes the triggers would be things people didn't even recognise, like one of Sheree's favourite television commercials. Or sometimes it might be kids playing in a park, laughing and running. It seemed that everywhere they saw joy, they saw overwhelming sorrow as well.

THE STRANGE gifts and phone calls Margaret received - often from people she didn't know or hadn't seen for years - added a further dimension to the surreal situation she was in. People would ring up out of the blue.

"Margaret, are you all right?"

"We're praying for you."

After a particularly nasty session with Robert one day, Margaret was sitting with her head on her desk crying, when a friend, Maria, rang.

"I have not seen you for three years. You are in trouble. I pray for you every night. What is wrong?"

Margaret went to explain but realised she could not.

People brought Margaret crystals to deflect Evil. They would walk in and say, "There's something wrong here. I've brought you this, you're not safe."

And yet they knew nothing about Robert Lowe. And Margaret didn't believe in all that stuff anyway. She was an atheist with her feet planted firmly on the ground. At least she used to be. She was surprised at the amount of things she was sent. Flowers, photos of St Michael, even some garlic. She found the gifts and calls from well wishers were of great consolation to her, even if she, and the people contacting her, didn't know what it was all about.

ROBERT ARRIVED for the next session on April 6 with a pile of handwritten notes in his knapsack. He had been doing a little homework and today he hoped to take some notes during his discussion with Margaret. Andrew Gustke and Alex Bartsch, in their T-shirts and jeans, were listening on a monitor. They took turns listening to Lowe and Margaret talking - they couldn't stand hearing his voice so they split the task. Andrew was sitting with the earphones on; Alex was sitting on the couch nearby when the session began. It was the same old routine. Round and round in circles, here we go again, thought Andrew. Lowe was talking about Lorraine, of how he missed her, of how he wished he could get back with her. Andrew told Alex what was going on. Alex cursed. He often fantasised about going in there and thumping Lowe in the mouth.

Andrew settled in for another mind- and bum-numbing eavesdropping session. He heard Lowe tell Margaret he now knew where Parkmore Street was as he had hitchhiked and been dropped off there recently - but he hadn't been there before. After some small talk about where Margaret went for the weekend with her husband John, Robert pulled out his notes. He said he had written down some thoughts about Sheree Beasley. Robert said he was detailing a scenario to save his marriage. But Margaret soon saw he was indirectly seeking information. Robert knew she had been talking to Lorraine, who had been constantly talking to the police. He was hoping to learn what they had said about the offender or the crime scene.

Robert began reading from a set of notes he had brought with him in his floppy knapsack.

"I wrote down here I- I've, you know, I've pulled up in the car near the milk bar where a cou- two kids were arguing."

Margaret felt her lips tighten. "Mmm," was all she could say.

"Alex!" Andrew called. "Come and listen to this." Andrew ripped off the earphones and flicked a switch on the radio. The speakers came on, propelling Lowe's rich, cultured voice around the policemen's flat. The voice was completely devoid of emotion.

"Umm, I left the left hand door open. I didn't go into the milk bar and I asked - because they were arguing - I asked if she wanted to, want a ride (sic)."

"Mmm." Margaret thought it was best just to listen and not say anything unless she had to. She had endured six months of torture to see if Robert was a murderer. Now it seemed he was going to confess to it. But then, you never knew with Robert Lowe.

"She just got straight in," he continued.

"Mmm."

Andrew and Alex were excited. It didn't sound as if Lowe was making his story up. It sounded real.

"And umm, and aah, I put a seat belt on. I had a- helped her put her seat belt on and then we went over Chinaman's Creek and at that stage she began to get aah, uptight or worried and thinking where she was going or whatever she was going to do. So I did a U-turn, I came back along the main highway at least I think it, there is another road goes right around but I wouldn't know where that road goes."

"Mmm." The impact of what Robert was saying was starting to hit home. Margaret was trying to ensure Robert would not notice her frock shivering, or the tears brimming in her eyes.

Andrew and Alex were gaping wide-eyed at each other. A witness, Catherine Brown, had come forward months earlier to tell police she was driving along the Nepean Highway on June 29 when she noticed a small blue car suddenly brake and do a U-turn on the highway for no apparent reason. At the time it was a seemingly useless piece of information. Suddenly it was a vital piece of evidence. If he was making up this confession, how the hell did he know about the U-turn?

At that moment, both men *knew* Lowe was Sheree's killer. Alex turned to Andrew and said, smiling, "That's got to be the greatest guess of all time. He turns the right way into Nepean Highway!"

In between listening to Robert's dronings, the detectives would occasionally ask each other questions about Robert's scenario. *Why on earth would you say that? Why put it in your scenario if it's a bullshit scenario?* They were so excited they couldn't get the smiles off their faces.

Lowe continued trying to sell his notes as 'What might have happened - if I did it'. He was still trying to temper the truth with a possible believable scenario. And he was enjoying teasing his therapist. The inscrutable voice droned on, in the room, and through the speaker.

"Came back along the high- main highway, umm, and I was going to take her back when she started coughing and spluttering and things and then it went quiet and I panicked and I thought, 'Well, what's happened you know? I pulled into the side, into the foreshore area and realised that you know, she wasn't breathing properly at all."

"Mmm."

"And umm, so I didn't know what to do. So I was, I was going to go, take her back to where I picked her up and I thought 'Look, I can't do that, cause I don't even know where she lives anyway."

"Mmm." Margaret was ashen-faced.

"So I took her up Arthur's Seat, and I'm not quite sure of my geography there. I haven't got a sp- haven't got a Melways down there."

"Mmm." Margaret couldn't believe the tone of his voice. He might have been describing how he prepares the same breakfast every morning. There was no remorse, no tinge of regret or guilt. Just a voice.

"Took her up Arthur's Seat and I just kept going, I didn't know what to do with her. Umm, first, um, reactions were possibly to dig a damn, a umm, grave."

"Mmm, yep."

"And then aah, I could easily do that. It was the easiest thing. I didn't have a spade with me."

"Mmm."

"I could've still have done it but I thought, aah, well that's going to take time and everything else but that's, that's...Actually the place I've stopped has a drain running underneath the road...

"Mmm, mmm."

"And I just thought 'Well'. I went down and had a look and it was fairly well hidden umm, hidden enough to jam the body in. So I carted the body out and…"

"Mmm."

Neither of them used Sheree's name. For Robert, it was because Sheree was never anything more than an object. Margaret depersonalised her but for different reasons. She knew she would not be able to talk about her - or even stay in the room with this man - if she let the picture of her pretty face, in her playclothes, force its way into her consciousness.

"I didn't take any clothes off because what is the purpose of taking the clothes off when the girl's dead? Umm, perhaps if the clothes are missing, I don't know what clothes are missing. If they, you know, I might have to alter that. Aah, so I just jammed the body in there. It was a tight fit. I don't know what size the pi- pipe is, I don't know if- tight fit or not."

"Mmm, mmm."

"Umm, I thought 'Goodness,' and just panicked and then headed back to Melbourne."

"Mmm."

"Couldn't give you any detail or anything but, umm, what else can I do? I mean I could fill it in. I mean, I obviously have to go and have a look and see how- what size the pipe is, where the roads go around there because, umm, people could ask all these questions."

He was still pretending he didn't know the area even though Lorraine had already told the police six months earlier that he had gone pineconing there with her. Margaret finally felt she could speak without a sharp cry escaping from her lips.

"Well, of course, then ask all the questions, Robert but you can't sort of umm, I told you I wasn't going to let you sacrifice yourself, you know, and you can't make something up in umm, you know, yeah."

Robert didn't hear her. He was a little glassy-eyed.

"I said, you know, how big is the pipe for instance. I don't know if it's a pipe the size of that chair and I don't know how big she was. Wa- was she a big girl or small girl and I'm sure she'll be able to get in the pipe but must be a fairly small pipe because-"

"Mmm."

"- I..."

"I don't know anything myself Robert."

"Her body wasn't washed out for three months or two months," he said matter-of-factly. "That's the point. Yes."

"So it wouldn't have been loose."

"Mmm."

"It would have been stuffed in there."

"Mmm, mmm. Yeah it would have to have been you're right......"

"It must be a fairly small pipe."

"Mmm, but when you say this Arthur's Seat thing - is this place by Arthur's Seat? You said you went by..."

"Behind Arthur's Seat."

"Yeah."

"It's the road, there are probably various roads to Red Hill but I believe that day that we came - went round the back there. We ended up, up the top of Arthur's Seat."

"Mmm."

"Now I'm not certain Marg but I believe, and I've had a look on, on, Melways some time ago-"

"Mmm."

"If you go into the store again but that comes around through Arthur's Seat at the top where the umm..."

"Yeah I, I don't know the- I do know the area. It's like, you know, you go like, you saying you go around and you know it's Arthur's Seat and I know that's Red Hill but-"

"I mean it's got that lift thing -"

"Yes."

"- going up and-"

"That's right."

"- the road goes backwards and forwards underneath it like that."

"So this drain is behind Arthur's Seat is it?"

"Mmm, mmm."

"And you're saying, there in your story, that you, you stopped there and you were by the drain or something?"

"Mmm."

"Right. Well, what are you saying in your story now Robert, that you think happened to her?"

"Really must of, aah, choked..."

"Mmm." Another wave of nausea ripped through Margaret. She had heard Peter Reid talking about how he had killed a policeman but it was never, ever like this. Firstly there was the unreality of it. *My God, he did it.* And there were the awful details he was giving without showing any emotion at all. Margaret knew if she showed any emotion, or told him to stop, he might not go on any further. So she sat and listened, her heart beating as if she'd just run a marathon race. In their secret room, Alex and Andrew were holding their breaths as they stood right next to the speaker. They were drinking in every single word.

"I can't say I suffocated her and I mean why would I want to suffocate her?"

Margaret cleared her throat. "No exactly, Robert, this is what I'm saying to you is that, aah, I mean look, let's face it, what you've just said there is, is an accidental death. There's no doubt about that at all."

"Mm."

"I mean it's as they said, you know it's an accidental death, it's a panic situation and that is it."

Robert was thinking as he listened to what Margaret had to say.

"Mmm."

"And that's as much as, as one needs to say. There's no intent, aah, you certainly wouldn't have picked her up to, to murder or molest her. It was like I said to you before in my little scenario there, that just a little bit of, I don't know."

"A bit of fun or whatever it must have been," Robert offered, smiling.

"Hmm?"

"Not fun but a... something."

"Bit of a prank ..and a bit of 'take her for a ride' and one thing and another."

"There, I put her in there with her, with her clothes on and I know there's certain bits of clothes that are missing and I think her helmet is missing. Is it or, or...?"

Margaret saw him coming.

"Oh, it was cleared in the paper that the helmet was missing, Robert and the, umm, tracksuit."

"Okay, well, aah, have to say I took the helmet off in the car. I mean you'd be stupid burying a girl with a helmet on wouldn't you?" Andrew and Alex swore again.

"You couldn't. I think you're probably right that perhaps even a helmet wouldn't have got in that, in the, aah, drain."

Margaret was terrified by this talk. Mostly she was disturbed by the off-hand way he was discussing Sheree's death. But simultaneously she hoped he kept talking about it. Perhaps this whole shocking episode would be over when she knew once and for all what had happened.

"Drain, no," Robert went on taking notes.

"It would have been very noticeable..."

"So had to have taken it off."

"Yeah. What have you done with it?"

"Well, do you think or somebody thinks, the dumpmaster. I don't know where there are any dumpmasters around that place," he lied. "I mean, any of the dumpmasters in shopping centres and things, don't you?"

"I don't think so Robert. I think in places like that like where there are tips and things there are often lay-by areas with dumpmasters in them. It's often those sort of situations where you've got a lay-by."

"Yeah."

"And with a dumpmaster in."

"I'm not sure if dumpmaster is a good example but umm, I only say that because Lorraine said that didn't she?"

"I think, I think the police have said Robert, cause you went and dumped all those clothes and that pornography in the dumpmaster."

"You reckon that's the reason?"

"Yeah."

Then Robert said he dumped the items in a dumpmaster at Mount Waverley shopping centre.

"Yeah. Is this where the police found, found the pornography?" Margaret asked.

"Part of it, yeah."

"It was in the Mount Waverley bin."

After talking about dumpmasters and rubbish bins for a while Margaret tried to pick up the threads again.

"But what's, what's another scenario Robert, that could've happened to the clothes and the helmet?"

"Well, the helmet I could've kept in the car and I could've taken it back towards Melbourne and just put her in a dumpmaster there."

"Mmm. Which dumpmaster?"

"Well, Brandon Park Shopping Centre."

"Mmm."

"I'm sure there's one there."

"Mmm."

"I don't know if there is or not but a lo—, lot of these dumpmasters now in the new areas are actually ec- enclosed in the building."

"Mmm."

"Rather than being sat outside, they're actually enclosed in the building."

"That's right."

"I don't know if they're only sitting outside, Brandon Park's got a lot of renovations and ah, the dumpmasters may actually be enclosed now."

"Mmm."

"I have to go around and have a look see if there are any sitting outside and then if there's none there, well, I'll have to go find one somewhere else."

"Robert, I can't collude with you in making stories up. We're, we're conspiring."

Robert sighed. "I mean a dump ... master's only one option."

"Mmm."

"As far as the clothes, the helmet um," he paused. Margaret heard the clock ticking. It was much slower than her heart beat. "A helmet is a hard thing to, to hide."

"Mmm."

"I don't know what colour...Was it blue or something?"

"It was pink Robert, come on."

"Pink." He wrote the word down in his notes.

Sheree's grandfather Neil Greenhill.

Sheree's great-grandparents Joy and Leslie Greenhill.

Sheree's grandparents Jill and Anthony Mandile.

POLICE NEED YOUR HELP!

Police investigating the Homicide of 6 year old Sheree Beasley in the Rosebud area on 29/6/91 are seeking public assistance in apprehending those responsible.

A body of a child believed to be that of Sheree Beasley was located on 26/9/91 alongside the Mornington-Flinders Road, Red Hill, near the intersection of Sheehans Road.

The vehicle fitting the description below is suspected of being involved.

Anyone with any information should contact Crime Stoppers on (03) 865 5000 or Rosebud Police on (059) 86 0444.

DESCRIPTION OF CAR
SMALL HATCHBACK DESIGN
EITHER TWO OR FOUR DOOR
MID BLUE COLOUR.

YOUR INFORMATION IS STRICTLY CONFIDENTIAL

The flier police used to try to gather information from the public.

BODY IN DRAIN

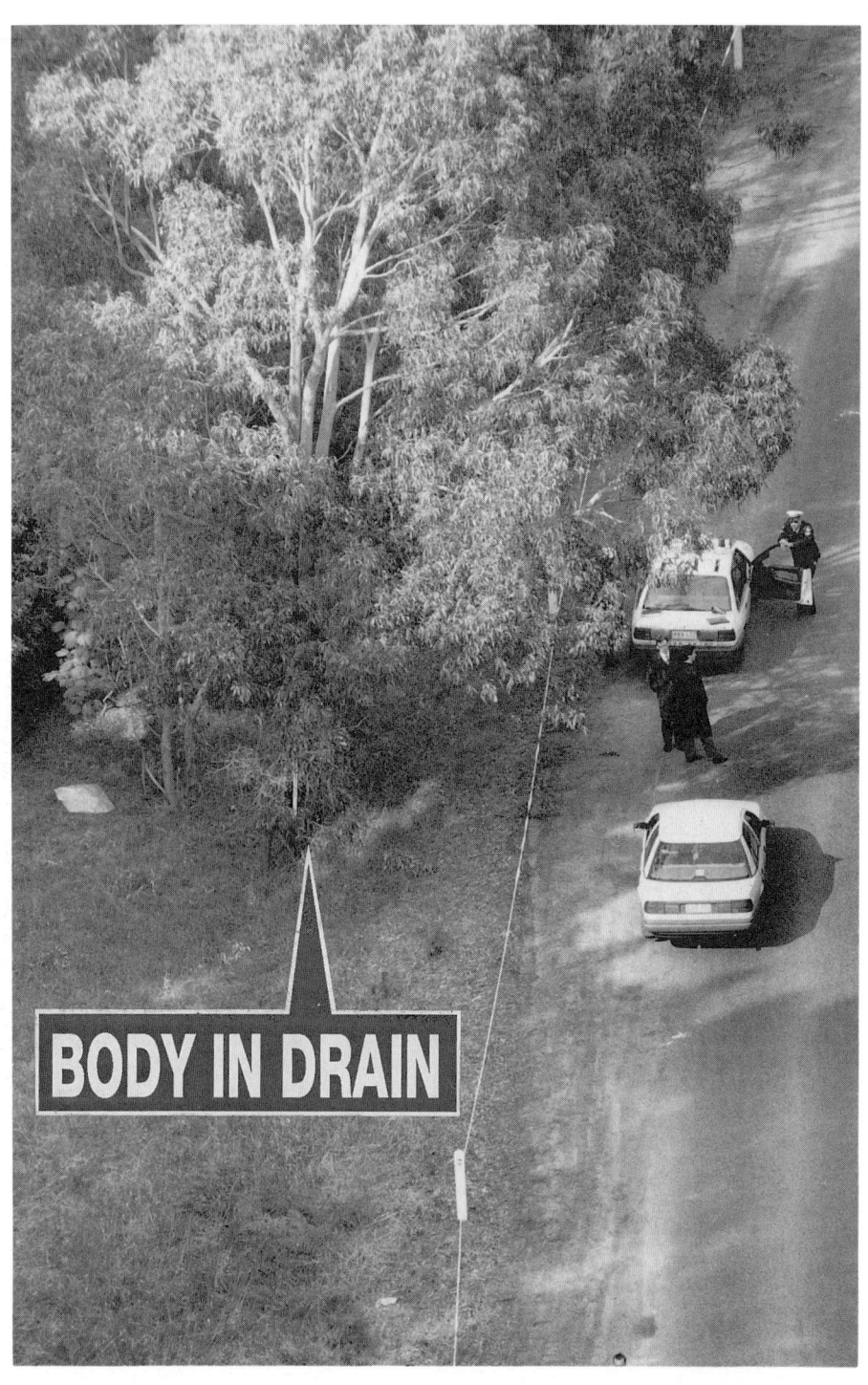

This aerial photograph shows how close Sheree's final resting place was to Mornington-Flinders Road. The police later learned Lowe had previously been pineconing there with his wife.

Kerri, Steve and Neil hear of the discovery of Sheree's body in the drain at Red Hill.

Detective Chief Inspector Peter Halloran.

Detective Senior Constable Murray Gregor.

Professor Stephen Cordner.

Left to right: Detective Snr Const Paul O'Halloran, Det Snr Sgt Paul Hollowood, Det Snr Const Alex Bartsch, Det Snr Const Andrew Gustke.

Robert Lowe being interviewed by Paul Hollowood on December 19, 1991.

Lowe confidently initials alterations to his statement...

...he gets agitated when Hollowood persistently questions him...

...flustered, he confronts Hollowood at the end of the interview.

"You know it was pink."

"Sorry, I didn't know, honestly, they might've said but I didn't know. Um-"

"- There's enough photographs of her around with her pink helmet and her pink parachute clothes on."

"Yeah, I know."

Margaret changed tack again to see how much Robert did know.

"All right. Where's the, where...where are we, with helmets, pink helmet- difficult to, um, difficult to get rid of."

"You can't throw it in the sea. It would've- it would float."

"(You) can weight it down."

"Ahh (pause) could and ... you know, where would I have all the rope and things like on me or, or, or string or whatever like that to weight it? You know it would roll and things like that, wouldn't it? How would I get out to the place? You know if I'm gonna w—, weigh it down off the shore, how am I gonna get out that deep?"

"Off piers."

"Yeah. Off piers, yeah. Off piers. But you just think, you know, a lot ... in the summer where people would've found it and it could've been covered over with mud and slush and sand and - but you just think that, you know, a lot of people dive under these piers and things like that."

"It may come to light yet, Robert."

"Well, I hope it does."

"How about, um, taking it away with you?"

"What- the, the helmet?"

"Mmm."

"What- to, to see where - what I did with it, so to speak?"

"Mmm. What?"

"To see what was supposed - well, I used the words 'To see what I did with it' so to speak."

"What do you mean?"

"Well, ah, are you saying 'Take the thought of the helmet away'?"

"No, did you take it away to Bendigo?"

"Oh! No."

".. there literally."

"Could, I, if I had done something like that, Marg, I couldn't possibly have had that helmet at home. The kids were in and out the car on the weekend and I cleaned the car out." Then he decided to move on.

"Not a problem. I could've thrown it away and what about the clothes? The clothes could be put anywhere, the clothes would be fairly easy to dispose of just dig a, dig a, dig a hole in the sand somewhere."

"Mmm."

"They'd be easy to dispose of."

"Mmm."

"Actually even the helmet - but I didn't have a- I didn't have a spade on me, so I can't go digging holes. But if it's sandy you can dig."

"Yes but you can't go ... Robert, you're in your car now and you're t-, you're pressed for time.

Alex and Andy looked at each other again. *Why would he say he didn't have a shovel on him?*

"Yeah."

"You can't wandering round digging holes in sand and looking for places and piers and ropes." Margaret felt the over-inclusive account was fact dressed up as fiction.

Robert had said that he was manufacturing a story. Margaret tried to call his bluff.

"I am not, under any circumstances, going to save your marriage. And I, I know you flew at me the other day when you said I said I'd put your marriage back together and I'm probably able to do that better than anybody. But I'm not going to save your marriage at your expense, it's too great a sacrifice, Robert. It's a perversion of justice for one thing and I can't be party to that."

"It's a perversion of justice but, ah...."

"Well, I can't be a party to that."

"I'm not asking you, I'm just working through possibilities."

"All right, you're not. I accept that I, ..."

"Marg, you can take your weight off that."

"Mmm, mmm."

"But ultimately it will be my decision."

"Yes."

"But I'm just just looking for some ... support advice for it."

"All right, it's absolutely your decision. I've got no problems with that at all ... Okay."

"But I'm looking for alternatives, I'm looking -"

"- Well there are alternatives Robert, it's -"

"- I'm looking how I c— can atone for that, that's the broad aspect."

"This is atonement you know, per se, I said because you've, you know you've brought your family up to be very Christian and honest and live by those very Christian moral standards. It's a sort of a bit of a, ah, you know a trap because, because you've done that they're in this bind now."

"Yeah. Mmm."

"Because you're the sort of family you are, your moral principles, the whole family's, are very, very high."

"Yeah almost too high."

"Yeah, yeah but you know, you brought them up like that in a way and then, as I say, because, there's the greater capacity for good, the greater capacity for evil, Robert. I really believe that. Do you?"

"Yeah yeah, I do."

The conversation came towards the end.

"Well, we don't have to go any further than this here, Robert, at this point in time or even at any time at all but, ah, suppose it -"

"- Doesn't get us anywhere Marg, though, does it?"

"Well, it does and it doesn't, you know, it's, it's a start and we have to look at it as a complete option."

Robert raised the possibility of a clairvoyant being able to find out who the real offender was. He talked about a blue car being identified by two witnesses. Then he said he was only trying to work out the scenario to help Lorraine, Benjamin and Jonathan.

"I don't want to collude with, in you sacrificing yourself," Margaret said. "Then you reassured me and that did give me a little bit of relief."

"Yeah, it's my decision."

"All right. Well, as long as I can keep believing, hanging on to that, Robert, that's fine."

"Yeah, and it's not your decision, you're not involved. So breathe deep breaths. But what I'm trying to do is to; as you know and, and you even encouraged me a little bit to do, but there's no commitment at all. Is, that, is to try and make up a sort of; no, not try and make up a story..." He still needed to drag Margaret in with him.

"No, no. Please don't use that phrase, Robert."

"It is an option. Therefore, I have to look at it and work it out."

"I'm not going to sit here and help you make up a story, you know. I will listen to what you have to say..."

"That's what I'll be trying to do, though."

"Well, you can't do it, you can't do this, Robert."

"Well, how else can I help Lorraine and-"

"Oh, dear it's a mine field..."

"I mean, this is what I'm trying to do."

"All right."

"I'm trying to do it, not to sacrifice four years or whatever it is. I don't for a moment say I'm going to do it. But I've got to look at it."

"It's an option isn't it? As you said, it's an option."

At the end of the discussion, he tried to strengthen his position.

"They haven't got anything on me, Marg. It's all circumstantial. When it comes to Sheree Beasley and getting her into that car, I know I didn't do it..."

Then they arranged to go to Red Hill on Monday, April 13. Robert said he needed to check out some details there.

The instant Robert left, Margaret, still shaking, went downstairs and told her son-in-law she couldn't go on any more.

Alex called in. Although the detective had heard every word, Alex had Margaret go through the game of trying to remember the relevant information from the conversation with Lowe. She told him a few things that Robert had said. Then she said: "Is it true? Is that scenario true?"

Alex said: "I don't know, I wasn't there." It was almost a Robert Loweism. What he said was the truth. But he damn well *thought* the scenario was true. He just couldn't tell Margaret. At least, not yet.

"What do you *know*?" she demanded. She was shaking.

"I'm not going to tell you," the detective said. "I can't tell you because this is on-going. You're getting the story off him and that's what we want to hear," Alex said gently.

Alex felt for this poor woman but he knew that by telling her anything at all could only pull her further into the sticky mess she was in. It was a real sticking point. Secretly he felt that probably only made things worse for Mrs Hobbs. She was doing her damnedest and probably now felt that the police knew very little about the case at all.

He was right. Margaret had wondered from the very beginning if she was perpetuating the police investigation. She was terribly fearful of that. To compound her problems, she was acutely aware she was thinking on her feet, making decisions off the top of her head. The police never told her what to do or say. She was flying blind and making all these awful decisions at the same time. And she knew enough about the law to know she was now in dangerous territory. And now that Robert had come up with some detailed movements relating to Sheree, the police wouldn't tell her if it was right or not! "Lonely" was too cosy a word for what Margaret Hobbs was feeling that day.

Andrew and Alex rushed back to Homicide and told their crew what had happened. Paul Hollowood wasn't overly excited. It was interesting and sounded promising. But, as he reminded them, it still wasn't enough. There was still a long way to go.

THROUGH THE Salvation Army in Rosebud, Robert had befriended Richard Guy from The Broadway in Rosebud. They liked each other. Richard knew Robert was a suspect for the Sheree Beasley murder but couldn't believe such a nice man - a man who knew his scriptures so well, a man who now was running a bible class for the Salvos - could do such a thing. Why, Robert even came to visit Richard at home. In fact, he was now visiting often. Robert would use Richard's Olympia typewriter. Just type a few notes, then leave. Richard didn't know what Robert was typing; he thought he was just typing letters. Eventually he told Robert to take the typewriter and use it at Florence Avenue. He could return it when he had finished.

Lorraine and the boys went to Rosebud one weekend when they knew Robert would be out of the unit. They tidied up, looked around, and Benjamin noticed the typewriter. He quietly sat down, put a blank piece of A4 paper in the roller and typed out every key on the board, lower and upper case. Then he folded the paper, put it in his pocket, took it home and hid it. Benjamin was worried - worried sick - that his dad had killed a little girl. He thought getting the standards might be being a bit melodramatic - it was like something out of an Agatha Christie novel - but just in case a confession or anything else for that matter turned up one day in relation to Sheree's disappearance, he was making sure that all bases were covered.

ON APRIL 9, at another session with Margaret, Lowe gave further details of his confession and said he left Sheree's panties and T-shirt on the body before pushing it into the drain. Margaret asked him if he had said anything sexual to the little girl which might have frightened her. He said it was possible but he didn't touch her except when he tried to revive her.

He said he was checking libraries and newspaper cuttings for information to put into his "confession".

Afterwards Margaret spoke with Alex about the trip to Red Hill.

"I'm going to go. What do you think?" Margaret asked.

"Up to you," Alex said, hoping she would.

Two days later, he was at work when Margaret rang him.

"Alex, I have a friend who watches my car so nobody steals it and he reckons these blokes got into it and left without taking it. Do you know anything about that?"

Alex thought quickly.

"To be honest, we've got a tracking device in the car just to make sure that you're going to be safe," he lied. "He may be a murderer and if something happened to you, we'd never be able to live with ourselves."

What was really installed, under power of a warrant, was a listening device. If Lowe said anything incriminating during the drive, it would be recorded.

ONCE OR twice Robert had seen or heard the surveillance police following him in the nine months they were on his tail. Given that, he probably assumed he was being bugged as well. He put on an outstanding performance while he was waiting for Margaret to pick him up in Florence Avenue on April 13.

At 9.57am, the hidden listening device in the unit picked up Lowe "praying", just before Margaret arrived.

"Listen to my words, Oh Lord, consider my (inaudible) and listen to my cry for help My King and My God. For to you I pray and I am crying for help Lord. Listen to my cry for help. I cry for help that you will prevent me, Lorri, Benjamin or Jonathan having to go to court or to the inquest. I cry for help that you will find and bring to justice Lord the person who did this to Sheree Beasley. Lord, I cry out to you, I cry out to you."

Then he started to cry and wail.

"(inaudible) that the person can be dealt with, later be humiliated Lord. Praise God you can do this. I know you can do it Lord." Then there was a lengthy pause. Robert felt the Lord needed a bit more urging. Sounding like the rugby coach he had once been, he called louder.

"Lord, I know you can do it. Please show me in time, Lord, that you can do this and will do it. Lord, it's important, vitally important and as you know it's be done in time, plenty time."

"Please do it, Lord," he pleaded between sobs. "Please do this so that Lorri and I can, can... listen to my cry for help, Oh Lord."

Then he started singing in his best church choir voice: "Oh Lord, most high I praise you Oh Lord, with all my heart. I will tell of your wonders, I will be gladdened with your (inaudible) I will sing praise to your name. Oh, oh, God."

Then he began whistling cheerfully, as if he had not a worry in the world.

Margaret arrived in her blue Commodore followed by more than half a dozen surveillance police. Robert got in the car and they drove off. Robert was armed with several newspaper cuttings showing the site where Sheree's body had been discovered. He also had his typewritten notes he had presented on April 6. He asked for the use of Margaret's *Melways Street Directory* and then at his insistence they went to visit Bill Bates, one of Robert's new friends at the Salvation Army so he could vouch that Robert was a decent man.

Then they set off in earnest so Robert could "manufacture" the confession, visiting the sites the *real* killer had visited. When they left the church Robert directed her onto the Nepean Highway and told her to turn left.

He pointed out Parkmore Road and directed Margaret to turn into it, and indicated the Lighthouse Milk Bar.

"Did you see it?" he asked. Margaret nodded. Robert was acting like he was on a school excursion. He was excited and talking with purpose.

He pointed to the huge pine tree on the east side of Parkmore Road and said that was where he had picked up Sheree. He told Margaret how he got out of his car, grabbed her and strapped her in. He said again too that Sheree and "the boy" were arguing and he was going to take Sheree for a ride. Robert could barely stop talking. He said he believed Sheree's mother lived "along there somewhere", pointing further up Parkmore Road. He told Margaret to drive up Parkmore Road a bit further, turn around and head back towards Nepean Highway.

She did as she was told. Being at the actual site where Sheree had been abducted from, and now sitting next to the man who did it, was rocking her to the very core. She noticed her hand shaking on the steering wheel, all the while trying to maintain a steady exterior.

Robert directed her to turn left into the Nepean Highway. After they drove for a few seconds, he said, quite clinically and in a factual manner, "She began to panic at this point." He said he had then turned into the foreshore opposite Miriam Avenue and did a U-turn in order to take Sheree home. He said he had intended to drop Sheree off at the freeway end of Parkmore Road and directed Margaret to turn into it.

He asked Margaret to return to Parkmore Road and do the route again. As they did so, he said he would say he did a U-turn further along the foreshore because if Lorraine found out he had turned into the foreshore so near to the unit she would always remember it. Then he told Margaret to do a U-turn on the foreshore before telling her to turn right into Elizabeth Street, left into Eastbourne Road, then into Jetty Road and then right and left onto the freeway.

He said Sheree had quietened down as he was driving along the freeway when he had told her he was taking her home. But Sheree had become hysterical when he went past the turnoff.

"And there's no evidence," Robert said excitedly. "The police will never find any evidence of anything in the unit. I thought I'd eliminate that...She died in the car."

Margaret was struggling to control the car on the road. Robert then said he had pulled into the side of the freeway just short of the Matthew Flinders bridge. Margaret did the same.

"She begins to panic," Robert recounted. "So this is when she really begins to panic. I realised that she is, she's passed away, she's choked or (inaudible). Anyway, I can clarify that." He jotted down a note on a pad and then put it back in his bag. "Here that she's - I find that she's dead."

Margaret hoped Robert wouldn't see the tear running down the right side of her face. She knew if he saw her crying he'd stop.

"She's dead now," he said. He said he had panicked and told Margaret to drive along the freeway to Boundary Road and then into Mornington-Flinders Road.

As they approached the area between McIlroys and Sheehans Lane, he asked her to slow down, saying, "It's along here somewhere." He directed Margaret to drive to Sheehans Lane and then turned and returned to the opposite side of the road.

"Recognise this bit?" Margaret asked.

"I've never been, I can't, Marg," Robert said of the spot where he once went pineconing with Lorraine.

He told her to stop opposite a gateway marked "Wilgunya" saying that was the spot. He got out of the car and told her to come. Margaret said, "No, I'll stay in the car."

He walked through the gateway whilst Margaret sat alone, trying to collect her thoughts. Robert had left his notes and diary on the seat. Margaret started thumbing through them while she waited for him to come back. She noticed her right foot on the accelerator was shaking violently.

Robert walked about near the drain for about 15 minutes, out of Margaret's sight. But Steve Batten saw him. The Senior Constable from the Victoria Police Audio Visual Section had been hiding about 200m away in dense bush since early morning, waiting for Lowe to walk into the trap. Steve was recording Lowe's every movement on a video camera.

Robert walked back to the car and told Margaret it looked like the burial spot as there was a drain there. He then directed her to drive towards McIlroys Road and do a U-turn. Then he ordered her to stop directly outside the gateway. Margaret realised he wasn't even acknowledging her presence. Robert was reliving what had gone before. He was oblivious to everything except his own fantasy, his own recollection.

He got out again and walked around the outer area before returning to the car.

Referring to the newspaper cutting he said he thought it was the spot.

He said he needed to check which way the body had gone into the drain as this could be checked. He told Margaret he had got down on his bottom and kicked the body down into the drain. He would say he said a prayer similar to: "God forgive me for this terrible thing I've done. Please look after this child, or something like that."

Margaret was now driving with one hand hiding her tears and the other on the steering wheel. She took a quick sideways glance at Robert and saw him filling in the details in his notes. Margaret was quite sure he was having an orgasm as he sat, wriggling on the edge of the car seat as he relived Sheree's death.

As he kept writing he said he left the singlet and underpants on the body and had taken the tracksuit and shoes off and dumped them in a dumpmaster at Glen Waverley shopping centre. As they drove, Margaret asked Robert a few more questions. She noticed he was very much reliving the abduction and she spoke to him in the present tense.

"What's your intention of picking her up in the first place?"

"Mischief," he said, without hesitation.

"Mmm."

Then he checked himself. "No, I don't know if a (inaudible) mischief could I?"

"Mmm."

"Is it enough to pick a girl up for mischief?"

Margaret asked him if he had thought Sheree would be distraught.

"She was happy to get in the car."

"Why? Who would let a little girl go like that?"

"She's had an argument with that little boy who was there."

"How do you know they were arguing?"

"I don't and the mother could come up and say look, they never argued but they could have been arguing about that," Robert offered.

The Murder of Sheree

"What are you saying? That she wanted to be saved from this argument because you can't trick a little girl? I mean, you know, getting into a stranger's car..."

"Well, I could have had some lollies there, ah, I did. It would have looked, you know, if I had been seen putting a girl into the car it would look bad, you know, she could have yelled and screamed or anything. "

"Hmm, but you claim she got in herself."

"Well, I just said, 'Hop in. Hop in and I'll take you for a ride'. I say that."

As Margaret pulled up in Florence Avenue, he said he would have to check again to see how the body was found. He completed the notes he was taking with "the drain was smallish".

They walked back into the unit and Margaret saw he was as high as a kite. He was terribly excited, chattering away about the drain and Parkmore Road, the prayer. Then he checked himself and said to Margaret, "Oh, you've gone a bit pale."

"Yes," she said flatly, "I feel like going now." She drove off and then pulled over to the side of the road and vomited.

As she drove home, totally drained, Margaret wondered how she had not seen before that Robert was a complete psychopath. She knew a psychopath was a person who lacked conscience, remorse or guilt. They have very insular personalities and seem to have very little anxiety or depression. They can bring on emotional responses at will. And that was what Robert was superb at. She recapped the performances he had put on for her over the previous seven months. Crying, weeping, wailing. And yet, all the time, Margaret had known it was all a sham. She realised he was a cardboard cutout. She said to herself, aloud, "He's not real." She was never able to find the real man under the shifting facades. Once or twice she had pushed him to a point where she saw a glimpse of something. But he was so heavily defended! She only ever got a few bricks out of the wall and saw a very sad, tragic figure. But within minutes, not only were the bricks back but they were mortared up. Impenetrable.

Margaret had the same nightmare practically every night. Her unrealistic belief that she should have done more to stop Robert committing further crimes, for example, after the Flinders Street incident, manifested themselves in nightmares. Nightmares about saving children. Margaret was surrounded by children. But a swelling mob of angry people were trying to kill Robert. While Margaret tried to save the wailing and clawing children, she was busy trying to rescue Robert from his attackers as well. The nightmare would build up to a frenzy as she tried to be in two or three places at once. Then she would wake in a lather of sweat.

That night she had a nightmare that was even more horrifying. She was in a strange, shimmering yet faded place. There were no walls, no boundaries, no sky. Just murky light that somehow kept shifting on the periphery. Margaret was carrying a heavy weight in her arms. She looked down and saw it was Robert Lowe. She was staggering under the weight. Men wearing dark suits, some with sunglasses, were closing in on her from all sides until they threatened to envelop her. Then they stood still, somehow menacing her with their silence and stillness. Margaret was crying. It felt as if her feet would soon start to sink through the floor, if that was what she was standing on. She turned to the men.

"Please help me. I can't carry this anymore," Margaret said through her desperate tears. The men didn't move. They just watched her with stony faces. Robert was looking at her with the hint of a smirk on his face. She struggled to keep him up but her arms felt like they were about to break. She tried one last time to hold Robert in her outstretched arms but he fell with a thud to the floor. Margaret instantly turned to the men and said, "Please help me," but they all ignored her. They quickly closed in and started to kick Robert on the ground. They kicked viciously as if they wanted to kill him. They kicked him - hard - in the head, the groin, the back. No matter how hard the kick, Robert showed no emotion at all. He just bounced backwards and forwards on the ground, blood flowing freely from his mouth, nose and even his eyes. Then the men all turned to Margaret in unison. Robert lay motionless but conscious. The man closest to Margaret said, with utter contempt, "Do you know who this man is?"

Margaret knew, and they knew she knew. But she thought it was unfair what they were doing to him.

"You can't kick him when he's down" she protested. They all turned back to their work and Margaret woke with a start. She thought it was such an obvious dream.

That night, half a world away, Daniel Vander Lugt of the Radio Bible Class in Grand Rapids, Michigan, was adding the finishing touches to his letter to Robert Lowe. Lowe knew Lorraine had always held the Radio Bible Class in high regard and as another means of emotionally blackmailing her into accepting him back home, he had written to the US chapter, seeking a favourable letter to show to his estranged wife.

But the response he got was not what he was after.

Vander Lugt reiterated he had not recommended Lorraine divorce Lowe, but had stated it was possible she had grounds for divorce.

Then the letter continued...

> I only know that you - by your own admission - have been in court on 9 occasions during the past 23 years for offensive sexual behaviour. This seems to indicate a serious problem.
>
> Unfortunately, your letters don't give me the impression that you are "sincerely and humbly" repentant regarding your behaviour.
>
> Instead, you seem to rationalise it, trying to convince me that it really isn't very bad.
>
> The implication seems to be that other people have exaggerated its significance.
>
> Honestly, I doubt whether a minor offense would have resulted in your being brought to court on 9 occasions.
>
> In fact, your own words imply that there were many other occasions when your offensive behaviour didn't result in prosecution. ("I get caught when an adult is suspicious but I always walk away at 2 strokes at the most.")
>
> You stated that God has 'cast your previous sins as far as the East is from the West.' Certainly God's Word does assure us of the unconditional forgiveness of our sins when we sincerely repent and ask God's forgiveness.
>
> In your case, however, since you apparently have continued in the same sin, it doesn't appear that you ever really repented.

```
I'm afraid that it is possible that your past
involvement with the church and Christianity may
have been largely insincere, having as its main
purpose a desire to disguise a serious sin that
you were unwilling to confront and eradicate.

As I wrote in my previous letter, you need to
recognize the seriousness of your sin.

Its consequences have caught up with you. Your
wife and those who know you well have the
responsibility of deciding how they will deal with
you.

I hope that it will be possible for your marriage
to be saved.

But I can't be honest and imply to your wife that
she is obligated to remain married to you,
regardless of your behaviour.
```

HARDLY A week went by without Neil Greenhill dropping in to the Homicide Squad office. He could not hide his grief, nor could he deal with it. He wanted to know how the investigation was going and whether there were any suspects. Everybody at Homicide would have loved to have told him about Robert Lowe, but they simply couldn't. Every time Neil left Homicide, the men would talk about how they wished they could help him. They knew the only way they could help would be to make an arrest and get a conviction. His visits steeled their resolve.

THE NEXT session between Robert and Margaret was April 28. After talking about Lorraine again, Robert said: "You know, that scenario thing?"

Margaret looked up at him. "Have you got it on you? Well, what sort of thoughts did you have? I think we can virtually remember it, Robert. What were you saying?"

"What I was thinking, I've got to the point where I needed to go to the library to see which way the body was put in, you know, that type of thing."

"Well, I'm not certain whether you're going to find that thing out from the papers, Robert, and the other thing too is that they may well not say."

"I've just got this idea, I don't know why, where, it's just not relevant but it is relevant, Marg, because it is the only point of contact that the police know anything about, isn't it?"

"Yes, I would think so."

"So if I say the body went in one way and came out the other end, came out the other way, you know, that's a big mistake."

"Mmm."

"I just, I want to have a good look at that. I really do and I've got time to do it."

"Yes, you've got time to do it, but um..."

"I want to - go on."

"I was, well, I'm not, I'm just thinking you saying that that is the only sort of thing that the police would be able to check. I guess, this, whoever did it."

"Might be clothes and shoes, I'm not sure about that."

"Yes, yes, yes, yes - will those sorts of things, Robert, will make what was left of the body, and we've already talked about that, there are other little things that may have to be sort of fitted in there."

"Some thoughts?"

"Well, there are things that probably aren't relevant. That there are sort of things that I might be asking you like (pause), going down. We've got plenty of time Robert, don't worry about time. We'll have another cup of coffee and things like going down to the unit that day. Did you form any intent that day of picking anyone up?"

Robert liked this talk. That was the sort of question the police would ask him.

"Oh, okay, good. Well, I could say, you know, just do my usual wandering. I often do. Now I don't say I could ever say I intended picking someone up because I've never, ever intended picking someone up but on the spur of the moment and the situation presents itself, it just happened. That's how I would have to word it."

"Well that's the way it just does happen, isn't it, Robert? That you see the target and it triggers off the intent which may not have been conscious."

"Mmm."

"But you were talking about doing a U-turn and turning into Parkmore Street (sic). Now whereabouts in Parkmore Street (sic) were these kids?"

"Well I think (pause) now I don't know where Mrs Greenhill or whatever her name is lives. Maybe I should look it up in the phone book because they were obviously going home and that home may be straight across the top of Parkmore, further down the Nepean Highway and if it was they wouldn't have gone down Parkmore. Do you see what I mean?"

"I'm sort of visualising it."

"No, no, look the shops firstly were an awful long way from Parkmore Street (sic) weren't they? Do you remember that?"

"Yes."

"Now if we hadn't gone there that day I would have presumed the shops were very close to Parkmore Street (sic), so it's a good job we went because we had to go a lot more, a long way down to those shops so those kids have walked from the shops across the entrance to the freeway to Parkmore. Now, depending where they live, I mean, they may just continue over the front of, top of Parkmore further on down the Nepean Highway but she may live, 'cos we had a look there was some streets, little ones, I don't know if they had names, off Parkmore, don't you remember that? We went down there."

"We turned around in one, didn't we?"

"Yeah. When we went down Parkmore, there were some little streets off. But look, the point is, I think they just went along the top of Parkmore."

"Where would...you say you picked her up in Parkmore Street (sic)?"

"On the corner."

"On the corner?"

"I think there is a phone booth. Near the phone booth on the corner and I think that's what the papers say."

"And how about the kid who was with her? I mean, what age would you estimate he would be?"

"Well, they said he was supposed to be 10."

"Well, how old would you estimate he might have been?"

"Oh, I'd say 9 or 10. Nine, say 9. I don't know, he was a big kid or a little kid but presumably they're much the same size I would think."

"They were the same size."

"Well, I would think so. Kids."

"Yeah."

"She is 6 and he is 10. Well, she's not likely to be playing with a big 10-year-old, is she?"

"Mmm."

"They were most likely to be similar size. She might be a big 6-year-old and he a small 10-year-old."

"Well, what can you say about what he was wearing."

"I didn't notice. I wasn't looking at him. I was looking at the little girl and she had bright colours on."

"Which were what?"

"Which was a tracksuit. A pink and green tracksuit was it or just a pink tracksuit?"

"I don't know."

"These are the things I got to, pretty, check colours of tracksuit."

"Well, you're saying that it was pink in, pink in some of the colour, were you?"

"Well often they are, aren't they? They have got a little bit of something else in them."

"You can have two tone tracksuits, yeah."

"And actually her photograph has been around Rosebud. I think it's taken off all the (pause) the photograph of that tracksuit has been around Rosebud in shop windows and things like that for months."

"Mmm, mmm."

"I've often thought of getting one and then I've thought, no, it's wrong, it looks as if you're guilty."

"Yes. How about the (pause) you were saying you picked the girl up. You put her in the car."

"There was still a lot of Christmas (sic) shoppers on the highway."

"You picked the girl up, you put her in the car, fastened the seat belt. And what happened to the boy then?"

"No, he (pause) how many bikes were there? One bike, or did he have a bike? You don't know?"

"If I tell you - Robert, I know nothing about this at all. Do you know what would happen to me? Sort of I read...in the papers and I've never pursued any details."

"I haven't either, Margaret."

"No. So you think there was one bike?"

"Yes. Yes."

"And where, where (pause) was she pushing that? What was happening with that when you got in the car?"

"He was pushing it at that stage. She was pushing it. It was his turn to push it with groceries in it. Matter of fact he might have been riding it, I don't know. And nobody else knows so I can make up that story, can't I? And I think there's just one, there's only one bicycle everybody talked about it as far as I know and I think it was her bicycle."

"And what was in the, the-"

"Groceries, it was, I wouldn't know, didn't go and check the groceries I didn't even notice what was in the basket. I wasn't looking at the bike, I was looking at the little girl to get her into the car and the boy, what happened to him I don't know. I just took off as quick as I could. He was slightly separate from, from her. I didn't notice really what he had on probably plainer clothes, I suppose...duller clothes or something you know and I don't know what happened to him. It was winter so he probably had long pants on or something like that. He might have had a raincoat on - something like that I didn't notice. No interest. He had the bike and the groceries. I don't even know he had groceries but he had something in it. And um, I can't say she was eating a lollie or anything because a lollie paper would have been found there wouldn't it because the police were very quickly onto that. So I just left him there. Goodness knows where he came from and what he was doing. Might have been on his way home I suppose but the girl was, I got her pretty quickly into the car. I put the seatbelt on and I did that because I put that in my statement. I could change it but I think it tends to make sure that she intends to stay in the car. Oh, I was being nice to her and she was quite willing to come in the car, and there's no problem there because I think they'd had a disagreement and she was quite happy to go for a run around the block. So I sort of took off with her normal speed."

"Did you do a U-turn?"

"No, because I'd already done a U-turn. If I've done a U-turn which means I've got to head back to Portsea again so I didn't do another U-turn no. Now thinking about not doing another U-turn anyway, that's the way it happened. The boy could well have taken the registration number of the car. If I'd wanted the boy not to see the number plate of the car I would have done a U-turn because the front number plate or he would have if I'd driven away, he would have actually. It doesn't make much difference because he never got the number. As far as I know he didn't get the number plate and he didn't do much about getting the number plate. So I just, I didn't do a U-turn no, I just kept going straight back towards Rosebud which actually goes over Chinaman's Creek towards Portsea is what the paper says."

"Now when the witness saw the child at Chinaman's Creek were you aware that she'd been seen then?"

"No, no, no. I frankly didn't have a conscience about me much."

"Why?"

"Oh, I carried away for the thing of the moment. I haven't done anything wrong. Pick a girl pup and just drop her back home again. Sure, theoretically it's wrong and morally it's wrong but I hadn't done anything wrong. Oh, I had actually you know, yeah, it would be classified as child stealing and actually it was quite a long way. Chinaman's Creek is quite a long way. It's probably you know, three kilometres. It's not as if I was just going around the block. Going around the block is not necessarily child stealing. That one in Essendon, you saw that didn't you that day and that was a six year old."

"Mmm, that was child stealing, yeah."

"I don't know what happened to that but, um..."

"He's been charged with indecent assault and child stealing."

"Has he?"

"Mmm, yes."

"I notice the Karmein Chan detectives are interested in him."

"Yes."

"But not the Rosebud one. Or according to the paper."

"No, yeah, so go on."

"Why wouldn't the Rosebud ones be interested? Aren't they interested?"

"Perhaps they were."

"Yeah, perhaps they were. I don't know."

"Perhaps they were, Robert."

"Perhaps that's a little bit similar, isn't it?"

"Mmm, it was a bit foolish, you know, an ice cream man. So what are you saying? You're up at (pause) you've turned around?"

"Yeah, I've turned, I've turned you know and I've down to Chinaman's Creek and I didn't notice the people there. I mean there were lots of people along the side of the road who would notice and..."

"What was the traffic like?"

"A little bit heavy because the car was going slowly over Chinaman's Creek. It was a little bit heavy. This was a Saturday and the holiday makers down there at the weekend. The traffic goes fairly slowly along the Nepean Highway especially mid afternoon. People won't go to the summer beaches but they were going out. It wasn't raining I think, I don't know if it was or it wasn't but anyway people were out. Mid Saturday afternoon so people get out supposedly. So then I went...she at this stage was getting very agitated she still had her stack hat on. She was agitated and I said, 'Okay, hold on', you know because there was much traffic I couldn't do a U-turn. You can't do a U-turn on the Nepean Highway so I thought I'd go around to the left which is the natural way. If you go to the right, there's no turn to the right except into the sea or into the foreshore. So I turned into the left and went along Elizabeth which changes its name to Eastbourne Avenue which is the way we came as far along Jetty Road and I thought, this is the way to go without getting back onto the Nepean Highway which gets clogged. Just go along Eastbourne Road and the freeway and down and drop her off at home. Or not at home but far enough from home somewhere near the shops or something like that. But when I crossed Jetty Road and went and looked - turn off, turn off the freeway, down to where Parkmore Street (sic) is, next to, where it wasn't a turn off, there's no turnoff there and she recognised (pause) I wonder if she would recognise that but anyway I have to watch that because if her parents didn't have a car she wouldn't go on the freeway too much. But I suppose..."

"I think she's got grandparents."

"Yeah, yeah, that's right, who have to come on the freeway. So I had to explain, 'Sorry, look the road just doesn't go off that but so I'll have to go up further,' and she panicked, she really did panic. I told her to be quiet you know and I said, 'It'll only be another ten minutes', I said. I said, two minutes originally from Jetty Road down there but because there was no turn off we went up and we kept going and she really got into a fluster at this stage and she took (off) her seatbelt. No, no, she didn't take her seatbelt off. Okay, I could say she started to take her seatbelt off. I might have to change that a little bit. She started to take her seatbelt off, well, but she could have jumped out of the car so (pause) and then she, this confuses two issues actually, then she started coughing and spluttering and choking so then I took the seatbelt off, would be the better thing I think. Go back to the original. Then I - "

" - Did you pull in? Had you pulled in?"

"Yeah, I just then pulled in. I pulled into the side, oh, a couple of hundred metres short of an overhead bridge just before a barrier and she sort of leaned forward, so (pause) and the coughing stopped and I said, (pause) 'What's the matter?' or words to that effect and she didn't answer and I, just having been leaned forward I lent her back and realised that she was in a lot of trouble. In fact it was just as if her heart had stopped beating. So I tried mouth to mouth resusci -resuscitation, resuscitation but I was never very good at that. I think you've got to lay somebody out flat and I didn't do that. I've never. I never got her out of the car. So I left her there for a second and then went over to flag someone down on the motorway. I tried for a few seconds and realised that nobody could care a damn. Everybody just kept going and here's a man. If it was a woman who tried to flag someone down, people would stop. But a man trying to flag someone down, nobody will stop. So I went back to try and - "

" - Do you remember any particular person you tried to flag down. Any particular car or anybody noticed you?"

"I couldn't think...something a little bit unusual like a ute..."

"A ute?"

"Could be a ute...you remember those sort of people.'"

"Yeah."

"You know I've been hitch-hiking, you know the ones that do stop and the ones that don't."

"Yes."

"And I could mention something like that and nobody was going to... and I could be there half an hour trying to flag someone down, realised - so I thought I'd better go back and see what I could do myself. So I lay her across the seat. You can do that - or can you? I'd better have a look at a Toyota Corolla. I can't remember what's between the two seats, whether you can do that or if it's one of those partitions and you can't or I put the seat back, right back, that might be better. Put the seat right back and tried to undo the top of her tracksuit and tried to massage. I don't know what you massage, just the stomach or something like that isn't it? Or here, don't you? The heart's here, isn't it?"

"Mmm."

"I sort of tried to pump it or something like that. Blow or breathe air into her mouth and I think you hold her nose, nostrils together with the head as far back as you can."

"You'd taken the helmet off?"

"Yes, although I haven't said that in the report, I know."

'I think you did."

"I said it later, yeah, I said it very much later."

"Did you notice what type of strap there was on the helmet?"

"Just a normal, um, you know all straps are the same I think. Just a normal sort of um plastic type strap I think."

"What, buckle or press-studs or what?"

"Um, the boys have got a helmet and it's one of those, it's it's yeah, it's a buckle. The boys have buckles I think yeah, there's a buckle but it doesn't have the prong going in it so that's what it would have to be."

"Did you notice any, was there any sort of logos or anything on the helmet?"

"No, in fact I didn't much, pay much attention to the helmet. What, it was a pink helmet wasn't it? Or was that the tracksuit?"

"Mmm, mmm."

"Now, I don't want to go into that because I think I wasn't looking at the helmet, I was looking at her."

"Mmm, okay."

"The helmet was tossed in the back seat...and I don't, didn't want to know about it."

"And then what?"

"Then I realised I couldn't you know, there was nothing really I could do. I couldn't get off the freeway to go down to the hospital, Rosebud Hospital, it means I have to keep going and I didn't know where the next turnoff was, that could be another five minutes plus say fifteen minutes back to the Rosebud Hospital. Knowing the Rosebud Hospital, there is not a doctor, there's a nurse but there's not always a doctor. They have to call him in. And that's another twenty minutes and you have lost that life. But I don't think you can retain somebody for twenty minutes after they've been, you know, and they ask all the questions, how did this happen, so my goodness this is going to lead me into far more trouble. I've got to be back home. We're going to Mildura. I don't want to sacrifice that, I've been building up to this for months and you know, and if I went and reported myself I'd lose the whole trip to Mildura for the kids and Lorraine and...now that was a prime, that was a priority as far as I was concerned and that's true. Um, so Rosebud Hospital was ruled out. I had to get back fairly soon because I hadn't anticipated wasting time. I'd spent half an hour. So what do I do? I have to go and go somewhere where perhaps I don't usually go. Not on the normal way back. So I turned off the freeway, found this other road, went up somewhere behind Arthur's Seat and there were a few houses along this road I was going, Boundary Road, and the houses sort of petered out and I kept going and I thought, 'Well, if I turn right at the end here and just show that it's not on my, my own way home' and I don't know why I really turned down there because, um, I'll have to think about where the body was found because it's an unusual place for so many houses being around. I mean, I would have done it where there weren't houses around and another thing is you cannot see the drain from the road you have no indication there's a drain there. So I can't use, I suddenly saw this drain and it's in the middle of..."

"You would have seen the drain if you'd have driven down there."

"If I'd driven down there, yes."

"You're just looking for a concealing spot?"

"Yeah. It was fairly bushy, tall trees, fairly bushy. So I drove down there, yeah, slowly. Drove down, parked the car, had a look to see whether I can put this in the bushes somehow. I haven't got a spade on me for digging a (pause) because I walked in, had a look around, having left her in the car at this stage, and I saw this drain, looked at it, and looked through it, oh yeah, you know, it was adequate, not very long but adequately long enough anyway. I didn't know if she would fit in there because it was a fairly small type drain but then she wasn't very big herself because I came back and looked at her and I thought this was, I'd be, you know, this was a real possibility and I can stuff it up with branches and things like that at the other end. Cover it all over. Who would know? It could be months before anybody was (pause) so I then got her out, got the body out, took her shoes off, took her tracksuit off because it was very identifiable and just left her singlet and pants and maybe socks and carried her down there. Said a short prayer."

"What did you say?"

"'Forgive me Lord for the terrible things I've done. Please look after this life...and I'll speak to you later about it Lord' or something, I don't know. Perhaps not that. So I put her headfirst into the drain and she fitted because her shoulder's her broadest part, therefore if I could get her shoulders in, the rest would go in and the shoulders just fitted. Now this is the part I got to...whether she was in fact doubled up or not but let's just leave it like that. Her head went in first and her feet last and I could push on her feet to push her further down, push the body further down."

"Robert, how do you know she was dead at that point?"

"Well, she wasn't breathing. I checked her pulse there was no breathing, there was no pulse rate. There are other places you can feel the pulse too. I am just trying to think. But obviously the wrist is the most noticeable and I tried both wrists. There was nothing happening."

"You said she was very pale."

"Yeah, well, she lost her colour, which, blood gone out of her cheeks, I think that's right anyway. Yeah, cheeks kept red because the blood movement in it. I don't know. But anyway she'd gone pale so it looked as if, that there was just no life. There was not even any coughing and her breathing that was..."

"How did you feel when you were putting her in the drain?"

"I closed her eyes by the way."

"Hmm, how about body weight? Was she..."

"...Just the same."

"Floppy or what?"

"Yes, still floppy, still floppy, it was only twenty minutes I suppose at the most."

"Right."

"So it takes... it's about an hour, isn't it before the body hardens up or two hours or something you know. Twenty minutes should be nothing. So she was still there and she was quite pliable to be able to get into the drain and, um (pause) um, so I put her in there and I got a whole lot of branches, sods, turf, kicked some turf and stuffed it all in."

"In the entrance?"

"In the entrance. I didn't do anything on the other side, go around the other side and look or stuff anything in but I pushed her fairly well. As far down as my foot would take her. If there was a branch hanging around, I suppose I could have found a branch and pushed her further. Maybe I did that. Wouldn't I have time to break a branch off or you know maybe there was one."

"Was one lying around?"

"Unless one was just dry enough to push it further down, which, I did that so she was pretty well concealed and pushed all the sods and branches and everything else like that too so people couldn't see it and it would just appear an open drain from anybody who wants to come in, coming past."

"Right."

"And from there I just got back in the car. The clothes, the tracksuit the pair of shoes. I'm not happy about the pair of shoes. Perhaps I'd better leave her with shoes on."

"Well what sort of shoes were they?"

"Look, I didn't, I'll just have to say I didn't take the shoes off. I mean, in the decomposed state those shoes could have been washed away or something but if I took them off I'd have to say I unlaced them or unclipped them. People ask what type of shoes. So I didn't take much notice in the shoes. If I'd have took them they'd have been in the car. I would have time to look at them and examine them. So I left the shoes on. It also gave me greater pressure to push the body down the drain."

"Um, all right."

"So um with that I had the helmet and the tracksuit in the car, that's all. So I got in the car, drove away as quickly as I can. I didn't want the car to be seen there too long."

"You don't think anybody saw you around. Were there any?"

"No, because you can't actually see cars going along the main road down there."

"Mmm, mmm."

"I couldn't see your car when you were parked there."

"Oh, right."

"Couldn't you know, it's just the angle of the road, it goes around a corner at an angle like that from there down here. You were parked there at one stage I think I could just see the roof of you but you were, you know, (pause) so I then got out of there pretty quickly and headed back towards Melbourne, or to Melbourne and I thought what I'm going to do very carefully about the tracksuit and the helmet and I decided that um since the dumpmasters get dumped or emptied at least once a week, or sometimes, you know, two or three times a week, a commercial one, I should put it in the bottom part of the bottom of one of those because I haven't got a spade to dig a hole and bury them. Now, I don't know, sniffer dogs or something like that could sniff it out, especially the clothing, the tracksuit. I didn't want that risk although I could bury the things a long way away. Who would look up in say Springvale or something like that but the thing is... ...accidentally...Karmein Chan's body was found accidentally."

"Mmm, that's right."

"Sniffer dogs or horses or whatever you know, things be excavated or something like that. Somebody wants to bulldoze something and anything could happen. So I thought, you know, once it gets into here and then gets on a communal tip and buried, well, it's gone."

"It's gone."

"So that's what I did. I didn't know where the tips were in Brandon Park which is the local shopping centre but I did know there was one down near Safeway in Mt Waverley...now what I did actually, I had a look around in the bin and there was already just bits of wrapping paper and thing s like that, plastic sheeting and things like that, um, so I gather, got that, I made two separate parcels."

"Hmm."

"No, I didn't, I stuffed the tracksuit in the helmet of the head in the..."

"Mmm."

"...Head part of the helmet."

"Mmm."

"So it's just one. By doing so it would take less time and if anybody saw me wrapping things like that, you know, so I just put them all together, covered in this um, plastic layers of them, and um, the bin was quite full of quite a lot of cardboard and um plastic and things like that and so I just lifted it up and just pushed it."

"It was just all cardboard and plastic? Nothing else in there?"

"Ah, there were other things. Um, I looked through some of the rubbish bins down the road but the bins there, so I, I know what is in a typical Safeway bin. A lot of fruit and vegies and um, lettuce and some corn. They're not in that time of the year, um, but there were vegetables and all there, all kinds of things but the vegetables straight on top but underneath were layers of cardboard and plastic which is typical of that. There's so much wrapping all this stuff comes in."

"Mmm, mmm."

"Ah, so I just lifted it up and was able to pretty well drop it right down. It's not a big parcel. It's only the size of a you know, of a helmet and ..."

"Mmm."

"And so it was dropped down, um, the lid was ah, the lid was down so I was able to lift it. It wasn't locked or anything like that so, sometimes they're locked, sometimes they're not um, so I was able to drop it down and um that was the end of that."

"Hmm."

"So, without timing it, it must have been about half past four, ten minutes, quarter of an hour to get home, no problems, I just went straight into the garden got the lawnmower out."

"Did you?"

"Still got time for the lawn or whatever and pick up some of the twigs."

"Mmm, mmm."

"Lorraine was busy typing and I crept inside first actually and saw Lorraine. She was busy typing but I didn't want to make an issue out of it so I just went out in the garden and um and then come the five o'clock, no it's the five thirty news that night so I just kept going til it was dark. I'd say quarter past five, five, quarter past five, um, came in, I think the kids came back, ooooh, about half past five and saw this thing and the story just continues on so..."

"Did you um, did you have any muddy clothes or anything?"

"No, it's fairly grassy there where I went down, it was fairly grassy."

"Mmm."

"Well, I must have had mud, maybe just, just, um not muddy clothes, the body was never really laid on on the ground, um, and there was no blood."

"Mmm."

"Body was never laid on the ground, the body was always in a car or in the drain."

"Mmm."

"So my clothes were not muddy."

"Hmm."

"Um, my shoes would have been muddy but um I got most of that mud off. I took the shoes off and I cleaned them actually as I was home then when ah, nobody was around really."

"Hmm."

"And actually with this, ah, us cutting the grass um, nobody said anything about my shoes, but because I'd been mowing the grass and everything else like that, they got dirty and muddy anyway."

"Yeah, mmm, mmm."

"So nobody said anything. As you come in, you, you take your shoes off and just, just normal. Take your shoes off either outside and, um, and ah, wait for them to dry - might. Marg, those shoes weren't exceptionally muddy, well, well, no, no, when I got home I would have changed into my gumboots, I know I would have done that."

"Mmm, right."

"So I took my shoes off and I don't think anybody made any, you know, perhaps I just scraped the excess mud off, off the shoes and I got straight into my gumboots cos I'd only mow the lawn with gumboots on, protection for your legs, you know."

"Mmm."

"Ah ah, and ah, so the shoes were just what - whatever. Mud on the shoes were cleaned off then and, ah, when I came to clean the shoes later on - actually they're only old shoes anyway, they're only runners."

"Mmm."

"There weren't these shoes, they were only runners so they tend to get mud on them anyway, so."

"Mmm, that was okay."

"That's all right...it was fairly clean actually down there where the body was, you know, it was well grassed."

"Mmm."

"Bushy, there was no mud, although we didn't go in the winter, I know. There was a drain which suggests it might have flooded."

"Mmm."

"But you know, there's no evidence of mud, I don't think (pause) it's just that, it's just a normal amount of winter mud, you know, it wasn't as if I..."

"Mmm."

"...got it on my clothes. There was no need for it on my clothes. Shoes are about the only thing and, ah, nothing else was said after that, after 5.30 news. Nobody made a big fuss out about that. We turned the news off the for rest - I made sure the news was turned off for the rest of the night. I can say, 'Yes, I think it was turned off for the rest of the night'."

Later...

"I didn't want to hear about it so I turned the news off and didn't hear anymore. Didn't hear about it anymore."

"Mmm, you didn't think about it when you went away?"

"I want to get it out of my mind, now I was going to enjoy my holiday, although obviously I must have thought about it, I guess."

"Hmm, hmm."

"I didn't want to think about it but I thought about it, yes I did. Um, hmm, you know, if I'd been interested in that I would have been listening to news reports, wouldn't I? Probably."

"Possibly, hmm."

"But Lorraine said here the whole week away she never saw, never gave it another thought. She didn't hear anything."

"No."

"And I didn't."

"When you were driving around Robert, were you conscious of anybody at all seeing you? Was there any time when anybody paid any attention to this, do you think?"

"I could make something up, I could say somebody who was um, when I was picking the girl up you mean?"

"Any time."

"Well, nobody would be conscious of it other than..."

"Mmm."

"But picking the girl up, that's the only time."

"Mmm."

"I mean, if I drive around just looking for girls, it's nobody. I mean, it's just a car driving around, you know?"

"Yes, but you're saying that you, it was just a spur of the moment thing."

"Mmm."

"Sort of triggered off by..."

"Mmm."

"The sight of these kids."

"Yeah."

"All right. Mmm."

"Any other delving questions, you know, hard ones? If, if you think of it, you may not, you may think of something later on. I mean, there will be um, questions which will be..."

"I think there's suggestions Robert about ah, that we talked about in our last session about any sexual suggestions that you might have made to her to frighten her."

"I don't want to admit to that or say I did it because - two things that you've said today. I didn't want to do anyway but two things you said was the boys or Lorraine, one of them, or all of them is as scared that I have murdered the girl for manslaughter and that I sexually interfered with her and I have never, never sexually interfered with any girl anyway."

"I know that."

"Um, if I admit to sort of manslaughter the boys or Lorraine will, might breathe a sigh of relief."

"Mmm. Mmm."

"But if I include in that that I sexually molested her or, or suggested to her, that would take away some of the sigh of relief."

"Mmm, all right."

"So I don't want to cause them more trouble than it's worth."

"Mmm, mmm."

"Me and my story. Nobody knows that I've said anything or not."

"Except you and me."

"Except you and me, that's right but she could panic for reasons other than um, anything like that."

"Hmm."

"Just the fact that I'm taking away…"

"Well, children today who are picked up by men, you know, Robert, in today's climate, they, ah, have been warned and expect something dreadful to happen to them."

"Mmm."

"I'm only saying to, um, our kids constantly, ah, warning them."

"Yeah."

"But they don't know what - their expectancy is either, I mean it could be rape, it could be murder. I mean the worst, worst kids could probably think of is, is actually murder. Being killed isn't kids, at that age. Being taken away from their parents is enough and, and ah, you know how children are when they're just lost, how they …"

"Hmm, hmm."

"It's certainly been, it's an unknown because we tend to warn our kids and and not go into explicit details."

"Sure."

"So there's a great fear of the unknown too."

"Mmm. So there's probably no need to add anything further as to why she panicked because of something of the unknown. Would that be correct? I mean, I don't need to say I sexually…"

"You don't have to include that at all. We don't know what she was thinking. We can imagine."

"Well, if there's no suggestion of sexual interference on her as you say, just taking her away from home or taking her away and she not knowing you know when she's going to be taken back, not trusting me that I'd take her back. Here I am, I promise you'll be back in two minutes and then she's not going to be back in two minutes."

"Mmm."

"I don't know how long. I'm then going to you know that that's enough to…"

Robert was sitting on the edge of his seat and Margaret could see by the look on his face and his manner that he was really sitting back in his blue Toyota Corolla.

"Mmm."

"To um…"

"There's no suggestion Robert that you may have got agitated with her yourself and…"

"Slapped her or something?"

Now Margaret could see Sheree sitting next to him, terrified, pleading for her life. She prayed that no gasp of disbelief would burst from her lips.

"Mmm."

"I haven't, but I could. Certainly I could have raised my voice to her. 'Look, I've told you that I'm going to be there. I've told you I'm going to be there in two minutes or so. Now just be quiet. Shut UP!"

Margaret flinched and sat bolt upright, hoping Robert didn't notice her reaction. She struggled to hold back the tears.

"Mmm."

"You know, just a hard, firm - a voice would be enough to terrify her wouldn't it?"

"I would think so."

"Under the circumstances?"

"Yeah, mmm."

"I wouldn't hit her."

"Not even a back hand? 'Be quiet!'?"

"I don't know. But it would only be one-handed because of the sort of driving the car. Yes, it could have been, yeah. Yeah, that would shock her, wouldn't it?"

"Mmm."

"Yeah, just sort of a backhand off the tummy and then across the top of the head. I wouldn't hit her on the face but on the top of the head I could have, you know, clip on the top of the head. I've done that at times with the boys."

"She still had her helmet on though, didn't she?"

"Ah yeah, that's true. Ah um, yes, these are the things you know I would have fallen for that. It's hard to take a helmet off before that. I could tell her take her helmet off, I could tell her to take her helmet off, going on the Elizabeth Avenue or Eastbourne Avenue."

"What for now?"

"No, it doesn't make sense. No, no real reason. 'You'll be home soon. Listen, take you helmet off.' That doesn't make sense, does it? Um, she'll want to keep her helmet on as some protection, wouldn't she? Probably if she had panicked or if you had panicked but no, no, I wouldn't. I mean, hitting her across even the face, the chances are that I'd miss the face and hit the helmet and hurt my own finger so I'm not going to do that so I'm going to hit her across here and I don't think I'd ever do that, you know Marg? I mean, if you hurt someone, if you hit her anywhere near the stomach or the chest, you hurt someone without it, it doesn't have the same effect of what you're trying to do."

"Mmm."

"If you clip them across the top of the head or the face to bring them to…"

"She's being very hysterical though, isn't she Robert at this point in time? You may be panicking yourself to shut her up."

"No, I probably got to clip her, you know, somewhere, I said, grab her by the shoulder and shake her."

"Mmm."

"One hand, stop it, or something."

"Mmm, mmm."

"That's what I'd be more likely to do."

"Mmm."

"Because hitting her across the chest I don't think, has the, has the same effect as hitting someone across the um face. Across the face says shut up immediately, across the chest, they feel the pain and the, the blow and it doesn't register that they have to shut up crying."

"Mmm."

"Would you say that's right? All right?"

"Did you notice whether she had anything in her hair."

"No, she had her helmet on."

"No, but I mean you took the helmet off at some stage. When did you notice, when you put her in the drain whether she had her hair in a ponytail or a..."

"No."

"Or some ribbon. Slide?"

"I was only looking at her face Marg."

"Mmm, mmm."

"What she had in the back of her hair or in her hair made no difference."

"Mmm."

"She had a, I didn't really look for a ponytail."

"So she went in face up?"

"Mmm."

"Mmm."

"I couldn't put her face down on the concrete you know."

"Why?"

"Well, when you bury someone, they go in face up, don't they?"

"Mmm."

"In a coffin."

"Hmm."

"And you wouldn't want a nose and a mouth and a chin on a cold piece of concrete."

"But is she dead?"

"You think of it as a human being."

"Mmm, all right."

"I put her in the normal way, someone is buried face up."

"Hmm, mmm."

"So I didn't notice her hair...didn't, didn't, didn't register you know, I, I, just wanted to put that all...did I only just wanted to put it out of my mind."

"Mmm, mmm."

"Blank it out of my mind."

"All right."

"There are trick questions like that you know, not, not trick - whether she had her helmet on, when I hit her across the head, you know and other things."

"All right, well if you can you think about some of these things and..."

"Mmm."

"We'll go from there."

"If I come out on a bit of a high today, well I have..."

"Hmm."

"But I've got to keep my spirits up."

One topic of homework completed, Robert moved on to Lorraine and the boys. The only emotion Margaret saw was exhilaration at reliving the crime. She felt sick to the core. She nodded at the right time, she said the 'mmms' and 'yeahs' but she had trouble concentrating. She struggled to keep calm until he left. She realised now, with her head spinning, and a wave of nausea ripping through her, that it wasn't just a charade after all. He had actually done it. He had killed Sheree.

ROBERT STRODE in on May 8 with his completed confession and showed it to Margaret. She felt certain if the police were watching him and knew what he was up to, they would march right in and arrest him there and then. But it didn't happen. Robert was very nervous. He went to the toilet several times, something he had never done before in therapy.

When he settled in his seat again, Margaret told him to take his confession to the police. Robert was aghast. He couldn't believe what she was saying.

"No," Margaret said. "I think you should go to the police with that statement."

The Murder of Sheree

"I mean, the only reason I was going to do it is because of, because of her health and her..."

Margaret stared at him, frowning. Robert stared back. He was still amazed. The only noise in the room was the ticking of the clock. Lowe broke the silence.

"No, I can't go in and just say I'm doing it for my...." He groped for the word but he was stuck. Then he smiled a little and said hopefully, "I know you're pulling my leg."

"I'm not pulling your leg. I'm not pulling your leg," Margaret said forcefully, then she raised her eyebrows at him as if to say, "Come on, do it."

"I would never do that." Robert talked of his fear of going to jail. "There's always the fear of getting bashed up and all that type of thing, of course. But they (the police) cannot tie me in, just because Lorraine says I wasn't home and she's got the mental breakdown or whatever it is. Just be -"

In a flash Margaret realised what he was up to.

" - ah, now I've got it. You're waiting for her to have a mental breakdown so that she'll be too sick to testify against you. Is this what you're waiting for?"

"I'm not. I'm not. I'm not. I don't...."

"You're hoping."

"That cross - "

" - You are hoping that she's going to be so sick that you will wear her down to a point where she can't testify against you."

"I, I...the thought crossed my mind yesterday for the first time. It crossed my mind yesterday," he said in monotone. Margaret was disgusted. After hedging around her suggestion several times, then flatly refusing to go to the police, Robert finally agreed to leave the confession with her. When he left, Margaret slumped in her chair. Just a few minutes later, Matthew Wood came in to check on her and see if she had any information for the police. She handed him the 'confession'.

Not long after he left Margaret's clinic, Robert was arrested at Box Hill for shoplifting a packet of M&M sweets. He was taken back to the police station where the officers found, to their amazement, a confessional statement about the Sheree Beasley murder.

While Lowe was protesting his innocence in the interview room ("I was just on my way to take them back, I'd forgotten I had them"), the uniformed police rang the Zenith task force. Alex told them to photocopy the confession and put it back, so Lowe could continue working on it.

In subsequent sessions with Margaret, Robert tried to withdraw from the confession. He tried to get her to promise to say that he hadn't written it. Then he admonished her for calling it a confession. He preferred 'document'. Pedantic as ever, he preferred the adjective 'fictitious' to be used as well whenever the confession was mentioned. Then he told Margaret he only did it to show Lorraine, not for any other purpose. He said it was just 'an option' when he compiled it. Now he wanted to walk away from it. He continually reiterated that he had not killed Sheree.

A FEW DAYS later Robert moved out of Florence Avenue. The police did not know where he was living. Not that it was a major concern in terms of arresting him if they needed to. He was still consulting Margaret Hobbs regularly and could have arrested him there if and when the time came. But Paul Hollowood wanted to know where he was staying. He gave Murray Gregor the task of finding Lowe's new address.

AT ANOTHER session on May 15, Margaret asked Robert if he had done any further work on his 'scenario'. He said he could only 'pad it out' now. He asked for suggestions in relation to how Sheree died but Margaret told him it had to be from him, nobody else. He said he didn't like admitting things of a sexual nature took place but he would think about that. He talked of praying for the body of Sheree and of giving her a decent burial in order to 'minimise any outburst that he might get from the Greenhill family.' He then added that he 'hadn't meant to kill the girl' and the 'outcome is something gone drastically wrong and I panicked'. It was more fuel for the brief Murray Gregor was trying to piece together.

MURRAY WAS enjoying a rare day away from the Beasley investigation. It was a glorious day. It was a warm and sunny Sunday afternoon and there were crowds of people meandering by the bay. Murray went for a stroll along St Kilda pier and then sat down at the pier entry,

The Murder of Sheree

taking in the view. Moored yachts, kids on rollerblades, pretty women, lovers arm-in-arm, families with kids carrying balloons. Some people walked by with knick-knacks they'd bought at the craft market on The Esplanade, just a minute's walk away. Then Robert Lowe walked past wearing a striped, polo neck shirt, light coloured slacks and cheap runners. He was almost strutting, standing very erect, and walking at quite a reasonable pace. His face was set and he looked straight ahead. He certainly was not taking in the sights. He was a man with a purpose.

Murray followed him to Jean Jacques by the Sea, a trendy eatery just off Jacka Boulevard. Suddenly Lowe stopped and stood about three metres outside the entrance to the nearby women's toilets. There were a lot of kids there, playing outside the toilets on the grass and running in and out of the toilet block. Lowe stood transfixed, watching the children, then he looked around at the crowds moving about. He stood still for three long minutes, watching, his jaw still set. Murray was in no doubt that Lowe was captivated by the children and was drawn to them like a moth to light. Murray moved back to the traffic lights on Jacka Boulevard and watched. Lowe then walked to the same traffic lights where Murray was standing and waited for the lights to turn green. He was only two metres from the off-duty detective but he didn't notice him in the crowd of pedestrians. The lights changed and Lowe walked up Cavell Street next to Luna Park, then along several back streets, while Murray followed at a discreet distance. Lowe then turned into the Florida Lodge Backpackers Hostel in Grey Street, St Kilda. *Beauty!* Murray thought. *Gotcha!*

The following day Murray asked to see the lodgers book. His finger flicked down the list of names until it stopped at Robert Arthur, of 111 Messines Road, Wellington, New Zealand. That was Rick Lowe's address - Robert's brother. And the handwriting was obviously Robert Lowe's. Murray saw that Robert had stayed there on May 2, 9 and 15. He looked up at the advertising signs and saw straight away why it would appeal to Robert. At $7.50 per night, it was the cheapest backpackers hostel in Melbourne.

ROBERT CAME in with his knapsack and a plastic bag. He sat in his leather chair and looked at Margaret. She wasn't looking forward to another session. She had lost weight. She wasn't sleeping. Some of her

The Murder of Sheree

hair had fallen out.

Robert started again on Sheree.

"Margaret, do you really think that I could put a child in a drain to be consumed by maggots?"

She looked at Robert and just as she was about to speak, she saw something small on the back of the chair, just behind his left shoulder. She got up from her seat and saw it was a little caterpillar. She thought she would pick it up, crush it in a tissue, and throw it in the bin. As she reached for it, she saw it was not a caterpillar but a maggot. Recoiling in disgust, Margaret looked down and saw, crawling along the side of the chair, hundreds of little maggots, making their escape from the plastic bag at Robert's feet.

Margaret flew into a rage. She stormed to the door, flung it open and shouted at him.

"Get out, Robert. How dare you! Get out." Her finger and outstretched arm showed the way.

Robert stood and began mouthing apologies.

"Stop it. Just get out. Get out NOW."

Reluctantly Robert traipsed down the stairs. Margaret looked at the chair again and saw maggots everywhere. She couldn't believe how many there were. Nor could she believe that he would bring them in. A sick thought crossed her mind - she wondered if he had brought her a souvenir. Slowly she opened the bag and saw inside a crawling mass of white pupae. With her fingertips, and trying not to gag, Margaret picked up the bag and feeling dizzy, clambered down the steps and threw the bag into a rubbish bin. She sprayed it, and her room. There were maggots in the carpet and inside the lining under the chair. Then she walked into the waiting room downstairs and saw maggots crawling up the chairs and up the wall. A small white trail moved across the ceiling high above her.

Frantically Margaret continued her spraying and then returned to her room. Robert entered. Margaret drew a breath and told him to leave.

"But where's my bag Marg?"

"Robert, get out. I demand you leave."

"But where's my plastic bag?"

"Don't be stupid, I've thrown it out."

"You had no right to do that. That was my property. I demand to know where it is."

"It's in the bin downstairs. Now leave."

Robert was angry.

"You had no right to do that." He stomped from the office, down the stairs and after retrieving his bag from the bin, he left. Margaret was in shock for some time. Murray Gregor and Matthew Wood were wondering what the hell was going on in Lowe's mind.

Two days later Robert came in to Margaret's clinic and went up the stairs past the waiting room. Immediately behind him trailed a malodorous gas that filled the waiting area, causing several patients to cover the noses and mouths with their handkerchiefs or whatever they could get their hands on. Later they told Margaret it smelled like sulphur. They ran from the room and out into the street to see what the smell was, expecting to see a garbage truck. But there was nothing there.

DURING THEIR sessions, Robert had spoken enthusiatically to Margaret about the joys of rummaging through dumpmasters, particularly outside the Safeway store in Rye. He told her how exciting it was to find vegetables and other foodstuffs that had passed their use-by date, yet still looked good enough to eat. Sometimes there were surprises, like the time they threw out packaged meat that was still fresh. He sounded like a kid at a lucky dip.

But Lorraine didn't know Robert was behaving like a vagrant in his scruffy clothes. She almost died of shame when she took the boys for a drive down the Nepean Highway one afternoon, only to see her estranged husband fossicking in a rubbish bin outside the milk bar near Truemans Road in Rosebud. Benjamin watched his father as the car drove past and felt humiliation, and anger. It was a graphic depiction of how far his father had fallen. He never wanted to speak to him again.

On August 22, 1992, in a pathetic last-ditch attempt to get back with his wife, Lowe sent two parcels of scavenged food and a $10 note by taxi to Lorraine. He also enclosed a note professing his love for her. She threw it in the bin and then she wept. She couldn't believe this was happening. Why couldn't things go back to the way they were before?

The Murder of Sheree

ALEX BARTSCH had been tied up with other murder investigations but by late August he was back on the Beasley case. His next job was to take a statement from Margaret Hobbs. He knew it would be difficult for her. He knew she still had loyalty to Robert and there was still the issue of ethics.

At 9am on August 28, 1992, he approached her. She reluctantly agreed but by the time she reached page five, she told him she didn't want to make a statement any more.

Margaret had an overwhelming desire to go to the drain in Red Hill to pay her respects to Sheree and Alex offered to take her. He couldn't help notice how much Margaret had gone downhill in the five months he had known her. She was pale and shaking - a stark contrast to the confident woman he first met. He was very concerned for her welfare.

He drove her to Rosebud, retracing the route Robert had taken her on. Then they drove to Red Hill. Alex stopped on the shoulder of the road and the pair alighted and started walking to the drain. Alex gestured to it while Margaret stood watching.

"I don't feel well, I don't feel well," she said, her voice trembling. Then she took off. Her knee buckled a little and as she started to run, she careered into Alex. Then she ran to the car.

Alex walked around near the drain for a few moments and then got back into the car. Margaret was already in the drivers seat. She was crying openly and shaking. Alex looked at her with sympathy. He really felt for her. He was glad the tear he was shedding was on Margaret's blind side.

They sat in silence for a few minutes, thinking of the horror of the past 14 months. Mostly their thoughts were with Sheree. They could picture her last moments alive and now they could picture Robert Lowe, busying himself down there, just next to where they were parked, fussing and pushing Sheree's lifeless form into that filthy pipe.

They gathered themselves and then drove off. Margaret took Alex a bit further down the road and showed where Robert had turned around and told her to come back.

Alex looked at Margaret out of the corner of his eye. She was on a different plane to him now. She was gone. She had blocked out the terror and was functioning like a robot.

The Murder of Sheree

They got back to Victoria Parade at 12.30pm. Margaret got out and Alex headed back to the Homicide Squad. That was the day the repugnance of the crime, the shocking realisation of what had happened, became real to him. Before that it had been a serious investigation into a frightful murder. But he knew now that this one had scarred him for life.

CHRISTINE DOGAN was at a barbecue with friends when the conversation turned to the disappearance of Sheree about 14 months earlier. Christine, a young mother from Rye, was talking to the wife of a policeman about the abduction. Christine spoke of how she had seen a distressed girl in a blue car on June 29 but said it couldn't be Sheree because she had a helmet on. It was then she heard something that made her blood run cold. The policeman's wife told her that some sections of the media had mistakenly reported that the helmet was found near Sheree's bike. But it wasn't. Sheree had still been wearing it.

Murray Gregor had been visiting witnesses and taking statements. Then he was at his desk in Homicide one day when he received an Information Report from Crime Stoppers, stating a lady on the peninsula had seen Sheree in a car the day she vanished. Murray looked at the IR and wondered why people took so long to ring up. He thought it was probably a 'crazy'. Over the months he had received plenty of information about Sheree, but a lot of the information was from people who hadn't seen a thing. They simply enjoyed talking to police and being 'involved' in the investigation.

Murray visited the Crime Stoppers caller. Christine Dogan struck him as being extremely level-headed. She told him she had seen a blue car on the day of Sheree's abduction. She had been driving south along the Nepean Highway towards Rye when she saw a little girl in the car crying and looking at her. When she stopped next to the car at the intersection with Dundas Street, Christine had looked past the girl with the helmet on and peered at the driver. She described his clothing, even down to the type of stripes and the colours on his shirt.

Murray was surprised, and very interested. It appeared to be very genuine.

"Do you think you'd be able to pick the car again?" he asked.

"Yes, I would," Christine said, without hesitation. But Murray was sceptical. *Oh yeah, I'd like to see this one*, he thought.

He took Christine for a drive around the streets of Rye and Rosebud, to see if she could pick the type of car. After about 15 minutes, Murray took his witness through the Rosebud Plaza car park. He got a little start when Christine jumped and pointed. "That's the car," she said. "That's the exact model. The same."

And it was. In fact it was one of the cars that had been eliminated from the car file. Murray was amazed.

"Are you sure?"

"Yes," Christine said, "but it's a different colour. It's a darker blue."

And she was right. This was an ice blue which is a lighter colour. Murray was very happy. He thought it was incredible.

Christine told the detective the reason she paid such particular attention to the abductor's car was she liked the colour and the shape. Then she had noticed Sheree with her helmet on, sitting with a person she thought was Sheree's grandfather, staring straight ahead, ignoring her cries.

Murray took a statement from Christine, detailing her observations, and then asked her if she would be able to pick the driver of the car if she saw him again.

"Yes, I'm confident I would," she said. But despite her earlier performance, Murray was a bit dubious. That would be too much, he thought, although he realised that sometimes there are witnesses with a remarkable recollection.

Murray prepared a photoboard of the different shades of blue the manufacturers used on Toyota Corollas. She picked Azure Blue, the colour of Robert Lowe's vehicle, and said, "That's the closest to it. I thought it was a bit darker but that's the closest."

The trip back to Melbourne for Murray was a thoroughly enjoyable one. He couldn't wait to tell everyone in the office what had just happened.

IN THE LATTER half of 1992, the surveillance police and the telephone intercepts and listening devices were withdrawn. Other squads had been screaming for the dogs to work on jobs for them, jobs that had been on hold while resources were thrown at the Sheree Beasley investigation. Now, after 12 months, it was time to allocate them to other areas of the force. And Paul Hollowood could not justify keeping the phone tapping and the bugs in place. It seemed to Paul the information gathering from bugging Margaret Hobbs's office was now on the down turn. Now his men spent most of their time taking statements and working out which evidence could be used against Lowe - that is, when they weren't working on more recent murders. Margaret was on her own.

```
To Jonnon,
I give you full and due warning that the best
situation for you, I believe, is to have mum and I
together. I most likely will not be around and you
will have to live with that accusation yourself
and from your peer group. God doesn't make marriages
and families to break them or murder a marriage or
his own creation. His ultimate warning is that no-
one should break families and woe betide any person
who does.
```

ROBERT SENT letters like that to his sons and wife almost every day. Often his rambling letters twisted Christian principles as he emotionally blackmailed his estranged family. But he often mixed the 'teachings' with threats. Several times his letters to Lorraine foretold that if she divorced him something dreadful would happen to her. The letters were like a Chinese water torture, gradually grinding down her resolve and spirit. Almost hysterical, she eventually told the police to take all Robert's letters from the letterbox and open them themselves. Occasionally he would send cards that broke her heart; cards declaring his undying love. And now and then he would have bright, beautiful bunches of flowers delivered to her. He was trying to break her.

Then he started sneaking around his own home. Several times, Robert - now without a car - would travel to Glen Waverley and hide in the bushes outside his own front yard. Once Benjamin was driving the car out of the driveway when he saw his dad walking up Mannering Drive. Robert hid behind a bush when he saw his son. Benjamin sat still, watching,

The Murder of Sheree

as his father scuttled away down the street. Another time Benjamin was stopped at the intersection of Waverley and Watsons Roads when he saw Robert running toward the car along the road. Benjamin panicked and sped off.

When Benjamin walked to the garage on a third occasion and opened the garage door, only to see his father two metres away, facing him, it was the final straw. Robert wasn't doing anything - he was just standing in the garage. Both got a fearful fright and for a second or two stared at each other. Then Benjamin slammed the door and ran inside.

"Mum, he's in the garage!"

Robert went to the front door and Benjamin rang the police. Robert rang the doorbell and when Lorraine answered he tried to engage her in conversation. Then the police arrived and Robert left.

It was all becoming too much for Lorraine. She sought an intervention order to keep Robert away from the family home.

The matter was heard at the Oakleigh Magistrates Court on November 11, 1992. The court acquiesced to Lorraine's request. Her estranged husband was not permitted to go within 200 metres of their home in Mannering Drive; and he could not threaten, harass or intimidate Lorraine or the boys.

MARGARET LAST saw Robert in her rooms in November 1992. He told her he felt he was possessed by the Devil. He was planning to go to country Victoria to visit a group who could perform exorcisms. But for some reason, he never got around to doing it. He took a short holiday, occasionally ringing Margaret during his wanderings. Sheree was no longer on the agenda. Usually he droned on about Lorraine, the impending property settlement in the Family Court, and the upcoming divorce. In all, Margaret had seen him in her clinic at least 60 times.

```
My youngest daughter used to play with little
Sheree Beasley. When that girl died my daughter
asked me if her killer was a criminal and I had to
tell her, "Yes".
```

```
She said, "But Dad, you are a criminal". I had to
explain the difference. It wasn't easy to do.

Prisons are full of fathers just like me. Most of
us would string up the noose for any of those who
kill for sexual pleasure.

I've never met a child killer who wanted to change.
And I've met heaps of them.

By sending you this letter, I hoped to show that
even criminals hate these swine.
```

- Prisoner, (Dhurrungile),
Letter to the editor, *Herald Sun* January 10, 1993.

ON SATURDAY, February 13, 1993, Jonathan Lowe was to play cricket at Xavier College. Margaret told Lorraine that Robert intended to go and watch his son play. He was very proud of Jonathan's athletic prowess. Lorraine couldn't go - she was in hospital again. Benjamin decided he would go and look after his younger brother.

Benjamin, driving the family car, dropped Jonathan off at the school oval and then parked on an incline nearby so he could watch the action. It was a sunny, warm afternoon. After about half an hour, Benjamin drove down past the other oval and saw a man sitting in the schoolgrounds, watching the cricket. Benjamin squinted and looked hard. *Is that him? With the beard? Yes, it is.*

Benji was angry. His father had put his mother through the emotional wringer and didn't care about the family. He was furious his dad was now following him and his brother around, intruding. Benji drove out of the schoolgrounds and rang the police from a public phone box. He told them about the intervention order.

Robert left the schoolgrounds while Benji waited outside for the police. Then Benjamin lost sight of him, so he rang the police again. As he hung up, the divisional van arrived and Benjamin followed it around as it cruised the streets.

"If he turns up again, just give us a ring," the senior constable told Benjamin.

Benji nodded and then drove around again looking for his father. No luck. He drove back into the schoolgrounds and...there he was. Robert was sitting in the schoolgrounds eating a packed lunch. Benjamin grabbed somebody's mobile phone and rang the police.

Within minutes they were back, and they spoke to Lowe. Then they approached Benjamin who showed them a copy of the intervention order. They went back to Robert, sitting on the grass and Benjamin lost sight of them. He thought his dad had been arrested and that was the end of it. But as he went to drive out of the school, he saw them throw his dad to the ground.

All the kids from the cricket ran over to see what was going on. All except Jonathan, who was standing on the oval, alone. He could hear his father screaming and yelling as he wrestled with the police on the ground.

"Aaaahhh, don't hurt me!"

Benjamin heard it too and could see his father was overacting again, just like he did 18 months ago, laughing at a dull TV comedy. Most of the kids knew he and Jonathan were Robert's sons. Benjamin was embarrassed.

From the pack of watching schoolboys in their cricket creams came a voice:

"Oh, they've got Mr Cruel."

The police took him back to Kew police station where he was interviewed.

Lowe denied he was in breach of the intervention order. He was just watching his son play cricket. Then he was asked why he resisted arrest.

"I don't believe I resisted arrest. I believe I was just forced - thrown on the ground," he said in his most indignant and effeminate manner.

He was his old self-evasive, pedantic, irate, vague, defensive and uncooperative. And he lied non-stop.

When he was asked if he had anything to say in answer to the charges of assault by kicking, resisting arrest and breaching an intervention order, he said:

"If a person can't walk about freely without being hassled by the police.....I think if this is the state of the police force and this is all they've got to do, I think it's pretty shocking."

At the end of the interview, he was asked to stand. The sergeant took Lowe's photograph with a Polaroid camera. As soon as it was developed,

Lowe grabbed at the photo and bit the sergeant on the hand. He tried to eat the photo, destroying it in the process. Injured in his wrestle with the police, Lowe demanded to see the police surgeon. When the surgeon arrived, Lowe took a swing at him. He was later released on bail.

THE WORD had come down from the top that the brief had to be completed by the end of February. Paul Hollowood, Murray Gregor and Paul O'Halloran spent many days, working from 8am to midnight, putting everything in order. They had to get on top of the brief before they were swamped with more new work. It was imperative the brief be compiled and they get an answer one way or the other. They guessed they had enough evidence to charge Robert Lowe but they knew they would have to get an expert legal opinion. It was an unusual case.

Paul Hollowood determined which witnesses and exhibits were needed, and in what order they would be listed on the brief. He also worked on the overall summary of evidence, which eventually ran to 22 pages. Murray Gregor was responsible for gathering the witness statements together and chasing up statements that had not yet been obtained. Paul O'Halloran's job was to read the mountain of transcripts obtained from listening devices and compile a summary of each conversation, some of which had run for hours, between Margaret Hobbs and Lowe. As February drew to a close, Alex Bartsch was called in to help too, even though he was on recreational leave. There were hundreds of exhibits and 210 witnesses. And now the crew was on call for fresh homicide cases.

Finally the brief was complete. With the transcripts of conversations from Margaret Hobbs's clinic, together with the witnesses statements, the brief ran to 7,000 pages. It was one of the biggest-ever murder briefs in Victoria's history. Murray was rapt when the job was over. He had never worked so hard in his life. He loaded the brief onto a trolley, loaded it into a car and drove to William Street Police Headquarters. He took the lift to the Legal Advisor's Office and left the brief with Denis Grace.

Two weeks later Denis rang Homicide and asked to see Paul Hollowood. Paul and Murray went to his office and had a cup of coffee while they chatted. The men were waiting with bated breath. Murray felt they had enough for a circumstantial case but Paul was worried there

The Murder of Sheree

still wasn't enough. He knew there wasn't likely to be any more.

Then Denis said, "There is no doubt that Robert Lowe is going to be charged with something. It's just a matter of what charges we're going to give him."

Murray punched the air. "Yeeeesss!"

The men discussed a murder charge, the issue of kidnapping, and other legal issues. Finally Denis said he would write up the charges: Murder, kidnapping and unlawful imprisonment.

Murray wheeled the brief back to his office. Paul and Murray were quickly surrounded by their workmates. Murray told them what had just happened. The news was sweet, sweet music.

CHAPTER TWELVE

◆

THE SPECIALIST kept an eye on Lorraine, sometimes aspirating small cysts in her breasts with a needle. In February 1993, after he found another little lump, he suggested Lorraine have it taken out rather than worry about it. At the back of her mind was the letter Robert had sent her two weeks earlier, despite the intervention order. He had written that if Lorraine continued with her 'unforgiving spirit', God would punish her and she would get cancer - or at least some deadly fate would befall her. Lorraine decided to have the cyst removed.

She went into surgery at the Waverley Private Hospital as a day case - not carefree, but at least knowing there was little to worry about. The specialist was almost certain everything was okay. When Lorraine came around from the anaesthetic, she asked if everything had gone all right. The surgeon told her more radical surgery was required to remove what had been left behind. She had cancer.

At first she decided against further surgery. It seemed a good cop out and she didn't care much if she lived or not anyway. She was exhausted with worry. There were the money troubles. And everything else. She still wondered if Robert was Sheree's killer. She felt ashamed and she didn't know what to do anymore. But, as usual, it came back to the same thing - 'What about the boys?' She couldn't leave them alone to face all this.

Lorraine went under the knife but told the surgeon she didn't want any after-treatment, even though it was fairly radical surgery. All the glands in her armpit were removed, along with a large portion of her left breast, but the surgeon fashioned the shape again with muscle. Lorraine had told him she wouldn't allow the surgery otherwise. She was prescribed Tamoxifen but it made her so nauseous she stopped taking it after a few months. And there was no way she would have chemotherapy. She had lost enough already. She wasn't going to lose her hair too! But because the glands under her arm weren't involved, chemotherapy wasn't necessary anyway. It was an invasive ductal cancer, which was not a good type to have, but it had been caught extremely early. It was the best luck Lorraine had had in two years.

MURRAY GREGOR was still amazed at Christine Dogan's recollection of the little blue car she had seen on the Nepean Highway. After all that time! Having several people identify the car was a great start but nobody had positively identified Robert Arthur Selby Lowe. Murray wanted to know if this woman with the phenomenal memory could pick the driver of the blue Corolla.

After talking to Paul Hollowood and getting the go-ahead, Murray tried to compile a series of photos of men of similar age and appearance as Robert Lowe. The police usually compile a "photoboard" of similar looking people for witnesses hoping to identify an offender. But there were no face-on head shots of Robert Lowe to use. And Christine Dogan had only seen him side on.

Undaunted, Murray re-viewed the video-taped interviews between Lowe and Paul Hollowood. He picked one section which showed Lowe with his face fully visible but showing more of his left side than his right. Then he spent several days combing the St Kilda Road Police Complex and other office blocks in the area. He found eleven men - public servants and members of the public - of roughly the same age as Lowe. Then he had them sit in an interview room, adopting exactly the same pose as the chief suspect, where they were videoed. When all the "suspects" had been filmed, the Audio Visual Section compiled a tape which showed each man for several seconds before moving on to the next. Lowe was man number four.

Murray knew it was a long shot but still he went to see Christine. She had moved from Rye to Swan Hill, about 450 kilometres north-west of Melbourne. The policeman met the witness at the Swan Hill police station. After renewing their acquaintance, Murray set up a video recorder and television in the muster room. He pushed the play button and sat back to see what happened. The tape showed the twelve men sitting in the interview room. One, two, three. Then Lowe's face loomed large on the screen for several seconds and then moved on to number five and beyond.

When the tape finished, Murray said, "Well, that's it." Christine turned from the TV screen to the policeman. Authoritatively she said: "Number four". Murray nearly fell over. It was nearly 20 months since she had briefly seen Lowe driving along the Nepean Highway. That was just unbelievable. At last there was a witness who said Robert Lowe had Sheree Beasley in a blue car with him. Later Christine said number 10 was close too, but she leant more towards her first opinion. She was the only one who ever identified him.

ON MARCH 29, Murray visited the Florida Lodge in Grey Street to check if Mr 'Robert Arthur' was still staying there. He told the staff that Mr Arthur was suspected of committing a very serious offence. The detectives needed to know which room and bed Mr Arthur was in to effect the arrest. That way there wouldn't be any problems. Nothing would be damaged and nobody would get hurt.

Murray learnt the next day that Lowe had booked into room three. That night, just before he finished work, Murray rang the hostel to check if Lowe was still there. He was.

Murray hoped he didn't make a late check out.

THE HOMICIDE crew assembled at their St Kilda Road office at 5.30am. It was a balmy morning and some of the men wore short-sleeved business shirts. Paul Hollowood was there, along with Alex, Murray, Paul O'Halloran, Maurie Lynn, Mick Kelly, and Geoff Shepherd. They all felt pretty good. Everybody was excited but they tried not to show it too much.

Four guys hopped in one car, three in the other. Seven was a bit of overkill for the arrest of one, unarmed man, but they didn't want to miss out on this. It had been a long time coming. As they drove into Grey Street, a few of the men made jokes about how Robert's party was soon about to end. Both cars were full of anticipation. A few of the men smiled at each other.

The Murder of Sheree

They parked their cars down the hill and walked back to the Florida Lodge. There were hardly any cars on the road and nobody was about - just the seven lawmen walking towards a long awaited arrest. Alex thought it was so quiet it was almost eerie.

Murray rang the buzzer of number 37 and they were let in. The men walked along the hallway to room number three, then opened the door. The men looked into the small room. It contained only two sets of bunks, a chest of drawers, an old wardrobe and some bags and packs on the floor. Three of the four beds were occupied. On the bottom bunk on the left slept a Japanese tourist. On the top, a Swede. To the right, sleeping blissfully on the bottom bunk, with his head facing the wall, lay Robert Arthur Selby Lowe.

The seven men shuffled quietly into the room. They could hardly wait for this. They were trying to keep quiet but some of them felt ready to burst. Every one of them would have come to work on their day off to upset Robert Lowe's day.

Murray Gregor took out his police identification badge - "Freddy" in police vernacular - and said: "Robert Lowe, wake up! Police!"

"We finally got here, Robbie," someone said cheekily.

Lowe stirred. "Yes?" he said and then climbed slowly out of bed. He was wearing only his dirty jockettes. He looked around at the detectives. He didn't look frightened, or even surprised. Instead he sighed, as if it all was a bit of a bother. Alex was surprised how much Lowe had deteriorated. He looked like an old vagrant. All the policemen noticed the filthy body smell.

The two startled tourists were peering over the edges of their beds. They'd seen nothing like this before. The Swede produced his passport from somewhere and timidly held it out but nobody looked at it. All the action was on the other side of the room.

In his deep, strong voice, Murray said: "You're under arrest for the murder of Sheree Beasley." The tourists' eyes were popping. "You are not obliged to say or do anything unless you wish to do so but whatever you do say may be given in evidence. Do you understand that?"

Lowe looked in Murray's general direction with disinterest.

"Oh, fair enough," he said.

The Murder of Sheree

A few of the detectives looked at each other and shook their heads.

"Where's your bag?" Murray said. Lowe pointed to a bag on the floor.

"Get dressed, you're coming with us," Murray ordered as he covered his nose. *God he stinks!* Murray saw a little grey airline carrybag on the floor next to Robert's bunk. Lowe spied the detective eyeing it.

"Look, I've got a book in it that belongs to a friend of mine," Lowe said.

Murray looked inside and found a book of hardcore pornography - Teenage Schoolgirls No 37. Murray just looked at Lowe and mockingly shook his head as he smiled cheekily. *You can't admit even the book's yours,* he thought.

From that point on Lowe remained virtually mute. He dressed defiantly, maintaining a superior air without exchanging so much as a glance with his captors. Murray noticed how Lowe avoided eye contact at all times. Murray smiled as he heard the handcuff ratchets tightening on Lowe's wrists as he bound him behind his back. It felt pretty damn good.

But Lowe took it all in his stride. Murray thought he might have been thinking, "Well maybe I was expecting this, but well, who cares? I've beaten everything else up 'til now and I'll beat this, too."

With the two tourists still agog in their beds, Lowe was quietly taken from the lodge and placed in the back seat of one of the cars between Paul and Murray. Alex drove.

In the rear vision mirror Alex noticed Lowe writhing between the detectives and assumed the handcuffs might be too tight. When he stopped at a red light in Lorne Street, he turned around and asked, "Are you all right?".

Lowe leant forward and gave a big, sarcastic grin. "I'm fine, thanks," he said.

Alex turned back to face the road. *Mongrel.*

They were back at Homicide by 6.25am where they took the suspect to an interview room. Murray took the 'cuffs off him and gave him a cup of coffee, which he thought was far more than he deserved. Then Paul Hollowood entered the room and started asking questions. But as soon as the interview began, Lowe asked to speak to his lawyer. After ringing Peter Ward - and on his advice - Lowe refused to answer any questions.

The Murder of Sheree

When told he was going to be charged with murder, kidnapping and unlawful imprisonment, he was asked if he had anything to say.

Quietly but firmly he said, "No, except I am innocent of those charges". Despite the gravity of his situation, he didn't appear to care. He certainly didn't look worried.

The police kept him in their office until they were ready for court at 10am. While they waited, Murray searched through Lowe's property. In his knapsack he found a newspaper article about the discovery of Sheree Beasley's body. They also found scribblings from the Scriptures, which Lowe copied constantly. Most of the quotes related to persecution.

Alex rang Lorraine to tell her the news. She was stunned. It was almost a relief in a funny sort of a way. Now Robert was no longer on the road, she could relax a little. Ever since Robert had left Mannering Drive, she had panicked whenever there was an unsolved murder or if somebody was reported missing. She found herself ringing Homicide on these occasions, checking to see if they knew where Robert was. She was terrified he would pick up another girl. But now all that sort of worry and pain was over. A new type was about to begin. Now she braced herself for the court hearings - and the shame. She was very ashamed. Many people hadn't known up until then that Robert was the prime suspect. She spent the rest of the day in a trance.

THE COPPERS were still on a high. They drove Lowe to the Melbourne Magistrates' Court for the charges to be formally laid. As they drove up Russell Street and crossed La Trobe Street, Lowe began to show some concern. He saw a gathering of TV cameramen and sound recorders waiting. Clearly peeved, he turned to Hollowood and said flatly, "Thanks very much, fellas." From that point on he kept his chin on his chest to avoid being photographed. To him this was still a big game of one-upmanship. He thought somebody had notified the media of his arrest. And for a man who was petrified of people finding out what he was really like, that was a dirty trick.

A small crowd had gathered near the TV people, opposite the Russell Street police station. Kerri's uncle Leslie Greenhill was among them.

"You fucking dog. You fucking bastard," someone yelled as Lowe was

THE MURDER OF SHEREE

taken from the police car, with a jumper over his head. Alex and Murray frogmarched him straight into the City Watch-House while Paul Hollowood brought up the rear. The three of them walked Lowe up to the desk sergeant, who entered the prisoner's particulars in the heavy, brown Watch-House Book. Lowe only answered his name, address and date of birth. And his religion. Otherwise he didn't speak at all. The policemen couldn't believe his facial expression. It was supremely arrogant, as if he had not a care in the world. Alex thought he looked very defiant but he detected some trembling. Very occasionally Lowe's nose twitched too.

The sergeant grabbed a Polaroid camera and told Lowe he had to take his photo. Under the Prisons Act, every new prisoner must be photographed before entering the system, he explained. Lowe was having none of that. As the sergeant aimed the camera, Lowe dropped his head and screwed his face up as tight as he could. He is unrecognisable in the photo.

He was lodged in the cells where he waited for his name to be called to appear in court. The detectives went into the court proper and waited. The TV cameras hovered outside on the footpath.

The main court room at Melbourne Magistrates' Court was in full swing. It runs with a kind of organised chaos. People - defendants, police, lawyers, witnesses, Salvation Army officers - walk in and out as justice is swiftly meted out. Every morning, the court, packed and noisy, hears tales of sorry drunks, kleptomaniac housewives and people who stole, bashed or threatened (but didn't mean to, their lawyers say). The bigger cases are handballed to the other courts outside and upstairs, while the main court, apart from hearing the simpler cases, deals with adjournments, and matters of bail when people have just been arrested.

Allison Harding, a court reporter with the *Herald Sun* newspaper, had just dashed to the court after hearing of the arrest. The court was no different than any other day. It was full with the community's flotsam and jetsam, the unlucky, the naughty and the plain bad, plus a few of the innocent victims. Kerri, Steve, Neil and friends were sitting in the back of the court with the homicide men. Kerri was crying.

Allison took her seat next to *Age* reporter Tim Pegler in the press

The Murder of Sheree

seats, opposite the dock where Lowe would soon stand as Chief Magistrate Sally Brown ordered the court cleared.

Everybody left, then re-entered, but only after being checked by court security staff and walking through metal detectors. Nobody wanted anything out of the ordinary to happen in the court. Mrs Brown had insisted on the extra safety measures when she knew the man accused of abducting and murdering a 6-year-old girl was in the cells just behind the wooden wall.

Defendants in custody stand in a large, elevated wooden dock - a good metre higher than those standing in the body of the court. Eight uniformed police and four protective security group officers stood in the dock and on the court floor. Kerri, Steve and Neil looked nervous, tense and angry. For nearly two years they had been tortured by a faceless, formless, nameless horror. Now the cause of their heartache stood defiantly before them. At least that's how they saw it, even though Lowe was only the *alleged* killer. They wanted to kill him.

Now the court was packed and hushed. All the seats were taken. People stood, lining the walls. Allison walked back into court after her satchel had been searched. She felt a tension in the air that was missing before the Lowe case came up. Just as she took her seat next to Tim and the other reporters, Lowe was led in by four court security officers. Every eye in the court was upon him. A few heads in the body of the court leant towards the person beside them and whispered. TV sketch artists scribbled madly. Kerri's crying became more audible.

Allison was surprised. Lowe wasn't what she had expected. She knew his age - 56 - but expected somebody who looked a bit younger. Lowe looked haggard but what shocked her most was he looked otherwise quite decent. *He looks like one of my friend's fathers*, she thought. *He looks like anybody's father.*

Lowe looked a little arrogant and completely unfazed. His nose twitched a little now and then. He only looked at the magistrate and his counsel, oblivious to the feeling in the court. For good measure, he stood with his hands on his hips, as if he was totally put out at having to stand and listen to the tripe going on around him. He looked even bored. That shocked Allison too. *For a crime that serious, somebody who was guilty* might look a little more daunted rather than standing there arrogantly.

Tim Pegler took an instant dislike to Lowe. The man in the dock was a little dishevelled but he stood erect, with his head held high. His manner said it all. *This is a bloke who is never, ever going to plead guilty*, Tim thought. Everybody was holding their breath. The court room that had sounded like a late-night bar room just a few minutes earlier suddenly fell silent.

The magistrate read out the charges. Murder, kidnapping, unlawful imprisonment. Pandemonium broke out. Among the shouting and screaming from the back of the court, the only word Allison could make out was 'bastard', repeated over and over. Just as the magistrate's stern looks caused the ruckus to subside, Kerri cried out, "He killed my Sheree". The shouting began again and the magistrate cleared the court. Lowe stood, still with his hands on his hips. The only people now allowed in were Sheree's extended family, the police and the media.

Barrister Peter Ward stood and spoke on behalf of his client. He was concerned for Mr Lowe's safety. He asked that his client not stay in the City Watch-House for the night. From the back of the court, Kerri called out, "He should be allowed in with the other prisoners".

The accused was not asked to plead to the charges. Mr Ward said his client would be vigorously defending all the charges and while not seeking bail at the moment, would apply for bail at the Supreme Court as soon as possible. The magistrate had no option but to remand Lowe in custody.

As he was being led from the dock back into the bowels of the City Watch-House cells, Lowe paused momentarily. Then he turned back to face the magistrate over his left shoulder and fired a passing shot, one he would enjoy reliving as he sat alone in his cell. In a flat voice, devoid of expression and somehow bereft of tone, he said: "Wrong person your Honor," confusing the magistrate's title with that of a judge.

The court erupted again. Tim Pegler heard cries of "Child killer", "We're going to kill you". From the indistinguishable general insults sprung loudly "cunt", "dog", "fucking bastard".

Kerri broke down completely in the arms of her new husband and uncle. When they left, the court opened again for the drunks, the disqualified drivers trying to get their licences back, and the petty thieves.

Kerri composed herself and faced a media scrum on the footpath outside the court. She was still crying as she spoke.

"It's been 21 long months since Sheree went missing. Now that somebody has been charged with Sheree's murder, I know that Sheree won't come back but I know she helped the police find him. May justice be done." She went on to thank the police for all they'd done.

The news of the arrest and court appearance had dominated the radio and TV reports all morning. As Kerri spoke, someone yelled loudly from a passing car.

"Hang him. Hang the bastard high." It would have made good copy but nobody was allowed to report what he said. It would have been prejudicial to Lowe's court case.

The homicide squad detectives went to the Olive Tree restaurant in South Melbourne for lunch. After 21 months, it was time for a well-earned break. They knew all too well that arresting a man for murder was only half the battle. Now he had to be convicted.

That afternoon Matthew Wood and Detective Senior Constable David Yeoman called in on Lorraine. They knew she would be feeling low. They found her in a trance, wandering zombie-like around what was once a home. Matthew thought the only way to help her was to make her face what had happened. They sat at the dining room table they had sat at so many times before.

"What was Robert arrested for?" Matthew said.

"You know," Lorraine said distantly.

"I want you to say it."

The word still sounded foreign as it leapt from her mouth.

"Murder."

Margaret called in on Lorraine that night. Lorraine and her sons watched the television news in disbelief as they saw Robert being led, handcuffed, into the City Watch-House. There were photos too, of their Rosebud unit. Oh, the shame. Margaret was a mess. In tears, she left, passing a number of visitors from Lorraine's church who had called around to check on her welfare. But by 9.30pm, the visitors had all gone. Alone in her bed, Lorraine started to cry. She wondered whether she should take Robert his pyjamas. She still couldn't equate the old Robert with the monster in jail. How she missed the man she thought she knew.

The Murder of Sheree

The police also searched the Rosebud unit the day of Lowe's arrest but found nothing of evidentiary value. All they found was $2500 in cash in a drawer beside the bed in the main bedroom. They rang Lorraine and told her to collect the money. She went to Florence Avenue with Benjamin and Jonathan the following day.

Lorraine approached the unit with dread. Now their holiday home would forever hold memories of the horror of Robert's demise, rather than joyous family days. Lorraine put the key in the security door, then pushed the wooden door open. Immediately she was swamped with a strong smell - a smell reminiscent of stale sweat. As she walked from room to room, she was cast back more than 20 years, to the Hudson St boarding house where Robert had lived. The unit wasn't just untidy, it was dirty. The fridge was stuffed with dozens of packets of frankfurts and yoghurt, Mars bars and margarine, all of which were well past their use-by dates. Lorraine knew they must have come from dumpmasters outside supermarkets. The plastic containers at the bottom of the fridge were stocked with rotten vegetables swimming in mouldy water. Dirty, empty ice cream containers were stacked high on the kitchen bench. On the kitchen table was a cheap vacuum flask Robert had bought which he filled every morning with boiling water to save electricity. The pantry was stacked with potato chips and sweets. There was no other food.

The laundry housed about a dozen bottles of unused hair shampoo. Lorraine wondered whether he had bought them, or stolen them and decided they had probably been shoplifted. Tentatively she opened the washing machine lid. It was full of cobwebs.

Robert's clothes were strewn about the place. All his shirts, underpants and trousers were filthy. In a daze Lorraine walked towards the bedroom. She peeked through the doorway at the bed. The blankets and sheets were thrown back. There was a stiff, brown mark on the mattress where Robert had lain. The bare pillow had a brown patch in the middle and was stiff and smelly. He had never washed the sheets. Lorraine was ashamed the police had seen the flat in such a state. On the bedside table she saw, to her shock and surprise, several pamphlets about breast cancer. She wondered why they were there. In the top drawer of the table, Lorraine found the $2500. Sitting alone, on top of the pile of dirty notes, was her

The Murder of Sheree

golden wedding ring. She heard a muffled sound and turned to see her two sons crying.

Over the next two weeks, from dawn until dusk, Lorraine and the boys scrubbed the flat from top to bottom. Everything felt so filthy. They threw out the mattress, the pillow and the blankets. For good measure, Lorraine threw out the cutlery, which was grey and slimy and obviously had not been washed in hot water. Out, too, went the crockery, the curtains and all the rubbish lying on the floor. The carpets were shampooed. The walls were painted. Lorraine made new curtains and changed all the locks. She wasn't just tidying up. She was erasing all memories and reminders of Robert. The clean up bill was just over $2500.

THREE WEEKS later the boss of the Prison Squad - Detective Senior Sergeant Greg Bowd - walked into the Homicide Squad. It is the Prison Squad's job to monitor what is happening in Victoria's prisons and investigate crimes committed by men and women in the system. Greg walked across the office and stood next to Alex Bartsch, who was sitting at his desk, wading through a mountain of paperwork.

"Alex," the senior sergeant said.

Alex looked up. "Oh, gidday Greg."

The pair talked for a few minutes, then Greg explained why he was there.

"I've seen Peter Reid. Thought you might be interested." He dropped some notes on the table in front of Alex.

Alex had mentally misspelled the surname. He wondered what on earth Peter Reed could say that would interest him. Alex remembered Peter Reed as the man who had shot at a policeman several years earlier and was also tried and acquitted over the planting of a bomb outside Russell Street Police station in March 1986, killing policewoman Angela Taylor in the subsequent explosion. What could a scumbag like that possibly say that would interest Alex? He started flicking through the notes and realised he was thinking of the wrong man. He didn't know much at all about this Peter Reid Greg was talking about but suddenly he was very interested. What he was reading was good stuff. There were 12 pages and they all related to Robert Arthur Selby Lowe. In a fashion,

The Murder of Sheree

Lowe had confessed to Reid that he had abducted Sheree. Reid had then gone to Bowd via a prison officer.

"Sure, I'm interested," Alex said. He asked Greg to organise a visit to Reid in Pentridge's K Division, which houses the worst criminals in Victoria.

Alex did a bit of homework on Peter Reid before he went to visit him and decided he was a real low life. He had committed murder, armed robberies, assaults, thefts, burglaries. He was an absolute shocker, and even in jail, his reputation was appalling. Alex thought it would be better to have the other Peter Reed as a witness. The more he thought about it, Alex realised he would be hard pressed to find anybody in the country, let alone the state, who would be less credible as a witness for the prosecution in a murder trial. He wasn't filled with much hope. Yet he had read what Reid had written and it seemed to be on the right track. It certainly required further investigation.

Alex first met Peter Reid in Pentridge Prison on April 23, 1993. Alex and Greg Bowd were led into the K-Division library, where they sat down. The room was only about four metres by three metres and two of the walls were lined with books. The room contained a table, four chairs - two on either side - and a big red button on the wall. When it was pushed it sounded a buzzer for the guards to come.

Alex and Greg sat down and watched the hydraulic door that leads to another side of life slowly grind open. A prison officer led Peter Reid into the room and then left, the door again moving slowly shut. Alex was shocked at what he saw, particularly after everything he had just read. Reid was a nervous little man. Short, balding, almost jockey size, although he had a strong, muscular physique. Alex was surprised at his timidity. There was nothing intimidating about him at all. Nonetheless, Alex was on guard. Knowing how deceitful Robert Lowe was, it was probable that he was using Peter Reid to muddy the waters about the case. Alex was worried that Lowe might use Reid to introduce some sort of wild card into the investigation and thus damage the police case.

Alex and Peter eyed each other across the table.

"Okay," Alex said coolly, his hands clasped in front on him on the table. "I am interested in what you have to say."

The Murder of Sheree

The maximum security prisoner wanted to know if he could have a computer. He wanted to be transferred to Barwon prison too, as it was less restrictive than K-Division. Alex had been expecting something like this. After what Reid had done to the poor Chan family, he expected nothing less. He didn't know what else Reid had to say but he wasn't about to start bargaining with someone who had killed a policeman - one of his own.

"I don't run the gaol," Alex explained. "If some guy from the gaol came to my office and told me how to run a murder investigation, I'd throw him out of the office. It's the reverse situation. I'm not telling them how to run the gaol. Peter, I can't make promises and I can't keep them. That's the way it's going to be."

Reid shrugged his shoulders. It was worth a try. They got down to business.

He told the police what they had already read in the notes.* That on April 6, he and Lowe were moved in together, despite both being in maximum security. He told how on April 16, Lowe had approached him and said he had to work out his defence for the trial.

"He told me he picked up a girl and she had died by accident. He took her to Red Hill," Peter said.

Normally a policeman tries to establish some rapport with a witness. But that's in a 'normal' case. This wasn't your average murder investigation - and Peter Reid wasn't your normal witness. Alex was unmoved. He just stared across the table.

"He killed Sheree with dirty acts," Peter said. Alex thought that was convenient. It painted Lowe in the worst possible light and made Reid look good at this first meeting. He looked impassively across the table at the murderer.

"He's just a cunt. He said she would have been submissive because she was the daughter of a prostitute."*

Alex had trouble controlling the look on his face. He felt like crying.

"He told me he had learnt his lesson - next time he says he'll use valium so she won't struggle. Can you believe that?"

---

* The notes and Reid's comments to the police formed the basis of the evidence given by Reid in later court hearings.

Alex certainly could but he wasn't going to say so.

"He thinks I am helping him prepare a defence," Peter said to the unasked question. Then, by way of explanation, he added, "It's a pretty terrible crime."

Alex was impressed by his sincerity.

"Okay, just keep going and I'll come back in a couple of days."

There was no way he was going to be friendly with a cop killer. And it wasn't as if he was telling them something they didn't already know.

Three days later Alex and Greg returned to Pentridge and Peter Reid handed over more notes of his conversation with Lowe, plus some drawings of the abduction site - complete with notation "picked up girl here" - and a rough drawing of the route Lowe had taken with Sheree in the car. Alex was happy. While Reid hadn't told them anything new, it showed he wasn't lying. The route marked was exactly the same as the one Lowe had told his therapist.

Four days later, Reid handed over some proper scaled drawings of the spot in Mornington-Flinders Road where Sheree's body had been dumped. It showed the driveway - even the drain, showing which way it was tilted for drainage. It even showed where the car was parked nearby when Lowe jammed her body in the pipe. Peter was animated.

"Head jobs, that's how he killed her," he said effusively. "He told me 'dirty acts' - he won't say oral sex - that's how he killed her."

Alex squinted and shook his head. He felt a wave of revulsion sweep over him.

"He took her into here," Reid said, pointing to an isolated spot near the drain, "not far from where he buried her."

Alex and Greg produced a Nagra tape recorder and strapped it onto Reid's body. The detectives told him they needed to get some or all of the confessions on tape. With Peter Reid's track record, nobody would believe his uncorroborated word.

"The dirty acts. I'll get it on tape, no worries," Peter said.

"Just let Lowe do the talking," Alex said, and turned on the tape. He pushed the red button on the wall and watched as Peter Reid disappeared back into the gaol proper. As he watched the prisoner leave he wondered. *What's in it for him?*

The Murder of Sheree

On May 5 Alex was back again. He was dying to know if the 'dirty acts' had been mentioned on tape. He sat in the tiny library, waiting. Slowly, Peter Reid was brought in. A prison warder half carried him and plopped him onto the seat opposite Alex. Peter was as white as a ghost.

"Are you all right?" Alex asked.

"I've got the lot, " Peter said with resignation. "That's enough, I can't handle it."

The two men looked at each other across the table. Alex listened intently as the man looking at him sat in a daze. Then his mouth opened.

"I don't know how you coppers do this sort of thing," Peter said. He was shaking. "How do you listen to this shit all day and then sleep at night? I can't handle all this."

He went on to explain that he hadn't slept for three consecutive nights. He couldn't believe a man could kill a little girl and have absolutely no remorse at all. Lowe talked about Sheree as if he was describing a leaking tap. She was merely an annoyance. One that had taken away his wife, sons, livelihood and good reputation. In all his years in prison, Reid had never encountered anybody like Lowe. He said he had been to see Jenny Tuck, the prison doctor, who had sedated him. Alex was worried about him. He looked as if he was on the verge of a breakdown.

"Am I doing the right thing?" Peter asked plaintively.

"Just keep going," Alex said softly. "Hopefully we'll get there." Alex knew Reid couldn't last much longer. He looked shocking.

As he left the prison, Alex was feeling ambivalent. He was concerned at Reid's health and worried he might collapse, while also feeling elated at the admissions finally being recorded on tape. He drove back to homicide and handed in the tape to be transcribed. The next day he heard the news. The tape hadn't worked. It was absolutely useless.

Alex was concerned he was becoming too close to Peter Reid. And he was worried other members of the Homicide Squad, and the force, might spurn him for becoming chummy with a convicted police killer. He sought counsel with Detective Senior Sergeant Rod Wilson and told him of his concerns. Rod told him he had a job to do, an important job, and he was doing it professionally. He reminded the detective senior constable that no matter how unsavoury the task, he was doing it for a purpose. Any

The Murder of Sheree

thinking police officer would see that. It didn't matter that Reid had killed a fellow officer now. He could become the star witness against a man who had killed a little girl for sexual pleasure. End of story. It was just what Alex needed to hear.

On May 11 Alex executed a warrant at Pentridge, seizing 40 hours of security video tape which recorded Lowe and Peter working on the maps as they leant over a billiard table.

Two days later he was back again. Peter was on the point of collapse. He told Alex Lowe had described a dumpmaster bin in Mt Waverley as being the spot where he had dumped Sheree's clothes and pink bike helmet.

Alex thought it was time for one last shot at getting evidence of the actual murder on tape. He wired Reid up again with a hidden Nagra tape recorder and sent him on his way. Peter wanted to help but felt he couldn't handle it any more. Alex didn't want to push but gently he said, "Come on mate, do it again. Just one more time, then it's finished."

Alex then instructed the prisoner to try to talk about the murder again but not to go into the specifics of the case. That could alert Lowe to what was going on.

Lowe obligingly went through the scenario again but didn't go into the dirty acts. It was something he was trying to deny ever happened, even to himself.

Alex left, knowing he could not use Peter Reid again. He knew one more shot at Lowe would send him to the nuthouse. He knew now how Sheree had died but the evidence was not on tape. He wondered whether Peter's sworn oral testimony, without corroboration, would ever be admitted into evidence. He doubted it.

On June 16, after a number of fights with Lowe, Peter Reid was moved to another section of the prison. The authorities feared he might kill the alleged child murderer. He was treated for anxiety attacks and insomnia.

LORRAINE WALKED from the kitchen to the family room. Then she stopped and looked around, puzzled. She had come in here for something. What was it? Maybe if she retraced her steps she would remember. She walked back into the kitchen and stood looking back into the family room. She thought hard. No, it was gone. Her eyes absently wandered around the kitchen. The table the family had prayed at every morning was empty but for a small white doyley cushioning a wooden bowl of fruit. The chairs were empty. So was the family room. So was the entire house. Then she realised, with a shudder, so was her life. She couldn't face going out in public - she felt like a pariah. She wondered whether she had some unknown inadequacy which had caused Robert to seek sexual comfort outside the home, in the most disgusting way. Then she remembered the same Robert had comforted the aged and infirm in their homes. He might not have killed Sheree Beasley but he had certainly molested and accosted little girls for the past twenty years. Even he had had the good grace, in his capacity as church elder, to call on those experiencing tough or troubled times. Yet apart from Ross Brightwell and a few couples from the church, she had been completely wiped by everybody in the congregation. Did they blame her? She wondered what it was that stopped people coming to visit her in her most trying hour. She had learnt, as they had, about compassion, love, and helping others, without askance. She wondered whether the church people had written her off as a black sheep, just as Robert's family had all those years ago, or were they content to go to church on Sundays and live out their mundane and unthreatening lives for another six days. What was the point in learning about helping others when it was only a theoretical exercise? Not so long ago, Lorraine had been one of the most sheltered women around. Now she had seen not just a glimpse but a gutful of what happens in the real world, far removed from the pretty pictures in church books of men in robes standing in sandals near barren mountains and sandy deserts. She knew she would help somebody in similar circumstances. Then, with horror, she began imagining church conversations about her.

Inadequate wife. She must have known, how could she not? Maybe she's weird too. What about the boys? I wonder if he molested the boys too. You never really know what goes on in people's homes, do you?

Or maybe, they simply didn't know what to do. Maybe they all felt too embarrassed to come and talk to her. After all, what could they say? "How's Robert?" Humpff, hardly. The world she had embraced after leaving the brethren now lay in powder, beneath her feet. For the second time, everything she had believed in had been totally and utterly destroyed. Her faith was still, amazingly, very strong, but her lifestyle was gone forever. No more would she look forward to going to church and meeting other worshippers on the lawn after another enriching sermon. Now she did her praying at home. She didn't pray at a set time. She prayed for all this to stop, for Robert to be a decent family man, for another man to come forward to claim responsibility for the shocking murder. And she prayed for Sheree, a little girl she never knew, to come back. As she reflected on 1993, she hardly comprehended what she knew was true. She had married "forever and forever", yet her divorce had gone through early in the year. A thought was nagging her. She concentrated on it for a few moments and then stopped in her tracks. "Oh, that's right, I've got cancer," she said aloud. The cancer had resulted in her losing her part-time job because her arm was too sore to type. And then her husband was arrested for murder. She wondered what was next. Through the fog she walked into the family room, stood for a few minutes staring at the feature brick wall over the fireplace and then, aimlessly, walked back into the kitchen. What was it she was going to do?

IT WAS FIVE months since Lowe had been arrested. Alex and Murray hadn't felt this good since that day. Armed with a set of continuity statements, some photographs of Sheree which would be produced at court and copies of Peter Reid's tapes, they drove to Her Majesty's Prison Pentridge in Coburg. They were shown to the small library and locked in while they waited for Robert Lowe. They joked a bit about how Robert would react to what was about to happen, then just sat still. Finally the hydraulic door opened and the prisoner, wearing his green T-shirt and green prison track suit trousers, was escorted in. He looked at them with that same superior air, yet not totally happy to meet their eyes.

Alex put some of the exhibits on the table. Lowe leant forward and looked them over, his nose twitching a little as he did so. Each pile of documents had a cover sheet describing who and what they related to. He was sniffing over the first statements like they were nothing.

"Show them to your solicitor," Alex said.

Lowe did not speak at all. He was trying to pretend they weren't in

The Murder of Sheree

the room, or if they were, they were simply not worth noticing. After all, they were only dim-witted public servants. He moved in his chair as if he was getting ready to leave.

Then, with not a little glee, Alex pointed one finger in the air, as a magician does before cleverly revealing another trick. He leant over and reached to the floor to pick something up. As he did so, he said, cheerfully, "Just a moment, Robert. I've got something else you'd *really* want to see." He picked up a folder which contained 16 pages and placed it directly in front of Lowe.

"You'll *definitely* want to have a look at these," he said, smiling.

Lowe looked down, his nose now spasming, and read: "Peter Allen Reid, K Division, Pentridge Prison, 353 0200". It was Reid's statement.

Alex and Murray watched the colour drain from Lowe's face. They quickly glanced at each other and smiled, while the man over the table sat transfixed, staring at the paperwork before him. As the realisation of what he was looking at overcame him, his twitching intensified and his heavy breathing gave way to panting. For the first time, the men saw a look of worry fill his face. Mortified, Lowe could not bring himself to even touch the documents on the table. It was the only time the men saw him rocked. The detectives thought this was exquisite. And it got better. Alex pointed the finger at the roof again, for his next trick.

"Oh," he said, with mock surprise. "And, you'll want to hear these, too." He leant down and picked up a box of audio tapes which he plonked on the table next to the Reid statement.

Alex could read Lowe's mind. *What the hell's going on here?* But still he didn't speak. On the tapecovers he read, "Peter Allen Reid/Robert Arthur Selby Lowe".

Murray and Alex were enjoying every bit of this.

"And you'll want to have a look at these, too," Alex said, plonking the photos of Sheree on the table. He knew normally they wouldn't have caused Lowe to even raise an eyebrow but with the shock of what he had just comprehended, he knew it might shake him. Lowe didn't look at the photos. His eyes were on the cover of Reid's statement. He was stunned. He couldn't bring himself to pick it up. Finally, without looking at the policemen, he spoke.

"Is that all you've got?"

"Yeah, you're right to go, Robbie," Alex said cheerfully.

Lowe was agitated now. He was smashing on the red button with the side of his fist to get the guards to come. He had lost control completely.

"Yeah, that's all we've got to say to you," Alex teased, smiling. Murray was smiling too.

Thump, thump, thump on the red button. Hard. Lowe was perplexed, and he wanted out.

"What's wrong?" Alex continued, showing mock concern.

Thump, thump, thump. The arm was in full swing now. He desperately wanted to leave the room.

"I don't want to talk to you," he said loudly. The door opened and Lowe quickly picked up his Homicide Squad souvenirs and walked out. With a cardboard box containing statements and photos of Sheree under his arm, Lowe limped away. He was buckling under the mental weight of the revelations. He had thought Peter Reid was a like kind and Peter Reid had exposed him. Having finally been comfortable enough to share with someone what he was really like, Robert Lowe now faced the prospect of the whole world hearing about it in a court of law. He couldn't believe it. Slowly, he lumped along the long concrete spine of the maximum security wing, which looks like a spindly, barren, concrete submarine, complete with small portholes at regular intervals. A few cells run off from the finger. Peter Reid stuck his face to the door of his cell. As Lowe hobbled by, Peter yelled tauntingly, "Have a read of that, Robbie." Then he derisively laughed the high pitched cackle of a witch in a children's play.

The eerie laughter reverberated around, and then along the concrete corridor, enveloping Lowe and his smirking guard before disappearing into the dead walls. Murray and Alex looked at each other and laughed.

"He's going to have a bad night tonight," Murray said, with satisfaction.

The Murder of Sheree

Robert Lowe
K Division Box 114
Coburg, 3058
27-10-93

Dear Mr Powell,

Thank you very much for your letter as a result of Gwen Hester contacting you. It was good of you to write and for her to pass the message on. It is a long time since we had contact - 25 years as I believe you say. But I remember those days *very* vividly. You and Mrs Powell were very kind to me then, you were Chairman of the Billy Graham '69 Crusade, through which I became a Christian, and I met my wife Lorraine at Scots (Church) on Christmas Day 1970, are 3 very good reasons for a clear memory then!

Life has been good to me since then, that is up until August '91 when I was first spoken to by the Authorities about the shocking happening that resulted in my arrest 7 months ago now. Since then it has been tragic in the extreme, especially with my wife and children leaving me at the suggestion of our Presbyterian minister. Had that not happened, I would rightly not be here, and not be charged. However I must face things as they really are.

As a result of your letter I wrote to Bill Brown and received an immediate reply. Bill has been most supportive of me. But the conditions of getting into this very secure part of the complex are difficult and restrictive - for good reason may I add. I have outlined these to Bill, although conditions have changed again this week so I will write to him again.

Briefly however, I am restriction to only one religious minister's professional visit, and I had nominated Ross Brightwell of Knox Presbyterian at his specific urgent request. However, he did not co-operate with authorities nor sought to help me so I allocated the position to Rev David Reid of Richmond Assemblies of God where I attended. Bill came in several times on his own initiative which I was most appreciative of. But I've been restricted to one professional who can come anytime, while others can only visit for an hour at a set time and day (now 9.45am - 10.45am on Mondays). Bill and others will be the latter.

May I add that if people haven't been in a jail before it can be devastating and as such I would not ask anyone to come unless urgent which it isn't at present. So the occasional 'Tonic Card' or similar that I thank you for together with fervent prayer is probably the best at this stage.

My committal hearing commencing Nov 15th will receive huge police media publicity. Lorraine sadly and maybe the boys are caught up in this as well. Naturally they are terrified. But the worst part will be what an inside prison criminal informer will say. It will be a mixture of disgusting lies and inflame the media and some truth to make his statement believable.

I know I have not done this and have never been involved. And God knows that. I am not lying and have a clear conscious before the Lord. But people will say otherwise, and lie.

I could say far more about this but I cannot because I am restricted by what I say. A copy of this letter and every letter I send, and receive is sent to the Homicide Squad and I do not want to say too much lest it is used against me. Even every phone call to my lawyers and any call is taped. I cannot discuss my defence with my lawyers without the conversation I have with any and everybody being recorded to be used against me by police. Obviously this is not fair justice but it is the way it is. I can't even chose my own lawyer unless I pay him cash which obviously I can't. With the lawyer I am allocated the decisions made are his decisions - not mine. Anyway, I will say no more, because there is nothing I can do about it.

Thank you for news of your family. I'm not sure what you're doing at present but I'll find out maybe in due course.

```
Please remember us as a family in your prayers.
Lorraine, Benjamin (18) and Jonathan (16) have had
to put up with far too much already. They've had a
lot of attacks on the house, snubbed and rejected
by friends, and molotov cocktails thrown at the
home. They are having to sell up and move out of
town. I can't say where.

I thank you for your interest. Should you wish to
further pursue the matter in any way please write
me again.

My sincere regards to Mrs Powell.

In Him,

Robert.
```

Margaret was sitting at home when the phone rang. She walked across the loungeroom, into the family room and picked up the handset.

"Margaret Hobbs," she said melodiously.

She recognised the voice instantly.

"You betrayed me," it spat. "You betrayed my family, you've ruined my family. How could you do this to me?" The poison words spattered out of the earpiece. Margaret tried to talk but the words wouldn't come. Robert wouldn't let her get a word in anyway. He railed long and loud about betrayal and deceit, rambling about the Peter Reid tapes before the line went dead. Margaret was shaking violently. . .

She had just finished drinking a glass of water when the phone rang again. Terrified, she walked over and reluctantly picked it up again, bracing herself for another tirade. Instead, she heard a sympathetic man's voice.

"Are you all right?"

"No, I'm not. Who is this?"

"Peter Reid, Margaret."

"Robert's just given me a terrible serve," she whispered.

"We know. The whole unit heard it."

Margaret asked him why he was ringing.

"Didn't you hear the phone go down?"

"Yeah."

"Well, who do you think took the phone off him?"

"Oh."

"I told him, I said, 'You talk to her like that again...'."

With Peter Reid on her side, Margaret thought that was the last she would hear from Robert. But the next day he rang her again.

"Sorry Marg..." he began. Then he spoke about Lorraine and the impending property settlements as if nothing had happened. Then he asked Margaret to visit him. He picked exactly the right time to ask. Margaret was experiencing enormous guilt over 'betraying' him. She felt she had to see the case right through to the bitter end, whatever that might be, to put it to rest in her own way. And his blast over the phone had affected her badly.

The first time Margaret visited him, he leant over and kissed her on the cheek. She was nearly ill. Most, if not all of the time, he spoke about himself; about the injustices of the divorce; of how people had condemned him without waiting for the guilty verdict. And that he had never, ever seen 'the little girl'.

But what consumed him more than the criminal charges, or being in prison, was the looming Family Court property settlement. He was desperate to retain at least half of whatever was going to be divided by the Family Court. He quizzed Margaret on what Lorraine was going to ask for in court; how she had no right to certain things. Occasionally he asked Margaret to send messages to either Lorraine or his brothers Rick and Graeme in New Zealand, who were to fund his criminal defence. Most times she helped him out.

Margaret visited Robert in prison about six times. At their last meeting, when Margaret had secretly deemed she would not be coming back to visit, she said: "Robert, if I ever find out to my own satisfaction that you've killed this child, I will never forgive you."

Robert smiled at her pleasantly and said, softly and reassuringly, "You will Margaret because you're a good woman."

As Margaret began to cry, he said, "Don't give evidence against me in court."

Weeping quietly, Margaret shook her head and left. He wasn't like anybody she'd ever known.

CHAPTER THIRTEEN

◆

THE PRISON van pulled to a stop at Frankston police station. It was Wednesday, November 10, 1993. Sergeant Keith Joyce was on hand with a few constables to take charge of the criminals due to appear in court during the day. It was the usual sort of crew. Seven men and two women. Five were on car stealing charges, two were druggies, and one - George - was an armed robber.

But before they could be removed from the van, the police had to remove one other prisoner. He was sitting in the dog box, a small, sealed area with just enough room for a man to sit down. Only prisoners who are at risk from other prisoners travel in the dog box. That meant they were either informers, or child molesters, or worse.

Keith opened the box and pulled out the prisoner. He saw an insipid, thin, grey-haired man who seemed to be in his early 60s. What Keith noticed most were his steely eyes. Every time Lowe looked at him, Keith felt the urge to look away.

He put Lowe in the holding cell inside the station and then went to help get the other prisoners out of the van. As he escorted George into the cells, the prisoner jerked his head back to where the van stood and said, "A dog or a spider?" Like all the other prisoners, he wondered who the mystery prisoner was.

"I can't tell you," Keith said.

"I think I know who it is," George said with a dark smile. "Can you put him in the cells with us?"

Keith looked at him for a second and then smiled. "Nah, can't do that." He knew Lowe wouldn't last two minutes.

Keith soon found out Lowe was there for an extension on an intervention order but that didn't make sense. He couldn't see how there

THE MURDER OF SHEREE

would be a need for an intervention order when Lowe was in prison, charged with murder. But then it was explained to him by one of the Court Network women that Lowe had made threats against his family and there were fears that Lorraine may be in danger.

When the hearing began, Keith saw Lorraine sitting on the edge of her seat. He could see she was upset but she wasn't crying. It seemed to Keith she was very strong in her resolve but her lips were shaking out of fear. She was sitting with Benjamin and several detectives. Keith noticed Lowe sitting in the dock, staring at his ex-wife. It surprised Keith that Lowe showed no emotion at all.

The hearing didn't last long and it resulted in a win for Robert Lowe. The intervention order would not be extended. He was driven back to Pentridge in a police car. He couldn't be kept overnight at the station with the other prisoners.

THE COMMITTAL hearing was due and the authorities were concerned about Robert Lowe's safety. It was decided the hearing would be conducted under tight security. Unfortunately, the only 'security' court available was the old Brunswick Magistrates' Court, a tiny old courthouse set back from the Brunswick Police Station in Sydney Road. Visitors walked along the concrete driveway and up three steps into the foyer of the small building where they were confronted by the clerk's office. On the left were the cramped toilets and an interview room. To the right was the courtroom which is entered from the rear. Five long pews in the body of the court filled the room. Immediately in front of the rows stood a long, worn wooden table for the prosecution and defence counsel. In front of the table, behind a raised desk, sat the clerk of the court. Immediately behind, raised higher, sat the magistrate behind a huge wooden desk. On the wall above the magistrate's chair stood the standard plaque on which was inscribed, on an unfurled metal ribbon, 'Dieu et mon Droit' - God is my Right. Also at the front of the court, on the magistrate's left, was what passed in 1993 as the 'secure' prisoner's dock. It was surrounded in reinforced plastic panelling about a metre high and two metres long. It had two chairs in it. Defendants looked as if they were standing, fully clothed, inside an overblown shower recess. On the other side of the magistrate's perch was the witness box, behind which was a door for easy access and egress. The witness box was just a couple of metres from the bar table and the same distance from the magistrate's seat. It was a small building. More than thirty people in the court would see it almost overflowing.

The committal began on November 16, 1993. Three Protective Services Group officers sat outside the courtroom door behind a large blue tin sign informing potential witnesses and gallery members that before they could enter they must proffer their names and addresses and submit to being searched. Failure to do so would result in being refused permission to enter. The media were there in full force. All the talkback radio stations and some of the music ones were represented as were the major daily newspapers and all the television stations. Most of the reporters were in the front row of the court. They were separated from the lawyers by one empty row. They sat behind prosecutor Geoff Flatman, who stood on the left near the witness box, and David Brustman, who stood at the other end of the table, which was only about one metre away, not far from the defendant's plastic screen. Not all the media could fit in the front row, though, and some were scattered around the court. Tim Pegler and Allison Harding were back in court, following the big story for the next day's paper. Both made it to the front of the public gallery.

Some of Sheree's family sat in the next row - Kerri, Steve, Neil Greenhill, Jill and Anthony Mandile. Interested spectators sat in the next few rows.

The clerk stood and told everybody to stand as magistrate Wendy Wilmoth entered the court. After it was announced the court was in session, Lowe was brought into the room and escorted to his plastic box. Someone shouted "dog" from the body of the court, then there was absolute silence.

The clerk read out the charges, then Geoff Flatman, a senior DPP barrister, and David Brustman, argued on some finer points of law for several minutes.

When argument was over, little blond-haired Shane Park, dressed in short sleeved shirt and shorts, walked to the witness box. As he stood there alone, a video tape was played which showed him talking to

Detective Senior Constable Peter Butland and pointing out where Sheree was taken on June 29.

"I was riding my bike around here, she said she was riding to the milk bar."

Shane's mother looked on with concern. He told the court he was in the same school class as Sheree. She wasn't very long. He saw Sheree coming back from the shop. She had a pink helmet on. She had milk on the handlebars but she didn't want it there. She put it in her basket. The milk was in a plastic bag. She had some lollies too.

"The man in the car said, 'Stop there'." Shane said he didn't know where the car came from. It was a blacky, bluey colour.

"She didn't want to get in the car," Shane said quietly. When he paused, there was silence.

"She didn't want to, so the man got out of the car and put her in the car."

Kerri sobbed quietly as she listened to the little boy talking about her daughter's last free movements. The other family members were crying openly. Shane continued bravely, despite his nervousness. His voice quavered a little but he didn't seem to get too upset. He repeated that the man got her off the bike and put her in the car. Sheree didn't say anything. The bike was left in the middle of the road.

Shane said the man put Sheree in the front of the car. In the passenger side. The man didn't say anything to Shane. The man did a bit of a "skidder" and he went off. The man nearly ran over the bike.

The boy said he went home and said Sheree had been kidnapped. He didn't remember what was said when he said that.

Cross-examined by the bearded David Brustman, Shane elaborated. The man had said to Sheree, "'Hop in the car please.' She didn't want to, so she got taken off her bike and gone in."

Shane said the man was big. Skinny and big and he had hair that was blackish, like purple. He didn't know how old he was, just had a normal face with white skin, jeans and a T-shirt and a jumper and a belt. He thought it was a blue T-shirt and black belt.

Shane's ordeal was over, everybody shifted in their seats and the court was adjourned.

Christine Dogan was the next witness. She told the court the girl she saw, while driving home to Rye that day almost two and half years ago, was very upset and distressed.

"This girl saw that I was looking towards her and she just stared toward me and kept crying," Ms Dogan said.

She said the man driving the small blue car was between 50 to 65. He just looked straight ahead and totally ignored the girl's crying. Ms Dogan thought that was strange because if he was the father or grandfather then he wouldn't have ignored the crying. She noticed the girl had her seatbelt on.

As Allison Harding scribbled her notes for the next day's news, she noticed how strong Ms Dogan's testimony was. She was a very good witness. She was so sure she was right, even after all this time.

THE NEXT MORNING, Alex Bartsch picked up Lorraine and drove her to court. She was to be the next witness. Lorraine was panicking and rang Ross Brightwell for a bit of support. "It's all in the providence of God, Lorraine," the churchman told her. Lorraine was furious with him. She muttered, "I'll providence of God you!" She wanted him to tell her everything would be all right. Caught up in the emotional whirlpool, she was getting angry at those around her who couldn't help her, instead of the man who had placed her in this predicament.

The police had told Margaret Hobbs they would pick her up when she was due to give evidence. As soon as she heard that she thought, *No, I'm not going to go*. On the Tuesday evening, her specialist rang and cancelled an appointment scheduled for the next day, the same day she suspected she should be at court. Margaret decided to go shopping instead of finding out if she was wanted as a witness. She was running away.

As she readied herself to go out, she was startled when the phone rang. She picked it up and answered as she always does.

"Margaret Hobbs." She said the surname with a little musical lilt. She looked up at the clock. It was 8am.

"Hi Marg. Robert here. It's very unpleasant down here."

Margaret felt as though she had been thumped in the belly. She felt the adrenalin rush through her body. Her heart was racing. That horrible voice continued its monotone. Flat, measured, menacing. Margaret had heard Robert speak like that before - on the day he described the "hypothetical" death scenario.

"You shouldn't be here," he continued. "It's too dangerous. Don't come."

Margaret quickly put the phone down and felt a wave of nausea sweep over her.

Why did he say that? Clutching her stomach, she staggered to the toilet and threw up.

What's wrong with me? she thought. *A voice can make me physically ill? A voice?* She paged Alex Bartsch and told him what had happened.

"What did he say?" Bartsch demanded.

"I shouldn't be at the court."

"I've got Lorraine with me, I'll call you back."

Lorraine was terrified. She arrived at Brunswick, dodging the media by being shunted in the court's back entrance through the police station. She waited in the prosecutor's office for a couple of hours. Lorraine had been told she would be first witness in but that was not the case. Geoff Flatman came in and spoke to her briefly before she was called in to the courtroom. Alex now had time to ring Margaret. She had been crying for a full hour.

"I'll come and pick you up," Alex said.

"What for?"

"You're on today."

"Nobody told me." Margaret was trying to sound defiant. She had been playing 'silly buggers' because she had been waiting for somebody to tell her. She was determined not to ask. So Alex told her. Andrew Gustke would come and pick her up as soon as possible.

Andrew went to Margaret's Belgrave home and found her sitting in her family room, watching a blue wren, who had made his home in the huge tree fern outside, standing bravely before his own reflection. Often she and her husband John sat and watched the wren and his hen dancing in the fronds, enchanted by their grace and beauty. Now she watched him with envy. How she wished she could jettison all this misery and fear.

Margaret had powdered her face but couldn't disguise her puffy eyes.

Luckily it was a hot day and she put the air conditioner in the unmarked police car on full. She was thankful it was a long drive. By the time she got to court 50 minutes later, she felt she was looking a little better. She still felt shaken to the core but she knew she would cope. After all, she wasn't on trial. Or so she thought.

With trepidation , and feeling a little dazed, Lorraine stepped into the witness box. It was ghastly. To her left sat the magistrate. To her immediate right, so close she could almost reach out and touch him, stood the prosecutor. David Brustman was only a further metre away, almost directly in front of her. It was claustrophobic. And across the room, between the magistrate and the lawmen, sitting behind his plastic shield was Robert, staring intently at her. Yet he looked bored. *Could this really be a court case about him murdering a 6-year-old girl? He couldn't care less!*

Lorraine had trouble focussing on the proceedings. She gripped the edge of the witness box so hard her knuckles went white. Geoff Flatman tendered her six statements which were all accepted into evidence. Then David Brustman quizzed Lorraine on the number of statements she had made; the first statement was totally contradicted by the last. Brustman wanted to know why there was such a difference.

"When I made that first statement, the police had just raided our home," Lorraine said. "I could barely remember what had happened." She was shaky but composed. Everybody except the magistrate and counsel had to strain to hear what she was saying. Her words barely passed her lips before they fell away. The court listened in silence. Nobody moved. There was only one person who didn't seem to want to hear what she was saying. And yet his freedom was at stake.

She was, she told Brustman, upset and shocked straight after the raid on August 13, and she had answered the police questions as best she could. She told Brustman her husband had told her he was home on the 29th. Lorraine didn't like Brustman at all; to her he looked evil and very nasty. She found it hard to look at him.

"He left the house at 7.45 in the morning," she said. Robert had taken a son to tennis, and then he went to a church meeting.

"I didn't see him again after that until around 5.30 when it was just getting dark. "

"Unless he was hiding somewhere, he was not home 'cos I walked around the house several times that day. I went out a couple of times to the shops," she said.

Allison looked up from scribbling her notes to see Lorraine looking forlornly at the floor while her ex-husband stared at her intently.

Lorraine also testified that Robert was obsessed with the Karmein Chan case and had prayed for the murdered teenager at church and at home. He was also obsessed with the Azaria Chamberlain case, she said, and he often claimed the police were always going after good church-going people.

When Lorraine told the court her then husband had washed his clothes that day for the first time in 19 years, Allison looked at another woman reporter and they both curled their lips in disgust. What a creep! How could he have not committed this appalling crime?

Lorraine waited for the next barrage of horrible questions but Mr Brustman sat down. The cross examination was over. When the court adjourned, Brustman approached Lorraine in the court foyer. The two security officers sitting at the table outside the courtroom jumped to Lorraine's side to hear what he said.

"Mrs Lowe, my name is David Brustman and I am defending Mr Lowe," he said. He looked as if he wanted to talk further.

"You could have fooled me," Lorraine said, and walked away. She thought Brustman had a very dark look on his face.

Benjamin knew his mum was giving evidence that day but he couldn't go into court in case he was called as a witness. During his lunch break, just before an exam at RMIT, he caught the tram from the city to Brunswick. He alighted in Sydney Road and walked to the west side of the road, away from the court. He stood still on the footpath and peered across the busy thoroughfare. He saw cameramen everywhere. There were crowds of people milling around, hurling abuse at the court and swearing. Everybody in the street was talking about what was going on. People were calling out, 'Hang him'. Benjamin waited until it calmed down and court resumed for the afternoon session before he went in with his mum.

Now it was Margaret's turn. She stepped up into the witness box and purposely ignored Robert Lowe. She wanted him to know she was going to stand firm but knew if she looked at him her resolve might diminish.

She wouldn't give him the satisfaction of seeing how upset she had been. Proudly she stood in the box, steeling herself for the onslaught. She knew she would be attacked for breaching confidentiality - that sacred thing she had herself jealously guarded for years. She briefly looked down and saw the hem of her dress quivering. She didn't think her shaking had been that visible. Lorraine was now sitting in the body of the court. She thought Margaret looked terrible. That surprised her. She thought Margaret would be more used to being in court.

Brustman began by asking Margaret how long it took to make her 82 page statement and what had happened when Geoff Alway and Dale Johnson had first approached her way back in August 1991. He asked how often she had had conversations with the police whilst she was seeing Robert. Margaret told him she had seen them "perhaps a once a monthly contact, even more - it was reasonably considerable". Her right foot, unseen by most in the room, was tap, tap, tapping.

"Were the visits by a police officer driving from somewhere to your rooms, knocking on the door saying, 'Hello, is Mr Lowe still your patient?' Is that the entirety of a visit, rather than a telephone call? It must be more, I suspect or suggest?" Brustman leaned forward, gaping for an answer. Tim Pegler thought he sounded a little smarmy.

"No, they were very often just that." Tim continued taking notes. Margaret's demeanour showed she was angry that she had to defend herself. She answered his questions sharply. It would be obvious to a blind man that Margaret didn't like Brustman at all.

"Some police officer would drive all the way to your rooms from wherever it is he or she is coming from, to ask you one question, the answer to which is "Yes" - are you saying that?" Brustman asked incredulously.

"Yes, yes, I see what you mean," Margaret said.

The clerk handed Margaret a glass of water. It was slopping all over the place.

What have I done? she thought. *They're attacking me.*

"Wasn't there a bit more conversation than that, Mrs Hobbs?"

"Yes, there was sometimes more conversation than that."

"Tell us what the more conversation was, please."

"Some of the conversation would centre around perhaps what was happening with Mr Lowe and myself. There was not much interaction at that point in time. I was finding this case extremely difficult to deal with and at times I needed to talk to people."

"If I was a police officer" - a few coppers looked at each other and raised their eyebrows - "I would try to ask you as much and get as much information out of you as I could. You accept that, don't you?"

"Certainly."

"I take it that is exactly what was happening?"

"No, that wasn't exactly what was happening at all."

"Weren't the police at all interested in what Mr Lowe was doing?"

"Yes, they were, but I was mindful of my position."

"What was your position?"

"My position was as Mr Lowe's therapist primarily."

"Would you take that just a little bit further?"

"Yes."

"Your position *viz a viz* the police - we know you're his therapist but what does that mean in terms of your position?"

"It means that my prime concern was regarding Mr Lowe's position. Myself with him, as a therapist and a client."

"Did the police indicate to you, at any stage in any way in any of these meetings and by any police officer, that they wanted to know what he, if anything, was saying to you?"

"No."

"Did you, Mrs Hobbs, in any way at all indicate to the police prior to November 1992, when you did... what he was saying to you?"

"Did I in..."

"I'll just repeat that. At any time between July 1991 and November 1992, did you in any way at all tell or indicate to police officers investigating this case, what he, Lowe, was saying to you?"

"Not in any great detail, yes, there was some kind."

"The answer's yes but not in any great detail?" Brustman looked around at the gallery. He was pleased with himself.

"Yes."

"What did you tell the police he was telling you?"

"I guess that much of my contact with the police would be adversarial. I was telling the police that in fact what Mr Lowe was telling me was confidential and that my first duty was towards the client."

"Are we to take from that answer that you didn't tell the police anything Mr Lowe said to you?"

'Not in detail, no."

Brustman let out a puff of air in mock exasperation.

"Your answers, with respect madam, are inconsistent. I'll just go a bit further. You've told Her Worship a minute ago, yes, what I was telling the police was, 'It is my patient and it is confidential'. Right?"

"Yes."

"That is in another form saying, 'I'm not going to tell you what he's told me'. Right?"

"Yes."

"Do I understand that to be the situation or are you saying, 'No, I did tell them certain things he told me?' Which one is it? 'I didn't tell them anything or I did tell them something?'"

"I did tell them some things, yes."

"What did you tell them?"

"I would have difficulty in recalling exactly what I told them but at times I was telling them that Mr Lowe was indicating that he had nothing to do with this matter and that was the main thrust of the comments."

"That's a very general way of putting something and it took about 20/30 seconds to say it; there must have been more you said than that?"

"No, not specifically."

"How many times did you tell the police, approximately if you obviously can't remember, Mr Lowe was saying he had nothing to do with this?"

"I wouldn't recall that."

"It was clearly more than once?"

"Yes, possibly more than once, yes."

"Why would you tell the police that anyway?"

"I was placed in a very difficult position of working with a client who by his actions and his statements to me was throwing grave doubt on myself in which way I should go with him and I guess that was the way it went. I was in an enormous dilemma for two years with this case in terms of my duty to the community and my duty to the client."

Just talking about the past two years brought the mental scars to Margaret's face. Nobody in the court missed the pain she was experiencing. Sheree's relatives sat a little taller in their seats. They had no idea what sort of evidence Margaret was going to give. They had heard she had visited him in prison after he was charged with Sheree's murder and despised her for it. Now it sounded like she was going to give evidence against Robert Lowe. Suddenly they felt they were on the verge of switching allegiances.

"Mrs Hobbs, did you know whether your office had a listening device in it?"

"No."

"When did you first find out about that?"

"About six weeks ago."

"How did you find out about that six weeks ago?"

"I was told."

"Who told you?"

"By the police."

"Which police?"

"Alex Bartsch."

"What circumstances; did he come and tell you?"

"Yes."

"'By the way madam, we bugged your office for a couple of years?'"

"Yes."

"What was your reaction to that?"

"I was horrified." It was clear she was.

"Can I ask you this; did you at any stage tell the police of this," and he waved Lowe's 'confession' in the air - "after he gave it to you?"

"At that point in time, when Mr Lowe gave me that document, I was aware that this was a very serious matter and again I spoke on the legal ramifications of it and I was told that I had a duty to present that document to the police. However, I believe, before I did that Mr Lowe was caught shop-lifting with it on him, so that circumvented that problem for me."

The ire was rising. Margaret was pulling herself up to her full height. She was flushed, angry, defiant.

"Do I detect, Mrs Hobbs, a certain animosity toward my client in the way you have answered that question?"

"I think it's toward you, sir." Margaret glared at him across the bar table. A smattering of spontaneous applause broke out among some of Sheree's relatives. Steve put his arms up over his head like a boxer who had just won a fight. Several others, Kerri included, gave Margaret the thumbs up sign. Yeah, Margaret was all right. She was on their side.

Brustman then asked why Margaret had handed over the confessional statement to the police.

"I don't believe I had any choice. I have no privilege in these matters at all."

"You say you didn't think you had any choice; what about the choice not to tell anyone that it's been given to you; did you think of that?"

"I wonder whether that's a serious question. Are you considering my position in this?"

"I'm actually very serious."

"No, I don't believe I had any choice."

She was then quizzed on which police she told she was going to Rosebud with Robert Lowe.

"Why did you see fit to tell police officers you were going down with your patient to Rosebud?"

"Because at that point in time it was clear to me, or becoming clear to me, that Mr Lowe perhaps was seriously involved in the death of a 6-year-old child. I am a facilitator and nothing more."

Later....

"Would you say that throughout the occasions you detail, this man Lowe trusted you and depended on you, given the number of times you say 'He rang me and talked to me and came', and all the rest?"

"Did he trust me and depend upon me?"

"Yes, it must surely be a situation -"

"- Yes, certainly."

"You would say that continues until this very day, right?"

"Yes."

"Part, if not a lot, of the trust and dependency that you've said he's got has to do with the relationship as it not only deteriorated but split asunder?"

"Yes."

Later....

"It is abundantly clear from all the times you detail and indeed from even the events today that this man, as you say, was dependent upon you and trusted you but I put to you that what you detail is almost a total dependence and trust; you're the only one he's (got) to talk about all sorts of things?'

"Mr Lowe was well aware that I was interacting with police; it was Mr Lowe who gave me permission to make the statement. It is Mr Lowe who seeks interviews with me and it's his own dependency that makes him dependent upon me."

"Why don't you answer my questions, Mrs Hobbs?"

"Have I not answered it?"

Later....

"You kept on telling him, let's get now to the divorce and his wife; you kept on telling him that unless he told the truth to you his wife would not have him back and so on and so forth?"

"No, that's not correct."

Finally, Brustman finished his cross examination with, "Mrs Hobbs, if I put it to you that you have acted unprofessionally with gross impropriety, what would you say?"

Margaret felt like a double agent or maybe a spy who'd been caught by the enemy. She retorted: "I would say, 'So be it'." With that, the barrackers erupted into applause, a few whistles were heard. There were a few thumbs going up to say, "We're with you."

Brustman was a bit puzzled and then turned to the body of the court with a look of mock surprise on his face as if to say, "What have I done? What have I said to offend this lady?" He didn't win over anybody at all. Margaret saw the police at the side of the court. They all had trouble hiding the smiles.

A couple of times Lowe reacted badly to her evidence, shaking his head and becoming frustrated at some of the things she was saying. Tim thought he was a prickly sort of a bloke. If he didn't like what any of the witnesses were saying, he tended to carry on like he was in a pantomime.

As she got down from the witness box, Margaret heard a smattering of applause from the body of the court. Outside the court, Kerri walked up and kissed her on the cheek.

"Thank you," Kerri said quietly. Steve kissed Margaret, too and Neil Greenhill shook her hand. Margaret wiped a tear away. She was deeply touched. She didn't know these people. She had never met them before. All she knew was their little angel was dead and they were recognising her for what she had done. Two kisses and a handshake had made it worthwhile, she thought. A few others came up and congratulated Margaret too. But in the back of her mind, Margaret was still very fearful and felt even more vulnerable. That had been the defence's first crack at her. Next would be the trial, before a judge and a jury. This was just the beginning.

THE NEXT MORNING Lorraine went back to court with Benjamin. They sat near the back of the court. More relaxed than the day before, Lorraine was now able to take in what was going on in the court. She took special notice of her former husband. His hair was unkempt and very grey. When they were married, he had used Restoria on his hair at night. Now it was completely different. Lorraine wondered if he'd done that so the witnesses would have trouble identifying him. She glanced back at Robert and did a double-take. She realised he was trying to get Benjamin's attention. He kept staring at him, and smiling and nodding. It made Benjamin angry. He wondered if his dad was completely mad.

Peter Reid was brought into court, escorted by police and security guards. As soon as Margaret saw him, she thought, *You've lost it Pete*. She could see the tenseness in his body, the tightness of his jaw. She knew he was very uptight.

Hmm, she thought, *this is going to get interesting. Especially for you, Mr Brustman.*

Allison Harding looked at the prisoner stepping into the witness box and saw a pretty scary ball of energy. He looked tough and mean, and very, very angry. She could see that when Reid glanced at Lowe, his face showed an expression of total disgust.

Geoff Flatman handed Reid his statement.

"Are the contents of the statement true and correct?" Flatman asked.

Peter Reid was a wild horse champing at the bit.

"Very much so," he said.

Tim Pegler could see how angry and upset Reid was. He eyed him very carefully. He was short but powerfully built with a huge chest and shoulders and big hands but a small head. Reid was balding, his black hair cut above the ears and a couple of inches long at the back. Tim thought it would be easy for Reid to hurt somebody.

Reid turned to Brustman. The cross examination was about to begin. The witness and his interrogator were only three metres apart. Reid's stance and manner said it all. *Come on, say something. Have a go.*

Tim was surprised at Brustman's manner. He was talking to Reid as if he was a dog. Tim thought he was baiting Reid to see what would happen. Allison knew why Brustman was being sarcastic - he was trying to discredit him. She thought Brustman was doing the right thing by his client. Brustman wanted to know how Reid was dealing with the police when he was handing over information.

"I was handing in notes and various items, maps that he had put together," Reid said. Then he turned and sneered at Lowe. The hate was obvious.

Paul Hollowood noticed Lowe was always looking smug. That was intimidating enough for Sheree's relatives who were trying to stare him out. They were flustered by the fact that he wasn't at all fazed by proceedings. To Robert Lowe it was an academic exercise. In his plastic bubble, he studiously took notes and looked totally engrossed in himself. He was acting the role of a man who knew the law. If anybody was watching him, they would see a professional man, a man who knew what he was doing. He showed no fear, no remorse, no concern.

Brustman's questioning continued. He asked Reid for some dates when he had had conversations with Lowe. Reid couldn't remember. Alex Bartsch looked on and thought, *Any wonder. He was a physical wreck at the time.*

"Can I refer to my statement please?" Reid said.

"No, you can't," Brustman taunted. He leaned forward across the bar table. The large media contingent took notes. Watching from the body of the court, Margaret was very concerned.

Calm down, calm down, she said to Peter silently. She could see the build up of anger. Brustman was speaking to Reid with complete and utter contempt.

Brustman established that 13 and a half years earlier, Reid was sentenced to life imprisonment for murder.

"Who did you kill?"

"A police officer, you knew that," he snarled at Brustman.

"Have you stayed out of trouble since?"

"No."

Then he was asked what trouble he had been in while in prison.

"Assaulting prisoners, assaulting officers, extortion, and various internal matters within the prison system." Brustman nodded. Reid was not the sort of person a jury would take kindly to. The lawyer then referred to a charge of threatening to kill.

"Who did you make the demand of?"

"You know who it was, Karmein Chan. Why play games, just ask me the question. You knew who it was."

"I'm sorry, I didn't get that answer, Mr Reid?"

"Karmein Chan."

"Is that who you made the demand of?"

"The family of Karmein Chan."

"Why did you do that?"

"Personal reasons which I won't answer."

"I'm asking you why did you do that?"

"Hey, am I here on trial or is your mutt over there on trial?"

The Magistrate intervened.

"Excuse me, Mr Reid -"

"- No, I'm not going to cop this. I'm not here on trial."

"You are in court under subpoena to answer questions," Ms Wilmoth said before David Brustman continued.

"The question, Mr Reid, is why did you do that?"

"Because I wanted someone killed, I needed the money."

"I beg your pardon?"

"I was trying to raise money because I wanted someone killed outside."

"Are you, Mr Reid, an *honest* person?" he said, sarcastically accentuating the word.

"No, otherwise I wouldn't be in gaol. If I was honest I wouldn't be in gaol, would I?" Reid said. Everybody's eyes were locked on the action. Reid's dislike for Brustman was almost palpable. Margaret could see a huge vein throbbing in Peter's neck. His face was getting dark. *Oh God, he's losing it.*

"Honesty has nothing to do with murder, necessarily, has it? That's what you're in gaol for?"

"All right."

From his plastic box, Robert was determined to attract his family's attention. Benjamin didn't want to look at him because he was wary about what people might think about him and what they might do. Eventually Benjamin did glance over at his dad and saw he was trying to attract his attention. His dad smiled and raised his eyebrows, as if nothing was happening. Benjamin just stared at him. He was very angry with his father. It was obvious that he didn't care about what was happening in court - it was as though he was somewhere else. Benjamin stared at him to show he was mad. Mad at what his dad had put the family through. Mad at having to endure the stress of going to court. Mad that the family had to break up. Mad at the change to his whole life.

Occasionally Robert became agitated at something Reid said. He would look at Lorraine and Benjamin and slowly shake his head from side to side. Benjamin was ashamed.

"Mr Reid, how much is or was, the reward which was posted in respect of the Sheree Beasley matter?"

"I wouldn't have a clue?"

"Wouldn't have a clue?"

"No."

"Sure about that?"

"Positive."

"Never heard of a reward?"

"Why don't you just ask me specific questions?"

"Just answer the question, please."

"I'm telling you everything I've got here is on video and tape, so it's not a matter of me lying, and you know that because you've seen and heard it."

The Murder of Sheree

"Would you please answer my question, Mr Reid?"

"I don't know anything about a reward."

To Tim it seemed, despite Reid's shocking past, there was a bit of honour involved in giving evidence against Lowe and sticking up for Sheree. Having his integrity questioned over the murder of a 6-year-old girl seemed to be the last straw. That was taking away his last shred of dignity. Reid got angrier and angrier, especially at the suggestion that he was in it only for himself.

Brustman continued haranguing Reid, taunting him in a sarcastic tone - as if nobody could believe anything Peter Reid said. Given his track record, that was a fair supposition.

"Is today, in fact, right now, the first time you've heard anything about it?"

Reid's voice rose. "Before today, or before I met Lowe, I never even got into the case of this poor Sheree." The name provoked more tears in the gallery.

"Of this what?"

"The case of Sheree. I've never even given it any thought."

"That's nice. Could you please listen to my question though? The question, sir, is this. Is today, right now, the first occasion you have heard of a reward in respect of this matter?"

"Yes."

Tim looked up from his notes and over at Lowe. He was looking pretty sanctimonious. Reid continued to glare at Lowe. Lowe returned the stare.

"Never heard of it before?"

"I might've discussed it with Robert Lowe at one stage, he might've said to me, look something about it, I just don't know, I didn't even give it any thought."

"You just told this court that everything you said with Mr Lowe is on tape."

"It is - "

" - Is there discussion - "

" - So why don't you go to the tape?"

"Please Mr Reid. Having said that Mr Reid, is your assertion that you might have discussed the reward with Mr Lowe also on tape?"

"No."

"What else is not on tape?"

"How do you mean? You were there. What are you trying to do? It's quite easy, you can get me upset, no-one's denying that."

Ms Wilmoth intervened again.

"Mr Reid, will you just restrain yourself for a moment, please?"

Peter was focused on Brustman. "Who looked after fucking Sheree, who looked after her? Who looked after Sheree, you mutt? I tell you, who looked after her? Not you. You mongrel."

He continued shouting as some of the security staff moved a little closer to the witness box.

"You mutt!" Peter shouted, leaning toward Brustman.

"Hey, very easy to upset me. I've never needed any reward for poor Sheree. You come back, you fucking mongrel. Don't ever suggest I need money. Don't ever suggest that." Gritted teeth, cold stare. Hatred.

Several people gave a start at the raised voice. Kerri and Jill Mandile sat with tissues to their faces. Both were sobbing.

Ms Wilmoth adjourned the court for a few minutes. Brustman was leaning forward on the bar table, pursing his lips. As the magistrate left the court, the inevitable happened. Reid shouted, "Who looked after fucking little Sheree?" his eyes bearing down into Brustman's. The small man's voice was loud and threatening. At that moment, he jumped from the witness box, lunging at Brustman. The lawyer jumped up with a start. He crouched behind his chair at the end of the front row, then moved further away towards the back of the court. Much of the gallery rose as one, with women screaming and wailing, people gasping in fear. A stampede for the door began at once, as Alex and three security officers quickly surrounded Reid. There was panic everywhere. Reid had shot and killed a policeman before. Maybe now he was going to do a lawyer in with his bare hands.

Lorraine had never witnessed anything like this in her life. She could not believe the anger, the shouting, the threats, people dashing around. She was frightened by the court proceedings. But Peter Reid - this was unbelievable. She didn't think Reid would go for her but she thought he could well kill Brustman or her ex-husband and the police might use

The Murder of Sheree

their guns. She didn't want to see that. She felt something dreadful was about to happen and had to get out. She leaned over to Benjamin, "Let's run for it," she said. They ran for the door and were carried along in the crush. Paul Hollowood could see Lorraine heading for the door. She looked so shaken he felt that if the crowd wasn't carrying her along, she would drop to the floor. As the crowd pushed and shoved, Brustman swept to the back of the court. Women were still screaming, yelling, crying. Lorraine was pushed through the doors by the flood of people, her handbag hitting a TV reporter.

"Are you all right, Mrs Lowe?" the reporter asked. Lorraine heard the question but no response came to mind. She ran straight into the toilet.

Brustman eventually ended up behind the last row of seats, while Reid was restrained by his minders. It seemed to Alex that Peter wasn't struggling all that much. He knew Reid was so powerful that if he wanted to get Brustman, or at least frighten him more, he could have. Tim and Allison had stopped taking notes in all the excitement. It seemed to them Reid was in protective custody in prison for everybody else's safety, not his own.

As the security guards hurriedly shuffled Lowe from the court, Reid shouted across the room: "You mutt, you will die in jail."

Steve Ludlow realised Reid was in more trouble. "Leave it Pete, leave it," he yelled.

Sheree's family were either crying or cursing Lowe. He showed no emotion as he left the court.

The reporters were spellbound. Brustman looked very frightened. Kerri was howling. Allison and Tim had covered courts all over Victoria for years and had never seen anything like this.

Reid was dragged from the court and everything slowly started to settle down. Margaret walked from the court - she had been one of the few non-police people to stay. She knew Peter Reid would never harm her. She went to check on Lorraine and Benjamin and was told Lorraine was in the ladies toilets. She found Lorraine lying on her back on the cold, tiled floor, where a woman was helplessly attending to her. Two police officers stood over them, watching. One of them climbed over the cubicle door to unlock it after Lorraine collapsed. As Margaret entered everyone looked at her.

"It's all right, I'm a friend," Margaret said.

The commotion was still bubbling outside in the foyer. Everyone was in a terrible state. The police surgeon went into the toilets and told Lorraine to take it very easy for a while. When she felt well enough, she walked into a coffee room to have a drink. A few other people were milling around, speaking in hushed tones. Lorraine sat in a chair, feeling more comfortable but totally drained, when a man walked up and stood before her. He had unchecked tears running down his face. Very quietly he said, "Would you be offended if I offered you a coffee? They have some made".

Lorraine nodded. The man walked over, made a cup and brought it back. Lorraine was moved. It had been such a long time since she had experienced this type of kindness. The man handed over the coffee and patted her on the shoulder. He smiled through his tears, and walked away. Lorraine was glad somebody knew how awful she felt. A uniformed policeman who had been watching from the doorway could see the puzzled look on Lorraine's face. He walked over to her and said, "That's Neil Greenhill. Sheree's grandad."

AFTER AN adjournment, the court reconvened. Media lawyers applied for, and lost, an argument to have the suppression order on Peter Reid's evidence lifted. Greg Bowd from the Prison Squad gave evidence, then Pentridge prison officer Robert Johnson. Peter Reid was next.

Wendy Wilmoth warned him if he carried on again he would be charged with contempt. Peter Reid, murderer, extortionist, and vital witness for the Crown, was to restrain himself and just answer questions. Tim thought Reid looked a little hangdog.

Reid apologised to the court. Then he calmly gave his evidence. He said all conversations with Lowe had been monitored by camera and the only two occupants in the unit were him and Lowe. Alex Bartsch sat right beside him outside the witness box, looking stonily ahead. He was totally annoyed. A man like Peter Reid had the potential to destroy the prosecution case with his earlier performance. What would he be like in front of a judge and jury?

Brustman continued his cross examination. He didn't sound sarcastic

The Murder of Sheree

anymore. He kept asking Reid for dates on which particular conversations with Robert Lowe had occurred. Reid was still struggling to remember. He kept turning and glancing at Alex as he searched his mind for dates. Alex would know. But Alex kept staring straight ahead. Reid gave his evidence of how he had spoken to Lowe and how Lowe had confessed his complicity.

Then, seemingly out of nowhere, Reid said, "He told me he made little Sheree perform oral sex on him." There was a collective horrified gasp. Kerri screamed. It was the first time she had heard that. It made her stomach turn. Kerri was supported by Steve as they left the courtroom. Lorraine saw a Protective Security Group officer walk up to Sheree's father, Anthony Mandile, and tell him he had to leave too. Lorraine was disgusted and felt so sorry for Sheree's family. Imagine hearing details like that about your own daughter. She looked across at Robert. He had showed no negative emotions throughout the proceedings. Often he talked and smiled to the men guarding him. He showed no shame, anger or distress at being accused of such acts. Lorraine sometimes thought he looked as though he was enjoying all the drama and attention. Now he was sitting there impassively with his eyes down. Everyone else was crying, or fighting back tears.

The court was adjourned. Lorraine and Benjamin got on a tram in Brunswick Street for the slow, surreal trip back to suburbia. They sat next to a young girl who was sitting with her family.

"Look at all the TV cameras, dad," she said. "What's going on?"

"That's the case about the blighter who killed the little girl," her father said. "What they need rather than cameras is a chain saw."

Lorraine shuddered and hoped the family wouldn't recognise her.

He used to be my husband, she thought. *I used to be proud of that.*

Benjamin sat staring out the window, away from the action. The shy, inexperienced boy, on the threshold of manhood, had led a sheltered life. Daily for the past two years, he had been hit in the face with the big issues most teenagers - and adults for that matter - shy away from. Death. Murder. Betrayal of the highest order. Now he was listening to people publicly deride his father, the man he had once loved. But the man he had seen behind that plastic screen was not the man he knew. Benjamin

The Murder of Sheree

blinked and suddenly realised where he was. He looked at the man with his family sitting opposite and offered a sad smile. It was a silent apology of sorts, as if to say 'We don't know him but if we did we wouldn't like him.' Then he turned his head and looked away from the court house to the other side of the road. He felt helpless and muddled. He tried to anticipate what would be the next shock in his life. He saw only shop windows, people with carry bags and trolleys, cars vying for parking space. That belonged to another world, a world he thought he would enter when he left school. Now he didn't know where he was heading.

That night he asked his mum about Peter Reid's evidence. The school and his parents had covered sex education but they had not covered the "sick side" of behaviour or sexual perversions. Lorraine tried to talk about it with Benjamin, who had been such a great support for her, but he went very quiet.

Later Lorraine trudged off to bed but did not sleep. She felt physically ill at what she had heard and seen in court. Peter Reid! What a performance! But even worse, the words that he said came from Robert's mouth! It was disgusting! Lorraine couldn't understand how Robert could do such filthy things while mixing with honest, good living people. How could he pretend he was a nice person too? She looked around the bedroom. She saw, on the bedside tables, pictures of the family. Of Robert and her, husband and wife, smiling, hugging. How could he jump into bed with her at night after what he did during the day? She began to feel guilty again. How could she bring two boys into the world to have to live with this? It wasn't as though it was a bank robbery or even a gun murder. It was a filthy murder - of a beautiful child - and committed for his 'pleasure'.

THE COURT adjourned for several weeks, resuming sittings at Melbourne Magistrates' Court. Jonathan Lowe returned from Queensland - he had been sent to Brisbane Boys' College to escape the fuss but after one term he was so lonely he came back home - and decided to go along to court. He wanted to know what it was like so he could prepare himself for his turn at the trial. And he wanted to support his mum. Robert was very keen to attract his son's attention by smiling, nodding and even waving. Jonathan thought it was a sick joke.

December 17, 1993, was the last day of the committal. Geoff Flatman summed up the prosecution case for the magistrate. It was, he said, very probative that Lowe had a prior fascination with child abductions, particularly the Karmein Chan case. Clearly the circumstantial case against Robert Arthur Selby Lowe was overwhelming.

"For this man to be innocent, he would have to be the unluckiest man alive," he said. "He was unlucky enough to be in the area at the time. He was unlucky enough to lie about it. He was unlucky enough to own a house nearby and know the area, he was unlucky enough to drive the same type of car as the one which took her. He was unlucky enough to look so much like the abductor that two witnesses identified him in identity parades, and he was unlucky enough to have an obsession with missing girls. He cannot give any satisfactory account of where he was. The lies go on, and on, and on, and on. They are all classic matters for a jury to decide."

He told Ms Wilmoth Lowe had denied he knew the Rosebud area or the milkbar Sheree had been to.

"He was a face known to the milkbar proprietor," Flatman said.

David Brustman then made a submission that there was no case to answer. There was no cause of death determined, no complete admissions by his client. The circumstantial case was "all very well" but there was no evidence that his client had killed Sheree Beasley.

Ms Wilmoth decided to commit Robert Lowe to trial and she asked him to stand. She asked him how he pleaded. He stood transfixed, apparently deep in thought, as the moments ticked by. The whole court was looking at him. Lorraine held her breath. It was as if he was groping around to see what all the fuss was about. It seemed he could not comprehend why people were so upset. Couldn't they see that he was in trouble? He should be the one people were worried about. Especially Lorraine, Benjamin and Jonathan.

After some time Lowe asked to speak with his barrister. Brustman jumped up and whispered to him in what appeared to be an agitated way, and then returned to his seat.

Robert raised his head high and stared along his nose at the magistrate.

"Not guilty," he said loudly and flatly, before being taken from the court.

No doubt recalling his past successes in Magistrates' Courts in cases of indecency, Lowe was supremely confident he would win again. He knew the ropes and the ways around the law. He knew he could win by fighting all the way and sticking to his story. But he'd never appeared before a judge and a jury before.

CHAPTER FOURTEEN

◇

PETER REID'S health improved a little after the committal hearing. He started writing to Kerri and Steve.

Dear Steve,

Now that I have had a chance to rest and sleep since Thursday I am now feeling a little better. You should be able to tell that I am better purely by my writing.

Believe me Steve, when you see and hear all the evidence I have against Lowe, you will then understand why the dog's lawyer tried so hard to discredit me. I do admit I did not handle the first half hour too well. I was unaware of him and I had no idea he was only fishing. It wasn't until later I learnt that he had NOT seen any of the drawings, tapes audio, tapes visual, Lowe's drawings and statements. Anyhow, yesterday I was put right on a lot of things and I assure you he's gone!!!

Steve, I hope you don't mind keeping in touch by letter for now, untill the trial is over, then I will add your phone number to my phone list. But should I need to contact you urgently I will have either my family or my architect tutor call you.

When I am not doing architecture, I am at my computer CAD station and when I am not doing that I am working on the dog, studying all the paperwork.

Yesterday he complained to the chief of 'K' (Division) that he was having trouble getting through to his lawyer that is assisting him in the court case he is involved in on an unfair dismissal (case) from his work.* The chief said, "Tough Lowe". The

---
* Lowe tried unsuccessfully to sue Maria George for unfair dismissal

The Murder of Sheree

screws keep me fully informed. I can see him every day but can't talk to him. Now that he is FULLY protected and in a unit with only rockspiders he seems to giggle each day, it's as though he has no worry in the world. This really makes me very angry. I'm sorry I never just killed him. I'd love to put dynamite in his mouth and light a 10 minute slow burning fuse. It would be the longest 10 minutes.

The dog is VERY fearful of Melbourne reading all about his life and what happened. He once said it would drive him to taking his own life. I personally will never give up till he is DEAD.

Anyhow, Steve, how are Kerri and you and the rest of the children and family coping? I do hope you all are OK. And I am also hoping that you and Kerri will be able to do an IMPACT STATEMENT where you can tell the dog what you think. Believe me, he gets no favours in here. EVERYONE knows who and what he is. He is known as MR ROCKSPIDER. It is rumoured very heavily that he is having sex with Chan, the Chinaman that killed the little girl way back. The little girl's mother was in a wheelchair. When I mentioned this to Alex he told me Lowe was a closet poof. I'm not surprised.

Well, Steve, I do hope to hear from you soon. I hope everything is fine with you all and have no worries mate. I will never stop. Never!!!

Take care, your friend.

Peter.

DESPITE UNIVERSAL predictions to the contrary, Kerri and Steve were still together three years after Sheree's murder. But they came close to breaking up a few times with the build-up of frustration and stress. Nothing mattered except Sheree's death and Robert Arthur Selby Lowe. Daily they would talk about him, curse him and then argue. They argued over trivial things - the dishes, what time the girls should go to bed, taking money out of the bank. Kerri was dead inside. She felt the pain but she couldn't put it into words. Every day, she could see Sheree in Robert Lowe's car, trying to get out, crying. She thought of suicide but that would be too hard on the girls and Steve.

Five months after Sheree was abducted, Kerri miscarried. Then she virtually stopped eating. She lost tens of kilos. Life wasn't worth living. She could no longer trust anybody. Lowe was a churchman and he killed her daughter. What's to stop the local doctor, the friendly cop, the smiling schoolteacher from being a paedophile in disguise, a serial rapist, or a drug pusher? Experience showed anybody could do anything. And the chances were they would do it to her or her family. She and Steve rarely went out, preferring instead to bunker down and wallow in their misery.

They tried to plan for life after the trial. Like Lorraine, Benjamin and Jonathan, everything in the Ludlow's life was put on hold. As far as they both could see, their lives were completely ruined.

Two weeks before Sheree was abducted Steve, a builder by trade, had organised a job in a Kalgoorlie mine. It would be tough, dusty and hot but it would be good money and it would be away from the bad memories of baby Shane. They were going to make a new life. Steve thought there'd be something wrong with him if he couldn't save 1200 bucks a week. They would have been laughing. Now there were no goals. What was the point? Everytime you get off your arse to do something life just smacks you in the teeth.

Kerri faced each day like a zombie, caring for the girls by rote. But often the scheduling, if you could call it that, was awry. Sometimes dinner was too late, sometimes it was burnt or undercooked. The girls often sat at the table together while Steve and Kerri sat in the lounge watching their black and white portable television in the loungeroom. In time, Community Services Victoria came in again to help with the girls. It wasn't that Kerri didn't love them. In a way they didn't want for anything. Kerri certainly loved them and showed it. But she was in an earth-bound purgatory.

She was suffering from severe migraines and she was prescribed Rohypnol and sedatives. By mid-1994 she was heavily addicted. Kerri was pleased when her doctor put her on the methadone program to try to kick the problem. She had been trying to come off the drugs so she would be well enough to understand what was said at Lowe's trial. In July 1994 she somehow overdosed on methadone and collapsed on the loungeroom floor.

Kerri went through a smooth tunnel which to her seemed like the inside of a bottle. At the end she saw something bright, a light. She was drawn inexorably toward it, not out of curiosity but by necessity. Then she saw Sheree come forward. Her daughter's face and torso filled all Kerri's vision. The doe eyes, the chubby cheeks, the cheeky smile, the lank hair. Kerri tentatively went up to her daughter. Strangely, Sheree spoke to her mum in a calm, strong, male voice. But for some reason it seemed right. Sheree sounded very content, very controlled and self-assured.

"The time is not right, " her daughter said. "You have to go back and do the thing that's got to be done." Kerri felt an overwhelming desire to stay with her daughter but instead felt herself floating away from her through the tunnel. This time she emerged in an expansive field of bright yellow daisies. It was a warm day. Kerri saw the rolling hills in the distance merge from green to gold to yellow where the land met the blue, cloudless sky. All she could see were daisies and grass that seemed to go on forever. It was very, very peaceful and she felt totally relaxed. It was the first time in three years Kerri had found a place to rest. She sat down and saw her daughter sitting opposite her, smiling back. Sheree looked beautiful. Kerri felt a warm sensation rush through her body. This was how it was supposed to feel all the time, she thought. She reached over and put a daisy chain in Sheree's hair and Sheree returned the favour. Sheree had a knowing look on her face as she smiled. When Kerri was a little girl she had tried to make daisy chains but the ends always broke when she pushed them with her fingernails. But these were thick and didn't break. Then mother and daughter talked for what could have been a few seconds or eternity. But there was no sound. Kerri felt as if she was watching a movie with the sound turned off. Despite the silence, or perhaps because of it, she thoroughly enjoyed the animated conversation. Words didn't matter anyway. As she sat in wonder, she suddenly felt herself floating away again, slowly at first but then accelerating, tumbling over and around, back along the tunnel, away from her daughter, away from the beautiful scenery, and the warmth.

As Steve gave his wife mouth-to-mouth resuscitation on the loungeroom floor, Kerri felt herself being dragged back along the tunnel, away from the light. The frantic paramedics gave her a dose of Narcan and she was instantly sober again. She sat there, holding her head, struggling to comprehend what had happened. She could tell by the people around her - her husband, the medicos, her daughters - that she had almost died. But she wanted to know just one thing. What was "The thing that had to be done"? Instantly she realised she had to be at the trial for Sheree. She knew if she went, she would be in touch with her daughter. It would be agonising, it would be heartbreaking, but for one more time she would feel reunited with her first-born. Kerri felt she already knew the outcome of Lowe's trial. After what she had just experienced, she saw the trial as Sheree's revenge.

As for the male voice that she heard come out of her daughter's mouth, Kerri had no doubts at all. It was the voice of Christ.

CHAPTER FIFTEEN

PETER Reid wrote another letter to Steve and Kerri on January 28, 1994.

Dear Steven,

I received your letter and was somewhat shocked as it was given to me by the Governor. He warned me that I should not try to take you for a ride, asking for anything in return for what I'm doing in court. I felt very angry that he mentioned it.

Anyhow, I want to reiterate to you Steven that I don't want anything from you and that due to the court case it would be very improper for me to do anything that could be seen in the wrong light.

Steven, I can't call you and I can't allow you to visit me. Let me explain. As you know, I am involved in a very hectic trial and if you were to visit me, big things could be made of it via Lowe's lawyer and I would run the risk of aborting the trial. With my background re K. Chan incident, I can't afford to do anything that could be taken the wrong way.

I am not allowed to give any of the evidence or transcripts to you, until AFTER the trial. To do otherwise would be breaking the law.

Steven I want to see Lowe convicted because I know what he did do, so I hope you can understand that by me having contact with you would lead to problems that would jeopardise the trial.

I am doing this for all the right reasons and I can't afford to put myself in a compromising situation.

I know you must be angry and hurting inside and I

can only say sorry I can't have any contact with you until after it is all over and even then Steven, I would not want you to visit me. It would not be right. But I will write!

I don't mean to hurt you but the Governor is right, my background is shit here and people could make plenty of me having contact with you.

I <u>promise</u> you this. I will stand my ground and I will tell the truth. My evidence is fully backed up. The courts will deal with Mr Lowe. Have faith.

I hope you understand my situation.

You owe me nothing, Steven.

Kind Regards
P.A. Reid.

CHAPTER SIXTEEN

BEFORE THE trial could begin properly, there was a voir dire - a small trial within a trial, in the absence of the jury - over contentious segments of evidence. Colin Lovitt, QC, for Lowe, had argued to Justice Philip Cummins that Margaret Hobbs and Peter Reid had tricked Robert Lowe into confessing to a crime he had not committed. He wanted the judge to rule that their evidence was tainted, that they were *agents provocateur* and that their testimony be ruled inadmissible. Without their evidence - tapes of Lowe confessing to vital sections of Sheree's disappearance - it was likely the Crown case would fail. Much rode on the outcome of this mini-trial. If the evidence was inadmissible, the case might be *nolle prosequied* and Robert Lowe could walk free for lack of evidence. Or he might face a full trial with an abundance of damning testimony coming from his own mouth.

Robert sat in the prisoner's dock, dressed in a faded turquoise wind jacket and no tie. He looked scruffy. He was delighted to see Margaret Hobbs savaged in the witness box for two days. His lawyers painted her as a master deceiver who had manipulated Lowe into confessing to something he hadn't done, purely to get his wife back. The inference was that she was an agent for the police. This was a worrying time for the witnesses, the family, the police. If Margaret's evidence was ruled out, the police case would be very shaky. With only circumstantial evidence against Lowe, corroborated by a cop-killer who, from prison, had blackmailed the parents of a missing schoolgirl, there might be no point in going on, after three hard years.

It was obvious from the questioning that Margaret was going to be in for a tough time at the trial. She was given a terrible hammering by the defence lawyers. They were determined to knock her about. She felt threatened and very, very alone. She felt terribly wronged and constantly on the back foot, defending what she had done. A disgusting by-product was that she had to relive her harrowing experiences with Robert. As Boris Kayser played tape after tape, highlighting sections of conversation in isolation where she had "manipulated" Robert into making a confession, Margaret tried to block out the noise. As some of the tapes were played, she stood with one finger in her ear. She didn't want to hear. Margaret was amazed at her own reaction when the first tape began and Robert's dull, wooden voice echoed around the court. She suddenly felt she was going to be sick. She turned to the judge.

"Can I have a break please?" she said urgently yet very quietly. She was pale as could be. Justice Cummins adjourned the court as Margaret ran to the toilets. As she threw up, the thought kept going through her mind. *Why is this voice doing this to me?*

When she returned to the witness box, Margaret realised she had to concentrate very hard on the questions, otherwise she got lost. Her major distraction was the accused. She felt evil emanating from him, an evil that permeated the court and its surrounds. His very being soiled the air around him and he contaminated those he came into contact with. She "felt" an aura around him that she knew was damaging her health and well-being. So mentally, she dehumanised him. Robert Lowe simply ceased to exist as far as she was concerned.

On the second day of the voir dire, Margaret's husband John sat in the body of the court, between his wife and the accused. Margaret felt a change in the room. She began to tune in more to the proceedings. Then, towards the end of voir dire, the fear left her. When she started to feel quite comfortable with being in court, she looked at Robert a couple of times. He looked completely bored.

Then her evidence was over. The defence argued to the judge that her evidence should be set aside because she had breached her client's confidentiality and misled him into thinking the sessions were confidential. It also argued that in the public interest her evidence should be disallowed. There were many people in the community, the lawyers said, who needed help for psychosexual problems. If those people knew their professional relationships were not confidential, they wouldn't seek help. A decision

The Murder of Sheree

on whether or not to admit Margaret's evidence would be made after Peter Reid gave his evidence.

Some observers predicted a repeat of his performance at the committal hearing. When Justice Cummins arrived in court, Lowe was already in the dock at the rear of the court, dressed in black pants, a grey jacket over a striped, open-neck shirt and white T-shirt. Lowe appeared composed, almost peaceful, apparently oblivious to the events unfolding.

Peter Reid, dressed in neat casual trousers and a beige sloppy joe, was brought before the judge and the lawyers, and surrounded by court security staff. He told the court Lowe had begun talking about Sheree's abduction about three days after he and Lowe were put together in K Division. He said he had coaxed more details out of Lowe on the pretext of helping him get a good lawyer. "More fool him for believing me," he said. He described Lowe as being cunning in some ways, but stupid in others.

Reid said Lowe had also confessed to abducting Sheree to two other prisoners. Lowe had also hinted he was responsible for another murder in Queensland. Reid said he had approached the Homicide Squad because he wanted to help them as part of his own rehabilitation.

Justice Cummins ordered the tapes be played, and told Reid he could step down from the stand. Prosecutor Paul Coghlan asked that Reid be held in the body of the court rather than be returned to the holding cells. David Brustman was on his feet in protest immediately, citing Reid's lunge at him during the committal hearing. Reid apologised profusely and was allowed to sit in the court only a few metres from the lawyer, with prison guards and protective services officers forming a human cage around him.

A prison surveillance camera had captured the action of one conversation, showing that Reid was not threatening or intimidating Lowe in any way. The other audio recording was made in the prisoners' cell. At times the words are almost swamped by a haunting opera soundtrack, which Reid advised Lowe would foil eavesdroppers. In the tapes, which ran for about 20 minutes, Lowe admitted to abducting Sheree and dumping her body, but tried to paint her death as some sort of accident. The final minutes of the tape were backed by the Vanessa Williams' song, *Save the Best Til Last*.

Under cross-examination, Reid said he abhorred Lowe's crime and

The Murder of Sheree

wanted to kill him.

David Brustman made much of Reid's past and Reid admitted he had been a liar from a very early age. Yet he broke down when asked about his extortion of the family of kidnapped and murdered schoolgirl Karmein Chan. He justified his actions by saying he had committed the crime to pay a contract killer. By proxy, he wanted to kill a criminal who was giving drugs to a little girl. Reid told the court although he wanted to help police, he had been reluctant to testify as he didn't believe his word would be any good in court. Sick of justifying himself and finally exasperated with the defence's questioning, Reid yelled "Why not let him go now? But if he's out on the street and kills another girl, how will you feel?" As Reid became more and more upset, a court official quietly replaced the glass of water on the edge of the witness box with a paper cup.

But Peter Reid didn't blow it. Visibly upset, he managed to stay in control. Justice Cummins ordered a short recess for Reid to regain his composure. During the adjournment, Lowe smiled in the dock and chatted to the tipstaff who gave him a glass of water. The carefree prisoner drummed his fingers on the dock rail slowly and deliberately, as if playing the piano.

Peter Reid continued his cross-examination without incident. When the voir dire finished, Justice Cummins ruled that not only was Margaret Hobbs' and Peter Reid's evidence admissible, it might be a good idea if Mr Lovitt considered his position as defence counsel as well. Lovitt had represented Reid in his murder trial in 1984 and the judge felt there would be a conflict of interest when Reid was in the witness box. Reid could be disadvantaged if his legal confidante of a decade ago was able to cross-examine him in the witness box. Lovitt retired to consider his position. Then he stood down.

After three years, Sheree's family, Margaret Hobbs, Lorraine Lowe and her sons, the police witnesses - and the police themselves - had geared themselves up for The Trial. They wanted it to be over so they could grieve properly. Some grieved for their little girl, some grieved for their husband or father, some for their careers and for a lost soul. Now it was put off for another month. It seemed like an eternity.

Robert wrote to his brothers in New Zealand on October 6, 1994.

Dear Rick and Graeme,

I have not been able to phone you this week due to prison staff strike and shortages, so we get locked up. Has Lorraine told you anything about her proceeding right thru' with the property/asset settlement? I believe it has been adjourned to 16 Jan. due to my trial.

When you told me her divorcing me was a big mistake, did she say anything in this area, or was it your opinion and why?

Concerning the trial, the Judge (Cummings) has insisted we continue on October 17 - Monday week, whether I have a Queens Councillor or Team Leader or not. Legal Aide Crown Law Commission boss Jim Care has told me in fairness it should be put off until next year when a qualified QC can be obtained. He said it was definitely no fault of mine nor Legal Aide this has happened as Mr Lovett had been cleared of any conflict of interest with the legal bar 'ethics board' as well as Judge Cummings himself publically. The defence team do not know why he changed his mind. Others are guessing but that's all.

Mr Lovett, who solicitor La Rosa says has an enormous capacity for speed reading, says any new QC would need minimum 4 weeks full time to get an understanding of the case and brief. Most briefs for this type of charge occupy about 20 pages. My brief is 8000 pages plus 250 audio tapes and audio visual tapes. It is said to be the biggest and most expensive the Police in Victoria have ever done. Yet the judge will not give us just time.

The QCs on the prosecution side have had 6 months. Judge Cummings is naming October 17 as the latest starting date that should enable the trial to finish before the Christmas break. ...the Judge even suggested junior barrister Brustman take the case. He has refused... However, yesterday Nunzio La Rosa brought in a barrister because there is no QC available in the whole of Victoria. He is the only qualified senior barrister available, and he

The Murder of Sheree

became available only because the case he was on fell through. But he obviously had no further commitments. He may be OK -I don't know, but he is not a QC which Legal Aide have approved funding me for because it's necessary...crucially he is being given 8-9 working days to prepare instead of the 6 months the Prosecution have had, or the 1 month minimum Mr Lovett said was only fair.

I've spoken to you before about the great injustices of being in jail. These include having correspondence and phone calls copied and monitored and private discussions even with lawyers being taped. I should be allowed the privacy and freedom to prepare one's own defence with lawyers and enquiries and contacts outside, at least equal to that of Police. In Britain, defence lawyers have gone public by obtaining all person charged with whatever the crime being allowed bail even on very strict conditions if necessary in order to prepare their defence. The sole exception is if the person has broken bail previously. How I've needed someone local to help me. I asked Graeme a long time ago but he was unwilling to pay - no response anyway. I can't even get myself a tie for court, and have had to borrow the one shirt I have which smells after 5 days (and I can't wash it)!

So with my QC Leader taken from me, no equivalent...being available plus only a few days for the only barrister not working...now being available, plus the gross and blatant injustices of the system here in denying me the right to a fair trial there is no chance of justice being done.

But now let me tell you what Mr (Deleted) and Mr (Deleted) said to me. They said, "There is no such thing as Justice. You will not get Justice. You will not get the truth. "Mr (Deleted) said Police manipulate and tell as many lies as crims, and prison officers say lawyers are just bad. There are no morals or justice. "It is all a mind game between lawyers and police."

No longer does one swear on the bible to tell the

truth the whole truth and nothing but the truth. So help me God." I noticed. Now one swears on the bible to answer a question truthfully only. That answer could be yes and the rest could be all a pack of lies. The people released after 9 and 7 years when ultimately found to be not guilty - one when after 9 of 15 years another person confessed, said the reason for the mistake was because witnesses tell or answer the truth - but not the WHOLE TRUTH - only half or a part of the truth!

Lorraine or even I might tell the truth but it counts for nothing. The police are prime examples - they say as little as possible. Yet they take my truth, turn it around, manipulate it and put it together in a story with other perhaps unrelated evidence and so convincing to a jury who believe the Police wouldn't lie, and yet because I'm already in the sentencing dock they presume I must be guilty. They forget the law that a person is presumed not guilty. The jury presume I am guilty and because it's a child they're already media encouraged to go for revenge.

I regret very much I ever listened to Lorraine, Hobbs and others and didn't stand up against them and do what Peter Ward said to say nothing. The church people were absolutely shocking. You may say it's easy to blame others but nobody is an island to himself. We all interrelate in so many different and various ways. I was stupid and weak in even listening to people I thought were friends. I'm here because of that - and they have all run away. I've learnt to trust nobody now - except God. You won't know or understand what I mean by that. A few pray for me, but they don't live in Melbourne to help me get a tie, for instance. But God is good and the future of my life depends on him.

I continue to pray for my family. I understand their need to be angry and my compassion for them is abundant. I wish them well and will always care for them but there's not much more I can say. Any content of this letter can be passed on to them if it helps at all.

I'm not at all pleased with all the family court

settlement problems being thrown at me when in the middle of my trial and the existing problems and injustices of losing a QC, no replacement, and no adjournment. I thought Lorraine would have a minuscule of consideration. I am human after all, feeling all the hurts and attacks, but maybe she is being encouraged by others to do this. She used to tell me to "Keep my heart tender toward God and each other". I presume she's still trying - bless her.

My lawyer said "Your only hope of justice is in Heaven".

Will try and phone. Thanks. In haste, sorry.

I think if the family persist in settling assets/property thru the courts that will indicate the completion of all contact with any of them - which the police will love.

I'll move on to my next family and let them do their own thing. Agree? What do you think?

I've got a lot of living to do yet.

Robert.

THE MONTH soon passed and after a few more legal arguments between the prosecution and the defence, a jury of six men and six women was empanelled to sit in judgment on October 27, 1994 - three years and four months after Sheree was murdered. Justice Cummins began by outlining the jury's duties. The judge spoke to the jury with empathy in a pleasant tone, occasionally smiling apologetically as he told them he understood the trial would be taking them away from loved ones, family, friends and work. He knew it would be a harrowing ordeal for all of them. Some jurors looked at each other and rolled their eyes, as if to say, "Why me?" No doubt it was a case most, if not all of them had read about, heard about, or seen on the TV news. The judge told them they were not to be influenced by what they had seen or read or heard. They must decide the case for themselves.

Emotions now were as high as they were the day Sheree went missing. As the judge addressed the jury, occasionally a juror would look out the corner of his or her eye at the man in the ill-fitting, dirty-looking, pale grey suit, sitting in the dock at the back of the court, beneath the public gallery. He was wearing his reading glasses, which had a black shoelace tied at each arm, draping the back of his head. They were part of the latest disguise, like the grey beard and fully grey hair.

On the first day of opening addresses to the jury, only journalists and lawyers sat in the body of the court. Soon, ordinary folk would sit in the upstairs gallery, watching 12 other ordinary people. They would watch how these jurors coped with the horror they knew was about to unfold. Like eagles from their safe eyries, they would watch to see if justice was done. These people had learnt in the past 41 months that there was an evil - a type of incomprehensible insanity that experts said was not madness - that was capable of destroying not just one little life, but every other life that was touched by it. They had seen and experienced the degrading, destructive, crushing sense of loss and futility Robert Lowe had forced into their lives. They couldn't wait for the trial to get under way.

Robert Lowe's high-wire act was about to begin. Having lost all the preceding rounds - his alibi splintered, his wife gone, being charged with murder and kidnapping, his "betrayal" by Peter Reid - he still thought he could deliver the knockout punch to the prosecution. Sheree Beasley was never a factor in this game. For Lowe, this was merely a matter of victory or defeat. Everything else was irrelevant. He sat in the court, acting the role of the distinguished elder gentleman, feigning complete disinterest.

When ordered by the judge's associate to stand he jumped quickly to his feet but he didn't know what to do with his hands. At first they were by his side, then clasped in front, then they hovered uncertainly near his pockets. He blinked nervously and his nose twitched several times. His lips were firmly set. His face showed not a glimmer of emotion. The dark, cadaver eyes darted about the court, flicking away instantly if they met a returned gaze. They revealed what Margaret Hobbs had suspected for a long, long time. He was a wax model, a cardboard cut-out.

The judge's associate read the charges.

"How say you Robert Arthur Selby Lowe? Are you guilty or not guilty," she asked.

Lowe swayed slightly to his left as if his knee had buckled but quickly straightened again. Boris Kayser, a ham-fisted, mountain of a man, stood and told the judge his client was not guilty. Then he asked the judge on behalf of his client if the court would make a ruling that the media be prohibited from reporting any child abductions in Australia that might happen during the trial. Philip Cummins smiled and said, in effect, no.

Prosecutor Paul Coghlan thought he was working with a strong case but there were some points he was worried about. He knew there could be problems if Lowe stuck by his story of accidental death. Yes, there had been an abduction and several people had identified Lowe from photo boards and had even identified him as the man they had seen with a little girl in the car. And yes, there was also a wasted, decomposed, mutilated body, found in a grubby drain. But if Lowe stuck to his story of accidental death, who could disprove it? How on earth could anybody rebut Lowe's version of events that Sheree had choked to death from fright?

Coghlan, a short man of stout build is affectionately nicknamed The Penguin by the police, for he looks a little like actor Danny De Vito, who played the role in one of the Batman movies. As Kerri and Steve sat in the upstairs gallery with Jill and Tony Mandile, Paul Coghlan stood before the jury, outlining the evidence he would put before them in the ensuing weeks. And he mocked Robert Lowe's input to the case against himself, perfectly paraphrasing what had dragged on in the previous three years and five months.

His introduction was a summation of what Lowe had told the police, Margaret Hobbs and then Peter Reid.

"First of all I wasn't there," Coghlan scoffed. "But if I was there, I wasn't there at the relevant time. And if I was there at the relevant time, it wasn't murder." The jury, sitting immediately to his right, listened intently. Some jurors fidgeted in their seats. One woman looked ill. Two other women looked briefly at each other without expression and then turned to briefly glance at the prisoner in the dock. Coghlan continued slowly, reading from his notes sitting on a large wooden lectern on the table before him.

"He gives a version of events which he hopes will be taken to be consistent with him being involved potentially in an abduction but not in a murder but perhaps in a manslaughter." As Coghlan described in detail Sheree's pink and purple tracksuit, her pink stackhat and pink bike, the jury nodded in recognition. Lowe sat, looking down, taking notes.

Many of the jurors frowned and looked at Lowe when Coghlan told them a small blue car, driven by the prisoner, suddenly appeared in Parkmore Road. He stopped the car, got out and called to Sheree, "Come here."

Coghlan told them how the police traced the blue Toyota Corolla hatchback and how Lowe had rung Andrew Gustke on July 30, 1991. He told of how police found Lowe had a holiday home near the abduction site after he had denied knowing the area. And he told of how Mrs Lowe said her husband returned home around 5pm that day and had later washed his own clothes. The colour had drained from every face in the jury box.

The next day - Friday - as he continued his opening address, Paul Coghlan played a tape of Lowe talking to Peter Reid in prison. Jill and Tony Mandile sat grimly in the public gallery in the seats they were to barely leave throughout the entire trial. The jury listened intently as Coghlan completed his opening address and played one of the Reid tapes. They heard Robert Lowe say: "I just saw the little girl and wanted to get her into the car. She was wearing coloured clothes." Jurors were at first mesmerised by what they were hearing and then began to look distressed.

On the tape they heard Lowe describe how he drove up and asked a little girl if she wanted him to take her home and she came willingly. He described how she appeared upset and incoherent and told him he was going the wrong way when he tried to find where she lived. Lowe was heard to tell Reid Sheree became more upset when he said he could not get off the freeway but would have to drive further on.

"She's coughed and spluttered and she's got herself in a real mess. I was pretty upset at this time. I was trying my best," Lowe said on the tape.

He described then how he pulled up at the side of the road and tried to calm her, saying it would be a bit longer to get her home.

"She didn't believe me. She's just coughing and spluttering and sort of leant forward and I tried to do what I could," he said.

"I looked at her and she had sort of gone all blue, blue round the lips. Just didn't bloody well seem right. I felt her pulse. Couldn't find a pulse. That really upset me."

Lowe said he wondered if he should take Sheree to hospital but drove the other way thinking, "What a mess."

The court heard him describe how he decided to dispose of the body and went to a road at the back of Arthur's Seat.

"It was just sheer panic. I thought to myself, 'I'll put her down here. I'll dig a hole or something like that'."

Lowe said he saw a drain running beneath an embankment.

"I tried to see if she would fit in there and it looked very tight. I had her clothes off and I said a prayer. I put her there gently...very gently, slid her in, pushed her in with my hands. Pushed her in a bit further then covered her up. Then covered the whole drain."

Lowe's voice, speaking in its horrible deep monotone to his fellow prisoner, went on.

"I said a little prayer...please Lord look after this life."

One juror looked about to cry.

"I closed her eyes and put her in the drain."

Several jurors started weeping. For a split second Lowe looked like he was verging on looking a little sad but it didn't happen.

Coghlan pointed out Lowe had disposed of the body because it would have proved how Sheree died if it was found.

"If in fact there was some accidental cause of death there was one way that the accused man might have established that," Coghlan said. "He might have done so by preserving the body. What he had to fear from the body being found was 'murder' and that is why he disposed of the body in the way he did."

After the luncheon adjournment, Kerri was called as the first witness. She was wearing a floral, calf-length dress. As she was escorted into the court, directly past the prisoner on her right, every eye in the court was upon her. She didn't look at Lowe. Just being in the same room as him made her feel dirty and nauseous. As she climbed the seven wooden steps into the witness box, the snake tattoos wrapped around her ankles became visible to all but the jury. She turned and faced them.

The Murder of Sheree

The judge was sitting above her and to her left, behind an ancient wooden bench. Directly opposite Kerri sat the jury. To Kerri's right and down below sat Boris Kayser. On his right was Brustman, Andrew Tinney the assistant prosecutor, and Paul Coghlan. Instructing solicitors, Nunzio La Rosa for the defence and Rod Gray for the prosecution, sat at the same table, facing their barristers, with their backs to the witness box.

Justice Cummins asked Kerri if she wanted to sit while she gave her evidence. She nodded. He smiled and asked if she was all right. Kerri braced herself and forced a grim smile, nodding quickly. Occasionally she squinted as she spoke. She had cried enough. She would not break down in front of Robert Arthur Selby friggin' Lowe.

She trembled as she answered a few short simple questions from Paul Coghlan about where the family lived in June 1991. She struggled as she described Sheree as a very independent little girl, who, on that terrible morning, made her own breakfast and her sisters' before she made a few trips to the shops.

Kerri said Sheree was "Healthy, nothing wrong with her, no particular illnesses." This evidence was led to counter what Coghlan knew would be coming. Despite her resolve and obvious courage, Kerri looked broken. The jurors stared sympathetically at her but looked away if Kerri looked directly at them. Some dabbed their eyes as she spoke. As Coghlan looked down for another question, and Kerri sat perfectly still, the only sound was the dull hum of the fluorescent tubes on the ceiling.

And Robert Lowe stared at her, as if listening to a professor describe some new, fascinating scientific discovery. Within minutes Kerri was gone, escorted from the court through a side door so she didn't have to walk past Lowe again.

Her husband was the next witness. Steve had been crying outside the court but he was determined to maintain his composure. He stood in the box and took the oath. In the dark grey suit he borrowed from his father-in-law Neil Greenhill, he told the jury how desperately he searched for Sheree the day she vanished. He felt that shocking pain in the belly all over again. He quickly turned to Lowe and glared at him.

The court was perfectly still, and silent, when Rod Gray brought into the court the pink bicycle Sheree had been riding - the same bike Steve

The Murder of Sheree

had given to Sheree as a Christmas present - and a pink bicycle helmet identical to Sheree's. As Steve identified them, he broke down, wiping the tears from his eyes with his thumb and the side of his index finger. Twice he turned and stared red-eyed at the prisoner, who was looking down, taking notes. Steve's look said it all. *If I get my hands on you, you're dead.*

He tearfully told, his voice trembling, how Sheree went out several times that day to the milkbar, running errands and checking if the mini-golf was open. He told how he had become concerned when Sheree hadn't come back after being sent off with $20. Then a neighbour had come to tell him she had found Sheree's bike in the street.

Paul Coghlan wanted to know if Steve had walked or driven to where the bike was found. "No, I ran," Steve said.

There was no cross examination. Having heard just two witnesses, the court adjourned for the weekend. If the jury were to ponder the case over those two days, all they had to remember was Kerri and Steve's brave testimony. And the little pink bike which sat just outside the juror's box. It stayed there for the duration of the trial.

KERRI HAD been feeling unwell but she was used to that. She was now clean of the sedatives and felt she should have been feeling a little better. At first she thought it was the pain of the impending trial - it was hard to judge. Her emotions were all over the place. That night, relieved at having finished her evidence, she consulted her local doctor. As soon as he finished examining her, she knew what he was going to say. In that instant she felt a mixture of joy and deep, deep sorrow. She was pregnant.

ON THE MONDAY, Shane Park and several others who had seen Sheree and the car gave evidence, including Danielle and Sueanne Marx and Christine Dogan. It was difficult for all of them, with the little pink bike and attendant pink helmet, sitting mutely but speaking volumes.

Shane, wearing shorts and turquoise T-shirt, stood looking wide-eyed at Justice Cummins as the judge asked questions to determine whether the boy understood the oath.

"Do you know why you've been asked to come here today?"

"No."

"Do you see that book in front of you, the bible? Do you know what it is?"

"It tells you about God and that."

The judge smiled. "Do you know that when you're in court you must tell the truth?"

"Yes."

Justice Cummins was not wearing his wig. Often throughout the trial, he took it off and placed it on the table before him. Perhaps it was uncomfortable, perhaps he was trying to make everybody more at ease.

"Do you know what happens if you don't tell the truth?"

"You get grounded or something?" Smiles everywhere.

"It's important not to make anything up. Just say you don't know if you don't know."

Shane took the oath and gave his evidence. He told again, as he had in the committal, what he had already told the police, that he was with Sheree when a man came and told her to "Come here". He tried his best to remember what he could of that far-off day. He concentrated on the questions asked of him. He testified that Sheree had spoken just once when Lowe told her to get in the car. Sheree had replied, "I'm not getting in the car for nothin'," before Lowe picked her up and abducted her.

Shane looked a little frightened but he was determined to do his best. After 15 minutes though, he became tired and confused. He didn't remember what he had said at the committal hearing and when making statements to the police. When defence counsel gently persisted in questioning him, he began to get upset. He appeared on the verge of tears but he insisted he had told the truth.

The string of witnesses continued, building the circumstantial case, jigsawing all the pieces of Sheree's last day. Danielle French-Marx, with her long, blonde hair and braces on her teeth, cried as she recounted how a young girl wearing a pink stackhat frantically attracted her attention and then gave her a terrible look. Then it was Danielle's mother's turn. Sue Marx maintained her composure but trembled and sounded nervous as she described that frightful day she was sweeping outside the hotel. She told how she had looked up and seen Sheree.

"I thought I read the lips as 'Help'. The fear on her face overrode everything. I sort of focused on that," she said.

Her evidence complete, she walked past the press benches and muttered "nightmare" while rolling her eyes at *Herald Sun* reporter Fay Burstin.

Christine Dogan stuck steadfastly to her story that she was positive she had seen Lowe's car and he looked like the man who was driving it.

She told Paul Coghlan's assistant Andrew Tinney, that "she was sitting side-on, looking and staring at me, and crying."

"She was looking at me - I just had no idea why she was crying."

The driver of the car, Ms Dogan said, was about 55 and looking straight ahead.

"It seemed like, to me, he just didn't hear her crying."

Andrew Tinney then asked her to describe the appearance of the man who was sitting next to the little girl in the car.

"At the time, he was very clean shaven. There was a bald patch on his crown."

"A bald patch on his crown?"

"Yes, at the top of his head. He had grey hair. He was wearing a pin-striped shirt with a collar. What I could distinguish from my car, I think he was wearing tan shorts, which - I can't recall too much, but I know the interior of the car was tan.'

"You said a pin-striped shirt. We've heard of pin-striped suits all of us, but what..."

"It's like stripes that are going horizontal, vertical and very light shades and make up little..."

"So they're stripes in both directions?'

"Yes."

"So sort of little checks, was it?"

"Yes, just making up little squares."

"What was the main colour of the shirt?"

"The main colour was a pale white - could distinguish to a creamy colour."

"Did you notice anything about any of his facial features?"

'Well, to me he appeared Australian but his nose was a bit long from side on, because he didn't sort of turn around to look at me, so what I saw was his nose was long and his chin looked a bit small."

Then she testified to viewing Murray Gregor's suspects' video tape at Swan Hill police station and having picked number 4, with number 10 being a possibility.

"I do lean towards No. 4 a lot more because I strongly say that it was that particular man that was driving that afternoon, even though it's a bit hard to distinguish when I saw him from side on." She could not be shaken from her testimony.

On Tuesday the court went on a "visit". Only the judge, his staff, legal counsel and the jury went and they drove past the Lighthouse Milkbar, the intersection of Parkmore Road and Nepean Highway, other reference points along Nepean Highway, Lowe's flat in Rosebud, the overpass on the freeway and Sheree's burial site at Mornington-Flinders Road.

The giant pine tree on which Sheree's bike had once rested was now gone, a victim of the reasoning that trees and power lines don't mix. A small wooden post now marked the spot where the bike once stood. Before the caravan moved to Winthunga in Mornington-Flinders Road, Red Hill, the judge directed the local police to check the site to ensure there was nothing there that might prejudice the trial, like graffiti or a bunch of flowers. They found a red, long stemmed rose laying across the entrance to the drain.

THE TRIAL was as much about the tactics as it was about the evidence. Paul Coghlan called only those witnesses he deemed essential as he didn't want to drag the trial out unnecessarily and lose impact. He called just 50 of the 210 witnesses listed on the brief. Boris Kayser couldn't attack many of the witnesses, like Kerri and Steve, or he would get the jury off-side.

Throughout it all, Lowe acted the way he had always acted in court. He was composed. When asked to stand each time the jury entered or left the court, he stood very erect. He was studious, head down, taking notes, just as he did with Margaret Hobbs in her clinic. He was carefully cultivating an image but he succeeded only in looking like a man who couldn't care less about what was being said about him. A man who didn't care about a little girl or her family.

The Murder of Sheree

Occasionally Justice Cummins addressed the jury on points of law or adjudicated on issues brought up by counsel. Sometimes he would look up at the gallery while he spoke, his eyes surveying the friends and family of Sheree. Kerri and Steve wiping their eyes or Jill Mandile and one of her daughters hugging each other for support.

On Friday, November 5 - the sixth sitting day of the case - Andrew Gustke told the court of his conversation with Lowe.

"The fact Mr Lowe came out with immediate responses and the tone of it gave me some strange feelings," he said. As he spoke, Lowe covered his face with a piece of paper to frustrate a newspaper artist.

Then came the video-taped interview with Dale Johnson. Apart from showing that Robert Lowe was an inveterate liar, the interview had not achieved much at the time it was conducted. But now it played a totally different role in the prosecution case. Robert Lowe now had a beard, wore glasses and his wavy hair was grey. As the jurors watched the interview on a television monitor, they continually looked backwards and forwards from the tape to the man in the dock. The TV Robert Lowe was dark haired, confident, verbose, while the grey haired man in the wooden dock at the back of the court was mute - and today looked a tad uncomfortable. Importantly, the man in the interview matched the descriptions given by the preceding witnesses.

Christine Malone told the court she was walking the dog with her daughter and young friend when she noticed an unusual smell in Red Hill. As evidence of the discovery of Sheree's body was given, Sheree's family became visibly more distressed.

"It smelt like a dead animal, very strong, like a dead dog or kangaroo," Christine said.

"I just kept walking because I had children with me," she said.

Upstairs in the gallery, Anthony Mandile began to cry and wipe his eyes.

Elizabeth Haworth described how early one morning, six weeks after Sheree vanished, she was on her way to her stables when she noticed a small, iridescent-blue hatchback parked near the drain. In cross examination, Boris Kayser told Ms Haworth he couldn't see much at 6am when he gets up and goes out to get the papers. The judge, who clearly liked Kayser, made a crack about Kayser reading law reports at 6am.

Kayser joked, "Actually I read the comics." Everybody laughed. It was a welcome relief from the constant tension. Lowe smiled. Then, head down in his own dark world, he started chuckling to himself.

Angela Chambers began to shake and became teary-eyed as she recounted how her horse shied at a puddle while riding along a horse-track near Mornington-Flinders Road. She looked closer and saw something that looked like a body. She went and investigated later that night with a friend who was a nurse who confirmed the grisly find before they called the police.

Crime scene expert Sergeant Brian Gamble spoke of what he found. Sheree's family flinched as he described finding the remains of a skull in the narrow drain, and flushing it out to find teeth and bone. Jill and Tony walked out of the courtroom, unable to listen to any more. Kerri looked as if she was about to faint. The tipstaff got up from his seat and with a glass of water in his hand, walked purposefully along the worn carpet and disappeared through the huge wooden doors that lead to the court foyer. He reappeared a minute later in the upstairs gallery and handed his gift to Kerri. She grabbed the glass without looking at him but she wouldn't leave the court. She had to be there for her daughter.

On Day Seven, Monday, November 7, 1994, Professor Stephen Cordner gave graphic details of Sheree's remains. The jury recoiled in horror. Boris Kayser asked about children dying of fright.

"I've never seen a child die from a heart attack under conditions of stress," the professor said. Photographs of the crime scene and the remains of the body were shown to the jury. They looked visibly upset as they were referred to print after print.

Professor Cordner said he would consider conditions such as epilepsy, asthma and a heart condition when discussing the sudden and unexpected death of a young child. Asked by Boris Kayser if it was possible for Sheree to have died of a heart attack as a result of stress, Cordner said it was not a possibility worth considering unless there was some underlying disease. He told the court he could not determine the cause of Sheree's death.

Maria George, Robert's former employer, testified Lowe had come and seen her looking for a log book for his former company car around New Years Day 1992. She had told him the police had it.

Then a host of Tai Chi aficionados gave evidence that they were exercising in the back yard next door to the Lowe household. Boris Kayser and David Brustman were trying to suggest that Lowe had been mowing the lawn at home. Kayser suggested to all the martial artists that a mower might have been running but they had not heard it due to their meditations. All of them disagreed. One man gave evidence of helping Lowe fix the side fence, but it was not on June 29. Lowe blinked and twitched and wouldn't look at them.

Lowe's former fellow parishioner Brian Lee gave his evidence of the strange telephone conversation with Robert Lowe, and of Lowe's behaviour after church on June 30, 1991. Lowe looked down throughout all his evidence.

LORRAINE WAS to give evidence the next morning. She lay in bed, unable to sleep after hours of tossing and turning. She decided to get up and have a drink, and maybe watch a little television. She flipped the covers off the bed and, in the total darkness, sat with her feet on the floor. For some reason she wanted to open the bedside drawer. She looked at it and saw that it wasn't her normal bedside table. The top drawer seemed to be much bigger than the one she was used to. She pulled the drawer fully open and let out a shriek. The whole drawer, which would have been about 60cm deep and about a metre long, was full of children's body parts. Dismembered arms, legs, hands, feet, fingers. She quickly slammed it shut and felt a hot flush surge through her before she broke out in a cold, clammy sweat. As she stood up, Lorraine felt her left leg go wobbly at the top of the thigh, tremble uncertainly for a second and then detach itself from her body. She fell heavily, face down, on the carpet. Desperate to flee, she began dragging herself along the carpet. As she did, her right leg dropped away. Her arms and torso felt like lumps of lead.

Her fingernails dug into the carpet as she tried to wrest herself away, but both arms pulled free from their sockets, leaving her lying face down unable to move. She sobbed and sobbed, unable to wipe her eyes. She felt that terrible fear of drowning, of suffocating, and she couldn't do anything about it at all.

When she woke, she sat in the family room, staring at nothing, until the sun came up.

LORRAINE LOOKED pretty in her pale blue blouse and shirt with white flower motif. Slowly she walked into the court, escorted by Senior Constable Helen Adams from Blackburn Community Policing Squad, and climbed the steps up into the witness box. Lorraine was visibly trembling as she gripped the handrail to steady herself. She faced the judge, then looked past him at the jury. She was obviously petrified. She glanced at her ex-husband - he wasn't looking at her - and she was wide-eyed with fear. She felt a strange magnetic pull towards him. Sorrow filled her as she thought, *I used to think you were a terrific husband*. A curious thought raced through her head. All she had to do, to get him off the charges, was to say, "Sorry, I made a mistake, he was home all day". But then she looked at Robert and thought, *I used to look at your hands and wonder what they'd done*. She knew she had to tell the truth. She couldn't live with a lie. As she turned her head back and looked towards the jury, she saw Sheree's bike. Lorraine thought it would be fitting for Sheree to walk into the court and just point at Robert before walking out again and put an end to the trial.

Paul Coghlan led Lorraine through her statement. She whispered, swallowed back tears, kept her head down. Whenever she looked up, her eyes darted around nervously. She was on the verge of tears. The startled women jurors looked on. As Lorraine continued her testimony, occasionally jurors sneaked furtive, sideways glances at Lowe who was watching the witness wearily. After 10 minutes Lorraine relaxed a little and spoke a little more freely but was still timid and girlish, and sometimes coy. Occasionally she was asked to speak up because she was barely audible. Kerri watched her carefully, weighing up her evidence.

Then it was time to hear some tapes. When Lorraine's telephone conversation with her husband on August 9, 1991, was played to the court - when she told him about the first time the police came to her home while he was in Sydney - she broke down. A violent spasm shook her whole body and she appeared to sob silently to herself. The jurors watched almost apologetically as Lorraine was led from the court by Helen

Adams after Justice Cummins announced a short break. Helen was half carrying Lorraine, who would have collapsed if she wasn't supported. In the dock, Lowe looked sick. He shifted uncomfortably and looked down as his former wife was led away. Kerri and the family looked on impassively.

When court resumed that afternoon, Lorraine was composed. She stood immobile as the conversation recorded on the telephone tapes continued. Then she described her husband's actions when he was taken away by Dale Johnson after the police went to their home in August 1991. She told the court how when the police had raided her home on August 13, her husband had left home apologising in tears, only to return later looking smug. The jury looked shocked and stunned.

She recounted how she had been home all day doing some computer typing and other odds and ends at home which included a little weeding in the gardening and doing the washing, particularly in preparation for the upcoming holiday in Mildura. She told of seeing Robert for the first time since he left just before dark when she called out to Benjamin.

"Did anything happen with respect to the washing machine in the house?" Paul Coghlan asked.

"Robert started it up again after tea."

"Sorry?"

"Robert started it up again after tea."

"Was there anything unusual about that?"

"Well, I noticed it because I was having such trouble getting the washing dry and it was the last straw to hear another load start up and I wondered what he was doing because I hadn't seen him do that before." Lorraine was twisting the fingers of both hands in front of her lap as she spoke.

"When you say you hadn't seen him do that before, was that through the whole course of your marriage?"

"Yes. Sometimes he'd run in with something when he heard me doing it, run in with something late, but..."

"On this occasion what feature of it was particularly unusual?"

"That he did it all himself. I thought I'd washed everything anyhow."

"Did he tell you what it was?"

"I questioned him about it because, I said, 'Do you really need to put it on because you're not going to get it dry before you leave to go away and we'll have a washing machine where we're going', and he said it was his casual things that he needed. I said, 'Well, can we wash them when we get there' and he said, no they were muddy and he needed to wash them."

"They were muddy and he needed to wash them?"

"I didn't see what they were. They were in the machine already."

Lowe face twitched spastically.

A tape was played of Lorraine talking to Robert when he was in Sydney in August 1991, shortly after Dale Johnson had first visited Mannering Drive. Lorraine told the court Robert had instructed her not to talk to the police.

She gave evidence of the day the police raided her home and Robert's subsequent crying and saying, 'I'm sorry'. Several jurors looked shocked and turned to look at Lowe, who was sitting with his head down in the dock. There was no expression on his face. She told of being taken on a ride with the police and pointing out the spot where she had gone pineconing with her husband. She gave evidence of how Robert and the boys had once gone sailing at McCrae.

When Lorraine was cross-examined about the area Sheree's body was found, Kerri became very upset. She sat with her head in hands. Even from the body of the court down below, her body could be seen shuddering noticeably.

THE FOLLOWING Monday, November 14, the judge told Lowe's boys that the law could not compel them to give evidence against their father. Both decided they would. Their mother had taught them that despite all the hardships that had befallen the family, honesty and truth were still paramount. Although the boys agonised for months about whether or not they should speak against their father, in the end it was an easy decision to make. They felt they didn't have an option. Benjamin testified nervously that his father had ignored a radio request for the drivers of blue Toyota Corollas to take their cars to police for forensic examination. Fidgety and softly spoken, Benjamin was shy and sometimes a little uncertain during cross examination. Both boys told how their dad was not home through the afternoon of June 29, 1991. Their mother sat next to Jill Mandile in the upstairs gallery. They did not speak to each other.

The Murder of Sheree

ON WEDNESDAY November 16th, Day 12, Margaret Hobbs was called. For weeks, she had had virtually no sleep. After the voir dire, she knew what to expect. Her doctor had told her she shouldn't give evidence. She had high blood pressure, a terrible vomiting cough and felt physically ill all the time. But she wanted to give her evidence and get it over with. She knew if she didn't go to court, she would only be putting off the inevitable. Unfortunately for her, she was an essential witness.

She was trembling noticeably as she climbed into the witness box. She was not allowed to testify as to why she was counselling Lowe, for the jury was not to know he was being treated for sexual problems - it could be prejudicial to him. Most of Margaret's evidence was covered by the prosecution playing snippets of secretly taped conversations with Robert Lowe. Time was suspended in the courtroom as everyone concentrated and strained to listen and transport themselves into that tiny clinic. When the court heard Lowe was enjoying the excitement of the police investigation and dodging the police, one woman in the gallery left the courtroom sobbing. Throughout Lowe's taped meandering, Kerri stared blankly at the ceiling, looking beaten. Lowe looked away or down at his feet the whole time. A video recording of Robert at the site was played as well. Then Margaret was recalled to the box and parts of the tape of their conversation on November 11, 1991 were played.

"She was apparently a very precocious little child," Margaret's tape-voice boomed round the cavernous courtroom. From the faces and the body movements in the upstairs gallery, it was clear many equated precocious with promiscuous. Feeling deep sorrow and extreme embarrassment, Margaret lowered her head. What she was saying sounded terrible. The tape rolled on.

"Very friendly. The sort who would get into a car." Jill Mandile looked outraged and angry.

Abruptly Kerri sat forward and looked down at the judge, shaking her head vigorously in protest. Margaret put her head in her hands and began to weep. She had made those comments to coax Robert into talking about Sheree. She had hoped he would pick up on the comment, agree with it, and talk about the abduction. Now, out of context, it sounded like she was blaming Sheree.

After she composed herself, Margaret ignored the jury. She felt terribly guilty. She felt she had destroyed Lorraine and Robert's marriage by being such a vital witness. And it was so hard to look anywhere near the jury while the pink bike leant against the front of the judge's bench. Margaret found it easier to simply focus on whoever questioned her. She did look at the upstairs gallery a couple of times to check that her husband John and a few supporters were up there. She didn't look at Lowe throughout the whole trial. When her tapes were played to the court, she was excused from the witness box, and permitted to sit behind the prosecutor. As Robert's monotone droned on and on in tape after tape, Margaret suddenly felt a strange, creepy feeling and realised she was sitting underneath him. She got up and moved forward a row, close to Paul Hollowood.

From another conversation, the court heard Margaret say, "It was an accidental death, she went into the car voluntarily, she's a very precocious little child." Kerri began to cry and Jill Mandile looked outraged. Margaret felt as if she was in a straitjacket. She wanted to tell the court why she had said those things but that was not what everybody was there for. People who had admired and supported her at the committal now found themselves hating her.

After the court adjourned for the day, Margaret approached Kerri in the foyer of the court. One of Margaret's supporters - a family friend - had given her a mauve rose to wish her luck before giving evidence. Margaret gave it to Kerri as a sign that she felt for her. Margaret didn't know it was Sheree's favourite colour.

MARGARET WAS sitting up in bed. She had been awake for a while, but she was very tired and she was sitting with her eyes closed, her head against the headboard. Her husband John was asleep next to her.

Aware there was some type of movement in the room, Margaret opened her eyes just as Robert plunged the scissors into her chest. She looked down curiously, unable to speak or move, and watched as the blades disappeared into her flesh, and then the blood start flowing. She had never felt such helplessness.

The screaming woke John, who shook Margaret violently until she woke too. John cursed Robert Lowe and made his wife a cup of coffee.

The Murder of Sheree

They sat in the loungeroom for about an hour. Margaret convinced her husband she would be okay, and he finally tottered off to bed. When John had gone, Margaret picked up Robert's bible from the coffee table. She had already spoken to some church people, seeking advice on what might be a suitable passage to dwell on to help her make it through the court case. By the lamplight, in the still night, she read the book of Psalms.

MORE TAPES were played over the next two days. The jury looked distressed. Jill Mandile sobbed constantly. Kerri and Steve sat with their heads buried in their hands for much of the time.

Margaret was heard telling Robert: "This confession you've made.....Robert seems to me, I'm going to be honest with you now..." There was a pause. The clock continued to flick its little red hand mechanically. *Tick, tick, tick.* "...seems to be fact wrapped up as fiction." *Tick, tick, tick.* Nobody's eyes seemed to be working in the court. Their ears had taken over and put them right inside the therapist's room.

Another tape was played. Lowe was heard to say: "Literally, if you want me to tell you the truth, I can tell you. I was involved. Yes. I could tell you I was involved."

Margaret and Lowe were heard agreeing to "work along that line" but Margaret told him she would not be involved in a conspiracy to pervert the course of justice and would not let him plead guilty to something he had not done.

The tape playing went on for four days.

Segments of the April 28, 1992, tape were played. Lowe said his prayer, after stuffing Sheree's body into the drain was: "Forgive me Lord for the terrible things I have done and I'll speak to you later about it Lord, or something. Perhaps not."

Mrs Hobbs told the court in a session recorded on May 15, 1992 Lowe had said putting Sheree in the drain and praying was almost like an attempt to give the child a Christian burial.

Lowe said in the same session, "But I thought now that's okay, say I'd done this terrible thing, but at least she'd been sort of looked after in a way. And the whole story is that I hadn't meant to kill her and the outcome is something drastically gone wrong and I panicked. But there's nothing I could do but bury her because the other things like hospital and things were out of the question, so I've tried to care for her. Any other person I kill I'd do that. I know it is stupid saying things like that. What's the point?"

Finally, Margaret finished giving her evidence. As she sat outside the court with her husband, she looked down and noticed her right foot tapping on the floor. She had noticed many months ago that every time she was under stress, her foot tapped like that.

PETER REID'S appearance in court - on day 15, November 21 of the trial - was an event. Surrounded by court security staff and police, he was led into the court. Reid was briefed by Alex Bartsch outside and then brought in. Paul Coghlan led Reid through his statement, and played excerpts of the tapes he had surreptitiously made in Lowe's cell.

Paul Coghlan's voice went on in its nasally whine, eliciting specific answers from specific questions as he built up the scene.

Reid told the jury that he took notes of his conversations with Lowe back in his cell after he closed the door. It was on Friday, 16th of April, 1993, he said.

He had had a number of conversations over four weeks, probably longer. He was in his second year of an instructional engineering course and was an architectural draughtsman. He said Lowe had told him he had gone to the unit to finish the tiles. Lowe had said he started at 11.30am and finished 30 minutes later.

"He stated he would - he had done it before and it was - he put it, a 'breeze'," Reid said. "He went to say that the next door neighbours were not around as he went to see how the old bloke was, he was apparently very ill with cancer...After this he went back to his place to clean up. He stated he left his house at about 2pm that Saturday. He stated he placed his tools in the boot of his car and headed to an area of about seven kilometres or more away and saw a girl riding - saw a little girl riding her pushbike all over the place. I did not ask him what he meant. He went on to say he pulled up away a bit to a T-intersection or a cross-intersection. One of the streets was Hume (sic) Highway Road or Street. He got out, waved for the little girl to pull over. He said that she had a blue and pink track suit on, with a pink and blue helmet. He stated that was from memory. He said that he told the little girl that her mummy said for him to take her home, as mummy was ill. The little girl was suss and Lowe said he opened the door, forced her into the front of his car. He said he placed the seat belt around her. He said he drove about 15 kilometres to an inland country farm area, and he forced her to do dirty acts. Lowe said that he never intended to kill her, and that she apparently started to choke as he forced her to do the dirty acts. From terrifying fear and the acts she was forced to do, she choked to death. Lowe would not comment much on the actual acts. Lowe stated that his sperm had gone all over her tracksuit so he got rid of her clothes and took them off her. At this stage he stated she was dead. Lowe said he went to the road, a sealed road, leaving her in her underwear, as he put it, forced her into a storm water drain. Lowe stated that on that side of the road was a farmhouse set back off the road. A long, low roof..."

"Sorry, just going back on that for a moment, on which side of the road was it?"

"Lowe stated on the other side of the road."

"Yes, go on then?"

"Was a farmhouse set back off the road, long, low roof and possibly a verandah on the front from the way Lowe described it. My mental sketch of the area is as such."

"In relation to that particular area, Mr Reid, did he later give you some detailed instructions and did you draw some fairly detailed drawings of that particular area?"

"He did. I asked him to draw some diagrams in his own hand and to describe to me as much as possible of the area, and I then from those sketches redrew a drawing of the actual sketch."

"In relation to what he was telling you on that particular day, what came next?"

"Lowe stated that he dumped her clothing into a dumpmaster. He mentioned the street in Blackburn, I think, I can't remember. Lowe stated that his car was taken by police but returned to him after four days. He also stated that on a few occasions police had interviewed him, I think he said Rosebud police station. One interview revolved around asking Lowe about his personal life, what football team he followed, and which his reply, St Kilda. What were his hobbies if any. He stated he was once talking to a councillor from, I think, Rosebud, and had noticed a car following him, so Lowe very secretly-like asked the councillor who they were, and the councillor said undercover police. Lowe asked him, 'How do you know?' The councillor stated he noticed them ages ago and he challenged them and they showed badges, stating they were undercover and looking for someone lost. From that day Lowe knew he was being followed.

"During this period Lowe stated that he went to the public library newspapers and collected all the media coverage on the missing girl to see if they had much on him. In fact, he was worried as to how much info you all had on him. He stated he was worried about his wife stuffing up his alibi, about being home at 1pm that Saturday when in fact he was not. He stated he collected the little girl at 2.30, 2.34. I asked him how do you remember this? He stated he just knew. Lowe stated that he never got home til 4.35 that Saturday night, but stated to the cops he got home 2pm. Lowe stated to his wife - his wife had divorced - he wanted her dead as she was working for the police. He stated she was very sick and wished she would die. He keeps raving on how he wants half of the house she's now in. That he will get his brother in New Zealand to take care of everything. That the girl's mother who is now apparently living in Queensland he would get her too. Lowe stated he had $2000 in a bank account. That the bank book or cheque book was with the legal advisers. That he would use that money to use to get the wife fixed."

"Just stopping there, Mr Reid. If you could go back for a moment to a place where I interrupted you on page 6 just below the diagram?"

"Yes."

"Did he say something to you about going back to check out the scene?"

"Yes."

"If you would perhaps read that piece out, please?"

"He stated he came back to check out about three days later the 'driving past' as he put it, but did not stop."

Peter continued telling the court what Lowe had told him.

"After that?"

The Murder of Sheree

"Lowe stated today that he did not go to Rosebud purely for fixing tiles. Lowe stated that he used the tile excuse to justify being away from his wife. Lowe made comment that he had been watching the little girl for some time, that she had been to the shops, to the same shops before."

A little later Paul Coghlan wanted to know about Lowe's car.

"I questioned Lowe further about checking his car, yes, cleaning his car, sorry and he made a comment that he had trouble cleaning a blood stain he had on the passenger front seat where he had the little girl. He said he first vacuumed the car on the Sunday and washed his car, his wife's car at the same time. He said he used a chamois to clean blood off the front, front edge of the front seat, he used detergent to clean it. I then asked him where the blood came from, he said, "The little girl vomited it up when she was choking.""

"Did you ask him when he'd been to Rosebud prior to that particular Saturday?"

"Are you referring to question 2?"

"Yes."

"Something made me ask Lowe if he had been to Rosebud prior to Saturday and he stated that he went to Rosebud the weekend before to deliver a fridge to the Rosebud unit. He states his son went with him. Lowe states that, then, that he took the opportunity to decide on what needed repairing in the bathroom."

"You continued talking to him?"

"Lowe stated that it was then that he first noticed the little girl walking along the roadside with her bike. She was walking towards Melbourne to the shop as Lowe stated. Lowe stated on the Monday, on the Monday Lowe decided to go back, he drove around for a while and on the Monday afternoon he saw the girl walking by again. Lowe followed her from the shop and followed her back to her house, just down from the shop. The following Saturday Lowe stated he went to Rosebud, not first and foremost to fix tiles but he used that to justify his movements to his wife. Lowe made comments that he sent, he spent very little time at the flat, that he had vacated the Rosebud unit at 12.30 and waited for the little girl to come to the shop. Lowe made his move when the little girl and the boy were on the way back."

"Did he say then something about saying something to the little boy?"

"Lowe stated that he did say something to the boy, 'Don't get upset, don't fight,' or words to that effect."

"Did he say where he'd driven to?"

"Lowe stated that he did drive into a little short, unsealed road. He has marked it on the map."

"Then the next point?"

"Lowe stated that at the place when the girl was choking, etcetera, he decided to take off her hard hat."

"The next point?"

"Lowe stated that he watched the girl's house and drew in where the house was located on the map."

"Did he make a comment about the little girl?"

"Yes, he said that, 'They say the little girl will be submissive, as the mother was a prostitute'."

"Did he say what the little girl had said, in point?"

"Take me home to mummy. I want my mummy."

Justice Cummins wiped the corner of his eye and looked vacantly for a moment down at the bench in front him. Peter Reid continued reading of how Lowe had told him that Sheree's tracksuit was covered in sperm and was dumped in a rubbish bin at Mt Waverley shopping centre. Of how Lowe had said Sheree was dead and how he had forced her into the stormwater drain.

A silent wave of disgust swept through the room. Jill Mandile stood up and made for the gallery door but her legs gave way under her. Desperate court officials rushed to catch her before she collapsed. Several jury members threw their hands up in horror, clasped their mouths and clutched their stomachs. Lorraine was nearly sick. Kerri ran out of the court, fled down the two flights of stairs, crossed the court foyer area and sat on a battered and worn wooden seat. She looked devastated but was not crying. She fumbled slowly in her handbag, not really knowing what she was doing. Finally she opened the packet of Winfield Red cigarettes and lit up. She took one drag, then stared ahead, exhaled and turned her head to one side. For a few seconds she stared at a reporter sitting next to her.

The Murder of Sheree

"What must she have gone through before she died?" she asked him. He didn't answer but simply put his arm around her.

Inside the court everybody was upset as Peter Reid continued reading untheatrically from his statement.

"Today Lowe also gave me a sketch of his flat in West Rosebud. Lowe made mention today if I would get rid of some ticket for a mini pot or a mini golf, apparently he is scared that it will prove he's been not only to the shop where the little girl was, but also to the shop next door where he used to use this - where he used this ticket. Lowe stated he was also concerned about identification from the shop owner where the little girl did her shopping."

Justice Cummins was forced to adjourn the court. The court security guards, detectives, uniformed police and other witnesses flooded into the open aired cobblestone courtyard in an attempt to escape the horror. Detectives who didn't smoke grabbed fags from their mates and lit up as quickly as they could. Several men went straight into the toilet but most of them only used the cold water tap as they washed their faces. One security guard kept blowing out air - ooooooofss, oooooofss - red cheeked and wide eyed. He could have just finished running around the block. He could not believe what he had just heard.

Kerri walked down Lonsdale Street towards the city centre, smothered again in that relentless numbness. The pain and grief was visible on her.

So that was what he did to Sheree. So that was how she died. Choked to death in the foulest possible way, by that piece of human scum.

Was there nothing that man - no, that thing, for no human could be so base - was there nothing he would not do? To a child? My little girl, my darling little girl.

As Kerri walked, people stared and tried not to walk too close. Most of Melbourne knew who she was and they felt sorry for her but she carried the aura of death. Kerri didn't see anyone or anything; just a jumble that made no sense. She felt sick and dizzy. She thought she could be losing her mind. She pinched herself on the back of the hand and felt nothing. Half an hour later her hand was sore but she couldn't work out why. It felt as if somebody had pinched her skin. She wondered for a while how that had happened.

The Murder of Sheree

Lorraine was escorted from the court and sat in a small room recovering. She thought she was all right about an hour later. She checked the media had gone and then walked out into Lonsdale Street. She was still dazed and didn't even realise she was crying. Alex saw her walk out and asked her to come to the police room for some coffee and a talk. But Lorraine wanted time on her own.

She walked down to Myer and had a coffee by the window of the Little Bourke Street store. Some puzzled Christmas shoppers stared as she sat there weeping. The holly, the gay streamers and baubles, the Santas and above all the air of excitement and expectation made her pain worse. *These people are gearing up for celebrations but what have I got to look forward to*, she thought. A few days earlier Lorraine had caught the train home from court but had to get off after a few stations because she could not stop crying and people were gawking. She didn't want that to happen again so she decided to walk, and think. She zig-zagged her way through the mass of shoppers along Swanston Street to Flinders Street, past the Flinders Street station clocks, past the spot where her ex-husband had menaced two little girls years before. Lorraine was repulsed and walked quickly across the Princes Bridge over the Yarra.

It was a lovely, warm afternoon and she walked through the gardens near the river. There was hardly anybody about and she could at least tidy herself up a bit. Lorraine kept walking - she didn't know why, or where she was going. She found herself outside her dad's old office in St Kilda Road and peered in the window. How she wished she could have gone inside and talked to him. She pressed her face up to the window and in her heart told him what was happening. Then she noticed the building was up for lease. With a jolt she observed there was nobody there. Feeling totally alone she continued walking south away from the city.

Trams rumbled past on St Kilda Road and their bells rang out at stops. Lorraine kept walking until she was confronted with the intersection of Dandenong Road and Chapel Street. As she watched a tram disappear along the tracks, she realised there was no path for her to follow now. She stopped and turned around and around. The whole world was swimming round her. She felt giddy. She turned to an old man behind her who was holding two black bags.

"How do I follow the tram on foot?" she asked urgently. For some reason that was very important. She didn't know why.

The man looked at her for a few moments. "It would be better to go back to the last tram stop," he said, motioning back to where Lorraine had already been.

Lorraine wearily began retracing her steps and suddenly realised she wasn't coping anymore. Her feet felt swollen and very, very tired. She had had nothing to eat since breakfast. Now just getting home was beyond her.

She found a public phone box and rang police psychologist Gary Thomson but she just missed him. It was now after 7pm. She decided to ring Senior Constable Helen Adams and just have a chat with her before going home. But Helen wasn't there. The CPS policewoman asked Lorraine where she was but Lorraine didn't know. She was asked and dutifully read out the number of the phone box. The policewoman talked and talked, about herb gardens, chives with pretty, purple flowers. Lorraine couldn't work out if she was going mad or the policewoman. Then Helen Adams came on the line and it was great just to talk to her and tell her what had been happening. In the middle of this conversation a man's hand reached over her shoulder and grabbed the phone.

"I paid for this call!" she protested. The sergeant took no notice. He spoke briefly on the phone and then put it down. He introduced himself as Lars Holden and then told her to come with him in the police car. Lorraine asked him what she had done wrong.

Later that night, after a series of long, detailed phone calls between a number of very qualified professional people, Lorraine was driven to the Melbourne Clinic and was admitted for the weekend. That was the first time she met Dr Andrew Stocky who became her psychiatrist. With the help of some medication she had her first good sleep in three years.

THE NEXT MORNING, Peter Reid continued his evidence, during which much of the public gallery was in tears. Two women jurors clutched handkerchiefs to their faces. Reid said Lowe had proudly boasted he had cleaned the driveway under the car after cleaning up Sheree's blood. Lowe had said he knew the drain area well and didn't want to go to a

The Murder of Sheree

busy area. Lowe also allegedly told Peter Reid he also wanted to 'fix' Sheree's mother. Almost in passing he mentioned that Lowe had said he had learned his lesson after abducting Sheree. Next time he would use valium and make his victims more pliable. In a reflex action in the upstairs gallery, Lorraine put her hand to her mouth and gasped as she remembered the conversation between Robert and Mark Bensen she had overheard in her loungeroom all those years ago.

Reid told the court he had to be removed from Robert Lowe in prison.

"I became very angry with him, I couldn't deal with the questioning any more, I was learning too much of the things that he did, and he then was subsequently moved to another area."

Then Boris Kayser began his cross-examination of the witness. Reid stood passively facing the lawyer. Kayser launched a fierce attack on him taunting him, belittling him, ridiculing him.

"Mr Reid. How old are you?"

"Thirty eight."

"Since the age of 17, how many years have you been in prison?"

"A fair length of that time.

"How many?"

"All but about six months."

"All but about six months."

"Yes."

"So that you're a person who is experienced in the survival skills of prison. Right?"

"That would be correct, yes sir."

"One of the survival skills of prison is first of all you don't discuss your case with anyone, unless you think you can trust them, do you?"

"Well, I disagree with that."

"Do you?"

"It depends what part of the prison you're in."

"Well?"

"What type of company you're in. Some people hold the law in the criminal code that you don't discuss your cases with other people, other people just quite freely just speak openly about their cases. It happens every day."

"Right, well, let's just examine this proposition of yours Mr Reid. You were in K Division at the time, weren't you?"

"Yes, that's correct."

"You were in K Division which used to be called Jika Jika?"

"That's correct."

"Top security?"

"High security, sir."

"That is a section of the gaol which is built of concrete off the ground, is it not?"

"Yes, sir. Pylons and concrete slabs, yes."

"There are video cameras that monitor the day rooms and corridors?"

"Yes, sir."

"Also the yards, the exercise yards?"

"No sir, there's no - not that I'm aware of there's no monitoring equipment in the yards."

"When did you move into K Division?"

"I couldn't give you a date, sir, I'd have to refresh my memory."

"Roughly how long had you been there at the time Mr Lowe came in there?"

"It could have been under a year, I can't recollect. It could have been under a year or just a bit over a year."

"The reason you were there?"

"I was there for protection and security, sir."

"Protection and security. Is this the reality, Mr Reid, that you in your time in prison have had disputes and disagreements with other prisoners?"

"That's correct."

"You'd had disputes and disagreements with prison officers?"

"Yes, that's correct."

"You'd engaged in violence against fellow prisoners?"

"Yes, I have, sir."

"You'd engaged in violence against prison officers?"

"Yes, I have, sir."

A juror fidgeted in her seat.

"As a result, you were what is called in prison parlance, a management problem, weren't you?"

"That's correct sir."

"Mr Reid, you told the jury yesterday that Mr Lowe told you, amongst other things, that the abduction of Sheree Beasley occurred at a cross or T-intersection with Hume Highway, Road or Street. That's what you told the jury yesterday, wasn't it?"

"Yes, sir."

"Bit of a slip on your part, wasn't it, to record Hume Highway Road or Street?"

"No, I went off the words of Robert Lowe, what he told me."

"He told you it was the Hume Highway Road or Street?"

"Yes, sir."

"He didn't tell you it was Nepean Highway Road or Street, did he?"

"I can only recollect what he told me, sir, and I wrote it down as he told me."

"Right well, the Hume Highway means something to you, doesn't it?"

"Hume Highway."

"The Hume Highway?"

"At Rosebud?"

"Not at Rosebud. The Hume Highway, the road that goes from Melbourne to Sydney. That means something to you, doesn't it?"

"Yes."

"Because in 1983 or '82 was it?"

"Yes, sir."

"You were driving a car along the Hume Highway weren't you?"

"Yes, I was."

"Nearing a particular town or city?"

"Sir, I -" He turned to face the jurors. "Ladies and gentlemen of the jury. I killed a police officer at Seymour - close to Seymour, the town of Seymour and that's what I'm doing time for." Some of the jurors looked stunned.

"It was close to Seymour?"

"Yes."

"You were driving which way - towards Sydney or north or south?"

"Driving north towards Sydney."

"Were you going on a hunting trip of some sort?"

Lowe's cell mate Peter Reid.

Lowe hides his face from the media as he is escorted to the prison van from the Supreme Court.

The Supreme Court during the trial.

David Brustman, defence counsel.

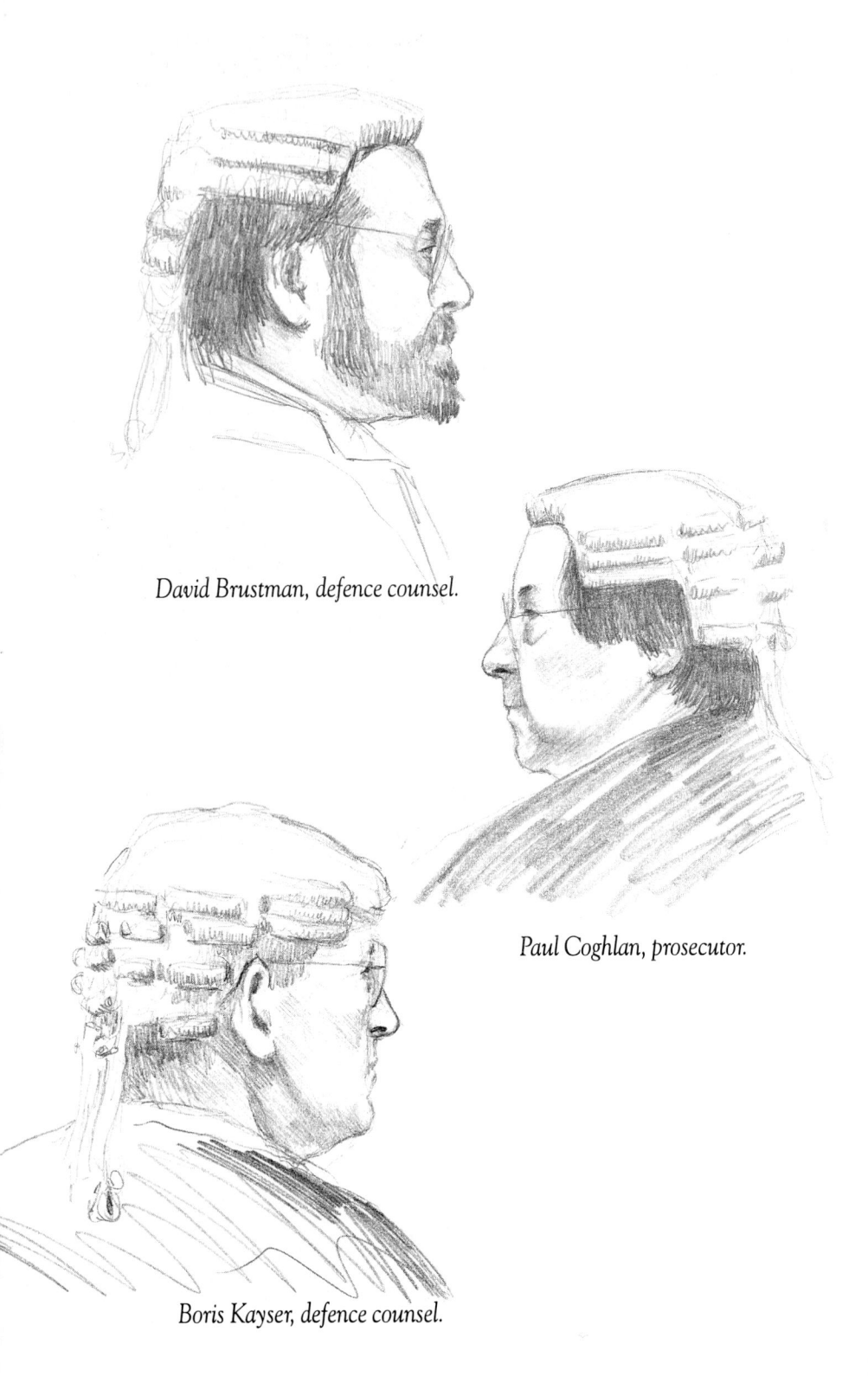

Paul Coghlan, prosecutor.

Boris Kayser, defence counsel.

The trial judge - Justice Philip Cummins.

Lorraine Lowe giving evidence against her husband. Lowe watches impassively from the prisoner's dock.

Neil Greenhill comforts his daughter as she fronts the media after Lowe is sentenced to life imprisonment.

Sheree's extended family and her father Anthony Mandile (left) look on as Lowe is driven away in a prison van.

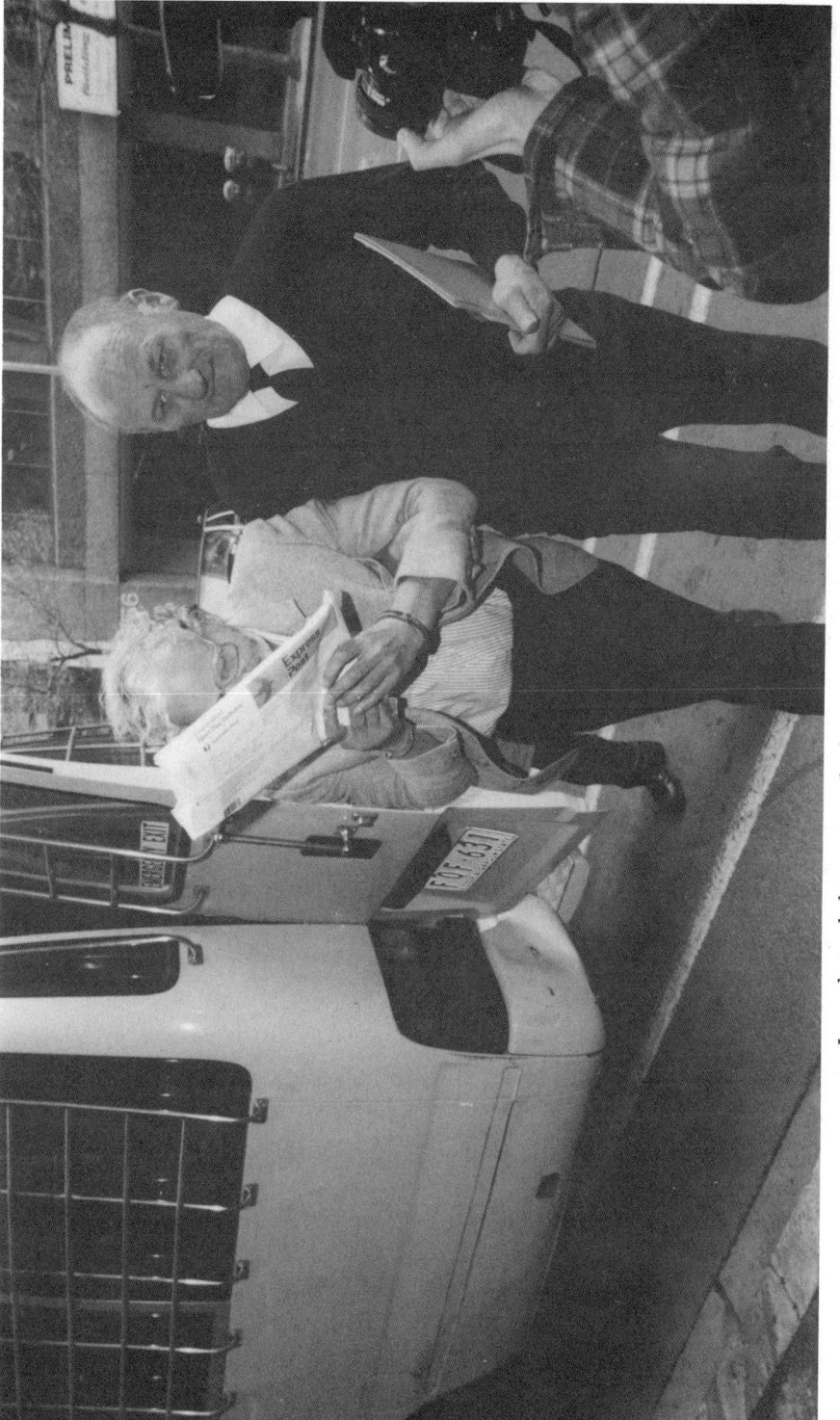

Lowe being led into court for his appeal on September 30, 1996.

SHEREE JOY MANDILE (GREENHILL)
25. 2. 85 - 29. 6. 91
TRAGICALLY TAKEN AGE 6 YRS.
BELOVED DAUGHTER OF KERRI & ANTHONY
LOVED SISTER OF CRYSTAL, JACINTA, SHANE (DEC.)
AND RHIANHON

A BEAUTIFUL SMILE, A HEART OF GOLD
THESE ARE THE MEMORIES WE ALL SHALL HOLD

"No sir, I wasn't."

"Did you have any firearms in the car?"

"Yes, I had firearms as I was going back to Sydney to join up with some people to get some prisoners out of an escort van."

"What - you were going to perform an armed raid on a prison escort van?"

"You could call it that sir, yes."

"What else do you call it?"

"Well..."

"You call it what you want to call it."

"Breaking prisoners out of a van."

"With guns?"

"Yes, sir."

"Loaded guns?"

"Yes, sir."

"How many guns did you have in your car, as you were approaching Seymour?"

"I had the one, sir."

"What was that?"

"I think from memory a Lee Enfield 303."

"Were you a member of the Army Reserve?"

"No, sir, never."

"Where did you get the gun?"

"I got it from a person who is now deceased."

"You acquired it?"

"Yes, sir."

"Does that mean you begged, borrowed, stole or bought?"

"No, I was sent down from Sydney - up from Sydney down to Melbourne to collect a case of guns from a certain person in Melbourne. When I got to that address, the case of guns wasn't present. There was only one and I got hold of that gun and kept it with me."

"You were sent down to acquire an arsenal of firearms, were you?"

"Yes, sir."

"How old were you then?"

"I would have been in my 20s sir."

"In your 20s?"

"Yes."

"Having acquired the Lee Enfield, did you acquire .303 ammunition?"

"I already had ammunition of all sorts, sir."

"You had ammunition?"

"Yes."

"You're driving back to Sydney, bent on reeking violence on prison officers in Sydney, weren't you?"

"They wouldn't have been prison officers doing the escort, sir."

"Who would they have been?"

"Police."

"So you're driving north to Sydney, bent on reeking violence on police officers in Sydney. Right?"

"Yes."

"When alongside you comes an unfortunate member of the Victoria Police Force, doesn't he?"

"Yes, he did."

"A traffic policeman wasn't he?"

"Yes, sir."

"On a motor bike?"

"On a motor cycle, sir."

"Were you speeding?"

"At the time, yes I was sir."

"What speed were you doing?"

"I can't recall from memory, it's been so long ago. It would've been in the range of 130 - 140 ks an hour."

"Along comes this traffic policeman. Right?"

"Yes."

"Draws alongside you?"

"No, sir, the police officer -"

"- Gestured to you to stop?"

"The police officer came up behind me, raised his lights, then I took off at a higher speed. The police officer caught up with me, came alongside and -"

"- Just a minute, please, if you don't mind. So you increased your speed in an attempt to get away from this police officer?"

"That's correct." Reid was now frowning and becoming a little upset.

"Did you know the police officer?"

"No, sir."

"Had he ever done anything to you?" Kayser asked casually.

"No, sir." Reid's cheeks were flushed.

"As far as you knew he was married, had kids?"

"I didn't know that, sir. It didn't even come into my mind."

"Of course it didn't. You didn't care either, did you?" he sneered.

Peter Reid looked around to the judge then back to Kayser.

"Excuse me, am I on trial here for murder?"

"Just answer the questions please," Kayser said.

Paul Coghlan objected to the style of cross-examination but Justice Cummins ruled against him.

"Proceed Mr Kayser," he said.

"If Your Honour pleases," Kayser said as he turned back to Reid.

"You didn't care either, did you?"

"It didn't come into my mind then, sir."

"So here he is, as far as you know, doing his job. That's all he was doing, wasn't he"

"Yes."

"You're trying to get away from him and he is chasing you on his motor bike, isn't he?

"Yes, sir."

"Then he drew alongside you, didn't he?"

"Yes, sir."

"He asked you to stop?"

"He waved his hand, pull over." He showed the hand motion.

"Waved his hand to pull over. He waved his hand to pull over, did he? You didn't pull over, did you?"

"No, sir, I didn't."

"You took your Lee Enfield?"

"No sir."

"What did you do?"

"I drove off again at high speed. He then pursued me further, came up alongside me again. I then slowed down to allow him to come up beside me. I reached over, grabbed the Lee Enfield rifle, cocked it, with it between my legs."

"You cocked it between your legs."

"Yes."

"What, you pulled the action back, did you, the bolt back?"

"Yeah, the thing at the end, the bolt."

"You know what a bolt is, don't you?"

"There's two parts. The gun is a lever action but you've got to pull back a bolt as well."

"You cocked it?"

"Yes, sir."

"You knew what you were doing?"

"My intentions then were -"

"- Just a minute, answer my question please, Mr Reid. You knew what you were doing?"

"With regard to the firearm or - ?"

"- Yes, the firearm."

"I hadn't any experience with firearms ever before, no."

"Mr Reid, if you had no experience with firearms that is not - but did you know what you were doing when you cocked it?"

"Yes, I was loading the rifle."

"You were deliberately preparing a firearm to be in a position where you could fire it, weren't you?"

"Yes, sir."

"You'd slowed down?"

"To let him catch up, yes."

"You thought that's what this policeman wanted you to do?"

"No, I knew it was the only -"

"- Just a minute. Did you think that that's what the policeman wanted you to do, to slow down and stop?"

"Well, I can't read his mind. I don't know sir."

"Of course you can't, but when he waved to you to pull over, did you think that he was asking you to pull over and stop?"

"Yes, I knew that, sir, yes."

The Murder of Sheree

"Did you slow down?"

"When he waved his hand?"

"You told us you did."

"When he waved his hand?"

"Yes."

"No, I sped off."

"You sped off and then you slowed down?"

"Yes."

"You slowed down after you cocked the firearm or before you cocked the firearm?"

"After, sir."

"After you cocked the firearm, so you made sure that you were in killing mode before you slowed down, is that right?"

"It wasn't my intention."

A couple of the detectives in the body of the court looked at each other but didn't speak. They wondered what the jury was thinking.

"Wasn't it?"

"No."

"If it wasn't your intention, why did you cock that gun?"

"I wanted to shoot his tyre out."

"I see. You cock the gun, you slow down and along comes this innocent traffic policeman again, doesn't he?"

"Yes, sir."

"You killed him, didn't you?"

"Regretfully, yes, I did, sir."

"You took that Lee Enfield rifle, you pointed it at his head, didn't you?"

"No, I didn't sir."

"At his chest?"

"No, I didn't."

"Didn't you?"

"No, I aimed it at the wheel."

"Aimed it at the wheel did you?"

"Yes."

"How far away was this man when you blew him off this earth?"

"About from here to that police officer there." He pointed at a policeman standing nearby.

Paul Coghlan jumped to his feet.

"Your Honour, I do object to the excessive language being used."

The judge looked down at Mr Kayser.

"I think the expression, Mr Kayser, is not appropriate for court."

Kayser nodded his head slowly, just the once.

"I'll rephrase it. How far away was this policeman when you fired at him and killed him? As close as that gentleman?"

"One and a half metres to two metres."

"Was he still on his motorcycle?"

"Yes."

"Was the motorcycle still moving?"

"He slowed to my pace then."

"You were moving and he was moving?"

"Yes."

"You anticipated, didn't you, that once you slowed down he would come to you, didn't you, Mr Reid?"

"Yes, that was the intention of doing it." Reid was clearly annoyed at this line of questioning. His eyes were burning.

"As soon as he got within range you killed him, didn't you?"

"I aimed at his wheel, sir, there was never any intent to kill him, never."

"Where in fact did you hit him?"

"He was hit in the helmet."

"Hit in the head was he and you were aiming at his tyre, were you?"

"Yes."

"That is nonsense, isn't it, Mr Reid?"

"Well, I think Mr Kayser if you had have got the transcripts you would have realised that forensic when they did the test on the gun, they admitted in court that when they aimed at an object they could never hit it, but when they aimed away from the object they hit it."

"Mr Reid, you are the man who was on his way to Sydney, bent on an expedition to attack a prison van staffed by police officers to try and break people out of police custody, that's you isn't it, at that stage?"

"Yes."

"You were in the state of mind where it really didn't trouble you to kill a police officer, did it?"

"That's lies." Reid was getting very worked up.

"Is it? Did you think that the police give up their prisoners in Sydney without a fight?"

"I was to be a driver, that was all I was to do."

"Answer my question, please. Did you think that the police in Sydney would give up their prisoners without a fight?"

"It was discussed that they wouldn't, yes."

"You were prepared to take part in the shooting of police officers in Sydney, weren't you?"

"No, I was their driver only."

"Driver only of a vehicle containing accomplices who were to be armed, is that right?"

"I was the lead car to slow the truck down."

"Did you have accomplices?"

"Not in that car, I was to be on my own."

"Was the plan that there were to be others involved in this attempt to break prisoners out?"

"Three other car loads."

"Were they to have people in them?"

"I didn't have much to do with them. All my job was -"

"- I'm asking you the plan. Was it that they were to have people in them?"

"I can't answer that because I don't know."

"Mr Reid, the reality's this, isn't it: that you thought the odds were that there would be people in those cars, didn't you?"

"That's a fair - yes, I could answer yes to that. Yes."

"The odds were and the intention was, I suggest to you, that those people would be armed?"

"I'm led to believe that their backup car's armed, but not the officers on board the truck."

"No, the people in your group?"

"Yes."

"They were to be armed, weren't they?"

"Yes."

"They were to be armed with weapons like you had?"

"No, shotguns."

"Pardon?"

"They were supposed to be shotguns."

"Mr Reid, as a result of that you stood trial in the Supreme Court in Melbourne in June 1983, didn't you?"

"I take your word for that, because I can't remember the dates, yes."

"But you will remember the sentence, surely?"

"I'll never forget it."

"Wouldn't think you would, with respect," said Kayser, with no respect at all. "It was that you be imprisoned for the term of your natural life, wasn't it?"

"Yes."

"You were also convicted at the same time on a count of using a firearm to resist arrest, weren't you?"

"Yes, I was."

"You were also convicted at the same time on a count of attempted murder?"

"Yes."

"Did other police attempt to apprehend you?"

"Yes, they did."

"Did you use your Lee Enfield on them too?"

"Yes, I did."

"You did your best to kill them, didn't you?"

"Yes, that I do admit."

"You've got a lot of prior convictions for dishonesty, haven't you?"

"A lot."

"Yes?"

"Yes."

"For violence?"

"Yes."

"For armed robbery?"

"Yes."

"Two counts?"

"Yes."

"Assaulting other prisoners?"

"Yes."

"Assaulting prison officers?"

"Yes."

"Then in 1989, on 28 July, 1989, you applied to this court to have a minimum sentence set in respect of your life term, didn't you?"

"Yes, I did."

"This court set a minimum of 21 years?"

"That's correct."

"That means, as you understand it, doesn't it Mr Reid, that 21 years is a period which must be served?"

"That's correct."

"Before the Parole Board can consider you for parole?"

"Yes."

"It doesn't mean, as far as you are aware, that you will get out after 21 years, does it?"

"That's correct."

"It's up the Parole Board, isn't it?"

"Yes."

"You know, don't you?"

"Yes, I do."

"That the Parole Board from time to time gets reports on prisoners; you know that, don't you?"

"Not when you're doing life, sir."

"But you're doing life with 21 years' minimum, aren't you?"

"But the life is the head sentence that the Parole Board act on."

"Of course it is, and what I'm asking you is this: you know, don't you- you believe that when and if the Parole Board considers your case -"

"- Yes -"

"- They take into account your behaviour whilst in prison?"

"Yes."

"They take into account, as far as you believe, whether you've been a management problem?"

"Yes."

"Whether you've been violent?"

"Yes."

"Whether you've committed other offences whilst in gaol?"

"Yes."

"And generally the Parole Board as far as you believe -"

"- Yes -"

"- ask the question 'Do we think it's safe to let this man out?'. That's what you believe in general is involved, don't you?"

"That's correct, yes."

"You believe that in order to have any chance of getting out after 21 years you've got to convince the Parole Board that it's safe to let you out, don't you?"

"Yes."

"Mr Reid, you also, don't you, believe that you've got to convince the Parole Board that you no longer are a murderous person?"

"Can you please rephrase that question?"

"I will. You believe, don't you, that if the Parole Board thought that you were still of a murderous state of mind, the sort of person who could commit murder, you believe the Parole Board wouldn't let you out?"

"No, I disagree with that because there'd be other -"

"- Do you? -"

"There'd be other factors that have to be taken into consideration."

"Of course there are."

"Many, that I'm not in control of."

"Of course there are. One of the things that would help you though to persuade the Parole Board to let you out after 21 years - and just pausing there, what is your earliest possible release date, Mr Reid?"

"Calculations of what we call remissions that we now do get."

"There are no remissions any more, are there?"

"Yes, on - when officers go out on strike everyone gets four days taken off their sentence."

"Apart from that you've got no remissions, have you?"

"Yes, accumulated 56 days, I think, from memory."

"What is your earliest release date, roughly?"

"14 June, 2004."

"That's in ten years?"

"Yes."

"That is something that you want to achieve, release on that date, if you possibly can, don't you?"

"Be crazy to say not. Yes, I agree with you."

"I'm asking you?"

"I agree with you."

"No, not whether you agree, I'm asking you?"

"Yes, I would love to be released."

"On that date?"

"Yes."

"Mr Reid, you however, whilst in gaol, besides committing offences of violence against other prisoners and prison officers, you've committed other offences, haven't you?"

"Yes, I have."

"In fact, on 9 December 1991, you were convicted at the Melbourne County Court of making a demand with a threat to kill. Is that right?"

"Yes, sir."

"For which you received a sentence of five years?"

"Yes, sir."

"That five years, is that concurrent with your prison sentence?"

"It will be concurrent, but it'll be up to the - I think the Parole Board did state to me at one stage seeing me not - about a year and a half, two years ago, that the five years will be taken into account on my behaviour. If it declined any more the five years will be added on as cumulative."

"They told you that? The Parole Board told you that, pretty soon after December 1991, didn't they?"

"Yes, they did, sir. Actually it was recorded by the judge too."

"Pardon?" Kayser was leaning forward with his head tilted slightly to the right.

"The judge made mention of it too, Justice Nathan."

"Maybe he did, but what I'm concerned about is that certainly was told to you by the Parole Board within six months at the very outside of your conviction in December 1991?"

"That's correct."

"So you knew at that stage that the ball was well and truly in your court in so far as whether you would have an extra five years added to your minimum 21 year sentence, didn't you?"

"Yes, I did, sir."

"The problem, Mr Reid, I suggest for you, was that that conviction, making a demand with a threat to kill, was a pretty serious conviction, wasn't it?"

"Very, yes."

"Indeed would you agree it is not overstating it to say that the crime which you committed on that occasion was a callous crime?"

"Yes, I did."

"That what you did, Mr Reid, was to ring the parents of the late Karmein Chan, didn't you?"

"Yes, I did."

Several jurors eyes widened. Some took a quick glance at the juror sitting next to them. Robert Lowe was smiling at the floor. Kerri was looking at the ceiling directly above her.

"You did that from gaol?"

"Yes."

"You knew, didn't you, that sometimes telephone conversations coming from the gaol are recorded or monitored?"

"This time it wasn't. It was the result of a prisoner going up and handing notes to the prison officer as I was actually doing the call."

"So you were safe. You could make your phone call from gaol confident that you wouldn't be recorded?"

"Yes, because we had the normal phone system in then and they didn't have the monitoring system they've got now." Reid's anger was gone. It seemed he was prepared to accept what was coming on the chin.

"Clothed with that confidence, you rang the parents of Karmein Chan?"

"Yes, I did."

"What sort of demand did you make? What demand did you make of them, Mr Reid?"

"I can't remember now the exact amount. I honestly can't remember it, because I put it straight out of my head. It was something that I wanted to try and bury."

"Is it?"

"It was a substantial amount of money."

"What? In excess of $100,000?"

"No, sir."

"In excess of $50,000?"

"No, I think it was down in the range of five or ten."

"Down in the range of five and ten; coupled with a threat to kill?"

"Yes, sir."

"In other words, you don't pay me this, I will kill you?"

"That's correct."

A woman in the upstairs public gallery shook her head.

"That's what you said to these distraught people?"

"Kill them?"

"Yes, or who did you say you would kill?"

"We were talking about the little girl."

"Who did you say you would kill? Tell the jury."

"The little child."

"Karmein Chan?"

"Yes."

"You wanted that money for a particular purpose, didn't you, Mr Reid?"

"Yes."

"You wanted it to pay to have someone murdered?"

"Yes."

Someone in the gallery tutted.

"Mr Reid, can the jury take it that your quiet acceptance of these propositions demonstrates that you can be quite calm about this sort of thing?"

Reid turned slightly to his left so he was facing straight past Sheree's pink bike at the jury. He spoke directly to them in a soft, contrite manner.

"Up until three years ago, ladies and gentlemen of the jury, I would never have stood before you like this, because I -"

"- Can the jury take it -?" Kayser cut in.

Reid turned to Justice Cummins.

"- Well, I'm trying to answer Your Honour, please," he said.

The judge said: "I think you asked for this, Mr Kayser."

"If Your Honour pleases," Kayser said, and stood and waited. Reid began his speech again, speaking politely, with his hands clasped in front of him.

"Ladies and gentlemen of the jury. I was the lowest person you could have ever met. I've done every conceivable crime you could have ever thought of and I would never have come before you, because just to believe a prisoner of my background you would never have done it."

As he spoke, his eyes moved from juror to juror. They were all transfixed, staring back at him, dropping their gaze only when his eyes met theirs.

"You wouldn't have believed a word that come out of my mouth. For the past three years, I've been in a rehabilitation program. I've got a lot of good values, a lot of good morals that I hold now and I can only say that today and what I've told you so far I did with the intention of either having it on video or here, because I knew that I could never come here with no evidence to back my story up."

"Right, okay, thank you," said Kayser, hurrying on, for that sort of talk was doing nothing for his client. "And that, Mr Reid was a matter which you took into account, I suggest; your state of mind I suggest was that you considered - this is in 1993 in April and May - you considered that your credibility was zero; is that right?"

"Yes."

"You considered that no one would believe you, unless there was a tape recording or video of a conversation?"

"That's correct."

"Is that right?"

"Yes."

Reid then told how when he first met Lowe in K Division, another prisoner had told Lowe that he shouldn't discuss his case with anybody. Reid confessed he had told Lowe he knew a bent lawyer who could help him prepare his defence.

"Mr Reid, you were carrying on a charade with Mr Lowe, weren't you?"

"Yes. I led him to believe that I was working for a lawyer and that I could get anything done for him that he wanted."

"That's why you told him, 'Look, I want a full description, full description of the bathroom at Rosebud', didn't you?"

"Yes."

"And I'll draw it?"

"Yes."

"We'll get the plans?"

"Yes."

"Then we'll be able to confound your wife with anything she says, words to that effect?"

"Yes."

"Really to put it in the vernacular, you wound him up, didn't you?"

Reid turned to the judge.

"Can I answer that the way I want to answer that Your Honour or do I…"

"I think we might just stick with yes and no for the moment, Mr Reid," the judge said. "If you don't agree with Mr Kayser's colourful description, you don't have to agree with it."

"No, I didn't wind him up."

"See you, I suggest to you, saw Mr Lowe as an opportunity to assist your position, didn't you, Mr Reid?"

"I deny that, I deny that."

"You saw him as an opportunity to be manipulated to help yourself?"

"I deny that." He shook his head.

"You saw him as an opportunity to be able to say to the prison authorities, I am rehabilitated?"

"I deny that." Both voices were raised. Nobody dared move.

"Do you? You've told this jury yesterday, you told this jury that Mr Lowe said to you that he committed 'dirty acts', you said."

"That's correct."

"Tell me something. Did you regard that admission as important?"

"Very important."

"Very important, isn't it?"

"Yes."

"In fact, it's such an admission you would regard, wouldn't you, as extremely important even?"

"Is that present tense question or past tense?" Justice Cummins wanted to know.

"Then, sorry, I withdraw it. You regarded such an admission as extremely important, didn't you?"

"No, there was one other that was more important than that, but I'm not allowed to talk about it today, I was told not to. That was the second most important factor." (The judge had ruled at the beginning of the trial that no mention of Lowe's fascination with the Karmein Chan would be allowed into evidence.)

"Mr Reid, did you regard the alleged admission that Mr Lowe had committed dirty acts on Sheree Beasley as important as evidence?"

"Yes, I did."

But the admission of dirty acts was not on tape because the tape had failed. Mr Kayser then tackled Reid head on.

"Mr Reid, over the years in gaol you've learned, haven't you, how to manipulate people?"

"Yes."

"Indeed, that is one of the survival skills which you have?"

"Yes, everyone has that sir."

"I suggest to you especially in the prison environment?"

"Yes."

"Tell me something; on that last tape what it refers to and starts off, not starts off but very early on, 'Tell me again what you told me yesterday'?"

"That's correct."

"Before that you discuss with Mr Lowe that the lawyer was very happy with the drawings, right?"

"Yes."

"Then it got around to the topic of Mr Lowe's wife's health."

"Yes."

"What happened in relation to, that's the 12th?"

"Right."

"In relation to Mr Lowe's wife and conversations relating thereto, Mr Lowe told you, didn't he, that he'd been told that his wife had had radical loss of weight."

"Yes, I think Margaret Hobbs or someone told him."

"And it appeared from what you could gather from Mr Lowe that Mr Lowe had been told that his wife, her health had declined dramatically?"

"That's correct."

"She was very sick?"

"He told me that."

"By this stage you and he are very chummy, aren't you?"

"We were from the first day he got in there."

"You took advantage of that?"

"Well, no, I didn't. See, I look at it this way, if -"

"- Just grapple - wait a minute, please -"

"- I'm allowed to answer -"

"- Mr Reid, just wait, please. You sought the opportunity, didn't you, to try and have on tape what would sound like a confession, that's what you wanted, didn't you?"

"I had three lots of tapes -"

"- Is that not what you were aiming at?"

"Yes, that's what - yes. Yes."

"Let's just focus on this last tape, right?"

"Okay."

"The day before, you and Mr Lowe had discussed what Mr Lowe had been told about his wife's health, state of health?"

"Yes."

"You, I suggest to you, told Mr Lowe that it sounded to you as if his wife had cancer?"

"Yes, that's how he described it to me and then I said, 'Well, what about the loss of weight, how's it she can lose weight so quickly?'. He said, 'Because she's got cancer', I said, 'Oh, sorry to hear it'."

"I suggest to you that you were the one who volunteered the diagnosis of cancer?"

"Excuse me?"

"No, excuse me, Mr Reid, answer my question please."

"Excuse me?"

"What's the answer to it?"

"I did not describe cancer to him at all. He made a phone call to Margaret Hobbs and Margaret Hobbs I think suggested somewhere along the lines that she was losing weight, she was very ill and I did ask your client what was she ill from and he said cancer."

"I suggest to you, you were the one who said it was cancer after having described to you the dramatic loss of weight. That's right, isn't it?"

"I don't agree with that."

"I suggest to you that you were the one who suggested cancer, right?"

"I disagree with that."

"It's obvious, isn't it, that Mr Lowe appeared to be very upset about the state of his wife's health? That's on the tape?"

"Second most. He was second most upset to that."

"Did he appear to be upset about his wife's health?"

"Not as much as he was to getting his house, half the money of his house."

"Really?"

"He paid more - a lot of attention to that more than his wife. It wasn't until the last few days before this last tape that he became very agitated about his wife apparently losing weight, very ill."

"Finished?"

"Yes."

Kayser suggested Lowe had told Reid that Margaret had coerced him. He suggested that Margaret Hobbs had told Lowe that he had to make up an account about the abduction and death of Sheree. If he could convince his wife that he wasn't a murderer, that he didn't kill Sheree and didn't sexually interfere with her, then there was a chance Lorraine would have him back. Reid denied that Lowe had said anything like that.

"Didn't he? It's possible that he did?"

"No, I would have remembered that last part about getting his wife back, because I do recall at one stage in our discussions in the first ten days when he was there that he was concerned more about regaining half of the house, and who was going to share up with the Rosebud flat or something. He was more insistent on getting half the money for that, and he - I was trying to tell him, 'Well, you know, what can you do? You've got to contact your lawyer and make sure you can come up with some sort of deal'. He was more interested in getting money at the start, and about who was going to get the house and who was going to get this than what he really was about the health of his wife."

The witness described how he had drawn up detailed maps and sketches of the burial site, Parkmore Road, the holiday unit, and so on. Reid said he had first asked Lowe to describe his Rosebud bathroom so he could sketch it purely to see if there really was a Rosebud unit.

"You said that Robert Lowe came back to check about three days later by driving past (the drain), as he put it, but he didn't stop, right?"

"Yes, that's in my notes, sir, yes."

"Yes, of course it's in your notes What I'm putting to you is this: that your notes contain some elements of truth but I'm putting to you that there are quite a few concoctions, and this is one of them?"

Reid shuffled from foot to foot and stared at Kayser.

"So what you're saying to me is - so I understand this correctly - is that the man's picked the girl up, she's just died, he's dumped her -"

"- No, what I'm saying to you is this. That you've made it up that he said that he came back to check about three days later by driving past but did not stop - that's what I'm suggesting to you. That you've made it up?"

"I deny that."

"And I suggest -"

"- I deny that strongly."

"I suggest to you - do you know, by the way, where Robert Lowe was three days later? Do you?"

"Not from memory, no."

"Do you think the police haven't checked out where Robert Lowe was three days later?

"I don't know police procedures. Without knowing that I can't give an honest answer. I don't know."

"Would it shock you to know that he was in northern Victoria three days later?"

"I wouldn't know."

"I suggest to you that's why -"

"- I can only go on what he tells me."

"I suggest to you that's why you put that verbal in. 'Stated he came back to check it out about three days later by driving past as he put it but did not stop'?"

The Murder of Sheree

"I deny that."

"Sperm all over her T-shirt, the tracksuit?"

"Well, why else would -"

"- I suggest you made that up?"

"Well, why would he want to get rid of her clothing for?"

"Exactly. Well, why didn't you ask him that on the tape?"

"Because that was the last tape and all that stuff had been covered."

"Had it? I see. So this is also more stuff. The allegation that the girl's tracksuit was covered in sperm, that is also on the failed tape, is it?"

"It could. I might -"

"- Is it? Yes or no?"

Justice Cummins intervened. "I think he might also be entitled to say he doesn't know."

"Thank you Your Honour."

"I don't know." Reid was getting upset again.

"Is that the answer?"

"I don't know."

"You don't know?"

"No." David Brustman watched intently from his seat next to Kayser. He was about the same distance away from Reid today as he had been in Brunswick Magistrates' Court.

"All right, you've just made that up, I suggest."

Reid's cheeks were flushed again. In a loud, angry voice, he spat out his reply.

"No, I haven't. You were there I suppose, you know everything. All I know is a little girl was killed by this person." He nodded his head in Lowe's direction. Lowe was staring calmly. "I heard everything he said and I won't stand here and be told I'm lying when you weren't there. You were not there. I heard what this little girl went through. I heard what she went through. She went through hell, because of him. She went through hell."

"No, you've answered the question, Mr Reid," said the judge. "Thank you very much."

Kayser continued.

"That being so, Mr Reid, why didn't you get him to say anything like that?"

"Because I thought I had it all covered on all other tapes."

"Mr Reid, I suggest to you just put on a bit of play acting?"

Some of the police were ready to pounce if anything happened. Reid's lip was curling.

"You think so? You think it's very funny that a little girl dies? Do you think it's funny the way she died?"

"Mr Reid, I put to you that you are now carrying on an act?"

"No, I don't like being called a liar, when I know I'm not lying."

"I suggest to you that you took statements that Mr Lowe made and twisted them about?"

"Then you go get hold of the video tapes and play them and see if I'm telling lies. There's 64 hours you can view and I'm pretty sure the jury will view them too. Sixty four hours worth."

"Your Honour, it may be that this witness would need a little rest over lunchtime. Perhaps he can then learn to listen to questions?"

"No, I don't need a rest. Not from you."

"I think the answer is no in one word," Justice Cummins said with a hint of a smile.

"Thank you, to which question, Your Honour?"

"To the question about whether it was on the tape or not."

"Thank you."

At 1.09pm Justice Cummins excused the jury. When they left, he explained to Mr Kayser why he had cut in earlier in the cross examination.

"Mr Kayser, I didn't want to intervene on the witness' behalf at the word 'No' for the answer but I was concerned that the witness might start talking about what was on the 64 hours that he spoke of being possibly other matters. I intervened for that reason."

"Your Honour, he's itching to do it, with respect."

Paul Coghlan looked at his learned friend Mr Kayser and then said, of Peter Reid, to the judge, "He's been very patient so far."

"I thought a monosyllable was safer than a speech," the judge said.

They adjourned for lunch. When court resumed, Boris Kayser continued on the same tack of baiting Reid, in an effort to destroy his credibility.

"I suggest to you, Mr Reid, that you were the person who said to Mr Lowe, 'Look, anyone you want get rid of, all you've got to do is say the word'?"

"Yes."

"Anything you want to get rid of?"

"Yes."

"All you've got to do is say the word?"

"An innocent man wouldn't have answered me the way he did."

"Is that right?"

"Yes."

"The reality of life in gaol is that there are certain power groupings, aren't there?"

"Yes."

"A long term prisoner like your good self, you've got to join a power group, don't you?"

"No, I've never had to belong to any group, I've always stood on my own, I've never belonged to any gang and I think even you Mr Kayser who has been before me before knows that to be very true. I've never -"

"- Is that right, have I'?"

"Yes, you have."

"Have I?"

"Yes."

"When?"

"When you were defending Greg Brazell when he stabbed me."

"Stabbed you? Stabbed you?"

"The same man that you - the same - the same -"

Justice Cummins held up his hand. "Let's not go back into history here," he said but Peter Reid continued addressing the defence lawyer.

"The same man, you very said that did it, and then he stabbed a governor six weeks later and then got out and killed a girl with a knife, the same very man."

"You're imagining things Mr Reid. That was Mark Brandon Read, Chopper Read."

"Excuse me, very wrong." Reid was adamant.

"Was it?"

444

"Your Honour, it'd take -"

"- That's all right."

"It'd take me five minutes to clarify that."

"We've got to stick to this case," the judge said.

Reid spoke deprecatingly to Kayser.

"See, you don't like that, because you've got to prove that now."

"You've got both your ears, Mr Reid," Kayser said. "The Mr Read I cross-examined didn't have any ears."

"Well, then, I suggest to you that the DPP will be able to prove it. Boris Kayser, the same man I wrote a letter to. Remember?"

"Press on," Justice Cummins said.

"Fame is a terrible thing Your Honour," said Kayser, smiling, before he went on to suggest that Reid's notes were simply a concoction. Then he quizzed Reid about the conversation that was taped but the tape hadn't worked.

"So you actually gave the tape to Mr Bartsch, is that right?"

"I think I could've, yes. Yes, I did."

"Mr Bartsch went away?"

"Yes. Oh, he had a talk with me. I can't remember the conversation, but we had a talk and then he left - he left and then I came back and was placed back in the unit."

"Naturally you told him about the dynamite things that were on it?"

"Yes, yes."

"What dynamite things did you tell Mr Bartsch were on it?"

"I told him the fact about the - well, there's one I can't mention, Your Honour, because you told me not to. There was one about the oral sex, there was one about the girl being promiscuous, which were his words. The next time he was going to use valium."

Then it was time for Paul Coghlan's re-examination of the witness. In answer to a question, Reid again turned to the jury.

"It was important to me at the time, when he was telling me things for the first three days ladies and gentlemen of the jury, it was a sort of touch and go affair. He told me a little bit, then I had a listen and I'd think about it. The next day I'd come out and I'd say, 'Remember that conversation we were talking about yesterday, I thought about it last night, something doesn't ring true', and that pattern kept going and kept going and kept going, and I got this story one day, and this story the next day, so I decided to compile notes because I realised that when I'm going back to my room I wouldn't remember everything he said, so it was important to me to notate down his words."

Coghlan wanted to know more.

"Yes, but he did say those words in the form, 'This is what happened', or did he say it in the form, 'The police say this is what happened'?"

"No, he - his direct line was, 'This is exactly what happened' and I said, 'Right, I'll get you a bent lawyer, we'll get you off. What do you got to get rid of?', all things like that. It was just me playing a person who put myself as law as he did to become a person who would do anything that he wanted, and it was he, in fact, who suggested first up that there was a lot of evidence that he needed to get rid of...."

The man who had behaved so poorly at the committal hearing had been an impressive witness in the Supreme Court. Alex breathed a sigh of relief, as did everybody associated with the prosecution. Now the prosecution case was over and the defence did not call any witnesses. But what had the jury made of it all?

FINALLY, THE prosecution, the defence and the judge had turns in summing up for the jury. Paul Coghlan pointed out the inconsistencies in Lowe's story. He summed up the accused's defence.

"(He says) 'I wasn't there. But if I was there, I wasn't the murderer.' He simply can't have it both ways," Coghlan said.

He urged the jury to use their common sense. Jurors looked at Lowe, with long, considered gazes before their eyes wandered up to the gallery, as Coghlan outlined Lowe's web of lies.

"The strength of the case is not a single piece of evidence, but the evidence in combination." He was talking about Shane Park, the witnesses who had seen the blue car with a man identified as being Lowe driving it, the lies to the police about his past and his association with the Mornington Peninsula. He was talking about the testimony of Lorraine, Margaret and Peter Reid. The tapes of Lowe talking about the crime. The video of him returning to the scene of the crime. But mostly he talked about Lowe's lies.

"Odd that church members could remember Lowe saying he was going to Rosebud that day but he'd forgotten himself," the prosecutor continued.

"Odd that he could describe in graphic detail where the family were standing in the room when watching news that night but he couldn't remember where he was for a few critical hours that day."

Concerning Lowe's comment, "Thank goodness I was home by 2pm," after seeing the 5.30pm news, Coghlan said there would have been more appropriate things to say like, "I didn't see the police cars and helicopters," or "That must have been after I was down there".

He pointed out Mr Lowe had washed his clothes for the first time in 20 years of marriage - "because he didn't want anyone else to see them after he got down on his knees to push the body in the drain".

When the court was adjourned, Lowe had an animated argument with his counsel outside the court. The tension was really starting to show. Some of the court security staff smiled.

On Tuesday, November 29, 1994, Justice Cummins summed up the prosecution and defence sides of the case, gave his own summation and then charged the jury to retire and consider its verdict.

CHAPTER SEVENTEEN

◆

AT 4.30PM the judge called the jury back into court and told them he would empanel them for the night. The forewoman and the woman next to her looked at each other in surprise, giving the impression they were not far off a verdict anyway. As they silently filed out to the jury room, they looked at nobody in the court. Robert Lowe stood in the dock, watching them intently, leaning slightly forward, his head held high, his jaw jutting out an inch or two in their direction.

Look at me. I am in your hands. Acquit me. You must. You must.

He had gambled on this for the past three and a half years. As the last juror left the court, Lowe relaxed, as if a steel rod had been removed from his spine. Now he leaned casually forward on the wooden dock.

Outside it was raining. Although it was the eve of summer, and only mid-afternoon, cars were slushing through the wet, noisy streets with their headlights on. The air of expectancy of impending summer. Everybody was keen to talk about the rain. Few talked about the jury. Nobody slept well.

The next morning Lowe turned up in court with a little schoolbag. He was confident he would be soon going home. A rumour went round outside the court that some other prisoners in the prison van had threatened to bash him, but nobody knew for sure whether it was true. Benjamin Lowe found a three foot length of iron pipe behind the Lonsdale Street exit door and pointed it out to the security staff who took it away.

While Lowe waited in the dock for the jury to deliver its finding, police, witnesses and Sheree's relatives and friends stood in the cobblestone courtyard, shuffling uneasily, unconvincingly reassuring each other the verdict would be guilty.

What if he got off? He would just walk out of the court!

The Murder of Sheree

Some of the detectives were chain smoking. Anthony and his parents, Kerri, her mum Marie Doolan and her husband Bruce, Neil Greenhill all stood around, petrified the jury might bring in the wrong result. A reporter bumped into Paul Coghlan in the toilets.

"How's it going?" the reporter asked.

"If only we had a cause of death," Coghlan muttered as he washed his hands. He looked concerned. He rearranged his wig slightly in the mirror.

Outside, corny jokes were told and laughed at. Non-smokers had a drag. Shoes were suddenly interesting things to look at. Nobody could stand still for long. Some were beginning to wonder if there was enough evidence. Too late now.

Then, just before lunch, the jury was set to return. The word went out to the lawyers, and through them to the police and through them, the family and media. And the rumour was it was a verdict, not a hung jury. Lowe was either innocent or guilty. It was about to end.

Justice Cummins came into court with a small smile. Very solemnly the jurors filed in, filling the front six seats first. Every single one of them was expressionless. Lowe was standing to attention, his eyes watching each one intently. Everybody stared at them for some sign. Knots in the stomach.

The judge smiled at the forelady who gave a nervous, half-hearted grin back that quickly dissipated into a grimace. Her head quickly jerked to her left, her eyes darting up toward Kerri for a split second. Kerri covered her mouth with her hands. The Mandiles were holding each other tightly. Extra security guards were now standing in the front row of the upstairs gallery. Then the forewoman turned back to the judge's associate who stood and read aloud, "Ladies and gentlemen of the jury, have you reached a verdict?"

The forewoman paused for a second or two.

"We have," she answered. Her head didn't move but her eyes flashed around the room, stopping at the lawyers, then the media, then the wall opposite her, then the judge and back to the associate. Her hands gripped the front of the jury box.

Some jurors started crying. Several others were rolling their eyes. One juror held one side of her face in her hand, her hair awry and wild. One

The Murder of Sheree

man had red eyes. They were all drained, physically and emotionally. None of them looked at the prisoner.

In the gallery, Kerri was straining forward to hear. The room was silent but for the humming fluorescent tubes. But it was impossible to tell whether they were upset at sending a man away for good or because a little girl had died and nobody knew who the murderer was. At the back of the court, next to the packed media benches sat several policemen who had not worked on the case since the early days in Rosebud in 1991, along with several of the homicide detectives including Paul Hollowood, Alex Bartsch, Jeff Calderbank, Andrew Gustke and Geoff Shepherd. They sat still and tried, unsuccessfully, to look calm.

Robert Lowe stood to attention like a tin soldier.

"How say you on the charge of kidnapping?" the associate asked. "Do you find Robert Arthur Selby Lowe guilty or not guilty?"

For a split-second it felt as if the air had been sucked out of the room. Jill Mandile clutched a handkerchief to her face. Everybody froze.

The forewoman faced the associate but as she opened her mouth to speak, her eyes flicked across to the judge. Several jurors looked up at Kerri and Steve as the verdict spilled out.

"Guilty."

The gallery erupted. Sheree's relatives and friends shouted abuse at Lowe, standing below them in his wooden box. Police, press and other observers let out an audible gasp of relief and smiled at each other.

Lowe showed no emotion other than a little rapid spasm in his nose. His eyes blinked uncontrollably for several seconds, then he was still.

"On the charge of murder, how say you? Is he guilty or not guilty?"

All went still again. One male juror wiped the corner of his eye.

Another juror quickly looked up at Kerri. His head slowly moved back towards the judge but his eyes wouldn't shift from Kerri. Then very slowly, a sympathetic smile appeared on his closed lips. Then slowly he turned back to look at the judge and wiped his eyes.

The forewoman looked at the judge too.

"Guilty," she said firmly.

There was cheering, jeering, clapping, abuse.

Kerri shouted, "Suffer Lowe. Sheree got her revenge this time. Rot in hell, Lowe."

Jill Mandile stood and shouted, "God's never going to forgive you and we won't either."

The court security guards up in the public gallery were on full alert, standing between the family and the railing.

Justice Cummins sat still and mute. After everything Sheree's family had been through, he could allow them at least the opportunity to vent some of their anger. Lowe was quickly taken from the court.

The judge thanked the jurors for their time. They smiled back at him, some like children who had just finished watching a horror movie and were trying to pretend it had not scared them. They rose quickly and started filing out of the room again. All of them glanced up at Kerri and Steve, giving small smiles or quick nods of the head. Then they disappeared.

Lorraine was gob-smacked. She heard the verdict and then she had seen everybody's reaction to Robert. It was still totally incredible. She became aware of a high-pitched whistle inside her head, then she felt giddy before collapsing on the floor. An ambulance was called and the paramedics tended to her after everybody else had filed out of the public gallery.

"God, did you feel the tension in that courtroom," one detective said to a reporter outside after the verdict. "I've never experienced anything like that." Detectives shook hands with each other, with Neil Greenhill, Anthony Mandile, Kerri. There were tearful smiles all round. Now the focus shifted from what would the jury say, to how long would he get.

The following day, December 1, 1994, Alex Bartsch was feeling on top of the world. The jury had done the right thing and no doubt Lowe would be behind bars for a long time. There was one person Alex wanted to talk to about that verdict. He drove to Barwon Prison.

He asked for Peter Reid and was taken to a small holding room. After a 10 minute wait, Peter entered the room. He was looking a bit grubby - he had been doing some pottery. Alex noticed Peter didn't look too well. His face muscles seemed to sag a little on the left side of his face and he was a bit 'down'. He found out later Peter was suffering from Bell's Palsy.

The cop killer looked at the cop for a second. Peter held out his dirty hand and said: "Do you want to shake my hand?"

"Of course I do," he said, and held out his hand. The two had never touched before. In normal circumstances Alex probably wouldn't have minded anyway. On this day he welcomed it. The two men looked at each other as they shook hands. They both realised what unlikely bedfellows they made in their combined fight against Robert Lowe but they didn't talk about it. Peter was getting emotional.

"Thanks," he said. "You were a gentleman."

Alex told him what the judge had said.

"They believed you mate," he said. "The jury believed you."

Peter was very happy. He didn't cry but the tears were welling.

"Thanks for helping me. And for believing me," he said.

"Thank *you*," Alex said. Alex felt good for him. At least, out of all the shit things in his life, this was one positive. Alex had hated him at one time. Now he didn't and he knows he never will.

Then they walked to a huge hall, where Peter was to return to the bowels of the system. The prisoner was walking across the hall when he stopped and turned around.

"Thanks mate," he said.

"Yeah, no worries."

Then cheekily, Peter said: "See, I got to call you mate and you didn't even say anything." He laughed loudly.

Alex smiled. "Yeah, okay."

Peter called out, "I'll see you in about 10 years." He slowly took a few more steps across the hall and stopped in the doorway. Then he turned around to face the detective. He was forcing a grin but he looked as if he was about to burst into tears. Then from about 10 metres away he gave Alex a wave - a loose, slow salute that stopped abruptly. Then he turned and walked away.

Alex just stood there, transfixed, and thought as he watched him walk away. *If there is a ledger up there somewhere, Peter, this time you would have got a few points.*

CHAPTER EIGHTEEN

NEIL GREENHILL had agonised for days over a victim impact statement to give to the judge. He wanted the world to know what Sheree meant to him in life and what devastation her death had caused. On Friday, December 2, he brought his letter to the court to give to Paul Coghlan. He wanted the prosecutor to hand it to the judge. He had written:

> Sheree Joy Mandile (Beasley) to her family was a very special and unique child. She was <u>not</u> influenced by others, Sheree had the ability to influence others.
>
> A little girl, with an eternal smile, that touch of cheekiness, you couldn't help but love her. A mind which seemed much older than her six years. The "big" sister to Crystal and Jacinta. The first, and special daughter to Kerri. Loved and adored by all her relatives. Here was a six year old, with everything in life, in front of her.
>
> A six year old so cruelly deprived of the most sacred thing, - life, itself. Robbed of the chance to grow, and wear those "special" party dresses and go to parties. Robbed of the chance to live and love, to form those special relationships, as she grew older. Gone is the chance to see a special flower bloom, and to share that precious life with her Mother, Father, Sisters, Great GrandParents, GrandParents, Aunts and Uncles. So tragically, Sheree was robbed of her innocence.
>
> This crime, the crime of a perverted monster, has touched the very heart of a country's innocence. In the words of the parents of Ebony Simpson, he (Robert Lowe) will get bed and breakfast, while we get the life sentence.

The Murder of Sheree

On 29th June, 1991, Robert Arthur Selby Lowe changed my life, as he has with all of the relatives of Sheree Mandile (Beasley). Such was the devastation, caused by Lowe's murderous, callous, cruel and selfish act, that he has left, in his wake, a trail of emotional wreckage.

I will try to explain the repercussions on the survivors of this horrible act. Changes take place in our personalities. Lost, is a sense of happiness, guilt sometimes consumes a smile. Relationships are tested to the limit between husband and wife, parents and their children, these relationships suffer due to the anxiety and stress going on in our minds and bodies. Tolerance levels are shot to pieces. Due to our own level of emotions nobody can say or tell us how to grieve, or how long we should grieve for. This depth is only measured in how we individually loved Sheree. And we all loved Sheree.

We have suffered, possibly, every parent's worst nightmare, a child missing, firstly the numb disbelief, that this bubbly six year old was missing, not believing that Sheree could have been taken, for the worst. Then as the hours drew into days we still couldn't believe that anything bad could happen to this child of life itself. This six year old who held grown ups in the palm of her hand.

As time passed, some of us, in desperation sought the help of clairvoyants. Rightly or wrongly, in our desperation and frustration, of not knowing, we were seeking answers, or help, or more importantly, HOPE. I spent night after night, tossing and turning, in bed, not ashamed to cry openly, when thoughts crossed my mind that, what if the worst had happened and somebody had left Sheree's body out in the open, there for the mercy of the elements. This tormented me. Thoughts of suicide entered my head as I questioned life itself. Religious beliefs suffered. How could a God let something like this happen?

The Murder of Sheree

Then on the night of Thursday, 27th September, all of our hopes were completely and utterly shattered, with the discovery of a child's body, being found at Red Hill. There were no other children missing. Our worst nightmare had arrived.

I have never seen so much distress amongst family members, or felt the pain of anguish like I did that night. That night alone, to see the suffering of a mother, my daughter, hyperventilating in front of my eyes, other members so distressed and helpless, having to wait through the night until the following morning for confirmation of the police report. For that night alone Robert Arthur Selby Lowe deserves to pay the maximum penalty possibly allowable to him.

For three years and five months our emotions have been put through the "wringer". Just when our anxiety levels seemed to level out, they were constantly assaulted. We have been tested to the limit.

All of this time, Robert Arthur Selby Lowe - (worst of all) has shown <u>No Remorse</u>. He is an evil coward who preys on the young. There is no forgiveness for this fiend. He is false, he is a lie. I can only hope, that in his incarcerated future, that when he tries to sleep, he will be tortured by a child's sobbing "in his mind".

And that - in the shadows of his cell if he catches what he thinks is movement out of the corner of his eye, he will know that he is sharing space with the ANTI CHRIST - For he is Robert Lowe's companion, for eternity.

Kerri was right. Sheree is having her revenge.

(Signed) Neil Greenhill

Grandfather of Sheree

Now May She Rest In Peace

The Murder of Sheree

Tears smudged the word 'Grandfather'.

But Justice Cummins didn't want to see Neil's impact statement. As soon as he walked into court, it was down to business. Lowe sat in the dock, still wearing the grey ill-fitting suit, the jacket buttoned uncomfortably. He looked a little grey himself but otherwise unaffected. Still he wore his spectacles with the tatty black shoelace. Jill and Anthony Mandile couldn't see him from the upstairs gallery. Lorraine Lowe and Margaret Hobbs weren't there. Kerri's mum Marie was the first of Sheree's family to arrive. The homicide men were dotted around the court. Several of the men, including Andrew Gustke, sat behind Paul Coghlan. Paul Hollowood and Alex Bartsch sat at the rear of the court with their backs to the side wall. Directly across from them, just three metres away, stood Robert Lowe, the man who had dominated their lives and their thoughts for over three years. The man who had destroyed scores of lives around him.

The judge's associate stood and read out Lowe's prior convictions to him. As she read each conviction in his dirty past, he would nod, just the once, while his eyes wavered uncertainly from her to the media seats and back again. As the litany of filth was read out, and as he continued to acknowledge he was the author of the crimes, some of the gallery upstairs gasped and started whispering, shocked. It seemed to go on and on and on.[*]

Lowe's eyes were focused on the judge but for the first time, the cockiness was gone. He looked for all the world like an errant schoolboy standing before the headmaster after having committed some terrible schoolyard sin that warranted expulsion. His eyes showed fear. The rigidity in his stance was gone, too. As he looked at the judge, his eyes, almost against their will, flicked occasionally to the full press box. Each time he saw someone watching him he quickly looked away and back to the judge. His lips dropped a little, he looked a little sad.

Robert Lowe sat down as Boris Kayser stood to ask for a minimum jail term and that the sentence not be a crushing one. He told the judge that life imprisonment with no minimum should only be set for cases which had exceptional circumstances.

---

[*]Lowe's prior convictions are listed at the rear of the book

"- I agree with you," the judge cut in, while staring at Lowe.

Boris argued that although Lowe's 'moral culpability' was extremely high, it was not of the same degree of moral culpability as the intent of killing 'with direct murderous intent'.

An artist began sketching Lowe so his face could be shown on the television news. The prisoner saw the artist and picked up his own notebook, obscuring the left side of his face.

The judge politely listened to Kayser's submission and then told Robert Lowe to stand. Gripping the front of the dock with both hands, Lowe slowly drew himself up. He was slightly stooped. No longer was he fit looking - tall, wirily muscled, healthy. Today the suit looked too big. His eyes could have belonged to a frightened dog. His jaw was clenched tight and he watched mutely as the judge stared at the upstairs public gallery for a few seconds before bringing his gaze back down to the prisoner's dock.

Justice Cummins took off his wig and sat it on the bench before him. Then with his clear, strong voice, he began his sentencing of the prisoner.

"Robert Arthur Selby Lowe, shortly after 2pm on Saturday 29 June 1991, there was at Rosebud a scene of innocence; a six year old girl riding a pink bicycle, wearing a pink crash helmet, and looking at the front wheel turning around. That is how one woman driving from McCrae to Rosebud described what she saw. The little girl with the pink helmet was looking at the wheel going around of her Christmas present, given to her by her loving parents, Kerri and Stephen Ludlow, six months before.

"Unknown to her you had been watching her. You had been in Rosebud the previous Saturday and seen her. You had gone back on the Monday and followed her. And then you went back on Saturday the 29th under the pretext of fixing the tiles in the bathroom of your Rosebud flat to kidnap her.

"What you did was every child's fear and every parent's nightmare. You inflicted on two families a terrible legacy. Your own good family was still in Glen Waverley. That morning you had been to a prayer meeting at your local church at which you are an elder. You dropped your young son Jonathan off at the Wheeler's Hill campus of Caulfield Grammar to play school tennis. You had left your wife working, typing medico-legal reports as an assistance

The Murder of Sheree

to the family. Your sexual interests fuelled by an interest in the Karmein Chan abduction led you to Rosebud to abduct this little girl.

"A six year old boy, Shane Park, a school friend of Sheree's, gave evidence that he and she were riding their little bicycles at the T-junction of the dirt road, Parkmore Road, Rosebud and the Nepean Highway. You told her from your car to get off her bicycle and she said, 'I'm not getting off the bike for nothing'. Intelligent and brave, all at the age of six years. You got out of your car, took her off the bike, bundled her into your car and in a skid drove off."

The judge paused for a minute, then looked up at the ceiling. His chin was quivering and his eyes were heavy. As he cleared his throat, his associate, sitting with her back to him, started to cry. Her eyes met Alex Bartsch's and he thought he might start too. The judge regained his composure and went on.

"A series of witnesses along the Nepean Highway leave with us a haunting, indeed indelible, imprint on our minds of the fear and distress of that young girl. A girl outside a motel at Rosebud said of Sheree in your car, 'She was kneeling. Her face was to the window. She was miming something. She gave me a terrible look.' The mother of that girl said of Sheree when her daughter said, 'Look mum', her body was very straight but she turned her head to make sure we saw her. Her lips said, 'Help'. The fear on her face overrode everything.

"You, Mr Lowe, had determined to force yourself upon her and having kidnapped her, you took her away and you forced yourself upon her.

"I am satisfied beyond reasonable doubt that Peter Reid, a prisoner of Pentridge Gaol gave truthful evidence before this jury when he said that on 16th April, 1993, you said this to him: That when you drove into Parkmore Road you told the little girl that her mummy said for you to take her home as her mummy was ill. The little girl became suss and you forced her into the front of your car. You drove to an inland area and forced her to do dirty acts. That she choked from you doing dirty acts. From terrifying fear and the acts she was forced to do, she choked to death."

Again the judge stopped. He looked up at the public gallery again, then higher to the ceiling. He appeared to be on the brink of tears. Several reporters were wiping tears from their eyes as they furiously scribbled. The tipstaff was lost in thought, staring at the floor. Almost imperceptibly, Lowe was shuffling from one foot to the other. Now his hand covered his face. The judge and the sentence was not his concern. It was the media. Justice Cummins composed himself before continuing.

"Mr Reid said you were uncomfortable using the words 'oral sex'. You used the words 'dirty acts' in their place. You told Mr Reid that your sperm had got all over her tracksuit, so you got rid of her clothes after you took them off her."

Lowe smirked. The judge didn't see.

"You then, with your feet, forced her into her final resting place."

Realising he was not avoiding the media, Lowe then unsteadily turned 90 degrees to his right so his back was to them. Then he turned his head hard to the left to try to look at the judge. Alex shook his head. Lowe couldn't even show any self-respect at this dark hour. He was as pathetic as he was disgusting.

"On Exhibit X in this trial, the film of the walkthrough by the surveillance police on 13th April, 1992 when you had taken your therapist to the scene of Sheree's final resting place, I directed that part of that film be excised so that the jury did not see it. The part that I ordered excised in the interests of your fair trial was one of terrible poignancy. For in that resting place there was a small floral tribute - still on 13th April, 1992 - from those who loved Sheree. Her final resting place was a cold concrete cylindrical drain, 30 centimetres wide, not even wide enough to contain her other Christmas present from Christmas 1990, her pink bicycle helmet.

"The jury went on a 'view' in this case. I gave directions through my associate to the local police to ensure that on the view there was no visible protest at Rosebud and that at Winthunga, 1331 Mornington-Flinders Road, Red Hill, there was no thing there to divert the jury from its task of acting as judges of the facts. Even on that day the police had to remove a floral tribute from that drain. That is where you left her.

"The pathologist, Professor Cordner, gave evidence that there was no tracksuit on the girl, that there was a white T-Shirt, a red singlet size 5, and no underpants.

"There has been a major police investigation into this case and I commend Inspector Hollowood* and the Homicide Squad and the Zenith Task Force and the local police for the comprehensive persistence with which they have investigated the death of this little girl.

"In the end your conduct assisted them because of a series of lies and half-truths you told the police over a period of time. The odyssey of those lies and half-truths I will not rehearse in this sentence. It is familiar to all here present - Walter Scott wrote in 1808:

'Oh what a tangled web we weave
When first we practise to deceive.'

"YOU WOVE A tangled web around yourself, which eventually captured you." Lowe nodded once quickly. "You have shown yourself, Mr Lowe, to be very intelligent, very articulate and very manipulative in your dealings with the police."

Lowe was now standing facing the judge, his face hidden from the media with an A4 size notebook.

"On 13 April, 1992, you went with your therapist, Mrs Hobbs, down to Rosebud and to Red Hill. She described your conduct as you went through the charade of pretending to her you were retracing not your steps, but some other person's steps, as one of excitatory participation. You were excited in reliving your crimes."

Lowe swapped his notebook for an A4 size orange envelope to hide behind.

"I consider you have utterly no remorse for your crimes. I reach that conclusion first on the basis of your conduct since, secondly on the basis of what is revealed by the numerous Exhibit X tapes of your discussions with your psychotherapist which show you to be egocentric and have utterly no care for the deceased, and finally, your excitement at reliving your crimes with your therapist on 13 April, 1992.

"This has been the most harrowing trial I have experienced. I have seen daily before me the suffering of two families. Your former wife, a good woman, I have seen suffering daily. Each of your boys, Benjamin

---

Paul Hollowood was promoted to Inspector during the trial

The Murder of Sheree

and Jonathan, gave evidence in this case, called by the prosecution. By virtue of a provision in the Crimes Act each of your boys could have applied to be excused from giving evidence against you. Neither boy applied, not because they were being disloyal to you, but because they were being loyal to truth and to justice. Both the boys one would be proud of."

Lowe was transfixed by the words he was hearing. He quickly nodded his head once.

"I have seen the suffering every day of Sheree's mother and of Stephen Ludlow and of Sheree's grandparents.

"Judicial sentencing must proceed according to principle. It does not vary according to emotion or publicity. It must be objective and measured."

Some lawyers sat staring at the books on the bar table, others watched the judge, spellbound.

"Thus I turn to the principles which judicially govern me in sentencing you. The first is the principle of reformation. The principle of reformation can be a most important and creative principle in sentencing, particularly with young offenders. Given your lack of remorse I consider it is of marginal utility in sentencing you in this case. The principle of deterrence both general and special is of significance. But in the synthesis of principles which governs judicial sentencing, which varies from case to case and from offender to offender, the two principles here pre-eminent are condemnation and punishment.

"The sentence I shall soon impose upon you marks the condemnation by the community of your conduct. It also is the punishment by the community for your conduct. The protective mantle of the law has a special application to innocent children.

"I consider there is in the end no real difference in moral turpitude between intentional murder and reckless murder in this case."

Kerri, Neil and his teenage daughters Adele and Harmony walked through the court foyer and up the two flights of stairs before emerging in the upstairs gallery. The judge looked up at them, as did his associate, the police and the reporters. Justice Cummins went on.

"If, as the Crown primarily argued, you inflicted oral sex upon this poor child and you then intentionally killed her, or if on the other hand, as may be the case, you killed her during the infliction of oral sex well knowing that that would be the result and not caring, in either event the sentence I impose upon you is necessary and appropriate.

"I am conscious that the Court of Criminal Appeal in the matter of Paul Charles Denyer by majority held in that case that a sentence of life imprisonment with no minimum was inappropriate. Respectfully it appears that that was because, given the age of the applicant, the statistical likelihood of that sentence would have been of the order of 50 years. That is not this case. You are now aged 57 years.

"Bearing in mind the restraint of judicial principle and applying to this case long-standing criteria of sentencing as I have expressed, on count one for the kidnapping of Sheree Beasley I sentence you to 15 years' imprisonment. On count two for the murder of Sheree Beasley I sentence you to life imprisonment."

A smattering of applause broke out in the upstairs gallery.

"The question arises as to whether a minimum term should be set. I bear in mind what was cited by Dawson, Toohey and Gaudron, JJ. in R V Bugmy (1991) 69 CLR. 525 at 536, citing R V Deacon (1984), 58 ALJR 367 as to minimum terms:

"The intention of the legislature in providing for the fixing of a minimum term is to provide for mitigation of the punishment of the prisoner in favour of his rehabilitation through conditional freedom where appropriate. Once a prisoner has served the minimum time that a judge determines justice requires that he must serve having regard to all the circumstances of the offence."

Lowe was staring mutely, hypnotised but he didn't seem to understand what was happening to him. His head was tilted very slightly to right.

"I bear in mind also what Jenkinson, J. said in Morgan v Morgan (1980) 7 A. Crim.R. 146 at 154, where His Honour said: 'The minimum term is the period before the expiration of which release of that offender would in the estimation of the sentencing judge be in violation of justice according to law, notwithstanding the mitigation of punishment which mercy to the offender and benefit to the public may justify.'

"Bearing in mind those principles, and being conscious of the exceptional course which it is to refuse a minimum term, and being conscious of the importance of mercy in the sentencing process, nonetheless given the facts of this terrible crime, given what you did to this innocent girl, I refuse to set a minimum term on the life sentence.

"You are sentenced to imprisonment for life on the count of murder with no minimum term. Life means life. Remove the prisoner."

In one movement, Robert Lowe, handcuffed in front, moved to his left, ducked forward and tried to shield his face. Court security officers grabbed him from either side as he scurried out of the dock and toward the door. He looked like the pervert he was, rushing away from the scene of some obscene exposure as a parent chased him. Above, while five uniformed police and security staff stood in the front row of the gallery, men and women yelled, shook their fists, and mouthed obscenities at the invisible man below them. The system that protects the accused had even prevented them seeing Lowe at his lowest, at the moment of his total demise.

Outside the court, Anthony Mandile shook hands with just about everybody and smiled.

"Justice was done," he said. "It feels good."

Neil Greenhill stood with his daughter. Kerri broke down completely and for more than 40 minutes sat on a lonely courtyard bench sobbing uncontrollably while her dad tried to console her. It was true after all. Sheree really was dead. Finally they composed themselves and hugging each other, they fronted a media scrum in Lonsdale Street.

Then they joined the homicide detectives and some family members for a celebratory drink at the Metropolitan Hotel in William Street. The family wanted to thank the police for their persistence and professionalism, and to toast the legal system. Justice had finally prevailed. At least not everything in the world had been turned upside down. It was really a proper wake. Sheree could rest now the man who buried her was also being buried alive. *Life means life.* At least it was something.

Kerri sat next to her former husband. They talked for a while and occasionally people joked - usually cracks about some of the more ridiculous things Lowe had told Margaret Hobbs, or the police, or Peter Reid. Then Kerri saw one man on the other side of the bar. A young man, say late 20s. He didn't take his eyes off her. Kerri leaned over and told

Neil about him. Neil went over and spoke to the man but when Neil sat down again, the guy hadn't moved.

"He was a juror on another case and he says he's got a special interest in Sheree," Neil announced, shaking his head. One of the detectives sprang from his seat, walked the 15 metres to the starer and spoke firmly to him. Very firmly. The man left.

They all drank, and talked, and laughed, and cried, until the early hours of the morning. For the homicide detectives, it was now all over and they would concentrate on more 'normal' investigations. For Sheree's family, it was time to move on and start again. Life without Sheree. They didn't know where to start. Every one of them was lost.

CHAPTER NINETEEN

◆

ROBERT felt moved to write to Rev Dr Powell. The reverend felt very sad when he read the letter.

```
Robert Lowe,
K2 Division, Box 260 Coburg 3058
6.12.94
(Four days after sentencing)
```

Dear Mr Powell,

I feel embarrassed and very saddened as I write to you because of the terrible position from which I write. I had genuinely hoped to write from a position of victory, but you will well know this is not so, and in fact I couldn't go any lower in any way. I am deeply saddened and shocked, but I will survive.

Thank you for sending me cuttings from The Age. I hope you are doing alright yourself and are home again. Thank you for the tonic cards too. I have so much appreciated your support and I certainly like to pray regularly for you.

I write now to see how you are, but also in an endevour to overcome whatever embarrassment or difficulty there is between us. The result of the trial is devastating and the "no minimum release date" is based on my age of nearly 58. I'm told if I was 40 or 50 or even 30 Yes, I'd get a release date.

I really do not want to go into the why's and whereof's of the judge's or jury's decision. I will leave that for another time when I am clearer of mind. But I do want to tell you I have not lied to you, not even partially, and I have not mislead you intentionally. I have told you the truth that I have never seen the little girl at any time, and what I can say now is there was never any Police evidence to say I was, other than what I have personally been entrapped or tricked into, conned if you like into considering a plea of guilt to a lesser charge on the condition I'd get my wife back. It was stupid of me to even consider it but I do love my wife and that was my mistake. Then an inmate has media inflamed that into a very nasty evil and wrong accusation.

If you come across further articles in The Age I'd appreciate your sending me them no matter how bad. Without these I would wrongfully believe friends and supporters I write to would think all is OK. But knowing others might read such articles enables me to be humble and quiet and considerate when writing them.

Thank you for your patience and support in the past. Should you wish to withdraw or withhold further prayers I'd well understand.

In the meantime.

God bless you all.

Robert.

Three days later he wrote to Margaret Hobbs.

Dear Margaret,

Excuse me please for this brief question of you - better me than someone else. I want to know please Margaret if you still have my bible in your possession. If you have I will arrange for someone to pick that up from you. I have a book of yours if you want it returned. I have not criticised you and I trust you will not of me either. I thank you for your past support.

Sincerely Robert.

The Murder of Sheree

Lowe received a letter from his brother Richard in New Zealand.

Dear Robert,

Well, what can one say?? At the time of writing, I haven't heard the sentence but expect it to be "Life" - whatever that means today.

I rang Lorrie. She was naturally distraught but has to now pick up the pieces - I guess distraught - not so much because of your problem but your reaction to the problem - lies, lies and lies. You just unfortunately couldn't help yourself.

Whether you did it or not (and I'm still not totally convinced you did) you just painted yourself into a corner and the result was inevitable. Unfortunately you only have yourself to blame - if you had been <u>totally</u> honest from the start you would have stood a chance - but your way?? - no chance at all.

If I had been on the jury, even as your brother, even I could not have said there was reasonable doubt for your innocence. The facts were indisputable and so were the lies, lies, lies. There was no way out and society and the Cherie's of this world have to be protected. There would have been an uproar on the evidence submitted if you had been allowed to go free - and the public have a right to protect their own people. This may be harsh but it is the real world - not a fantasy world.

Everybody close to you has tried to believe you but as I have said to you before, where do the lies stop and the truth start?? We all face this dilemma to a greater or lesser extent every day.

Lorrie thinks there may be an appeal by you. I could not support that at all. You must <u>NOT</u> appeal - unless there is new evidence which I am sure there is not. You cannot put your family through this again - it would be ridiculous, unfair and the final irony.

The Murder of Sheree

You may believe you are innocent - you may even be innocent - but nobody except you and God know that and upon the evidence submitted, plus the lack of evidence by the defence and you would mean once again the public would have to be protected and it would be a waste of time and put your loved ones through the most tremendous ordeal again - unwarranted.

So PLEASE -don't do it - for their sake as well as yours. In the fullness of time we will all know the truth - we are after all only human and can only judge things as they are put to us.

You cannot continue to blame the police, Margaret Hobbs, Reid or your family for your predicament - only yourself.

People now have to pick up the pieces in their own time and get on with their lives as best they can - so please let them.

I will always be your brother and have brotherly love for you - rest assured.

But please be sensible with your appeal. It's a waste of time.

Love as always,

Rick.

PS What also amazes me is your evidently total lack of emotion or remorse at the verdict - never any compassion. Hardly the actions of a supposedly innocent man. I just don't understand that.

TWO WEEKS after the sentencing, and just before Christmas, Robert Lowe lodged his notice of appeal. And even though Margaret had told him months earlier that Lorraine had collected the $2500 from the Rosebud unit when she cleaned it up, he reported the police to the Ombudsman. He complained they had stolen his money.

CHAPTER TWENTY

ALMOST everyone in Melbourne had heard of Robert and Lorraine Lowe. Now their property settlement was news. The *Herald Sun* newspaper won a plea for the results of their Family Court property settlement in April 1995 to be made public because of the public interest.

What Lorraine couldn't understand was why Robert wanted to split everything they owned fifty-fifty. She couldn't understand what enjoyment he would get out of that type of settlement. After all, he was in jail for life and by getting half the assets, he would deprive his own sons of the benefit of financial assistance. She thought he was being like a dog with a bone. He had to have his own way and it didn't matter to him who was upset or got hurt in the process.

Lorraine went to the hearing with Benjamin and several of the homicide guys, including Paul O'Halloran and Andrew Gustke. Lorraine was frightened Robert would get what he was asking for. After all, all she had heard about over the past three and half years were Robert's rights. Now he was fighting for what was lawfully his, she was concerned she would miss out. She wondered why he had to do this, to fight her like this. The only reason the hearing was listed was because Robert refused to let go of his entitlements.

But he was still full of surprises. When the court began, Robert asked for time to think about the matter further. After a 10 minute adjournment, he came back into the court and said he had decided to agree to Lorraine's wishes.

Lorraine kept the family home in Glen Waverley and the Rosebud unit, while Robert kept his interest in a family trust in New Zealand. Some life policies were to be divided between them. Caveats filed by Graeme and Richard Lowe and the Legal Aid Commission on the real estate were to be discharged.

Justice Fogarty said in his finding, "The effect of the orders is really that most of the property is to be transferred to Mrs Lowe. It appears to me that that is an entirely appropriate outcome in this case, which is a most tragic one. The circumstance of the police investigation of Mr Lowe and his subsequent trial and conviction imposed extraordinary pressures upon Mrs Lowe and her two children and they have gravely affected her health and made her life a nightmare over the last three years.

"It is to be hoped that the community will extend to her the sympathy and support to which she is entitled and it is to be hoped that this represents the final step in this tragic case."

Robert was seen to have finally done 'the right thing'. It seemed that there was, after all, a shred of decency in him. But he had done it for himself. On April 2, the day before the court hearing, Gordon Powell had written to him, pleading with him to withdraw from the Family Court battle. The reverend appealed to Robert on moral grounds, including the effect the case was having on his wife and sons.

```
This letter is to plead with you to withdraw from
the case for seven reasons.

1. As a Christian, it is time to apply the verse
you quoted to me, 1st Cor. 6; 7. "Why do ye not
rather take wrong?" You could honestly say you are
doing it because of your Christian principles.

2. In your letter dated March 2 you had a fine
passage about wanting to lift Lorraine out of her
'total misery'. You rightly speak of her
'devastating totally unfair experiences'. You wrote,
'I want to see her fears and doubts wonderfully
changed to love of herself, God and others'. A
first big step towards that would be to relieve
her of the worry of this court case.

3. I don't know how many friends you have left,
but I doubt if you will have any at all if you add
one straw to the awful burden Lorraine is carrying.

4. Nothing is more devastating to developing
personalities than to have the parents fighting.
```

The Murder of Sheree

To have it happen publicly in court is disastrous. It will take the grace of God to restore to your sons any affection for you. If you want them to hate you with a bitter hatred continue on in this court case. On the other hand, if you of your own free will withdraw, they may find it in their hearts to feel better towards you.

5. If you did the Christian thing and withdrew, it would really make headlines - good ones in your favour.

6. By shortening the court case it could save thousands of dollars and reduce the temptation Lorraine must feel to accept large payments for selling her story to the Press.

7. It would make at least one noble page in the book Wayne Miller is writing about you. I understand he is starting with your boyhood in England and then the story of your unfortunate sojourns in prison in New Zealand. His job is 'Chief Police Reporter' for the Herald Sun so he naturally writes up crime, but he strikes me as a decent chap and would highlight any noble act.

Very sincerely, Gordon Powell.

Robert basked in the glory of the good press for a few days. Then he appealed. He complained he had not had enough time to prepare for the court battle, and had been disadvantaged in prison by not having adequate access to a typewriter.

LORRAINE WENT for another check up and the doctor found four lumps in her breast. Because they had appeared so quickly, it was decided she should be operated on as quickly as possible. But first, she had to determine how radical she wanted the surgery to be. She was given four options, but the first two were never viable anyway. She could do nothing, which would mean a painful, lingering death. She could just have the lumps removed, but that was a band-aid approach to what was a very serious problem. The last two options, the real ones, were to have one breast removed, or both.

The Murder of Sheree

Night after night, Lorraine sat in the family room of her home, myriad memories surrounding her. Sometimes she imagined Robert behind her, walking about the house, readying himself for another bible class. She saw him sitting there with his sons, the fire roaring in the fireplace, as the rain tumbled outside. Sometimes she smiled as she recalled the journey she and her husband had taken together. Their first meeting, the engagement, the wedding, the birth of the boys, the lovely home, the church. But those memories now always dimmed and gave way to the darker ones. She could see Robert slapping his knee and laughing hysterically, watching some corny TV show while the boys wept in their rooms. She could see him creeping off to the laundry to wash the clothes he had worn when he murdered Sheree. Her spirit, or ghost, or whatever it was, seemed to be in Lorraine's home all the time. She could not forget this child and how her husband had killed her. The loss of a life. Such a deep loss.

Then Lorraine thought about her own losses. She had walked out of one life at 29, and began another, only to find in her 50s it was all a lie. She feared it was too late to start again. Her search for honesty and truth and the correct way of living would go on unrewarded. Perhaps the easiest way to go out would be to succumb to the cancer in her chest. At least it would be an end to the pain and the loneliness. But what on earth had she done to deserve all this?

On August 25, 1995, Lorraine had a double mastectomy at Waverley Private Hospital. She made the right decision. While the lumps showed cancer, the surgeon found further pre-cancerous growths that had been undetected in the other breast. She was gravely ill after the operation and it seemed to some of her visitors, who included Margaret Hobbs and the Blackburn Community Policing Squad, especially Helen Adams, that she had given up the will to live. High on pethidine, Lorraine greeted her guests groggily with just two thoughts on her mind. She was frightened that the following week, when Robert's Family Court appeal was listed for hearing, she could lose her home. And she was terribly upset that she had been 'mutilated' and lost her breasts.

The next day she began haemorrhaging. She was found in the nick of time, lapsing into unconsciousness, and raced back into theatre. The surgeon told her later that she was 10 minutes away from death.

The Murder of Sheree

Back in her private room, Lorraine lay perfectly still, acutely aware of the tubes protruding from her body, feeding the jars and bottles under the bed. Occasionally she noticed the flowers and cards sent to her from well-wishers and friends. Slowly she shifted a little in the bed and looked towards the window. Her mouth felt dry. Then, for some reason, despite the wonderfully warm and soothing sensation the pethidine was providing, something didn't seem right. Lorraine was vaguely aware something was wrong for a few seconds before she noticed the wisps of smoke licking the blankets and flicked up the side of the bed. Fire?! What next? She buzzed the nurse, who found that a night light in the wall under the bed had shorted.

Lorraine wondered if she was cursed. Then her mind went back to 1969, in her aunt and uncle's home, when the elders had tried to dissuade her from leaving the church.

Lord, we commit her to Satan for destruction of the flesh.

Staring at the wall, Lorraine only thought about that for a second. She knew Christ had defeated Satan at Calvary and the power of curses had been broken. But she knew she did not have the strength to go much further. Everything she had ever had, except for her two boys, had been taken away from her, even her womanhood. She knew the Family Court hearing would see her lose her house or the Rosebud unit. Or both.

But she was wrong. The court decided Robert had no grounds for appeal and the original orders would stay. It was Lorraine's first victory since Robert had been sentenced to life imprisonment. She wondered what was in store next, for if one thing was certain, it was Robert would never lie down and give up this senseless court action. She was sick to death of hearing about his rights. It seemed to her that he was the only one who had any rights. Sheree's were gone, he had seen to that. But Kerri, Anthony, Neil, Steve, Jill and Anthony, everybody associated with Sheree - what about their rights? Didn't they have a right to try to piece their shattered lives together, to try to make some sense of life? Lorraine couldn't find any rights that applied to them or to her. She wondered what the justice system was really all about. It certainly wasn't the victims and their families. And she wondered how fair a justice system was that cared only for the offenders.

CHAPTER TWENTY-ONE

◆

THE 'AVERAGE' homicide investigation in Victoria costs the taxpayer about $500,000, including the trial costs. The Robert Lowe investigation, though, was far from average. Most investigations take only a few weeks or months. This investigation, which took over 41 months from the day Sheree disappeared until the day the trial finished, cost Victorians just shy of $4 million. But Paul Hollowood knew the monetary cost was the minor consideration. He and his detectives had seen first hand the emotional devastation that had swept through dozens of people's lives. And he knew the wreckage could never be fully repaired.

What affected Paul so badly during the investigation was seeing the lives of so many people close to Sheree unravelling around him. There were times when he, and most of his men, wanted to go up to Kerri, to Anthony, to Neil and Denise, to Jill and Anthony, and tell them Lowe was the prime suspect and that it was just a matter of time before he would be arrested. But they couldn't do that.

The job had consumed everybody who worked on it. All the detectives carried Lowe around in their heads every waking moment, right up until the end of the trial. It was like a poison. They knew he was the psychopath every parent feared. Even these experienced detectives found it hard to come to terms with a man who didn't have any remorse at all. And Lowe hadn't complained to people that the police were investigating him - being followed actually excited him. The types of things that would normally probably bother somebody, even a psychopath, weren't bothering him.

Paul Hollowood never saw anything from Lowe that showed anything at all that might point to self-justification. All Lowe had done was ignore his crime, and that meant it didn't happen. Paul knew that what that really meant was, "I am the centre of the universe".

Throughout the investigation, there were times when Lowe had done something and the whole crew would sit down and just pose the question, "Why would he do that?"

And more often than not, the reply would be, "Because he's Robert Lowe, that's why". It became the easy answer to give but often it was the only answer. Often logic didn't come into it.

Paul was fascinated by Lowe's internal strength and his ability to ignore anything troublesome. It occurred to the policeman that it was an incredible mind that thinks it can believe in God while simultaneously manipulating Him to do what it wanted Him to. Paul often wondered what sort of person prayed to God and said, "I need to be forgiven for this God. I've forgiven myself and you should too."

Paul had always acknowledged mad and bad, like everyone else, but he had never really considered evil as a category of criminal. Now he believes it exists but it's like trying to visualise the universe.

What makes a person the way he is? Why does he do the types of things he does? What makes a man kill a child? While Paul doesn't agree with what killers do, he can see how the crimes happen, and why. But to be able to explain why Lowe behaved the way he did defied every type of rationalisation. Paul knew Lowe was the type of person people could accept and trust, except there was no good in him at all. The reason Lowe was 'good' - ie went to church, helped others, prayed - was to mask his bad side. It seemed to Paul that was what probably made a person evil. The ability to use goodness to mask vile deeds. Paul thought Lowe was the sort of person who could be studied for years and even then nobody could be sure they knew anything about him.

Paul knew Lowe was in a league of his own. Sometimes homicide hauled someone in and put them in the same category as, say, Julian Knight - a man who shot and killed seven people in a wild shooting spree in Melbourne's Hoddle Street in 1987. But Lowe had started up his own category. Paul didn't really know what made Lowe different. He wasn't sure that he would really want to know because he had never seen a case affect so many experienced, hardened men. The tight-knit crew had become noticeably niggly at times. They were always tired, working long shifts away from their families. Paul knew none of them would ever forget this case.

The Murder of Sheree

JANUARY 1995 saw Kerri on the move again. She took her four daughters and husband Steven to South Australia where they rented a home in the Adelaide suburb of Renown Park. It was a new start. Steve had his head shaved and grew a goatee beard. Kerri enjoyed walking down the street without people gawking at her but she was always aware of the tug of Sheree's and Shane's graves in Mornington Cemetery. She knew she would one day return to Victoria because of her daughter and son, but just for now she had to try to come to terms with the nightmare she had lived most of her adult life.

Every month carried a special gruesome anniversary. May was the month Shane had died. Sheree was murdered in June. September - her body was discovered. Four miscarriages dotted the calendar year. Now February marked the month that baby Steven, born on February 17, 1995, had died, just 90 minutes after he was born. Yeah, Kerri knew what life was all about. It's a bitch, and then you die.

After so much horror in her life, Kerri came to suspect she had been born for a reason. But try as she might, she could never work out what it was. Life was just one long episode of torment, pain, rejection, loss, grief, despair. Why was she put through so many trials and tribulations? Today she sees only evil and badness everywhere she looks. She mistrusts all men. She sees no point in worrying about the day to day matters of life because they no longer mean anything to her. From the age of 25, she has been more concerned with death, funerals, anguish, hurt. What does it matter what some politician says in Canberra, or how much the gas bill is about to go up, or who won the footy? What does it matter? She sees life as something that must be endured. It happens without love, without joy, without happiness. Kerri no longer sees her parents or grandparents. It is a lonely and sad life.

Yet she hasn't lost her faith in God. Not long after the family moved to Adelaide, Kerri and Steve decided to send Crystal and Jacinta to Sunday School every week. Kerri wanted the girls to know that there were good people, and beautiful things, in the world, and not just death, destruction and uncertainty.

Hanging on the wall just inside the front door of their home is a photoboard with seven photographs of Sheree. One of the photos was taken the day she was murdered. Large cut-out paper letters pronounce her to be 'Our Little Angel'. Kerri will always struggle to find a reason why Sheree had to die. Sometimes she thinks her daughter really was a little angel. The circumstances of her death touched every parent in Victoria, perhaps even in Australia. The night her decomposed body was found in that filthy Red Hill drain, parents everywhere hugged their own children and thought deeply about just how precious they really are. Sheree's death united in an intangible and invisible way, every parent in the community. They felt for her mum and wondered how they would cope in her shoes. They wondered with a shudder what Sheree's last moments alive were like, all the while thinking of their own kids.

Kerri sat, looking out the window of her home, daydreaming. She could hear the squeals of delight coming from the girls down the street, playing skippy and gleefully running about. She saw three girls, all about nine or 10, and thought absently *Sheree would be as old as you now*. She smiled as she thought of Sheree, who was going to buy her a brand new car when she was a rich and famous dancer. A tear slipped from the corner of Kerri's eye and dropped on her shoulder.

Steve walked in with the girls. Both girls were dressed in their best clothes and they were bursting with excitement. As they ran into the loungeroom, Kerri turned and saw the wild, bright eyes and the broad, toothy grins.

"Mum, we learned a new song today. Djya wanta hear it?" Crystal said.

Kerri wiped her eye and smiled at the girls. She nodded and said, "Sure."

"Jesus loves me, this I know, for the bible tells me so..." the girls sang. They were gently jostling for position to see who could get the most of their mother's attention. Kerri watched them sing and then listened as they chattered on about what had happened at church. She waited until they left the room before she went back to her daydreaming. She was glad they were happy. They still talked about Sheree from time to time, and Crystal still had her nightmares. Kerri wondered whether they would ever get over Sheree's loss. Then she snorted derisively to herself, for she knew they never would. Robert Lowe would haunt her, and her daughters, to their graves.

There would be no permanency in Kerri's life, for she knew nothing was permanent. There was no point working for anything because no matter what she achieved, it would be snatched away. She knew that. She knew her life would be a succession of rented homes, in different towns, for different reasons. The girls would go to a succession of different schools and have different friends. They would learn that everything is temporary - schools, houses, friendships, relationships - and life itself.

MARGARET CUT back on counselling offenders. She had lost her objectivity and was more concerned with working with victims of sex offenders. The work was much less lucrative but far more rewarding, and now she felt she knew exactly how the victims felt. She had endured a long, long nightmare with Robert Lowe. Margaret, trying to be all things to all people, had lost her health, her objectivity, and in some quarters, her reputation. As the months went by after Robert's conviction, she gradually reviewed the past four years. She kept it quiet but it dawned on her that she had been used as God's instrument in the war against Satan. She thought talking would draw ridicule but the more she looked at it, the more the evidence was incontrovertible.

She wasn't a committed Christian, yet during the period Robert was in therapy, she spoke often to church people to try to make sense of Robert's constant references to the bible. And when she couldn't sleep during the trial, dreading giving evidence against him in the Supreme Court the next day, she had sought solace in the Psalms.

The more she thought about it, the more it made sense. What better person to carry out God's work on earth and prove his might than a person with little religious conviction? It occurred to her that all her training in Wales, then in the prison system with some of the toughest and most sadistic men in the country, had merely been preparation for her battle with Evil, in the form of Robert Lowe.

She regarded professional confidentiality as the most important aspect of her job yet she had jumped the fence and given evidence for the prosecution, something that had always been unthinkable.

She thought of the odd collection of people who had come together over Sheree. At one end of the spectrum there was Lorraine Lowe, the prim and proper housewife who could never divorce her husband. At the other end was Peter Reid. It would be a hard struggle to find somebody less trustworthy, or more devious and treacherous than Peter, who had killed a cop and tried to extort money from a murdered girl's parents. Yet he had come full circle. Only Peter Reid and Robert Lowe had shared a morbid fascination with Karmein Chan's disappearance. Yet this case had allowed Peter to atone in some way for the terrible manner in which he had besmirched Karmein's memory. And he did it by working with the police.

And what about Christine Dogan, the woman with the phenomenal memory, who could remember not just the model but the colour and shade of the abductor's car after so long. And to then identify the offender after 20 months!

No, it seemed to Margaret that inside her clinic she had waged a battle with Robert, backed by the police, and Lorraine, and Peter Reid, with the thought of Sheree as her driving force. She thought of Sheree often, and wondered if she really was a little angel, who had been sacrificed in the fight against the Devil. Maybe she was wrong, but she didn't think so. It gave some semblance of sense to such a senseless act. And if there was someone as bad and evil as Robert Lowe, it was logical that there must be something equally good to counter it. Margaret began investigating which church would best suit her needs.

ALEX WAS sitting in a friend's kitchen, having a few beers. On the table sat several empty beer cans and two more that had just been opened. The air was thick with heavy blue smoke. An ashtray was full to overflowing. A few black marks from ash that had missed its target stained the doyly tablecloth. Salted peanuts were strewn about the table.

It was now two months since the trial and Alex's wife Cathy had just given birth to daughter Eliza. But Alex was depressed. He talked to his friend about the Lowe investigation. There had never been a debriefing for all the police involved. Alex found, to his surprise, that talking about it was very therapeutic. He talked about his involvement with Margaret Hobbs. He talked about Lorraine Lowe, Kerri Ludlow, Peter Reid. He talked for seven hours. Then his friend asked him how he felt about it all.

The Murder of Sheree

"It's hard to say," Alex said, dragging on another cigarette and absent-mindedly flicking some more ash at the ashtray but hitting only the tablecloth.

"You know, after the trial I was on holidays, doing the gardening, and I realised every now and then that I would start one job and five minutes later be doing something totally different," he said. His friend sat opposite, nodding, but not fully comprehending. He took another swig. Alex went on.

"It's like I can't concentrate any more. My wife says I'm not the person I was when the Lowe case started. Before, I was always bright and sunny - now I'm very cynical."

Alex frowned as he studied the burning end of his cigarette. Then with his head still down, he looked up and confided in his friend.

"Robert Lowe has changed me - without doubt. I'm a different person."

The mate shifted in his seat. He looked at Alex and then studied the ashtray. Mates don't often talk like this.

"When it was going on I handled it competently," Alex explained. "I did what I had to do. But now I realise it scarred me badly. And I don't even know how it has affected me. I don't know how but I know I'm wounded."

The mate wanted to know more but he didn't want to press the policeman. He tried to change course slightly.

"He was a religious bloke wasn't he? Are you religious?"

Alex was stepping up a gear. He hadn't talked about the case fully with anybody, even his wife, for he was having problems identifying what it had done to him. The beer and a ready ear were helping him sort out what he was feeling.

"I've got no faith any more. Any vestige of faith I had before this is gone," he said pensively.

"I've never really had religious faith but I was brought up in the Catholic system. But now when I hear people say things happened 'for a reason' I just blow up."

He took another drag on his cigarette and again flicked the ash, this time getting it into the ashtray. He sat as if listening to an inaudible question for a few moments before he spat out, "That's crap. They do not happen for a reason. They just happen. It's the old saying - 'Shit happens'. This stuff about Robert Lowe having done it for a reason, of Sheree having died for a reason, that's just crap. He is a low life. He took this little six-year-old girl and he murdered her."

Alex's voice grew louder. His mate looked away and reached for another cigarette.

"It happened because he can't control his sexual urges, not because there's some vengeful God in Heaven pulling the strings saying 'Sheree Beasley deserves to die', rah, rah, rah and this will make them a better person and so and so a better person, and they need to go through this."

Alex looked disgusted at the thought.

"That's just crap. Total crap. It just comes down to the fact that he couldn't control his urges and he has set this train of events into motion that affected everyone else. The pebble in the pond. The pebble drops in and the ripples just go on and on..." His voice trailed off. The friend cleared his throat and shifted again in his chair.

"Wanna coffee or something?" he ventured. Alex wasn't listening.

"I still don't know how badly it's wounded me. I don't know how and to what extent."

The friend forgot about the hot drinks.

"What about your missus? Do you talk to her about it?"

Alex shook his head slowly.

"No, not at all. I didn't want her to see it. I want to spare her from that. Oh, we did speak about it at times but never at a great level. But seeing what happened to Margaret Hobbs and particularly what happened to Peter Reid, I was genuinely shocked. It's ripped any last shred of faith out of me completely."

"Why?"

"I think a big part of it is because it was somebody who was totally helpless. If it was a man who was taken he would have had the chance to fight back. I think we sort of got so much more involved in the case. In a lot of our jobs, you're in and out of the job in a week or two - a couple of months at the most usually. It's not drawn out and long. You don't get to concentrate on the horror of it really. I suppose all murders in a way are much the same. But to me, up until this point, a lot of those jobs are just past, gone, and you're so busy and you're so swept up in getting the job done - and getting it done properly - that you never get a chance to concentrate on who these people are and what they're all about. But then you get something like this..." His voice trailed off again. He looked at his watch. It was 3.15am.

"It's interwoven with jobs at Seymour, Colac, in town. You try to forget about it, to keep it at the back of your mind but something happens and it keeps coming back at you again and again. It jumps back into the front of your brain."

Tears welled in his eyes.

"It goes back to that 'I want my mummy, I want my mummy'. You just think you hear your own children say that sort of thing and you know when your own child is upset. It really hurts me when my kids cry and I love being able to comfort them and hug them. What would it be like for them when they don't have anyone there to comfort them? And they're just left in sheer panic and terror and they lose all control. They have no control over the situation." The friend opened his mouth to speak, then realised there was nothing to say. Alex squinted as he continued thinking aloud.

"This is what for him would be the ultimate thrill. He is totally in control, without any fear of contradiction from anyone else. No-one else can step in and save the situation. He is the master of the situation. He's in control. If anything would make that man have an erection, a thrill, it would be that."

"Here he is," said Alex with derision. "The total master of the situation, and it just horrifies me to think that..." He was looking at the wall as he spoke.

"I can understand a man walking into a bank, sticking it up, and saying 'I need the money'. You don't condone it but you can understand it. You could understand someone burgling someone's house, stealing, or flogging someone when they're upset or mad. Or a crime of passion for instance - we get a lot of those. Catch someone in bed with their wife and they get a gun and shoot them."

The colour came to his face again and his eyes focused intensely on something invisible.

"But there's something about a child pleading with him, saying, 'Please, take me home, I want my mummy', so upset, you know - their world is so simple - that you wouldn't stop the car and say, 'Oh, I'm so sorry' and just kick her out and drive off. Just forget about the whole thing."

His voice rose half an octave.

"What would make a man continue on, sexually assault her, cause her all that pain and fear, and then bury her? And act like it didn't happen and she just didn't matter. The arrogance of all this play acting that has gone on since, I just can't understand it. If somebody cried, I'd put them straight out of the car."

Alex thought for a moment and then mimicked Robert Lowe's voice.

"'I didn't even see the girl.' When he said that - I'll always remember that - I was thinking, 'That'd be right too. How could you do it if you even acknowledged she was even there?'"

"I know it's convenient to say he's a psychopath but that's classically what it is," he said. "He's got the blinkers on. He sees himself and he sees his own gratification. That's what I can't get over. The callousness of it is just so enormous. It's what Cummins said, it really drove home. She lived in a different world and a different plane to us adults. She just had simple bloody pleasures and simple things and she just didn't stand a chance. It's just like squashing a bloody beetle. She didn't even see it coming." Alex's upper lip was curling.

"She had no way of fighting back, no way of...." he was momentarily lost for words. Then he gritted his teeth.

"It just makes me rage. I hate an uneven fight. It makes me rage to think that he can do that to someone else, especially when they're so vulnerable, when they've got no hope at all. And then to dismiss it as some sort of, a, a game!"

He mimicked Lowe's voice again.

"It's an aberration. It's a game. I made a mistake."

Alex imagined Lowe standing before him and started talking to the killer.

"It's not a bloody mistake Robert. I just want to grab you and go choof choof." As he spoke he moved his right hand as if he was slapping someone across both cheeks.

"It's not a mistake. It's a deliberate act. It's the ultimate act of power.

The Murder of Sheree

You had the chance to stop it. You were given ample time."

Alex fidgeted.

"This is the other thing. It's not like you snatched her off the street and grabbed her and shook her and she's dead and then you've said 'Oh God, she's dead. It's a horrible mistake'. I can't believe you were driving a car with this girl going berserk next to you for probably 15 to 20 minutes and you couldn't feel even the tiniest tinge of sympathy for her. Even if you had to do whatever it was you had to do - just give her the chance to be alive. Are you that callous that you made a mistake and you had to kill someone to cover your mistake? That to me is just...." Alex stared at the table for a moment with despair. Then he looked up at his friend. He spoke as if he was talking to somebody who had just entered a room halfway through a conversation.

"You can't forgive any of it but there are stages of that crime and there were a number of stages where he could have said 'Enough!', like having someone totally submissive and begging for their life and he can walk away and say 'Okay, it's gone far enough', but to then go and do that and to end her life, to me just......phew." Alex was exhausted.

"Do you reckon he went down to Rosebud that day to kill her?" the friend wanted to know.

"I have thought about that," Alex said. "I have no doubt he went there to do everything he did to her. He didn't pick her up to take her for a ride. Knowing him, given the circumstances, I'd say he knew once he had her in the car he knew he had to kill her. Once he had committed an offence that is going to be extremely embarrassing to him, she was dead once he dragged her into the car. Once the offence of abduction was complete, she was dead."

Alex looked like he had seen a ghost. The friend was staring blankly at the tablecloth as Alex continued talking without emotion.

"I think such is his ego and he had so much to lose by being discovered, not only would this have brought out about what he did about abducting a girl, this may have led to the entire sordid mess coming out in front of everyone. He would have been totally exposed. That's why he did it! That's why he killed her! Because he couldn't afford to get caught. To me, it sticks out like a beacon. Maybe when he was driving down the

Nepean Highway he wasn't going there to kill her. Maybe not but I'm sure he thought of the eventuality. 'What am I going to do with her once I've got her in the car?' 'What do I do with her once I've raped her.' 'I can't afford to get caught.' I can imagine him thinking that's the only solution - dead men tell no tales."

The men looked at each other for a split second and then both looked away. They cleared their throats and felt uncomfortable. Alex stood up.

"I'd better go home," he said. He looked at his watch. It was almost 3.30am. The friend walked Alex to the door and waved goodbye. He watched the policeman climb into the cab and wondered if he would stay in the police force.

ROBERT LOWE sits in his prison cell at the Melbourne Remand Centre, still amazed and hurt that his wife turned against him. He does not see that she told the truth, just that she didn't stand by him. He cannot understand why Peter Reid tricked him. He cannot understand why the police wouldn't give up. He cannot understand how Kerri and Anthony and Steve and Neil Greenhill and Jill and Anthony, and everybody else associated with Sheree were so devastated at her death. She was just a little girl.

And the humiliating irony, of which he is all too aware, is that he convicted himself out of his own mouth. Had he kept quiet, the police would have always suspected him but would never have been able to charge him. But he relished the excitement of the crime, the thrill at having killed and got away with it. He couldn't boast about it to his wife, his sons, anybody from church and certainly not the police. And he didn't have any friends. It had to be Margaret. At first, he just played games with her, dropping obscure hints, to see if she was bright enough to see how smart he had been. Sheree was never the issue. It was Robert's brilliance.

But it was a double-edged sword. As soon as people recognised his cleverness, it meant he must be found out. And Margaret, and all the police listening in, and all the people who read the transcripts of the tapes, soon saw what he had done. He had to give so much away for everyone to see, and eventually he trapped himself.

The Murder of Sheree

ROBERT'S APPEAL hung over everyone's head like a guillotine. It was expected in November 1995, then it was held over into 1996 while the Legal Aid Commission assessed whether it would get involved. Margaret Hobbs was terrified of testifying again. She didn't think she could stand the strain. For months she had been writing a book of her experiences with Robert Lowe. She hoped that in writing the book, she could record her thoughts and try to forget what she had been through. She wanted it to all go away.

Lorraine was sitting in her family room when the phone rang. It was Detective Senior Constable Paul O'Halloran with the news that Margaret had died in a car crash. Mid-afternoon on January 17, 1996, John Hobbs was driving with Margaret along Stud Road, near Dandenong, when John blacked out, something that had happened a couple of times in the past. The car careered off the road and ripped through a cyclone wire fence. Margaret's died instantly when the car then slammed into a tree. The jolt simultaneously roused John who spent several days in intensive care but recovered quickly enough to attend Margaret's funeral at St James Anglican Church in Langhorne Street, Dandenong. Matthew Wood, Harry Simpson, Paul O'Halloran and Alex Bartsch attended the funeral. So did Denise and Neil Greenhill, Neil's former wife Marie, and Jill and Anthony Mandile.

CHAPTER TWENTY-TWO

◆

THE PRESIDENT of the Court of Appeal, Justice John Winneke, with Justice Robert Brooking and Justice Alex Southwell, heard Lowe's appeal on September 30 and October 1, 1996.

Lowe's counsel, David Grace QC, argued that his client's conviction and sentence was a miscarriage of justice. The evidence of Margaret Hobbs and Peter Reid should have been excluded at the trial because they were police agents, Mr Grace said.

Paul Coghlan, QC, for the DPP, told the court it was clear Lowe was Sheree's killer but he had shown not one scintilla of remorse. The prospect of rehabilitation, he said, was non-existent "or at the very best, bleak". Arguing that Lowe should not be given a non-parole term, Coghlan said the community had a special responsibility for young children. A deterrent was needed - a minimum term should not be fixed.

The judges reserved their decision.

The court reconvened on Friday, November 29. Lorraine was there, sitting next to Andrew Gustke. Neil Greenhill sat red-eyed behind her, next to Paul Hollowood.

The prisoner was escorted into the court by two security guards and sat in the dock just a few metres in front of his former wife. He was wearing a light coloured jacket, dark grey trousers. The arms of his spectacles were still tied with a brown, worn shoelace. His closely cropped hair and beard was quite grey. Lowe looked relaxed, almost calm, and occasionally looked around the court indifferently.

At 10.05am the judges entered the court. Justice Winneke announced that both appeals had been dismissed. He then produced a copy of the judges' findings and adjourned the court. The hearing lasted less than three minutes. Lowe appeared completely unconcerned.

After the judges left, and as Lowe was being led downstairs to the cells, he called out.

"I've never seen, ever, Sheree Beasley," he said. He paused momentarily and then held a pocket-sized bible above his head. "On the Bible," he said. He then descended the stairs, and was gone.

"The crime was a vile one," the judges wrote. "If it has any redeeming features, Mr Grace was unable to draw them to our attention." It was fitting no minimum be set.

SHE WALKED the streets of Melbourne in a daze. She knew the city so well, yet she was lost. It had dawned on Lorraine long ago now that the road she had been following was not leading her to her intended destination. Now she didn't even know where she wanted to go in her life. Twenty years with Robert was an illusion. Now she wondered what lay before her and if there was any point going on. After all, she was 55 and couldn't imagine being alive much longer.

Later she sat in her family room and looked around. She was alone, yet the memories of Robert were so strong it was as if he was with her. She knew she would have to sell the house if she was to ever have a reasonable chance of starting again. But before she stepped into the future, she needed to know if there was any point. And before she could do that, she needed to reflect on what had happened to her, and what she had become. Four years before, Lorraine Lowe had her head buried in the sand. She knew there was a problem with her husband's behaviour but she couldn't comprehend it and she didn't really want to know, either. But she realised now that in ignoring the problem, it had only grown. Like a force ten tornado, it built up and finally hit her in the face, destroying her dream in the process. She wondered if Robert had ever really loved her.

Then she started to wonder if anything good at all had come from this terrible journey she'd been on. She knew only too well the bad. She thought about the police, who, ever since she had known Robert, she had treated with mistrust and disdain. She thought about Helen Adams, the senior constable from Blackburn Community Policing Squad, who had spent at least several days of each week over the past four years with her, trying to comfort her. She thought about Matthew Wood, Tony Jacobs and Alex Bartsch who had taken her sons to football games at Waverley Park and cricket matches at the MCG, usually on their days off, while Robert loitered near toilet blocks on the Rosebud foreshore. She remembered fondly how she had scores of silent phone and pager numbers that belonged to policemen and women who insisted she call them whenever she needed them. And she remembered the 600 letters and cards she had received from strangers who had read about her plight in the newspapers.

Then she recalled how she had spoken out about her husband's lies and how she had altered her statement several times over many months, as she gradually recalled what had really happened on June 29, 1991. At the time she wondered if she was doing the right thing by her husband, but now, after all the torment, heartache and grief, she knew she had done the only thing she could. Her health was badly damaged and her life had changed completely. She felt certain she had been tested by the Devil's power but her faith had brought her through. Not unscathed, for it had been a fierce struggle but she had come through with her faith and integrity intact.

Lorraine realised when she looked at people now, she tried to work out what they were hiding, rather than taking them at face value. She didn't think that was necessarily a bad thing, for she hadn't lost the ability to recognise the good in people. It occurred to her, as she looked out the window at the lemon tree and the boys cubby house that they hadn't used for years, that she had become somehow more worldly. She had seen another side of life that nobody could have ever explained to her. Cops. Courts. Prisons. The Law. Death, grief, misery. And fear. Fear of the unknown and fear of what she had been living with. She felt she had learned more compassion, too. Even though she had lost her dream life, she saw that at least she hadn't lost a child. She was in pain but she felt more for the Greenhills and the Mandiles and the Ludlows. She wondered how they would ever cope.

EPILOGUE

The following is a full list of Robert Arthur Selby Lowe's prior convictions.

BRITAIN:
North Riding (North East England): July 5, 1956.
Assault police with intent to resist arrest - Fined 10 pounds.
Taking and driving away motor vehicle without owner's consent - Fined 10 pounds.
Dangerous driving - Fined 1 pound. Disqualified from driving for two years.

NEW ZEALAND:

Wellington: March 6, 1959.
Indecent assault on a male - Fined 5 pounds.

Auckland: March 16, 1961.
Obscene exposure - Six months imprisonment plus 12 months probation.

Wellington: October 22, 1964.
Obscene exposure and being found in enclosed premises - Six months imprisonment.
Obscene exposure - Three months imprisonment. Declared a rogue and a vagabond.

Wellington: September 3, 1965.
Theft - Fined 15 pounds.

AUSTRALIA:

Richmond: August 5, 1969.
Wilful and obscene exposure - Dismissed.

Moonee Ponds: April 1, 1970.
Loiter for homosexual purposes - Dismissed.

Richmond: August 7, 1974.
Wilful and obscene exposure - Dismissed.

Hampton: December 15, 1981.
Indecent behaviour - Good behaviour bond.

Prahran: November 20, 1984.
Theft - Fined $200.

Springvale: December 12, 1984.
Offensive behaviour - Withdrawn.
Wilful and obscene exposure - 12 month $500 good behaviour bond.

Preston: December 21, 1984.
Offensive behaviour - Prosecution not authorised.

Mt Waverly: November 5, 1985.
Wilful and obscene exposure - Dismissed.

Broadmeadows: July 22, 1986.
Offensive behaviour - Fined $1000.

Prahran: April 1, 1987.
Theft - Fined $500.

Melbourne: November 9, 1990
Indecent Assault (2 charges), *Assault* (2 charges), *Offensive Behaviour* (2 charges) - Fined a total of $750.

Melbourne Supreme Court
Kidnapping - 15 years imprisonment.
Murder - Life imprisonment. (No minimum term set)

The following people were founding members of the Zenith Task Force at Rosebud police station. This list shows the office or station they were originally attached to.

Detective Inspectors
Laurie Ratz - "D" District
Dannye Moloney - Rape Squad

Detective Senior Sergeants
Dale Johnson - "D" District

Detective Sergeants
Geoff Alway - Rape Squad
Ken Heggie - Rosebud CIB
Graham Arthur - Major Crime Squad
Neil Beeson - Rape Squad

Sergeants
Matthew Wood - Transit Police
Gavan Wallace - Prahran police station
Wayne Salt - Fingerprints
Brian Gamble - Crime Scene Section
Ian Coutts - Crime Scene Section

Detective Senior Constables
Tony (Jock) Jacobs, Neil Merrick, Robyn Heal - Rape Squad
Harry Simpson - Mornington CIB
Andrew Gustke - East Bentleigh CIB
Brett Spence, Kate Foley - Parkdale CIB
David (Hedge) Noonan - St Kilda CIB
Lisa Anderson, Tracy Leitch, Glen Anthony - Springvale CIB
Peter Butland, Roger Puehl, Alan Dickinson - Rosebud CIB
John Bradbury - Stolen Motor Vehicle Squad
Geoff McLean - Frankston CIB
Cameron Duncan - Major Crime Squad
Jeff Kyne - Elsternwick CIB
Hugh Ellis - Cranbourne CIB
Bruce Harwood - Major Crime Squad
Stephen Cox - Hampton CIB

Senior Constables
Richard Shields - Frankston District Support Group
Maree Kepert - Frankston District Support Group
Mandy Hunter - Bureau of Criminal Intelligence
Helen Adams - Blackburn Community Policing Squad

The following men and women worked on the case from the Homicide Squad.

Detective Senior Sergeant Paul Hollowood
Detective Sergeant John Hill
Detective Sergeant Jeff Calderbank
Detective Senior Constable Graeme Ashworth
Detective Senior Constable Murray Gregor
Detective Senior Constable Paul O'Halloran
Detective Senior Constable Alex Bartsch
Detective Senior Constable Mick Flanagan
Detective Senior Constable Mercedes Galacho

Police, public servants and volunteers from the following areas also worked on the case.

Victoria Police
Bureau of Criminal Intelligence Surveillance Section, Mounted Branch, Air Wing, Transport Branch, Search and Rescue Squad, Audio Visual Section, State Forensic Science Laboratories (now the Victoria Forensic Science Laboratories), Victorian Institute of Forensic Pathology, Country Fire Authority, Southern Peninsula Rescue Squad, State Emergency Service

DETECTIVE CHIEF Inspector Peter Halloran was promoted to Superintendent in January 1996 and transferred to Traffic and Operations Support.

Detective Chief Inspector Laurie Ratz is now working at the National Crime Authority in Melbourne.

Detective Inspector Paul Hollowood is now the head of the Crime Intelligence Support Centre.

Detective Inspector Dannye Moloney is now the head of the Armed Robbery Squad.

After being promoted to uniform senior sergeant at Ballarat, Geoff Alway transferred back to the Rape Squad in mid-1995.

Detective Senior Sergeant Dale Johnson transferred to the Drug Squad and spent much of 1995 on long service leave with his wife and children, touring Australia. He resigned from the Victoria Police on February 23, 1996, after 21 years service.

After working at St Kilda Road police station for two years as a uniform sergeant, Alex Bartsch transferred to the Crime Intelligence Support Centre, where he works with Paul Hollowood.

Sergeant Matthew Wood transferred from Rosebud police station to Yarrawonga police station in June 1996.

Detective Senior Constable Andrew Gustke transferred to the Homicide Squad where he worked on the same crew as Detective Senior Constable Paul O'Halloran. Andrew later transferred to the Major Fraud Group. Paul was promoted to Sergeant and transferred to Prahran Police Station in 1996.

Detective Senior Constable Murray Gregor is working as a special investigator in Sydney, on secondment to the Royal Commission into Corruption in the NSW Police Service.

In 1995, Geoff Flatman, QC, was appointed Victorian Director of Public Prosecutions. In late 1995, Paul Coghlan was appointed QC.

LORRAINE LOWE still lives in Mannering Drive, Glen Waverley, with her two sons. She plans to sell the house soon. The Rosebud unit is on the market.

Peter Reid is still in jail.

Kerri and Steve Ludlow still live in Adelaide.

ROBERT LOWE spends his spare time in the Melbourne Remand Centre making stained glass windows. He is a regular in prison bible class.

THE KARMEIN CHAN investigation remains open.

In late 1995, DNA tests were completed on evidence found on Kylie Maybury's body in 1984. Those results are currently being examined. The investigation is continuing.